WARNE'S
EVERYDAY COOKERY

WARNE'S
EVERYDAY COOKERY

Revised by

CLAIRE HEWITT

FREDERICK WARNE

Published by Frederick Warne & Co Ltd
London 1976

Revised and reset edition
© Frederick Warne & Co Ltd 1976

ISBN 0 7232 1827 7
Printed in Great Britain by
BAS Printers Limited, Wallop, Hampshire

PREFACE

In the modern kitchen it remains as essential as ever to keep a book of basic well tried and well liked recipes; a book more for constant day by day reference than for the special occasion. *Everyday Cookery* aims at just such down to earth usefulness and as its long life testifies (it was first published in 1929) it may fairly claim to be as popular and well tried as the recipes it explains.

The list of contents, built up from past experience, indicates the wide scope of this entirely new and re-set edition. Apart from a complete up-dating particular care has been taken to choose a page layout which allows the main steps and quantities for each recipe to be seen literally at a glance.

Metric as well as Imperial units have been given throughout in the belief that in most kitchens both systems will be met with from time to time for some years to come.

London
October 1976

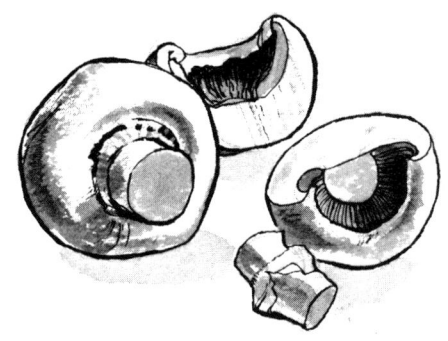

CONTENTS

THE IMPORTANCE AND SCIENCE
OF COOKING

The science of cookery is the knowledge of the values of food and the needs of the body. A meal should be planned so that there is a balance of the necessary food elements and it should be served in a palatable and digestible way. Food is made up of many nutrients:

1 Protein, the flesh-forming food which is needed for growth and repair of waste tissues. It is important to everyone, but particularly to growing children, adolescents, and athletes who are building up their muscle-power. Protein is found in eggs, cheese, meat, fish, nuts, milk, bread, peas, beans and cereals.

2 Carbohydrates, or starches and sugars, which supply most of the heat and power of the body. They include sugars of all kinds, cereals, bread, flour and potatoes.

3 Fats, which are an important source of energy, their fuel value being twice as great as that of protein and starch. The principal sources of fats are butter, margarine, lard, bacon, nuts and fish-liver oils.

4 Minerals, which are builders of tissues and sources of potential energy. Among them are: calcium, which helps the growth of bones and teeth, and is found in fish, cheese, milk, green vegetables and bread; phosphorus, which performs the same function and is present in most foods; iron, found in liver, kidneys, cocoa, fish, green vegetables; and salt and potassium.

5 Vitamins, substances present in very small quantities in food but which are vital in regulating all body processes.

Vitamin A is contained mostly in green vegetables, carrots, eggs, butter, cod-liver, liver and milk. Lack of Vitamin A is likely to cause a certain type of unpleasant skin disease, and also night blindness and in more severe cases, permanent blindness.

Vitamin B is subdivided into several categories, the main ones being: B_1 or thiamine, which is contained in bread, bacon, oatmeal, wheatgerm and brown rice; Vitamin B_2 or riboflavine, which is contained in milk, liver, kidney and yeast; and nicotinic acid which is found in peanuts, bread, yeast, soya flour, rice, beer, pulses, sunflower seeds, coffee, liver and meat. Vitamin B is needed to liberate the energy from food.

Vitamin C is found in blackcurrants, strawberries, oranges, lemons, grapefruit, gooseberries, cauliflowers, cabbage and potatoes. Vitamin C is easily lost from cooked vegetables which are over-cooked, or reheated, kept hot or cooked in too much water. Lack of Vitamin C causes scurvy, and is sometimes responsible for abnormal bone and teeth formation.

Vitamin D is obtained from fish-liver oils, egg yolks, butter and oily fish, such as herrings and mackerel. A deficiency of Vitamin D is liable to cause rickets.

Vitamin E is contained in rice-germ and wheat-germ oils, and green leaves. Lack of Vitamin E gives rise to failure in reproduction in the male and female.

Value of a balanced diet   As some foods are too rich in proteins and others contain too much carbohydrate and fat, the value of a mixed diet is easily understood. An ordinary daily diet should contain about 100 g (4 oz) of protein; 75 g (2–3 oz) of fat; 350 g (14 oz) of carbohydrate; and a little over 25 g (1 oz) of mineral salts; but the exact amount varies slightly according to the occupation, age, build and sex of the individual, and the influence of climate and seasons.

It is not enough just to arrange a balanced meal and to cook the food well. Food must look appetizing and the flavours and textures should go well together and also provide contrast. With many of the recipes in this book, suitable accompanying sauces and vegetables have been suggested as a guide to the beginner.

THE KITCHEN

Kitchen planning – kitchen utensils – cookers and their management – cooking by gas – cooking by electricity – cooking on solid fuel cookers – cleaning cookers – pressure cooking – casserole cooking – cooking on the spit – refrigerators – freezers – cleaning a kitchen, scullery and larder – cleaning utensils

KITCHEN PLANNING

The kitchen should be looked upon as one of the most important parts of the house. Kitchens are so varied these days that it is difficult to lay down hard and fast rules for their design. The first thing is to decide what the kitchen is to be used for: is it for food preparation and cooking only, and by a cook who likes to have the room to herself; must it combine with the laundry; will it be used for eating in – family only or for entertaining as well; as a room in which the children are to be encouraged to play or which the housewife can use for her hobbies, write at a desk, watch television, mix with the rest of the family. This decision is, of course, governed to a certain extent by the size of the room, and it is possible to find kitchens consisting of a few combined units fitted to one wall of a room, or, in complete contrast, kitchens converted from the entire floor of a house and furnished like a sitting-room complete with armchairs and carpet.

It is a help, however, to observe a few principles:

1 The kitchen should be well ventilated, if possible with windows that can be opened at the top. It is easy to install a ventilator or air extractor which will carry off all fumes and steam from cooking, and so prevent them from spreading all over the house.

2 The kitchen should be well lighted, the lights so arranged as to enable one to see well when preparing or cooking the food.

3 The lay-out should be chosen with a view to saving steps. It is helpful to arrange the work areas in the following order:

1 Store cupboard, refrigerator, etc.
2 Working surface for food preparation
3 Sink
4 Working surface
5 Cooker
6 Serving counter

It is important to have all equipment of convenient height, with easily cleaned surfaces.

In a large kitchen, a trolley will save much time and energy when assembling ingredients and utensils for cooking and when putting away the washing-up.

KITCHEN UTENSILS

The hardware department of any store offers a variety of kitchen utensils to suit every need, and in a wide range of prices. It is well worth while spending a little time searching for utensils that are of good design and will stand up to wear and cleaning.

Saucepans are available in various shades of enamel, to suit a favoured colour scheme, or in different qualities of aluminium, in cast-iron, in copper or in polished steel.

Pans should be chosen of a reasonably heavy gauge; these will retain their shape and help prevent food from burning. It is essential to have ground-base saucepans for use with electric cookers and solid-fuel stoves such as Agas, Esses and Rayburns, otherwise time and heat will be wasted.

Aluminium pans are durable and comparatively light. Enamel pans should be of good quality to stand up to hard wear without chipping. Care should be taken to avoid foreign makes that do not have a lead-free glaze. Some enamel saucepans with two grip handles are quite suitable to double as casseroles used in the oven.

Cast-iron pans are splendid for long slow cooking and perfect browning, but are heavy to handle. Before using for the first time, a cast-iron utensil must be seasoned. Wash and dry it well, then cover the bottom with olive oil to a depth of about half an inch. Leave for at least

12 hours, then heat oil very gently to frying point. Remove from heat, pour off oil and wipe the pan thoroughly with absorbent paper. It should not be washed after each use, but wiped while still hot with kitchen paper dipped in salt.

Copper pans are excellent for sauces. They are usually lined with tin. A check should be kept on the inside for signs of wear, and they should be sent for relining when necessary.

Stainless steel pans are very durable and easy to keep clean, but rather expensive.

Non-stick surfaces can be very satisfactory so long as they are not damaged by scratchy utensils or harsh cleaning. It is essential to use only special tools that have been made for use with these surfaces, and to wash them in soapy water without using powders or scourers. Pans that have become pitted and blistered can be sent back to the makers for resurfacing.

Several reputable makes of kitchen cutlery are obtainable in stainless steel, which is ideal for use in the kitchen since it neither stains nor rusts. It is essential to have sharp knives, and the best of these are the French makes, which are well worth the extra expense.

Ovenware is made in fireproof glass, fireproof pottery and enamel for casseroles and pie-dishes. They are all satisfactory, and the choice is a matter of individual taste, though it is worth remembering that enamelled cast-iron, while made to last a lifetime, is extremely heavy, and a large casserole when filled is quite difficult to lift.

Baking-tins can be bought in tin or aluminium, with or without non-stick interiors. Tin is cheap and quite adequate, provided it is dried carefully to avoid rusting.

Plastic is excellent in the kitchen for bowls, buckets and other containers, and is available in many colours.

Electric mixing- and beating-machines, toasters, coffee percolators, etc. are available in various designs to suit individual tastes.

COOKERS AND THEIR MANAGEMENT

The first consideration when choosing a cooker is the type of fuel that is to heat it. Gas and electricity are usually available in the town, whereas storage space for oil or solid fuel is not so easily found. Gas is quite often not laid on in the remoter parts of the country, but for someone who is really keen to cook by gas and does not live where mains gas reaches, it is worth considering bottled gas – the only difference being that space is needed for the cylinders, and refills have to be ordered regularly.

Solid-fuel cookers (Agas, Esses, etc.) and oil-fired cookers are much larger than most electric or gas stoves, and tend to raise the temperature of the kitchen, so are not always suitable for small rooms. However, they do have the advantage of a permanently warm oven and if a lot of cooking is to be done throughout the day, and food kept warm for irregular meal-times, they can be the most economical method of cooking. Many models heat the water system as well.

Having decided on the type of fuel to be used, visit the appropriate showroom, armed with the exact measurements of the space available. Study the models and the leaflets, taking into consideration the following points:

1 Amount of rings and size of oven needed. This will depend obviously on the number of people to be cooked for, but also on the amount of supplementary cooking aids used, e.g. toaster, rôtisserie, electric frying-pan, warming cabinet.

2 Price

3 Ease of cleaning

4 Additional features, e.g. ovens that switch on and off automatically, self-cleaning ovens – will they be used?

Split-level cookers, in which the hob and oven are separate units, may be more suitable for a particular kitchen or housewife than the conventional cooker but they work out more expensive. An oven that is fixed at the level of the outstretched arm saves bending and is especially useful to the disabled or elderly cook.

COOKING BY GAS

Many people choose gas because it is easy to regulate, quick and responds instantly to adjustment of the taps. Most gas cookers have rings and ovens that ignite automatically, and some have automatic timing devices to light and turn off the oven. Easy-clean surfaces are found on many ovens and some have self-cleaning walls and roof that give continuous cleaning action during cooking.

Never allow the flames to lick the sides of the pan, for this wastes gas and does not give any more heat. If a roaring noise is heard and the flame is yellow, turn the gas off at once and relight it as this indicates that the stove has lit incorrectly.

It is wasteful to use heavy saucepans for cooking by gas; use light, flat-bottomed ones, and see that the pans are clean underneath before they are used.

COOKING BY ELECTRICITY

Cooking by electricity is cleaner than any other method, and with experience, a certain amount of electricity can be saved by switching off hot-plates or oven before the end of cooking time, as the heat will remain at the same temperature for a while.

Most ovens are fitted with liners coated with a special enamelling process which helps keep the oven clean during cooking.

A fan oven produces even heating and allows large batches of food to be cooked at the same time at one temperature, which is particularly useful for the cook who likes to bake in bulk for the freezer.

Saucepans specially made for electric cooking with wide, flat bases give the best results, and use should be made of three-tiered steamers when possible.

COOKING ON SOLID-FUEL COOKERS

The familiar makes of solid-fuel cookers can now be obtained heated by gas and oil as well, but the principle of the old solid-fuel cooker remains the same: heat is always available as the cooker remains alight continuously; the ovens produce even, all-over cooking and no smell, and are self-cleaning; some models produce hot water as well.

It is essential to use ground-base saucepans, and it is possible to use up to three saucepans at once on a hot-plate.

CLEANING COOKERS

All cookers must be kept free from grease. In the case of gas cookers, if the burners become clogged, clean them out with a needle or fine wire. Take out all movable parts, wash them in hot water and soda and dry them with a cloth. Electric hot-plates should be wiped as soon as they are cool enough.

Ovens which are not self-cleaning should be wiped out with hot water and soda while still warm. Obstinate stains can be removed with proprietary oven-cleaners; the directions for use of these must be carefully followed as the cleaners are caustic. Solid-fuel cookers need no cleaning except for wiping the enamel casing occasionally and brushing the hot-plates with a wire brush to remove any carbonized particles of spilt food.

PRESSURE COOKING

A pressure cooker works by sealing in the steam, so that the temperature and the pressure inside the cooker are raised above normal saucepan levels. All foods cook very quickly by this method, without risk of losing the 'goodness' by fast boiling. Since the food is heated for a comparatively short time, it will be appreciated that this method is economical in respect of fuel consumption.

Cookers come in varying sizes; as a guide, a pan holding 4 litres (4 quarts) is reasonable for a family of four. For bottling, a high-domed pan holding at least 8 litres (8 quarts) is needed.

Instructions for use, together with specimen recipes, are supplied by individual makers. If care is taken to follow these instructions to the letter, a pressure cooker will give excellent results, but it is not ideal for the slapdash cook; food will be overcooked if the cooker is forgotten or the instructions disregarded. Cooking times are given for all dishes, but it must be remembered that allowance should be made in certain cases (e.g. tough meat must be given extra time). As a general rule, the time needed for cooking in a pressure cooker is quarter to one-third of the time needed for ordinary cooking.

Most types of food can be cooked in a pressure cooker, although jams and marmalades cannot be made completely under pressure as the liquid needs to be reduced. However, the first cooking of the fruit can be done in the pressure cooker, and then the sugar added and the volume reduced in the normal manner with the lid off.

The methods of cooking for which a pressure cooker is suitable are those involving moisture: braising, boiling, steaming or stewing. The rudiments of cookery used in ordinary cooking should be used for pressure cooking, e.g. vegetables will be **sweated** in butter in the open cooker before making soups, and meat browned in fat before braising. After these preliminaries, the pan must be removed from the heat for a couple of minutes before adding the liquid.

Very briefly, the method of cooking by pressure is as follows:

Measure the required amount of liquid into the cooker, and put in the prepared food. Less seasoning than normal is needed with solid foods, and it must be put on to the food itself and not into the water, since the water never touches the food as it does in normal cooking. Replace the cover and put the cooker on a high heat until the steam escapes freely (except in the case of cereals and milk, when a low heat is required throughout). Put on the pressure control and when, according to the instructions, the cooking pressure has been reached (usually indicated by a pointer or the sound of the escaping steam), lower the heat and begin the cooking time. When the cooking time is completed, reduce the pressure by running cold water over the sides of the cooker, or standing it in cold water, and remove the contents.

When cooking solids, the amount of liquid depends on the cooking time, and not on the amount of food to be cooked. Allow 250 ml (½ pt) for the first quarter of an hour and 125 ml (¼ pt) for each extra quarter of an hour. Never use less than 250 ml (½ pt) of liquid, and never fill the cooker more than two-thirds full of solids or half full of liquid, to allow for the compressed steam.

A pressure cooker is supplied with a rack to keep the food from being immersed in the liquid; soups and stews are cooked without it. Green vegetables will retain their colour if the water is brought to the boil and the pan filled with steam before they are put in the cooker and the lid put on. Root vegetables will cook considerably quicker if cut up.

In preparing milk dishes, bring the milk to the boil in the open cooker, add the cereal and flavouring and stir. Lower heat to simmering point, put on cover and bring to cooking pressure slowly.

Thicken soups and stews in the open cooker after the main cooking time is completed.

Most cookers are designed to give a constant pressure which is designated H (15 lb) inside the cooker, but in models where the pressure can be controlled, it has been found that preserves are improved by cooking them at the M (10 lb) pressure, and that sponge puddings are best at L (5 lb).

A pressure cooker can also be used to advantage in bottling fruit and making chutney.

Chicken food and pet meat is very suitable for pressure cooking as it reduces the unpleasant smell; a separate pan should be kept entirely for this purpose.

To clean a pressure cooker   A pressure cooker should be thoroughly washed in hot, soapy water before being used for the first time. Fill with warm water immediately after use. Never put cold water into an overheated dry cooker for fear of cracking it. Clean with a soap-pad and dry thoroughly. The vent tube must be kept clear and if necessary a piece of wire should be inserted to remove any obstruction. A light rub with a soft dry duster is usually sufficient to preserve the shine on the outside of the cooker, but it can be polished occasionally with a little metal cleaner.

Replacements of the safety valves and rubber rings round the lids should be made whenever necessary and at least once a year.

CASSEROLE COOKING

This is really a very ancient method of cooking. Casseroles are available in various shapes and sizes and are made of specially prepared glass, pottery or enamel. White china soufflè, ramekin and gratin dishes and scallop shells are classed with casseroles.

Advantages of a casserole

1 Less heat is required when cooking in a casserole, therefore the cooking is more economical.

2 Cheaper meat may be used, as the slow, gentle cooking softens the coarse fibres of the meat.

3 The food is cooked and served in the casserole, which saves labour and washing-up and helps it to be served really hot.

4 It is easy to keep clean and food does not readily burn in it.

A casserole is best for oven cooking. It is liable to crack if put over an electric ring or a fully turned-on gas jet unless used over a low heat with an asbestos mat under the casserole. This precaution does not of course apply to cast-iron based casseroles which may be used safely on any kind of heat.

Fireproof glassware   This can be bought in all shapes and sizes from small egg pipkins to large dishes in which a turkey can be cooked. It can be used for any kind of baking and economizes on fuel, as the food is not only cooked by the hot air heat of the oven, but also by the heat which radiates from the walls and bottom of the oven and penetrates the glass. As this radiant heat cannot penetrate metal utensils, cooking with glassware is achieved more quickly and with less fuel.

Almost anything can be cooked in a casserole: thick soups, such as *pot-au-feu* and French onion soup; stews; ragoûts; stewed or baked fruit and milk puddings. A casserole is more used for braising nowadays than a braising pan proper, which is rarely seen except in large establishments. A casserole is perfect for pot-roasting.

COOKING ON THE SPIT

Spit-roasting is one of the oldest methods of cooking, and has recently had a revival in popularity; spits are sold that are heated by gas or by electricity.

Most spits consist of a horizontal shaft on which the food is impaled, which turns under the heat, with a tray placed below to catch the juices; a few, however, are fixed vertically with the heat behind the shaft.

Some spits are fixed inside the oven of the cooker. These are not very satisfactory as the food cooks in a steamy atmosphere which will spoil its flavour, and the oven will be difficult to clean. The main advantages of spit-roasting are the excellent flavour given to the food and the labour saved with regard to cleaning the oven.

Spit-roasting can be used for joints of meat and birds or kebabs (small pieces of meat or fish and vegetables spiked on skewers), though for these, one has to have a special kebab attachment.

The booklet of instructions that accompanies each model must be followed for working the spit, but the principles of cooking on the turning spit are as follows:

The meat or bird must be seasoned and covered liberally with oil or melted butter. A bird can be stuffed if desired; meat must be of a compact shape, often a joint is best boned and rolled.

Red meat should be sealed by turning for 5 minutes under full heat, then reducing the temperature; white meat and poultry should be cooked steadily under a medium-hot fire, and constant **basting** is necessary; moisten the juice that gathers in the drip-tray with water if it looks like burning, and use this for **basting**.

Kebabs should consist of alternating pieces of dry and fatty food and should be threaded on to the skewers, brushed with oil or melted butter and cooked for 10–20 minutes, **basting** occasionally.

It is always important when starting to turn something on the spit to watch it for the first few minutes to make sure it revolves freely.

REFRIGERATORS

Domestic refrigerators can be operated by electricity, mains gas, bottled gas or oil.

Models are available in many styles and sizes and at various prices, to suit every need, the smallest having a storage capacity of 1 cu. foot.

When buying a refrigerator, it is well to bear these points in mind:

1 The choice of operating agent

2 The amount of space available for the cabinet

3 The number of people in the family and the amount of food to be stored (e.g. how many bottles of milk are used per day)

4 Is it intended to store vegetables, fruit and canned foods in the cabinet or will it be reserved solely for dairy produce, meat, etc?

Most refrigerators have a storage compartment for frozen foods which is marked with stars according to its coldness and the length of time frozen foods can be stored in it: a one-star compartment will keep frozen food up to a week, ice-cream for a day; a two-star compartment will keep food for four weeks, ice-cream for a week; a three-star compartment will store frozen food and ice-cream for three months. Some three-star compartments will actually freeze food for storage – this must be checked with the manufacturers. Never attempt to store ice-cream in an ordinary refrigerator cabinet.

Other features many refrigerators have include a butter compartment for keeping the butter cool but soft, a salad drawer and an automatic defrosting system.

Using a refrigerator   To make ice-cubes, or ice-cream quickly, the thermostat dial should be turned to maximum, or in the case of an oil-burning model, the flame should be turned high.

Once the ice is made, the thermostat or flame should be adjusted to give the normal temperature required within the cabinet. Thermostat numbers 3, 4 and 5 are usually found suitable for use in a temperate climate.

It is essential that there should be proper circulation of air within a refrigerator cabinet, and therefore it must not be packed tightly with food and containers.

Foods with a strong smell, such as cheese or bacon, and others, such as milk, which absorb odours readily, must always be covered. Salads and vegetables should be covered to preserve their crispness. Meat should be covered lightly in greaseproof paper, foil or polythene. Fish must always be placed in a covered container or wrapped in foil or polythene.

Defrosting and cleaning a refrigerator   With continuous use of a refrigerator, frost will form on the radiator, on the walls of the cabinet, and on the door of the frozen storage compartment. This frost must be removed periodically before it gets too thick. It is usual to defrost a refrigerator every seven or fourteen days, according to individual requirements.

To defrost, remove all food and containers from the cabinet, turn off the power, and leave the door of the cabinet open. The frost will melt in due course, and run into the drip-tray under the radiator. This tray should be emptied as required during defrosting.

When the process is complete, wash and wipe the drip-tray, wash the cabinet with warm water, and dry it well. Rinse the ice-trays and refill them with fresh water. Replace the drip-tray and shelves. Wash and dry all containers. Close the door, and restart the refrigerator.

When a refrigerator is to be out of use for any length of time, it should be defrosted and cleaned, and the door of the cabinet left open to prevent the inside from becoming musty.

FREEZERS

There are two types of freezer available, the chest type and the upright type, the latter often being sold in conjunction with a matching refrigerator installed either above or below it.

The chest type takes up more floor space than an upright one and it may be awkward for a small person to reach into the bottom or to lift out the wire baskets when filled with food. Choose one with a separate freezing compartment, if possible, as food to be frozen should not be in contact with food already frozen, which will happen in a one-section freezer.

The upright type usually fits better in a kitchen, and allows easy access to and sight of the contents. Its loaded weight puts great stress on a small area of the floor, so the strength of this must be considered. Some upright models have special quick-freeze shelves which are invaluable for freezing one's own produce.

Care of the freezer   The manufacturer's instructions must be followed carefully, but most freezers need defrosting only once or twice a year. Many firms have a 24-hour maintenance service and an insurance cover against loss of contents due to power failure. Should the latter happen, contents can safely stay for 24 hours in the freezer, provided it is not opened.

CLEANING A KITCHEN, SCULLERY AND LARDER

The kitchen, scullery and larder must be kept scrupulously clean. The walls and ceiling should be brushed regularly, and washed twice a year, taking care not to make them too wet.

All paint should be washed occasionally.

Floors should be washed once or twice a week, using a special detergent. Stains may be removed from tiles with scouring powder or soap-pads. Linoleum should never be made very wet.

Refrigerators and freezers, see p. 18.

Cookers, see p. 13.

Wooden tables should be scrubbed and bleached clean.

Clean the sink every time it is used with soap and water or a mild scouring powder, and flush very hot water down the drain. Occasionally flush with soda and boiling water. Never put anything down the drain that may clog it, such as grease, coffee grounds or tea-leaves. A sink-basket will catch the pieces that would clog up the pipe, and a sink brush must be kept near the sink. Both should be washed daily. Bowls used for washing-up must be kept scrupulously clean, and mops and dish-cloths must be washed out daily and boiled once a week. Paper cloths will save this chore and are very satisfactory.

The waste bin   Always line the bin with paper or a plastic bag. Drain the rubbish well before it is put in the bin. Empty the bin at least once a day. Wash at least once a week and if possible put to air. Disinfect with a safe household disinfectant occasionally.

The larder   Every week, sweep the walls and ceiling, and wipe all shelves with hot, soapy water. Wash and **scald** the bread-bin, vegetable rack and perforated meat covers.

If only wooden shelves are available in a larder, place a slab of slate or marble on one side to hold dairy produce. One window should be fitted with perforated zinc to admit air and exclude flies. Ventilators are also useful in a larder.

CLEANING UTENSILS

Saucepans   Directly the contents have been removed, the saucepan should be filled with tepid water. If food sticks to the pan or the contents have been burnt, soak in hot water until the food loosens, then scrape it off with a wooden spoon or rubber dish-scraper. Pans that are not made of aluminium can be boiled up with water and soda to get rid of stubborn stains, and apple or rhubarb peelings can be boiled in aluminium pans for the same purpose. It is very important to avoid using soda or scouring powders containing soda when cleaning aluminium pans, as they become pitted. For ordinary cleaning, regular use of wire-wool pads impregnated with soap will keep the pans in shining condition.

New pans and kettles should be filled with cold water and brought to the boil. Afterwards, they should be emptied, washed and thoroughly rinsed.

Omelette pans   Never wash these unless absolutely necessary. As soon as they are finished with, rub them all over with soft paper and wipe with a cloth. If they are stained or burnt, rub them with coarse salt.

Frying-pans and pans with wire baskets for deep frying   The fat should be allowed to cool and should then be strained through a fine sieve into a clean, dry bowl. The pan is wiped with kitchen paper and then with a dry cloth. The oil from deep frying can be used again.

Cake and bread tins, patty pans   Wash as seldom as possible, but wipe out when hot with a cloth. If they are washed, put near heat to dry.

Baking-tins   These can be boiled up with soda to clean off old grease if they have been neglected, otherwise regular cleaning with soap-pads will keep them clean.

Kettles should be emptied and flushed through regularly. Fur is removed from a kettle if some strong ammonia is put into it, then filled with water, and boiled slowly for about an hour. There are proprietary liquids on the market for defurring kettles, which are more suitable for electric kettles. Rinse well after either method and boil two lots of fresh water in the kettle before using it again. A marble or shell placed in the kettle prevents the formation of fur.

Knives   Wipe first with paper, then wash in hot water and dry. Never let the handles of knives lie in water. Non-stainless steel knives will need cleaning with wire-wool and soap or scouring powder. Store knives separately in a rack to preserve their cutting edge.

Wooden utensils, pastry boards, rolling-pins, salad bowls, etc. need special care. To prevent warping and cracking, clean immediately after use with very little water; never soak and never stand the article on edge while drying as this can cause warping. Salad bowls can be wiped clean only, and not washed, but flavours will become impregnated in the wood, so this is only satisfactory if you are always using the same sort of dressing.

Sieves and graters   Wash with a pot brush as soon as possible after they have been used, rinse well. Shake, wipe with a cloth, and hang near the window or fire to dry.

Mincers, parsley mills, etc   Dismantle when finished with and remove any pieces clinging to the teeth, wash in hot, soapy water, rinse and dry thoroughly, preferably near heat.

Pudding and jelly cloths   As soon as these are finished with, soak for an hour in hot water to which a piece of soda has been added. Rub them between the hands and rinse them in two or three waters. Hang them up to dry. Never use soap when washing these cloths. If very dirty, put them in a pan of water to which soda has been added and boil for half an hour. Rinse them well.

Pastry brushes, or any utensil that has been used with raw egg or milk. Always wash in cold water first, and remove egg or milk residue before using hot soapy water.

SHOPPING HINTS

Choosing meat – choosing poultry and game – choosing fish – choosing fruit – choosing vegetables – tinned, frozen and dehydrated foods – the larder or store cupboard – storing fruit and vegetables

There is no doubt that the best way of buying fresh meat, fish, fruit and vegetables is to shop daily, but most people do not have the time to do this, and one can be tempted to spend more than when shopping less frequently.

The time spent on shopping can be kept to a minimum with careful planning.

1 Keep a pencil and pad in the kitchen for noting when supplies need renewing.

2 Plan the week's menu before going shopping and list the ingredients needed in the order of the shops to be visited.

3 Keep an open mind about the type of fresh goods to choose, e.g. fish and vegetables, till you have seen what is available, reasonable in price and in good condition in the shops that day.

4 Plan to use the more perishable foods such as green vegetables on the day bought, and keep the others for later in the week.

5 Buy in bulk any commodity that is used a lot and will not deteriorate before it is finished.

6 If you stock up your deep-freeze with food for everyday use like butter or bread, plan to buy a load of one commodity on one trip and of another the next, so that the weight and cost of shopping is spread over the weeks.

7 It is not always economical to buy the cheapest goods, as they may be of inferior quality, but anything which is plentiful will be cheaper at that time and better in flavour and quality than when it is out of season.

CHOOSING MEAT

BEEF

The texture of the meat should be firm and elastic, the lean bright red, intermingled with grains of fat. The fat should be creamy and the suet white and firm. There should be little gristle in the prime cuts: a layer of gristle between the muscle and outer layer of fat indicates an old animal.

If meat has been deep-frozen, make sure it has completely defrosted at room temperature before cooking, or it will be tough.

All prime cuts of beef are tender and have good flavour. The coarse and medium cuts need slow cooking to achieve this, so choose your cut according to the method by which you will cook it.

An ox is usually divided into the following cuts, though there may be local variations:

Shoulder, chuck and blade (coarse cuts): need long, slow cooking; usually fairly lean and good for braising or stewing.

Top rib, fore rib, back rib (medium cuts): can be roasted on the bone or boned and rolled and used for roasting or braising.

Sirloin (prime cut): for roasting on the bone. Steaks cut from the upper part are grilled as entrecôte and porterhouse steaks.

Fillet (prime cut): from the undercut of sirloin. Usually grilled or fried as fillet steaks, *tournedos* or *filets mignons*, but large pieces can be roasted.

Wing rib (prime cut): sirloin without the fillet.

Rump steak (prime cut): for grilling or frying; plenty of flavour.

Topside (medium cut): economical as it has no bone; for pot-roasting or braising.

Silverside (coarse cut): can be salted or used fresh and either boiled or braised. Needs long, slow cooking. Has no bone.

Flank and skirt (coarse cut): good for stews, pies and puddings and give off a rich, well-flavoured gravy.

Brisket (coarse cut): has a certain amount of bone and fact; can be cooked fresh or salted, with or without the bone. Requires long, slow cooking, by boiling, braising or pot-roasting.

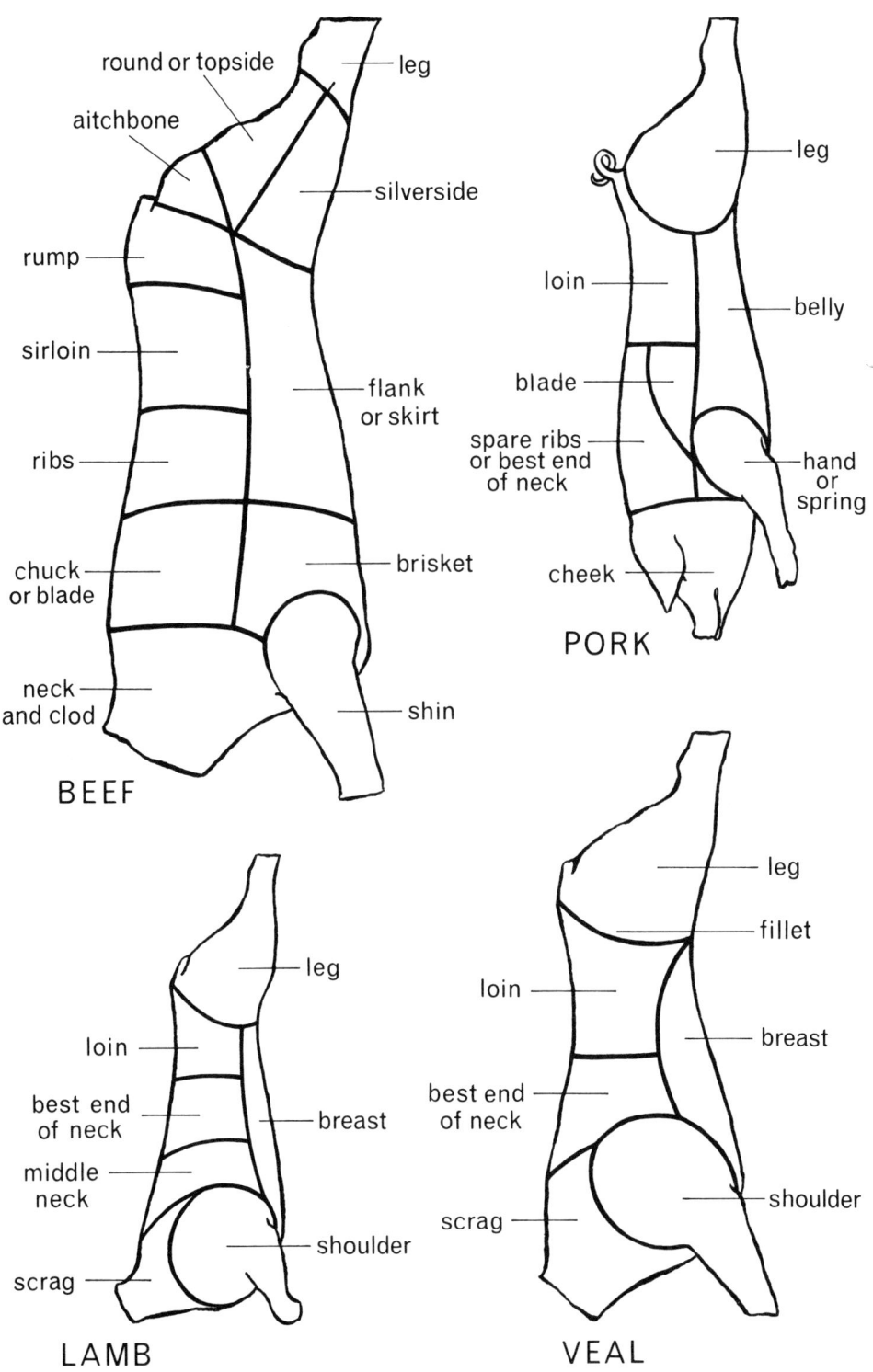

round or topside

leg

aitchbone

silverside

rump

sirloin

flank
or skirt

ribs

chuck
or blade

brisket

neck
and clod

shin

BEEF

leg

loin

belly

blade

spare ribs
or best end
of neck

hand
or
spring

cheek

PORK

leg

loin

best end
of neck

breast

middle
neck

shoulder

scrag

LAMB

leg

fillet

loin

breast

best end
of neck

scrag

shoulder

VEAL

Leg and shin (coarse cuts): contain a lot of gristle but are excellent for stewing.

Clod and sticking (coarse cuts): from the neck of the animal; can be stewed slowly or used for soups.

For meat on the bone and silverside, allow 200–300 g (½–¾ lb) per person; for boned meat allow 150–200 g (6–8 oz) per person.

Other portions of the ox, such as the heart, tail, tongue, liver, kidneys, sweetbread and tripe, which is the inner lining of the stomach, can all be used, as will be seen in later recipes.

VEAL

Two kinds of veal are sold: milk-fed veal, which is very tender, but expensive, and usually imported from the Continent, and grass-fed veal, which has more flavour but is less tender. The calf should not be older than eight to ten weeks when it is killed; if older, the meat will be coarse. The flesh should be dry, closely grained and off-white in the case of milk-fed veal, or pale pink for grass-fed veal. If it is moist and clammy or mottled, it is stale and should not be used. There is very little fat in veal, except round the kidneys, which should be well covered.

A calf is divided into the following joints:

Leg (prime cut): usually roasted, either on the bone, or boned and stuffed.

Fillet (prime cut): this is cut into thin slices on the bias from the top of the leg to make escalopes, or boned and roasted whole.

Loin (prime cut): this can be roasted on the bone, or boned and stuffed and roasted. It can also be cut into chops for frying, or escalopes may be cut from the underside of the loin.

Best end of neck (prime cut): cutlets for grilling, frying or braising.

Shoulder (prime cut): for roasting on the bone, or it can also be boned and rolled.

Scrag end and breast (medium cut): for stewing, boiling, and making jellied veal and veal moulds. Boned, stuffed and rolled breast can also be roasted or braised.

Hock and knuckle (medium cut): for boiling and stewing and making jellied veal.

Allow 500 g (1 lb) of shoulder, scrag end and breast with the bone per person; 250 g (½ lb) of leg or loin with the bone per person; 150 g (4–6 oz) of fillet per person.

Pie veal is often sold for making hot and cold pies, and consists of pieces of shoulder and breast, cut up ready for use.

A calf's head is a delicacy, usually served with parsley sauce. Calves' feet are also excellent when boiled, stewed or used for jelly. Veal makes the best stock for rich soups and gravies. The brains and sweetbreads are used in invalid fare and for light dishes. The kidneys can be used in stews, steak pies and puddings.

The liver is used according to any recipe for ox liver. The heart is stuffed, roasted or braised.

LAMB AND MUTTON

The colour of the flesh will vary from pink to bright red according to the age of the animal. The fat of home-produced lamb is creamy white, that of imported animals white and firm. In a young animal, the knuckle bone will have a bluish tinge.

Lamb is divided as follows:

Leg (prime cut): usually roasted, or boiled if lean. Can be divided into two, the shank and fillet. The shank is used for braising and stewing, the fillet for roasting whole, or cut up for grilling and frying. Chump chops are cut from the middle of the leg.

Loin (prime cut): for roasting. When two are sold together they form a saddle, which makes the choicest roasting joint. Chops are also cut from the loin.

Best end of neck (prime cut): used for roasting and as cutlets for grilling.

Middle neck (coarse cut): for pot-roasting and braising.

Scrag (coarse cut): for stewing and use in curries and hotpots.

Shoulder (medium cut): for roasting; pieces of shoulder meat can be used for grilling in kebabs.

Breast (coarse cut): can be boned, stuffed and roasted, or boiled, or can be used in stews if excessive fat is trimmed off.

Allow 260 g (½–¾ lb) per person of meat on the bone, 125 g (4–6 oz) of meat without bone.

The head and trotters make good soup, pies or stews. The heart, liver and lungs, in Scotland, form the foundation of haggis. The heart is also stuffed and roasted, and the liver made into various appetizing dishes. Mutton kidneys are considered the best.

DEER

Deer is cut up into four portions, namely: haunch, neck, shoulder and breast.

Venison can be tested by running a skewer into the shoulder; if this smells when withdrawn, the venison is high. Buck venison, which is in season from June to the end of September, is considered superior in flavour to doe venison. The latter is in season from October to the end of December. The fat should be firm, white and clean. The flesh should be dark and finely grained. It should be well hung (7 to 10 days) in order to acquire a game flavour. If the cleft of the hoof is smooth and close, the animal is young.

The haunch may be roasted, grilled, **sautéd** or braised. Steeping in a **marinade** before cooking improves the flavour of all venison.

PORK

This can now be bought safely at all times of the year provided it is refrigerated in hot weather. It should be pink with firm white fat and the skin, or rind, smooth and thin. Never buy pork with kernels in the fat.

The pig is divided into:

Leg (prime cut): for roasting. Fillets cut from the top are used for grilling and frying.

Loin (prime cut): for roasting, or cut into chops.

Spare ribs (medium cut): for pot-roasting and stewing; can be roasted or divided into cutlets.

Blade (prime cut): this is cut from the top part of the foreleg and used for roasting.

Hand and spring (medium cut): this is the foreleg and is suitable for roasting, pot-roasting and stewing.

Belly (prime cut): it is often salted, then boiled, or cut into slices for grilling or frying. It is a useful ingredient in making pâtés and terrines.

Allow 250 g (½–¾ lb) of meat on the bone and 125 g (4–6 oz) of boneless meat per person.

Pig's head is usually salted and made into brawn. The feet or trotters are boiled or stewed. The tongue is pickled or simmered slowly and served hot or cold. The heart, liver, kidneys and sweetbread are generally sliced and fried.

Bacon, gammon and ham are taken from pigs specially bred for this purpose. The sides or flitches of bacon pigs are salted down for about three weeks, and this makes 'green bacon' with pink flesh and a white rind. Smoked bacon is green bacon which has undergone a further curing process which will turn the rind golden-brown and the flesh dark pink. Rashers of bacon from the flitch are divided into back rashers (long, short and ribs) which are lean, and streaky (top, prime and thin) which are striped with fat.

Gammon and ham are both cut from the hind leg of the bacon pig but are cured in different ways, gammon being salted first. Gammon is divided into four joints, all suitable for boiling: gammon hock, middle and corner gammon and gammon slipper. Middle and corner gammon also make grilling rashers.

Bacon joints come from the forehock, which is often divided into three: the butt, lean and suitable for boiling; the small hock, for mincing or casseroling; and the fore slipper, fatty, but good for boiling. The best bacon joint for boiling is the collar.

CHOOSING POULTRY AND GAME

Turkeys   Choose a bird with plump, white flesh, a smooth back leg with a short spur; this indicates a young bird. The eyes will be bright and full and the feet supple if it is fresh. Allow 500 g (1 lb) approximately of undressed turkey per person. A frozen turkey will be oven ready, and the given weight will be less than the undressed bird, so allow about 350 g (¾ lb) per person.

Chicken   The young bird has a smooth leg and a short spur and a soft, flexible breast-bone. When fresh, the vent is close and dark. For roasting, birds usually weigh up to 2 ½ kg (5 lb), although capons can weigh up to 4 kg (8 lb) and are suitable for roasting. Allow the same weight per person as for turkeys.

Boiling chickens will be older and tougher birds up to 3 ½ kg (7 lb) in weight. These should be served in casseroles or made-up dishes.

Geese   In young geese the feet and bills will be yellow and free from hair. When fresh, the feet are pliable and the webbing easily torn; they are stiff when stale. When young, the underbill breaks easily when bent. A goose that is over a year old should never be eaten.

Ducks may be selected by the same rules as geese.

Pigeons, when fresh, have supple feet, and the vent will be firm; if discoloured they are stale. The legs should be pinkish in colour, the breast plump and fat.

Plovers, when fat, have hard vents; but, like almost all other birds, may be chosen by the above rules.

Hares and Rabbits   When hares and rabbits are young and fresh, the cleft in the lip is narrow, the body stiff, and the claws are smooth and sharp. In order to ascertain whether they are young or old, turn the claws sideways; if they crack they are young. The small nut under the paw should be well developed; this disappears in older animals.

Partridges   Yellow legs and a dark bill are signs by which a young bird may be known; they have a rigid vent when fresh. When this part is green the bird is stale.

Pheasants may be chosen as above. The young birds are known by the short or round spur, which in the old is long and pointed.

Moor Game   Grouse, woodcocks, snipe, quails, ortolans, etc., may be chosen by the rules given above. Young game birds have smooth pliable legs with short rounded spurs and supple feet. The feathers under the wing and on the breast of young birds should be soft and downy, and the long wing-feathers pointed.

CHOOSING FISH

The eyes of fresh fish are bright, the gills of a fine clear red, the body stiff, and the smell not unpleasant. Fish should only be eaten in season and very fresh. Oily fish and freshwater fish should be cooked as fresh as possible.

A **turbot** should be thick; the underside very white.

Salmon and **cod** should have small heads, very thick shoulders and small tails. The flesh of the salmon should be of a bright red colour, the scales very bright.

Herrings, mackerel, or **whiting** should not be bought unless they are quite fresh, and do not attempt to keep them even till the next day. **Cod** and **soles** may be kept for 24 hours.

Eels should be bought alive. **Crabs** and **lobsters** should be heavy and very stiff; if they feel limp they are stale. They are often bought alive. **Oysters** and **mussels**, if fresh, will close forcibly on the knife when opened. If the shell gapes in the least degree, the oyster is losing its freshness. When the fish is dead the shell remains open. Small 'natives' are the best oysters for eating.

In the case of most fish, allow 250 g–375 g (½–¾ lb) unfilleted for two people. For turbot and brill, allow 250 g (½ lb) per head. A lobster weighing 500 g (1 lb) will serve two portions.

CHOOSING FRUIT

Soft fruit should be bought on the day of eating and be dry. **Lemons** should be firm and light yellow; **oranges** firm and rich, deep orange in colour. **Grapefruit** will keep a long time if bought firm and light yellow, but are best eaten when golden yellow and those mottled with brown have the best flavour of all. **Pears, melons** and **plums** can be bought under-ripe and kept till ripe, but must be watched daily as they tend to go 'over the top' very suddenly. **Pears** will be ready to eat when the neck yields to gentle pressure. A ripe **melon** can be judged mainly by its smell, which should be full and not musty, and by its yielding gently to pressure on its base. Canteloupe, Ogen and Charentais melons will have a much stronger scent and be softer than Honeydew or water-melons. The seeds of ripe water-melons rattle when the fruit is shaken. Unripe **apricots** never ripen satisfactorily for eating, but tend to shrivel; ripe ones have a rosy bloom. The bloom on **peaches**, however, does not necessarily indicate ripeness. This is tested by the flesh round the stalk yielding to gentle pressure. **Apples** can be obtained all the year round, thanks to cold stores and imports. Until you get to know the characteristics of each variety, it is as well to ask the assistant to distinguish between crisp and soft varieties.

CHOOSING VEGETABLES

Green vegetables and **salads** should be crisp and not yellow, preferably eaten the day bought. **Beans**, runner and French, must be bright coloured and not too large, and should snap crisply in two when tested. On the Continent, the French beans are graded and sold according to size, the smallest being the most expensive. **Broad beans** should have green pods that are reasonably distended by the bean, but are not very hard and knobbly. **Root vegetables** must be firm. **Celery** should be large-stalked, smooth and crisp and is now sold green or white. **New potatoes** should be bought in small quantities and not kept for more than three or four days. The skin should rub off easily when rubbed with the thumb.

TINNED FOODS

Tinned, frozen and dehydrated goods are useful when a supply of fresh food is not easily available and are also useful in emergencies.

Always buy a reliable brand of goods and buy them from shops or stores of repute which have a quick turnover. It is not advisable to buy tinned goods in too large quantities, or to keep them in stock too long. Once a tin has been opened, the contents must be used as soon as possible, certainly within 48 hours.

Store tinned goods in a cool, dry place and empty the contents from the tins directly they are opened. On the whole it is better to buy small tins of the best quality so that the whole of the contents may be used up at once.

Tinned meat   Tins of tongue and ham are excellent for emergencies, used just as they are, direct from the tin, though they may also be cut up and used in fricassées, rice dishes, etc. Stewed steak is extremely useful. It is economical and may be used in pies or to make a stew with vegetables added, will curry satisfactorily or make a meat sauce for a pasta.

Tinned fish   All types of tinned fish are good for cooking, from the inexpensive mackerel and pilchards to luxuries like lobster and oysters. They can all be used in made-up dishes with great success.

Tinned vegetables   Some of these are invaluable for adding to dishes: tinned pimentoes, tomatoes and sweet corn are particularly useful. Sauerkraut, for those who like it, is good, as is cooked beetroot in vinegar for salads, and petits pois, especially if cooked in the French method (p. 194) with lettuce and spring onions. Other tinned peas, carrots, potatoes and mushrooms tend to have a very recognizable flavour and need to be used with discretion.

Tinned fruit   Certain tinned fruits, such as grapefruit segments, lychees, small seeded grapes, cherries, pineapple pieces, when mixed with fresh fruit, will enhance a winter fruit salad. Tinned pineapple is also very useful fried, as an accompaniment to rich meats such as pork, ham, goose. Tinned apricots may be used in the same way.

Tinned chestnuts and chestnut purée are excellent and save all the labour of preparing fresh chestnuts.

Tinned soups   Concentrated soups can be used undiluted for sauces; other tinned soups may be invaluable for emergencies and enhanced by the addition of a little cream or sherry or the blending of two kinds such as asparagus and green pea, or mushroom and celery.

FROZEN FOODS

The advantages of frozen foods are two-fold: they are labour-saving and they are of good quality, as the manufacturers only freeze the best.

The disadvantages are cost and a certain loss of flavour, though a fresh-frozen commodity, e.g. fish or vegetables, is certainly better than a stale 'fresh' one.

Always follow the instructions on the pack about storage and cooking.

Fish and vegetables should be used frozen, meat and poultry completely defrosted. Ice-cream should never be refrozen and only removed from the freezer at the last possible minute. Frozen pastry is excellent and only needs about an hour at room temperature before it can be used. Pies and pasties which are already prepared may be cooked straight from the freezer.

DEHYDRATED FOODS

Vegetables   Onions are perhaps the best of these; they are bought sliced in packets or jars and can be used straight from the pack in stews, casseroles and soups. Dried celery is also obtainable, as are dried, mixed vegetables.

Instant mashed potato has a place in all store cupboards; it will top a cottage pie in an emergency or can be piped to decorate a dish, and the better varieties are indistinguishable from fresh mashed potatoes.

Dried mushrooms, though not easily obtained, are the best form of preserved mushroom.

Dried peas, beans and lentils all keep well, but need to be soaked overnight in cold water before use.

Fruit   Dried fruits that are used as a dessert, e.g. prunes, apple rings, apricots, figs, peaches, must be soaked overnight in hot water and cooked in the liquor they soaked in.

Other dried fruits, used for cooking, e.g. sultanas, currants, raisins and dates, should be bought in small quantities and kept in a dry place, and will need careful cleaning before use.

Dried herbs   These are treated in a separate section (p. 42).

THE LARDER OR STORE CUPBOARD

The larder or store cupboard should be very dry and well ventilated. It should be lined with shelves. Narrow shelves about 38 cm (15 in.) apart are more useful than fewer, wider shelves, as it is difficult to see the products at the back of a wide shelf. Small tiers of circular shelves that revolve can be bought or made and placed in the corner of a larder or cupboard and are great space-savers. There should be jars or canisters for sugars and tins for keeping tea, coffee, biscuits and so on. Save empty sweet and biscuit tins for this.

Jams, pickles and **preserves** should be kept in the coolest part of the store.

Coffee should be bought in small quantities as it loses its flavour quickly; it must be kept in a tin with a tight lid. **Tea** should also be bought in moderate quantities and kept in a tin.

Tapioca, sago and **semolina** must be kept dry and close covered as they harbour mites. Keep in jars or tins and examine regularly.

Dried fruits   Store these in tins lined with greaseproof paper. They require watching, as they sometimes become infested with maggots.

Shelled nuts tend to go rancid if kept. Buy in small quantities and store in tins.

Spices and **dried herbs** are apt to deteriorate, so should be bought in small quantities. If the little bottles and drums are kept in alphabetical order in a shallow box or lid, they will quickly be located when wanted.

Salt must be kept very dry; the pottery salt containers shaped like a ship's funnel really do keep it so.

Candles and **soap** if bought and stored for months before they are used will last very much longer.

Tinned goods should be chosen carefully. The tins should be free from rust and bulges. They should not be kept too long and it is a good idea to write the date of purchase on each tin before storage to ensure this does not happen.

Care of perishable foods   Meat should be unwrapped and wiped with a dry, clean cloth as soon as it comes from the butcher's; in loins, the long pipe that runs by the bone should be taken out. If there is no refrigerator, meat that is to be kept hanging for some time should be sprinkled with pepper. In hot weather, a lump of charcoal in the larder will help keep the meat fresh. Meat becomes more digestible and tender with hanging, but lamb and veal cannot be kept as long as beef or mutton.

Cooked meat must be lifted from the gravy or sauce in which it has been served, and put on a clean dry plate with a wire cover, or wrapped in foil or polythene.

Frozen meat should be placed in a warm kitchen for several hours before cooking.

Hares should be hung head downwards without paunching if they have been freshly killed. In dry weather hares may hang for a week.

Rabbits must be paunched at once and should be used fresh. If they have to be kept a day or two, they should not be skinned until required, or they become very dry. They should be hung head downwards.

Poultry, if freshly killed, may hang for a day or two. It can be plucked at once and dusted over with flour and pepper, but not drawn until ready for use.

Game must hang for a few days. The length of time depends on the weather, as in damp, muggy weather it will not keep as long as in cold, dry weather. Young birds will not keep as long as old ones, nor will birds that have been badly shot or bruised. All game should hang unplucked and undrawn. A piece of charcoal placed in the vent helps to preserve game. Birds must not be allowed to touch one another while hanging. When the tail feathers pull out easily, the birds are ready for cooking, but if liked really high, they can be kept until they give off a pungent smell. Birds that are tainted may be washed in vinegar and water.

Wild duck and **waterfowl** should be used fresh, as they are very oily and so do not keep well. Small birds which are cooked without being drawn will not keep for long.

Venison should always hang before it is cooked; in dry, cool weather it may be hung for a fortnight. Before it is hung, it must be wiped well and sprinkled with black pepper. It should be examined daily and wiped dry and dredged with fresh pepper. To test it, a skewer should be run into the bone at the haunch. If, when withdrawn, it is not sticky and has no unpleasant smell, the venison is in good condition.

Ham and **sides** or **flitches of bacon** keep well in muslin or calico bags hung from the ceiling. They must be dusted over with black pepper and ginger before they are hung up.

Suet   All glands, kernel, skin or veins, and any discoloured portions should be removed, the suet dusted with flour and kept in an air-tight jar. Another method of keeping suet is to melt it slowly in a saucepan over minimal heat, preferably using an asbestos mat. When melted, it should be poured into a basin of cold water. When hard, drain off the water, wipe it dry, wrap it in foil and store in a cold place. Suet bought in packets already shredded can be kept in the packet in the refrigerator.

Lard must be kept in a closely covered jar.

Bones for stock, if not used immediately, should be baked or grilled.

Butter should be kept in the refrigerator; most models have a special compartment that keeps the butter less cold than the rest. One packet of butter can be kept out of the refrigerator in a special earthenware butter dish, so that there is always soft butter available.

Only **cream cheese** should be refrigerated, although it is possible to put some cheese in the refrigerator for a day or two if it is necessary to keep it from ripening too much before a certain day. In this case, it must be tightly wrapped in foil to avoid tainting the other food, and returned to room temperature for several hours before being eaten.

Milk and **cream**   All vessels containing milk and cream should be washed and **scalded** daily. As soon as they are emptied, cold water must be poured into them. This loosens the milk caked on the vessels, which hot water would fix. Later the bottles should be washed in hot water, then filled with boiling water, which should be left for a few moments. They should be emptied and wiped dry.

Milk quickly becomes tainted, so should be kept away from anything with a strong odour. All vessels containing milk should be covered and kept in the coolest place in the larder on a slate or stone slab if a refrigerator is not available. Earthenware covers for milk bottles help to keep them cool, and in heat-waves, it is advisable to stand bottles of milk in cold water if there is no refrigerator. Milk can be **scalded** in hot weather too as follows:

Put it into a double saucepan or into a jug, place the latter on a wire rack in a pan of cold water. Bring to the boil and cook for a few minutes.

Never mix a fresh lot of milk with that which has been in the house for some time, as it may all turn sour.

Cream may also be **scalded**. A lump of sugar will help to preserve it. If either milk or cream turns sour, it need not be thrown away; delicious little milk cheeses can be made with it, and scones, cakes and pastries are lighter when mixed with sour milk.

To make Devonshire Cream   Strain fresh cows' milk into large shallow pans or basins about 10 cm (4 in.) deep and let it stand for 24 hours in a very cool place. Then place the pans or basins on a hot plate and heat them very gently; on no account allow the milk to boil. As soon as the cream forms a ring round the pan and the undulations formed on the surface look thick, it is ready. Remove the pans from the fire, put them into a cold larder and leave for 24 hours, or in very cold weather for 36 hours. Then skim off the cream carefully.

Eggs should be stored in a cool place or in the refrigerator. Because the shells are porous, they should be kept away from food with a strong odour. Egg yolks may be kept for a day or two in a cold place if they are covered with cold water in a bowl with a lid on. Egg whites may be kept for the same time in a covered container.

It is a good plan to store eggs when plentiful, for use in the winter. There are various ways of doing this. If they are to be kept for a short while only, they should be smeared with Vaseline, lard or oil, and placed between layers of bran in a box. They should not touch each other.

Whole eggs may be stored in the freezer if taken out of their shell and put in a waxed carton, as may separated egg yolks and whites.

To preserve eggs in salt   Put them in strong earthenware jars in layers of coarse, dry salt.

The first layer of salt must be deep enough to allow the eggs to be placed in it, small end downwards, without touching the bottom of the jar. The eggs must not touch one another; cover with another layer of salt and continue alternate layers of salt and eggs until the crock is full. The layers of salt must be deep enough to keep the eggs from touching one another and the top layer must be salt. Cover the jar and keep in a cool place.

Eggs may be preserved also in waterglass, which is obtainable in tins with full directions for use. For this method, they are stored in a pail or large crock.

STORING FRUIT AND VEGETABLES

Vegetables for immediate use should be kept in wooden boxes on the floor in a cool place, or in wire vegetable racks. **Onions, shallots** and **garlic** are best kept in netted bags. **Parsley, watercress** and **mint** should be stood in water, which must be changed daily.

Green vegetables keep best if wrapped in newspaper; **lettuce** and **endive** put in polythene bags in the refrigerator or unwrapped in the special compartment provided for salads. **Cucumbers**, if sealed in a polythene tube, should be kept in this and cut through the wrapping as needed. The cut end of the cucumber should be covered with strips of peel, and it can be kept in the refrigerator. **Tomatoes** lose their flavour if refrigerated; they should be spread out on a dish or shelf without touching one another. The tops should be cut off rashishes, carrots and turnips. **Radishes** must be laid in a very little water for about an hour before using them.

Most fruit loses its flavour if stored in the refrigerator, though if soft fruits have to be kept for more than a day they should be cleaned and put into a fresh container and kept in the refrigerator. If **melons** are to be chilled before serving, they should be wrapped in foil before placing in the refrigerator, as their smell will spread to the other contents. **Bananas** should never, under any circumstances, be refrigerated. If **apples** and **pears** are to be stored for any length of time, they should be placed in special trays manufactured for this purpose, so that they do not touch each other, and kept in a cool, dark place, or wrapped individually in newspaper before storing in a box, and examined regularly. **Avocado pears** and **melons** that are not ripe can be kept in the airing cupboard and examined daily till ready.

Brands of **frozen vegetables** and **fruit** should be consumed within 24 hours, unless stored in the freezer or deep-freeze section of a refrigerator.

GENERAL COOKERY HINTS

Getting ready for cooking – tables of weights and measures – weighing without scales – measures for liquids – cooking temperatures – oven temperatures – oven positions – oven management – fridge and freezer temperatures – glossary of terms – usual accompaniments to serve with dishes – the art of using up – emergency dishes – herbs and spices

GETTING READY FOR COOKING

1 Read your recipe right through, making sure you have all the ingredients.

2 If the oven is to be used, turn it on at the required setting and arrange the shelves in the right positions.

3 Assemble the ingredients and cooking utensils.

4 Prepare the ingredients before starting to cook: measure, chop, peel, **blanch**, etc.

5 Prepare the containers if they need greasing or lining with paper.

WEIGHTS AND MEASURES

Exact conversions between imperial and metric measures would result in awkward, unmeasurable amounts. It has been decided, therefore, in this book, to follow the recommendation of the Metrication Board in taking the unit 25 g as the equivalent of 1 oz, and 25 ml as the equivalent of 1 fl. oz. By using these conversions, the resulting dish will be smaller in volume in metric measure than in imperial, and will, therefore need slightly less cooking time, and in the case of cakes, slightly smaller tins.

Large kitchen scales are obtainable that take weights up to 5 kg or 10 lb and are graduated down to 1 oz.

Smaller scales are available for weights up to 500 g or 18 oz and are graduated down to 5 g and ¼ oz.

Capacity measures are supplied in graded spoons and jugs.

	Imperial	Exact conversions	Metric equivalent
Weight	1 oz	28·35 g	25 g
	2 oz	56·7 g	50 g
	4 oz	113·4 g	100 g
	8 oz	226·8 g	200 g
	12 oz	340·2 g	300 g
	1 lb	453·6 g	500 g
	2 lb	907·2 g	800 g
Capacity	1 fl. oz	26·35 ml	25 ml
	2 fl. oz	56·7 ml	50 ml
	5 fl. oz (¼ pt)	141·75 ml	125 ml
	½ pt	283·5 ml	250 ml
	¾ pt	425·25 ml	375 ml
	1 pt	567 ml	500 ml
	2 pt	1136·5 ml	1 litre

1   5 ml spoon = 1 teaspoon
1 10 ml spoon = 1 dessertspoon
1 15 ml spoon = 1 tablespoon

WEIGHING WITHOUT SCALES

A breakfastcupful of moist sugar (pressed in) weighs about 225 g (8 oz).

A breakfastcupful of castor sugar (level) weighs about 225 g (8 oz).

A breakfastcupful of rice weighs about 250 g (9 oz).

A breakfastcupful of butter, lard or dripping weighs about 200 g (7 oz).

A breakfastcupful of flour, arrowroot, cornstarch (heaped) weighs about 200 g (7 oz).

A breakfastcupful of chopped suet (heaped) weighs about 125 g (4 oz).

A breakfastcupful of breadcrumbs (pressed in) weighs about 125 g (4 oz).

A breakfastcupful of sago, tapioca or semolina (heaped) weighs about 225 g (8 oz).

1 tablespoonful of flour, rounded, weighs about 25 g (1 oz).

1 level tablespoonful of sugar weighs about 25 g (1 oz).

1 level teaspoon of sugar weighs about 7 g (¼ oz).

1 level tablespoonful of rice weighs about 25 g (1 oz).

MEASURES FOR LIQUIDS

1 fluid lb or 20 fluid oz = 1 lb or 16 oz solid measure.

10 fluid oz = ½ pint = 1 breakfast cup or 1 tumbler.

5 fluid oz = ¼ pint or 1 gill = 1 teacup.

½ fluid oz = 1 tablespoon.

60 drops = 1 fluid drachm = 1 teaspoon.

Note: In the north of England, a gill is ½ pint and a noggin ¼ pint.

1 litre = 1¾ imperial pints or 35·2 oz.

1 American pint = 4/5 imperial pint or 16 fluid oz.

COOKING TEMPERATURES

Boiling   100°C (212°F); indicated by bubbles all over.

Simmering   96°C (185°F–205°F); a few small bubbles on surface.

Poaching   80°C (170°F–180°F); surface quivering.

Frying
Fritters and first frying of potatoes: 177°C (350°F) approximately; a **croûton** of bread will sizzle gently.
Croquettes, rissoles, large fillets of fish: 182°C (360°F) approximately; a **croûton** will brown in about a minute, and a light blue haze begins to rise.
Croûtons, crisping chips, small fillets of fish, whitebait: 199°C (390°F) approximately; a **croûton** will brown in 30 seconds.

OVEN TEMPERATURES

	Electric oven settings	Centigrade	Gas oven settings
Cool	200°F	95°C	¼
	225°F	110°C	
Slow	250°F	130°C	½
	275°F	140°C	1
	300°F	150°C	2
Moderate	325°F	160°C	3
	350°F	180°C	4
Fairly hot	375°F	190°C	5
	400°F	200°C	6
Hot	425°F	220°C	7
	450°F	230°C	8
Very hot	475°F	240°C	9
	500°F	260°C	

OVEN POSITIONS

Near top	Yorkshire pudding, pastry, small cakes, whisked sponges.
Centre	Meat, creamed cake mixtures, casseroles.
Near bottom	Milk puddings, large fruit cakes, casseroles.

OVEN MANAGEMENT

1 Place the oven shelves in right position before the oven is heated.

2 Turn on oven to required temperature setting about 20 minutes before food is put in. Most ovens indicate when the temperature is reached.

3 Unless the oven is fan heated, when the temperature will be constant throughout, the centre of the oven corresponds to the thermostat setting, the top being hotter and the bottom cooler.

4 In the case of cakes, batters and pastry, try not to open the door of the oven until at least two-thirds of the cooking time has elapsed, and then if it must be opened and shut, do so very gently.

FRIDGE AND FREEZER TEMPERATURES

4°C (40°F)–7°C (45°F)	Average temperature in main cabinet of refrigerator
0°C (32°F)	Freezing point of water
–6°C (21°F)	One-star frozen-food compartment in refrigerator

−12°C (10°F)   Two-star frozen-food compartment in refrigerator

−18°C (0°F)   Three-star frozen-food compartment in refrigerator and food
                               freezer at normal storage setting

GLOSSARY OF TERMS

Au gratin   Sprinkled with breadcrumbs and butter and browned.

Bain marie   A large container half-filled with hot water in which smaller vessels stand for poaching food or keeping sauces hot.

Bake blind   To bake a pastry case without a filling for 15 to 20 minutes in a hot oven. Line the bottom with a piece of foil, removing it before adding filling.

Bard   To wrap meat or poultry in strips of pork fat for cooking.

Baste   To spoon fat or juice over food while cooking to keep it moist.

Beurre manié   Butter and flour worked together to make a paste and used for thickening gravies, and other liquids.

Bind   Using egg or milk, to make a mixture of ingredients stick together.

Blanch   Either to dip vegetables or fruit for a minute in boiling water, before immersing in cold (used as a preparation for freezing or for skinning fruit); or to put in cold water and bring to the boil, then rinse in cold water to reduce strong flavours (used for some offal, and some bitter vegetables such as chicory).

Bouquet garni   Bunch of herbs for flavouring, consisting of thyme, parsley and a bay-leaf tied together, or in a small muslin bag.

Canapé   A slice of fried or toasted bread on which savouries are placed.

Chaudfroid   Coating of white or brown sauce covered with aspic for cold cooked chicken or meat.

Chine   To prepare best end of loin joints for carving by cutting away bone at the wide end of chops or cutlets to enable it to be divided into single ribs.

Clarify   **1** to purify dripping by boiling it up with cold water for 20 minutes, then allowing it to cool, when the pure fat will rise and can gently be poured off, leaving the impurities to sink to the bottom of the pan.
2 to purify butter by heating without browning until it is silent, letting it stand for a few moments, then gently pouring off pure fat as for clarifying dripping.

Court-bouillon   Mixture of water, herbs, vegetables and wine or vinegar, used for cooking fish.

Cream   To beat butter until it is soft and creamy.

Croûtons   Small cubes of fried bread.

Dredge   To sprinkle lightly.

En papillote   Cooked wrapped in oiled paper or foil.

Flake   To break up gently the flesh of cooked fish – best done with the fingers.

Fold in   To incorporate one ingredient into another by gently turning the mixture over with a spoon or spatula.

Glaze   Liquid brushed over a dish to give it a shiny appearance.

Julienne   Cut in thin, match-like strips.

Knead   To pummel a dough lightly with the knuckles to give a smooth texture.

Lard   To thread strips of pork fat or lardons into the surface of meat or poultry with a larding needle.

Liaison   Thickening agent for sauces and gravies, e.g. **beurre manié** (see above), **roux** (see below), with starch (flour, cornflour, potato flour or arrowroot), or with egg yolk and cream.

Marinade   A mixture, generally of oil, herbs, vinegar or wine, for steeping raw meat or fish in before cooking.

Reduce   To make a liquid more concentrated by boiling it till some of the water content evaporates.

Roux   Hot fat and flour mixed together and cooked to varying degrees of colour to make the base of white, blond or brown sauces.

Rub in   To incorporate fat into flour for pastry-making and some cake-making, by rubbing small pieces of fat lightly with the finger tips into the flour till the mixture resembles breadcrumbs.

Sauter   To cook in hot butter or oil, either from the raw state or in the case of root vegetables, boiled first and finished in the sauté pan.

Scald   To heat a liquid such as milk to just below boiling point or to pour on boiling water.

Score   To make incisions 1 cm (½ in.) apart on the skin of pork for crackling, or lightly for decoration on pastry.

Sweat   To cook slowly in a little fat in a covered pan to soften the food (usually vegetables).

USUAL ACCOMPANIMENTS TO SERVE WITH DISHES

The traditional accompaniments to many standard dishes are as follows:

Oysters, smoked salmon, potted shrimps   Quarters of lemon, brown bread and butter, and sometimes paprika.

Melon   Sugar, ginger.

Soups   With clear soups, and with minestrone, grated Parmesan cheese is often handed. With both clear and thick soups, small cubes of fried bread (**croûtons**) are served. With Mulligatawny soup, hand boiled rice to which a little turmeric has been added. With split-pea soup, powdered mint, very finely shredded and fried bacon are often served.

FISH

Poached fish is garnished with parsley and cut lemon; salmon with cucumber as well. A hot sauce often accompanies fish.

All fried fish, whole or in fillets, is usually served with some fish sauce and garnished with fried parsley and cut lemon.

Cod or turbot (poached)   Usually served with egg, shrimp or parsley sauce, sometimes with oyster sauce. Salt cod requires egg sauce and is usually served with boiled parsnips.

Salmon or turbot (poached)   Hollandaise, shrimp or lobster sauce, garnished with cut cucumber and lemon.

Salmon (grilled)   Maître d'hôtel or anchovy butter.
Salmon (cold)   Mayonnaise or tartare sauce.
Mackerel (poached)   Fennel or parsley sauce.
Mackerel or herrings (grilled)   Mustard sauce.
Skate (poached)   Brown butter or parsley sauce.
Whitebait   Cut lemon and thin brown bread and butter.
Red mullet (grilled or poached)   Parsley or tomato sauce.

MEAT

Beef (roast)   Yorkshire pudding, hot or cold horse-radish sauce, or grated horse-radish, clear gravy.
Beef (boiled, fresh)   Some green vegetable is usually served, or carrots, turnips, etc., pease pudding and the liquor in which it was boiled.
Beef (boiled, pickled or salted)   Suet dumplings, carrots, turnips, onions or leeks and the liquor in which it was boiled.
   Calf's head (boiled)   Parsley or brown sauce – sometimes brain sauce and boiled bacon.
   Mutton (boiled)   Caper or parsley sauce and carrots, turnips and leeks.
   Mutton (roast, saddle, loin or leg)   Redcurrant or cranberry jelly and clear gravy.
   Mutton (shoulder)   Onion sauce, baked potatoes.
   Lamb (roast)   Mint sauce, clear gravy.
   Veal (roast)   Boiled bacon or ham, thick gravy. Forcemeat balls are often used as a garnish.
   Veal (breast, boiled)   Parsley sauce and boiled bacon.
   Venison (roast)   Redcurrant or rowanberry jelly and thickened gravy.
   Pork (roast)   Sage and onion stuffing, apple sauce and thickened gravy.
   Pork (boiled, fresh or pickled)   Pease pudding, carrots or parsnips, plain white sauce or the meat liquor.
Boiled bacon   Cabbage or haricot beans, parsley sauce.
Ham (braised)   Brown sauce, pineapple rings, redcurrant jelly.
Rabbit (boiled)   Pickled pork, onion sauce.
Rabbit (roasted)   Herb stuffing, forcemeat balls, thickened gravy or tomato sauce.

POULTRY

Chicken (roast)   Grilled or fried bacon, watercress, bread sauce and thickened gravy.
   Chicken (boiled)   Egg or parsley sauce, boiled bacon, ham or tongue.
   Duck (roast)   Thickened gravy, apple, cranberry or orange sauce.
   Turkey (roast)   Grilled or fried sausages, bacon rolls, bread sauce and thickened gravy, cranberry jelly.
   Turkey (boiled)   Celery, oyster or egg sauce, boiled ham, tongue or bacon.
   Pigeons (roast)   Thickened gravy, watercress, served on toast.
   Goose (roast)   Apple or gooseberry sauce, thick gravy.

ROAST GAME

Guinea fowl   Bread sauce and watercress, thickened gravy.
   Partridges, grouse and ptarmigan, pheasant, quails   Bread sauce, fried breadcrumbs, clear gravy, watercress.
   Wild duck and widgeons, teal   Orange sauce or salad, clear gravy, watercress, cut lemon.

Hare   Redcurrant or cranberry jelly, forcemeat balls (fried), brown or port wine sauce.

Note   Fried potato chips or straw potatoes and a green salad should always be served with all roast game and most poultry.

VEGETABLES

Asparagus and sea kale (hot)   Melted butter, oiled butter or Hollandaise sauce.
   Asparagus (cold)   Vinaigrette or mayonnaise sauce.
   Globe artichokes   Oiled butter, Hollandaise or piquante sauce.
   Jerusalem artichokes   White or parsley sauce.
   Vegetable marrow   White, béchamel or parsley sauce.
   Cauliflower   White or cheese sauce.
   French beans and peas   Fresh butter, put over them after dishing.
   Broad beans   White or parsley sauce.
   Celery (boiled)   White sauce.
   Celery (braised)   Brown sauce.

THE ART OF USING UP

It really is an art to make use of any food that is left over and to present it in an appetizing and attractive way. This will obviously be a means of stretching the budget, and in some cases, will also be labour saving, as part of the ingredients for a dish using left-overs will be prepared and cooked already. Any food left from a meal should be put on a clean plate to be worked into some dish later on.

Half a bloater or kipper or a small portion of finnan haddock may be turned into appetizing savouries if the skin and bones are removed, and the flesh pounded with a teaspoon of anchovy essence and a little butter. Serve on small **croûtons** of fried bread or toast.

A rasher of bacon, small piece of ham or tongue, kidney or liver may be incorporated with a mince of any meat, poultry or game, and give flavour to rissoles or croquettes.

Use left-over rice, macaroni or other cereals in fish or meat croquettes, in kedgeree or as a filling for omelettes mixed with cooked mushrooms and a little cream. Plain boiled rice can be mixed with custard and topped with jam for a quickly made sweet, or steamed with eggs, sugar and cinnamon and served with pears (p. 209).

All bones and trimmings of meat, poultry or game should be used for stock, together with scraps of cooked or uncooked 'pot' vegetables. Every scrap of fat, cooked or uncooked should be **clarified** for use as dripping (p. 37).

Cold potatoes may be used in various ways. Cut into slices, they may be fried or **sautéd** or made into salads. If rubbed through a sieve, they are useful for making into fish cakes, potato or meat croquettes, potato bouchées (p. 161) or potato cakes (p. 294).

Cold cooked vegetables make excellent salad either alone or separately, or they can be made into vegetable cutlets (p. 199), patties or pies, or simmered in milk and sieved for soups.

Cold fish, meat, poultry or game can be diced or minced and combined with rice, or mixed into a sauce and served on toast, in vol-au-vent cases or in pancakes, or made into a pie with a potato topping, or curried.

Suet puddings can be returned to a basin covered with greased paper and re-steamed, or they may be cut into slices and fried lightly in butter and sprinkled with sugar and lemon juice.

Left-over jellies or creams may be melted down and put into smaller moulds.

Stale cheese, if grated, will keep in a jar in the refrigerator for a long time. Use grated cheese in omelettes, with or without snippets of bacon or diced, cooked vegetables; for a

Welsh rarebit; creamed with butter for sandwiches; blue cheese can be creamed with an equal quantity of butter and flavoured with a spoonful of brandy to taste.

Delicious mixed hors d'oeuvres and savouries can be made from scraps such as a sausage, small piece of pâté, cooked peas or beans, asparagus points, pickles, sardines, any left-over fish.

Gravy and sauces should be boiled up and poured into clean basins for use with made-up dishes. The addition of a spoonful of tomato purée and a spoonful of cream into gravy that is then brought gently to the boil will make a good sauce in which slices of cooked meat can be warmed up. If only a spoonful of gravy is left, it can be added to the stock-pot.

The water in which meat, ham, poultry, vegetables or cereals has been cooked can be used for making thick soups, gravies and sauces. Small quantities of sauces and gravies can be used for making up fish and meat dishes.

Uses for stale bread: all pieces of bread, crust or crumb can be used in various ways. Dry pieces in a slow oven till golden brown, then crush them with a rolling pin or mince them and they will keep for a long time in jars, and can be used for crumbing rissoles, croquettes, fish for frying, or with syrup in a syrup tart.

Stale bread, cut in cubes, small rounds, squares or triangles, and fried, may be served with soup or as **croûtons** on which to dish hors d'oeuvres and savouries and for garnishing mince and other dishes.

Slices of bread and butter can be used in bread-and-butter pudding, apple charlotte or into bread fritters as follows: spread the slices with jam or grated cheese, make into small sandwiches, dip into batter and fry in hot fat.

Stale cakes can be used for trifles or for Queen's Pudding (p. 236).

The peel of oranges and lemons can be used for flavouring various dishes, and will keep if the rind is grated on to salt or sugar and bottled, to be used for flavouring savoury or sweet dishes.

The remains of lemons, after the peel has been removed and the juice extracted, are excellent for removing stains from enamel pans or cleaning brass, if dipped in scouring powder.

EMERGENCY DISHES

Having to provide a meal unexpectedly should pose few problems if one has a freezer, but even without one, it is possible to provide an impromptu meal for the unexpected guest with very little effort, provided the store-cupboard has a few tins and basic foods kept regularly in stock.

The following ingredients will allow quite a choice of quickly made meals:

Rice, spaghetti, eggs, Parmesan cheese, tinned prawns or shrimps, tuna, ham and frankfurters, condensed soups (chicken and mushroom at least), tinned corn, peas and pimentoes, tinned grapefruit, gooseberries or raspberries, apple purée and half-peaches, tinned custard and cream, glacé cherries, a tube of tomato concentrate and packets of instant potato and dried onions.

It is also useful to collect a selection of liqueurs, rum and brandy and to save any left-over wine or sherry: these can transform a dish into something really special.

FIRST COURSES

Prawn cocktails: from tinned prawns and a sauce made of mayonnaise with a little tomato purée added, served on a bed of chopped lettuce; grapefruit cocktails: from tinned grapefruit served very cold with a liberal sprinkling of crème de menthe; soup: with a little cream or sherry added, and in the case of concentrated soups, thinned with a little stock; eggs: baked **en cocotte**, with cream.

MAIN COURSES

Risottos and pilafs; spaghetti; fricassées; tinned tuna in condensed chicken soup, on toast; Spanish omelettes with a filling of diced ham or bacon, onions, pimentoes and tomatoes; frankfurters baked in a casserole with a sauce of tomato juice, onions and peppers, or served plainly boiled with instant mashed potato and tinned sauerkraut.

SWEETS

Apple snow, from tinned apple purée and stiffly beaten white of egg; gooseberry fool with tinned fruit, custard and cream sieved together; banana cream from mashed, sweetened banana blended with a natural yoghourt and beaten white of egg; tinned half-peaches sprinkled with cinnamon and brown sugar and baked for 15 minutes in the oven in a little juice, and served with cream.

HERBS AND SPICES

Herbs should find a place in every kitchen, as they give a most delicate flavour to food. The temptation must be avoided to use them too lavishly or to mix them too freely. When they cannot be obtained fresh, dried herbs may be used, but the flavour of the fresh plant is better.

To dry herbs
 1 Harvest on a dry, still day, before the sun becomes hot. Wash the leaves gently if gritty, and avoid bruising them.
 2 Place on a tray covered in butter muslin, keeping the different varieties carefully apart. Place containers in a warm, dry place.
 3 Turn herbs gently once a day; they should be ready for storing after 4 or 5 days. Place in glass jars with a lid for a week. If moisture gathers on the inside of the jar, spread out the herbs on the tray again and dry for a further few days. When dry, strip the leaves from the stems and store in opaque containers.
  Herbs can also be dried by tying them in small bundles and hanging in an airy place.
  Chervil, parsley, basil, tarragon and mint can be frozen very successfully. Chop the fresh leaves finely and place in small polythene bags in the freezer. Use partly frozen.

PRINCIPAL HERBS

Basil The leaves should be used young and for flavouring omelettes, tomato dishes, and soups and sauces containing chicken or turkey.

Bay leaf is used, fresh or dried, for flavouring fish, meat stews, sauces, milk puddings and custards. It is a traditional ingredient of the bouquet garni.

Borage The blue, starry flowers can be candied for cake decoration; the hairy leaves are used in wine and fruit cups.

Bouquet garni consists of a sprig of parsley, a sprig of thyme and a bay leaf tied together or wrapped in a little piece of muslin.

Chervil has a good flavour for use with other herbs in omelettes, and a pretty leaf which makes a delicate decoration for savoury dishes.

Chives   A kind of onion which is used in salads, egg dishes, mixed with cottage cheese and in any garnish made with *fines herbes*. It should be finely chopped with scissors.

Coriander seeds are used in curries and chutneys.

Dill   Both leaves and dried seeds are used in cooking; the leaves in salads, fish dishes and sauces; the seeds for pickles.

Fennel is used for flavouring fish sauces and for herbal tea.

Fines herbes is a mixture of equal quantities of finely chopped parsley, chervil, chives and tarragon.

Garlic is a plant of the onion species. The spherical flower-heads which appear in June should be removed to encourage the production of large bulbs. The bulbs are composed of small divisions called cloves of garlic. Use garlic cloves sparingly, either crushing one before adding it to a dish, or simply rubbing the dish over with the cut side of a clove. Half a crushed clove is enough for a stew for four.

Marjoram (oregano) is similar to thyme and is often used instead of it. It can be used for seasoning meat, poultry, stuffings and omelettes.

Mint is used for making mint sauce. A spray is also added to new potatoes and green peas, etc., when cooking, or chopped finely and sprinkled over cooked carrots. Sprigs of mint are refreshing in cool drinks. Dried mint is served with pea soup.

Parsley is used fresh or fried for garnish, and in sauces, in bouquets garnis and, finely chopped, as an ingredient of *fines herbes*.

Rosemary   Use small sprigs of fresh rosemary to flavour roast lamb and pork, rabbit and grilled fish. Dried, it is used in stuffings.

Sage is used to flavour the stuffing of pork, geese, ducks.

Savory   There are two kinds, winter and summer savory. Both can be used either fresh or dried for flavouring soups, sauces and vegetable dishes.

Shallot is a species of onion, and has a mild flavour. It is used in delicate dishes in place of onions.

Tarragon is essential in a *fines herbes* mixture. It is used to flavour sauces, especially for chicken, and for salads and vinegar.

Thyme is a pungent herb, used in a **bouquet garni**, and for flavouring stuffings and soups.

SPICES

Dried spices should be bought in small quantities in order to keep the aroma fresh.

Allspice is used in pickles, meat dishes and cakes.

Chillis and chilli powder are very hot and spicy, and should be used sparingly in sauces and stews.

Cinnamon can be bought in sticks or powder. Used for flavouring hot drinks, apple dishes, cakes, and sometimes sprinkled over milk puddings.

Cloves are used whole for flavouring fish and boiled ham and tongue or for flavouring apple dishes and bread sauce, and ground in spicy cakes and puddings.

Curry can be bought in powder and paste form; the paste is the more satisfactory. The flavour is a mixture of different spices which vary according to the brand.

Ginger can be bought in root form, ground or crystallized. It is used in root form for preserves, and powdered for flavouring cakes, biscuits and puddings, and in mulled wines; in crystalline form it will flavour and garnish cakes and puddings.

Mace, which is the outer covering of nutmeg, is similar in flavour but milder and is used in **marinades** and cakes and puddings. It is usually sold powdered, or in blades.

Mixed spice is a blend of several ground spices and used in puddings, cakes and biscuits.

Nutmeg can be bought whole or ground. The whole nutmeg is grated when needed. The flavour is used for cakes and puddings, and sometimes sprinkled over baked custards and milk puddings.

Paprika is a mild red pepper, used lavishly in goulash, and often sprinkled over smoked salmon or cheese, egg and potato dishes for garnish as well as flavour.

Pepper Black pepper is stronger than white pepper and both are better used as peppercorns, either whole or ground in a mill when needed, rather than bought ready ground.

Cayenne pepper is very hot and must be used sparingly.

Saffron is bought in minute envelopes and used for cooking rice to flavour it and colour it yellow. It is emptied into the water that the rice is cooking in.

Turmeric is also yellow, and is used in curry powder and for flavouring pickles and some savoury dishes.

Vanilla can be bought as an essence, but for milk puddings it is best used in the pod, which is simply placed in the cooking liquid, removed, wiped clean and stored in a jar for using again and again. Vanilla sugar can be made by storing a pod in a jar of castor sugar, and using this for flavouring cakes and puddings.

STOCKS AND SOUPS

Care of the stock-pot – causes for failure in making stocks and soups – stocks – soups – clear soups – various consommés – fish soups – meat soups and broths – white soups and vegetable purées – cereal soups – cold soups

It is not always possible or convenient to have home-made stock to hand, so it is emphasized that substitutes can be used quite satisfactorily. These can be made from *bouillon* cubes, or from consommés mixed with water and sometimes wine, and from strained vegetable waters.

CARE OF THE STOCK-POT

But for those who wish to make their own stock, the rules for the care of the stock-pot are as follows:

1 Use a heavy pot for making stock.

2 Bones should be broken up in as small pieces as possible and browned in the oven or pot without fat before using.

3 There should be approximately 1 litre (1 qt) of water to 400 g (1 lb) of meat and bones.

4 See that all the ingredients are fresh and sound.

5 Put the meat and bones in cold water and soak for an hour or two before cooking. This draws out and dissolves the meat juices. Bring slowly to the boil without a lid, and skim off all fat and scum as it rises.

6 Wash all vegetables, scrape or peel and cut them into slices and add them after the stock has come to the boil. Cover the pan. The stock-pot should never go off the boil; its contents should simmer gently for 3 to 4 hours. It should be emptied every evening and the liquid strained off. All vegetables should be thrown away, but any bones from which all the goodness has not been extracted should be kept and returned to the stock-pot the following day. Stock will keep for a week if boiled up every other day, and kept in a clean basin in the refrigerator.

The vegetables used in stock are carrots, turnips, celery, onions and sometimes leeks and a **bouquet garni**.

Further flavourings are cloves and peppercorns. Too strong a flavour of vegetables detracts from the flavour of the meat, so care must be taken to avoid using too many. They must not be left in the stock after it has finished cooking.

Beef, veal, calf's head and sheep's head, ox cheek, and ox tail make the best stock. Mutton should not be used for stock for clear soups. Pork is too fat for stock.

Bones of any kind of meat make a good bone stock, but stocks made from bones alone should be used only for sauces; they are not suitable for clear soups as they impart an unpleasant flavour and a gluey consistency.

Fish bones and trimmings make an excellent stock for fish soups. Vegetables alone make a vegetarian stock.

CAUSES FOR FAILURE IN MAKING STOCKS AND SOUPS

Unsound meat and decaying vegetables will give stock an unpleasant flavour and cause it to deteriorate quickly.

If the stock is kept in a closed pan by the side of the fire without cooking, it will not keep well, and the goodness will not be drawn from the different ingredients.

If all scum is not removed from stocks and soups, it boils down into them and impairs both the colour and flavour.

If all trace of fat is not removed from stocks and soups, they taste greasy.

If stocks or soups are boiled fast, they evaporate and may boil away altogether.

If they are not kept covered while boiling, they **reduce** too quickly and much of the goodness of the various ingredients is lost in the escaping steam.

If thick soups and purées are not stirred occasionally with a wooden spoon, they are liable to burn. They must also be kept skimmed.

If the soup boils after an egg **liaison** has been added, the eggs will curdle.

STOCKS

Brown stock for clear soups
(Bouillon)

	Metric	Imp
knuckle of veal without marrow broken in small pieces and browned	300 g	¾ lb
shin of beef cut up	400 g	1 lb
water	2 l	2 qt

1 small onion stuck with a clove
1 small carrot chopped
1 small turnip chopped
2 sticks celery chopped
bouquet garni
3 peppercorns
salt

Method

1 Place prepared bones and meat in stock-pot, add the cold water and salt and bring very slowly to boil.
2 When just on boil, skim, add an extra 60 ml (½ gill) cold water and skim again.
3 Add chopped vegetables, onion with clove stuck into it, herbs and peppercorns. Bring to boil, skim, simmer for 3 to 4 hr.
4 Remove meat, strain liquor into basin and leave in a cold place till next day.
5 Skim off all fat when cold.

Note This stock can be used as broth or cleared for consommé (p. 49). If properly skimmed and cooked extremely gently, this stock requires very little clearing.

Stock for white soups

	Metric	Imp
knuckle of veal	800 g	2 lb
water	2 l	2 qt

bones or joints of a chicken
2 small onions
2 small carrots chopped
1 bunch herbs
2 bay leaves
2 cloves
salt

Method

Break up chicken carcass and make the stock according to the directions for the brown stock for clear soups.

Bone stock for sauces

	Metric	Imp
bones of any meat cooked or uncooked		
water	1 l to each 400 g of bones	1 qt to each lb of bones

bouquet garni
1 clove
2 peppercorns
2 small carrots chopped
1 stick celery chopped
salt

Method

Remove all fat from the bones and proceed for stock as before, simmering for 2 to 3 hr.

Game stock

	Metric	Imp
trimmings and bones of any kind of game cooked or uncooked	800 g	2 lb
shin of beef	400 g	1 lb
water	3 litres	3 qt
ham or ham bone	100 g	4 oz

1 turnip chopped
1 onion chopped
2 leeks chopped
2 sticks celery chopped, or ½ tsp celery seeds tied in muslin
2 carrots chopped
1 sprig each thyme, marjoram, basil, parsley, and a bay leaf tied together
1 blade mace
10 peppercorns
salt

Method

1 Remove all fat; put cut meat and broken and browned bones in stock-pot with game trimmings. Add cold water, bring to the boil very slowly and skim.
2 Add chopped vegetables, herbs and peppercorns, mace and salt.
3 Simmer gently for about 4 hr.
4 Strain through a sieve or soup strainer, leave till cold.
5 Skim off all the fat.

Vegetable stock

	Metric	Imp
water	2 l	2 qt
butter	40 g	1½ oz
onions sliced	150 g	6 oz
turnips sliced	150 g	6 oz
potatoes sliced	200 g	8 oz
carrots sliced	200 g	8 oz
leeks chopped	50 g	2 oz
celery chopped	50 g	2 oz
bouquet garni		
salt		

Method

1 Fry the sliced vegetables gently in the butter to a deep golden colour, stirring occasionally to prevent burning.
2 Pour over boiling water, add salt and **bouquet garni**, simmer with lid on for about 3 hr.
3 Strain through a sieve.

Note Stocks and soups can be made in the pressure cooker, but it must be emphasized that the cooker should never be more than half-filled with liquid, so it may be necessary to cut this down.

Stock for fish soups

	Metric	Imp
fish bones and trimmings washed	400 g	1 lb
water	1 l	1 qt
White wine	60 ml	½ gill
1 medium onion chopped		
2 sprigs parsley		
1 bay leaf		
5 peppercorns		
salt		

Method

1 Put all ingredients in a pan and bring slowly to boil.
2 Skim, and simmer approximately 1 hr or till liquid is reduced by about a third.
3 Strain off liquid.

Note Fish stock will not keep for more than two or three days, so a small quantity only should be made.

Place all the ingredients in the cooker and bring to the boil slowly. Skim and put on the lid. Bring the heat slowly up to cooking pressure, reduce the heat and cook for ¾ hr.

SOUPS

There are, roughly speaking, four types of soups with numberless recipes for each type.

1 Clear soups
2 Broths
3 Thickened soups
4 Purées

Clear soups and broths are made from a clear meat stock. **Clear soup** or **consommé** is generally **clarified** (see p. 37) and then garnished according to fancy. The consommé takes its name from the garnish.

Broths differ from clear soups, as they are not **clarified**, and the meat with which they are made is either served in the broth or used for a separate course.

Broths may be garnished with vegetables, rice or barley, and are more suited for simple meals than for formal dinner parties.

Thickened soups are made of fish, meat or vegetable stock, either white or brown, and even with milk and water. They are thickened with: (1) some cereal such as cornflour, arrowroot, and so on; (2) a **liaison** of eggs and cream or milk (p. 63).

Purées are made by rubbing the meat, fish, vegetables or farinaceous materials through a sieve, or putting all the ingredients in the blender, after cooking. Sometimes eggs, milk or cream and butter are added to purées.

Quantity of soup per head 175 ml (⅓ pt) is the usual allowance for dinner, but if a substantial soup is to furnish the principal part of a meal, 250 ml (½ pt) per head will be required.

CLEAR SOUPS

Clear oxtail soup

6–7 persons
Prepare the day before it is required

	Metric	Imp
2 small oxtails jointed		
brown stock (p. 47)	250 ml	½ pt
lean ham cut up thin	100 g	4 oz
butter	40 g	1½ oz
water	3 l	3 qt
carrots sliced	100 g	4 oz
onions sliced	100 g	4 oz
turnips sliced	100 g	4 oz
1 head celery diced		
1 bunch herbs		
1 glass sherry or port		
5 cloves		
5 peppercorns		
1 bay leaf		
salt		

Method

1 Put butter in a stewpan and gently cook prepared vegetables in it for about 5 min.
2 Add oxtail, stir well, then stock, herbs, ham, peppercorns and salt and stir over a quick heat to extract the flavour of the herbs, or till liquid is **reduced** almost to a **glaze**.
3 Add water, bring to boil, skimming well. Simmer for 3 hr.
4 Remove ox tail, strain the soup, and leave till next day.
5 Remove all fat, clear as for consommé (see p. 49).

6 Add glass of sherry or port and garnish with small dice of cooked celery, carrots and turnips. Add a few diced pieces of tail, heat and serve.

Consommé

4 persons

	Metric	Imp
brown stock (p. 47)	1 l	1 qt
lean minced shin of beef	100 g	4 oz
2 egg whites		
dash of sherry (optional)		

Method

1 Skim all trace of fat from cold brown stock and put in **scalded** pan. (Enamel is better than aluminium for avoiding cloudiness.)
2 Add the beef, and sherry, if used.
3 *To clarify the consommé:* drop in the softly beaten egg whites and whisk over a moderate heat till almost boiling.
4 Boil up again till froth rises in pan, draw pan to side and simmer for 20 min.
5 Strain through a clean **scalded** tea cloth, holding egg white back with a spoon at first, then allowing it to slide on to cloth.
6 If not quite clear, strain again.
7 Add more sherry if required, reheat without boiling. Season and garnish as desired.

VARIOUS CONSOMMÉS

Consommé à l'Italienne Clear soup garnished with cooked macaroni cut into rings, or with small fancy shapes of Italian pasta. Serve with grated Parmesan cheese.

Consommé à la jardinière Clear soup garnished with cooked turnip, carrot and cucumber cut into the shape of peas with a vegetable scoop. Add some cooked green peas and cauliflower sprigs.

Consommé à Julienne Clear soup garnished with cooked turnip, carrot, onion, leek and celery cut into strips like matches. All the vegetables, after they have been cut, should be put into a pan with 1 oz butter, over low heat, for 15 min. Shake the pan often, add the clear soup and simmer until the vegetables are soft. If preferred, the vegetables may be boiled in water and then added to the consommé. The soup is clearer but has less flavour when this is done.

Consommé aux œufs filés   Make a batter with 1 egg, 1 dssp flour, 1 tbsp milk and seasoning. Let it stand for 15 min. Boil up the consommé, and when boiling, strain the batter into it through a fine strainer and cook for 10 min. The batter should look like threads in the soup.

Consommé à la Portugaise   Clear soup garnished with finely shredded cooked leeks and French plums, stoned and stewed in stock. Allow 2 plums per person.

Consommé à la royale   Clear soup garnished with fancy shapes of savoury custard. The custard is made with 2 yolks and 1 whole egg, 125 ml (1 gill) of stock, seasoning. Beat up the eggs, add the stock, season and pour into a greased jar or cup. Steam very gently until the custard feels firm, 10 to 15 min. Let it cool, turn on to a board, cut it into slices and stamp these into fancy shapes with small cutters, or with a sharp knife cut out diamonds or dice. Put these into a tureen and cover with the boiling consommé.

Consommé aux navets   Clear soup garnished with small balls of cooked turnip.

Consommé aux pointes d'asperges   Clear soup garnished with cooked asparagus points.

Consommé au riz   Clear soup garnished with plain boiled rice.

FISH SOUPS

Conger eel soup

4 persons

	Metric	Imp
head and tail of a conger	about	about
eel	400 g	1 lb
milk	250 ml	½ pt
water	1 ½ l	3 pt
flour	25 g	1 oz
green peas shelled	200 g	8 oz
1 onion sliced		
1 bunch herbs (parsley, marigold petals, borage, savory, basil and lemon thyme,		
salt, pepper		

Method

1 Simmer eel in water, onion and herbs till it breaks easily with a fork.

2 Season with salt and pepper, strain soup, add peas. (There should be about 2 pt or 2 litres of liquid now.) Simmer till peas are tender.

3 Blend flour with milk, add and stir till boiling, then serve.

Haddock soup

	Metric	Imp
fish stock (p. 48)	1 l	1 qt
milk	250 ml	½ pt
skinned haddock fillet	300–400 g	¾–1 lb
peeled shrimps	100 g	4 oz
flour	50 g	2 oz
butter	50 g	2 oz
2 egg yolks mixed with a little cream		
1 French roll or slice of white bread		
1 tsp chopped parsley		
salt, pepper, pinch of cayenne pepper		
1 blade mace		

Method

1 Crumble bread and pour milk over it, mash it to a paste.

2 Add chopped parsley, filleted fish and shrimps.

3 Add warmed fish stock gradually, stirring continuously.

4 Season with pepper, salt, cayenne and mace.

5 Simmer, closely covered for ½ hr, then sieve or put in blender.

6 Blend flour and butter to a paste (**beurre manié**), and add bit by bit. Heat gently to boiling point, beating or whisking till smooth and thickened.

7 Remove from heat, add egg yolks beaten up with a little top of milk or cream, return to heat. Stir continuously till on the point of boiling. Serve.

Lobster soup (Bisque de homard)

6–8 persons

	Metric	Imp
1 small uncooked lobster		
fish stock (p. 48)	1700 ml	3½ pt
butter	50 g	2 oz
rice	100 g	4 oz
carrot finely chopped	50 g	2 oz
onion finely chopped	50 g	2 oz
4 tbsp brandy		
parsley		
thyme		
1 bay leaf		
2 wineglasses white wine		
salt, pepper, pinch of mace		
breadcrumbs		
a little flour		
a little cream		
1 egg		

Method

1 Melt 25 g (1 oz) butter in large pan and add chopped vegetables and herbs. Cook gently for a few minutes, add lobster cut in pieces across the body, cut side down.
2 Keep out any coral and pound with the rest of the butter, sieve and reserve.
3 Add brandy, wine and about 250 ml (½ pt) fish stock, cover tightly and cook gently for 15 min.
4 Cook rice gently in 500 ml (1 pt) stock till soft (about 30 min.).
5 Shell lobster, cut up meat, pound with half the reserved coral and the diced vegetables, well drained.
6 Add rice, pound again, then add half the stock and sieve all into a clean pan. Dilute with remaining stock if necessary.
7 Heat without boiling.
8 At moment of serving, add cream and a few drops of brandy.

Note Serve this soup with forcemeat balls made of the remaining lobster coral minced and mixed with breadcrumbs, mace, salt and pepper. Moisten with beaten egg, roll in flour, warm in soup and serve.

Oyster soup

6 persons

	Metric	Imp
fish velouté (p. 65) made with ⅓ stock, ⅔ milk	1 l	1 qt
cream	125 ml	1 gill (¼ pt)
24 oysters		

Method

1 Heat the velouté to simmering point.
2 Stir in cream, adjust seasoning.
3 Add oysters and the liquor from them. Leave for one minute. Serve.

MEAT SOUPS AND BROTHS

Chicken broth

6 persons

	Metric	Imp
1 boiling chicken cut up		
chicken stock (p. 47)	1½ l	3 pt
carrot diced	75 g	3 oz
leek diced	75 g	3 oz
onion diced	50 g	2 oz
pearl barley (soaked overnight) **or** rice	40 g	1½ oz
salt, pepper		

Method

1 Put chicken in pan with stock and salt and pepper to taste.
2 Bring slowly to boil, skim well.
3 Add barley or rice, cover and simmer for 20 min.
4 Add vegetables and continue simmering for 40 min.
5 Remove chicken, strain and serve.

Note The chicken may be served as a separate dish, coated with white sauce and accompanied by mashed potatoes.

Cock-a-leekie

6 persons

	Metric	Imp
1 boiling chicken cut up		
clear stock (p. 45)	2 l	2 qt
butter	50 g	2 oz
leeks washed and chopped	400 g	1 lb
water	250 ml	½ pt
salt, pepper		

Method

1 Melt butter in pan and brown pieces of chicken.

2 Drain off butter and add stock. Bring gently to boil, skim.

3 Add 250 ml (½ pt) cold water, season and boil up.

4 Add leeks and simmer for 2 hr. Remove all scum as it rises.

5 When ready to serve, take out the chicken, remove bones, cut the meat into neat pieces, place in tureen and pour leeks and broth over.

Note This soup is greatly improved by warming it up a second time.

French family soup (Pot-au-feu)

Soup and a main course for 6 persons

	Metric	Imp
water	3 l	3 qt
brisket	1200 g	3 lb
beef marrow bones broken up	400 g	1 lb
2 carrots sliced		
2 onions, each stuck with a clove		
½ head celery cut up		
½ cabbage washed and trimmed		
9 peppercorns		
1 turnip cut in 4		
1 bunch herbs		
salt		

Method

1 Wash meat, put in stock-pot with water and marrow bones; bring to boil slowly, skim.

2 Pour in a teacup of cold water to let the scum rise, skim again.

3 Add vegetables, salt, peppercorns, herbs and simmer for 3 hr. Season again if necessary.

4 Take out meat and cabbage and keep warm for main course.

5 Strain broth into a tureen, cut vegetables into dice and serve with broth.

Note The *pot-au-feu* is a standing institution in France and other Continental countries. The meat is usually served as a separate course, the vegetables being used as a garnish to either the meat or the soup.

Giblet soup

4 persons
Prepare the day before it is required

	Metric	Imp
giblets from 2 ducks or		
chickens **or** from 1 goose or		
turkey		
butter	25 g	1 oz
flour	25 g	1 oz
shin of beef cut up	200 g	½ lb
water	1 l	1 qt
1 onion sliced		
1 bunch herbs		
peel and juice of ½ lemon		
2 tsp mushroom ketchup		
salt, pepper, cayenne to taste		

Method

1 Scald and clean giblets thoroughly, skin feet, remove inside skin from gizzards. Cut into pieces.

2 Melt butter and fry giblets lightly.

3 Add water, bring gently to boil. Skim.

4 Add prepared beef, onion, lemon peel cut very thin, salt and pepper; simmer till tender.

5 Strain into a bowl, leave till next day.

6 Skim off fat.

7 Put about 25 g (1 oz) butter into a pan, melt and add flour. Brown, then add soup and bring it back to the boil, stirring constantly.

8 After 10 min. skim, then strain it through a fine sieve. Add ketchup, cayenne pepper and lemon juice and serve.

Note If stock is available instead of water, the beef can be omitted.

Hare soup

8–10 persons

	Metric	Imp
1 hare washed and jointed		
brown stock (p. 47)	3 l	3 qt
ham or bacon chopped	300 g	¾ lb
red wine	125 ml	¼ pt
1 tbsp redcurrant jelly		
2 onions sliced		
1 bunch thyme, parsley, marjoram		
2 blades mace		
2 rolls or slices bread crumbled		
salt, cayenne pepper		

Method

1 Put hare, ham, onions, herbs and mace in stewpan with the stock.

2 Simmer for about 2½ hr.

3 Pound all inferior parts of hare with ham. Keep the best pieces apart.

4 Skim and strain soup into a clean pan, add pounded meat, crumbs of bread and wine and simmer again for about ½ hr.

5 Rub through sieve, season with salt and a little cayenne. Add redcurrant jelly.

6 Heat thoroughly but do not allow to boil. Serve with forcemeat balls (p. 79) if desired.

Note The best pieces can be served as a stew with a little of the soup thickened as gravy.

Soup in haste

4 persons

	Metric	Imp
cooked meat minced	400 g	1 lb
water	1 l	1 qt
butter	50 g	2 oz
flour	25 g	1 oz
a few slices toast		
salt, pepper		

Method

1 Melt butter in pan and brown minced meat lightly. Add flour, stirring constantly and boiling water gradually. Season to taste. Cover pan tightly and simmer for ½ hr.

2 Strain through a cloth. Return to cleaned pan. At this point, a small handful of vermicelli may be added, in which case the soup should simmer for a further 10 to 12 min.

3 Put toast, cut in squares in tureen and pour soup over. Serve.

Mock turtle soup (thick)

8 persons

Prepare the day before it is required

	Metric	Imp
shin of beef cut up	1600 g	4 lb
beef bones	200 g	½ lb
water	4 l	4 qt
butter	25 g	1 oz
½ calf's head		
1 turnip sliced		
1 carrot sliced		
2 onions sliced		
1 glass sherry		
1 bunch herbs		
6 cloves		
1 blade mace		
very little flour		
salt, pepper		
forcemeat balls (p. 79)		

Method

1 Wash calf's head well, remove brains and tongue, cut away nostril parts and soak in cold, salted water for 1 hr.

2 Drain, put into a pan of fresh cold water, bring to the boil, drain and rinse.

3 Cut meat from bones of head, and tie meat up in a piece of muslin.

4 Break up bones from head and beef bones and brown in oven.

5 Put all bones and meat, cut in fairly large pieces, into a pan with the cold water. Bring to boil. Skim.

6 Add vegetables, herbs, mace, cloves and salt and simmer for 4 hr. Leave till cold.

7 Skim off all fat.

8 Melt butter in a pan, add flour and brown it.

9 Add the stock gradually and stir till boiling.

10 Add sherry, season to taste, and garnish with small dice of the cooked head, and forcemeat balls.

Note The rest of the meat and the calf's head may be used for some other dish.

Mulligatawny soup (thick)

6 persons

	Metric	Imp
chicken or rabbit jointed	800 g	2 lb
vegetable stock (p. 48)	2 l	2 qt
butter	50 g	2 oz
flour	25 g	1 oz

	Metric	Imp
cream or top of milk	125 ml	¼ pt
boiled rice	100 g	4 oz

2 tsp curry powder
2 tsp curry paste
2 onions sliced
1 apple peeled, cored and chopped
juice of a lemon
salt, pepper

Method

1 Melt butter in large pan and fry meat and onion till golden brown.
2 Add curry powder, paste and flour, fry another minute.
3 Add stock, apple and seasoning; simmer 1½ hr.
4 Bone meat, cut in small pieces and return to soup.
5 Add lemon juice and cream, more seasoning if necessary. Serve.
6 The rice should be served separately.

Note Coconut water much improves all mulligatawny. To make it, soak 100 g (4 oz) grated coconut in 500 ml (1 pt) of boiling water for about ½ hr. Strain into soup with stock. Use 500 ml (1 pt) less stock if using this.

Scotch barley broth

4 persons

	Metric	Imp
knuckle, scrag or middle neck of mutton	600 g	1½ lb
water	1½ l	3 pt
pearl barley washed	50 g	2 oz
½ head celery cut up		

3 onions sliced
2 turnips sliced
salt, pepper and cayenne

Method

1 Wipe meat, remove fat and skin.
2 Put meat, barley, salt in pan with water. Bring very slowly to boil. Skim.
3 Add onions and simmer for ½ hr. Skim well.
4 Add celery and turnips and more salt if necessary. Simmer for 1½ hr, skimming constantly.
5 Remove meat, cut a few pieces off bone and return to broth.
6 Skim to remove fat, adjust seasoning and serve.

Veal broth

4 persons

	Metric	Imp
scrag of veal cut in small pieces	800 g	2 lb
water	1 l	1 qt
boiled rice	100 g	4 oz
2 blades mace		
1 turnip cut up		
1 onion cut up		
salt, pepper		

Method

1 Put veal in stewpan with water, and bring to boil slowly.
2 Remove all scum. Add vegetables, mace and salt.
3 Simmer for 2 hr; strain through sieve.
4 Return liquid to pan, add boiled rice, simmer for 10 min. Serve.

WHITE SOUPS AND VEGETABLE PURÉES

In the case of vegetable purées and other soups in which the ingredients are sieved, an electric blender or emulsifier can be used very satisfactorily instead.

The goblet should not be filled more than half, so it may be necessary to blend the soup in batches. Turn on the machine to half speed at first, and increase to full speed if necessary. Two minutes is quite long enough for each batch. Make sure that there are no long pieces of stringy vegetables, such as spinach or celery, to wrap round the blades of the blender; chop these small if necessary.

The blender will produce a really creamy purée with much less effort and more quickly than sieving. If, however, you want to eliminate skins and pips from the pulp, e.g. with lentils or tomatoes, sieving is the only solution.

Artichoke soup

4 persons

	Metric	Imp
Jerusalem artichokes cut in pieces	600 g	1 ½ lb
white stock (p. 47)	750 ml	1 ½ pt
milk	250 ml	½ pt
1 turnip, 1 onion, 1 head celery, cut in pieces		
salt, cayenne, sugar to taste		
fried bread		

Method

1 Put the artichokes, turnip, onion and celery in the stock and boil gently till quite tender, about ¾ hr.
2 Rub through sieve or put in blender.
3 Return purée to pan and add milk, and season with sugar, salt and cayenne. If too thick, add extra milk.
4 Serve very hot with cubes of fried bread.

Inexpensive carrot soup

4 persons

	Metric	Imp
scraped carrots	400 g	1 lb
vegetable stock	1 l	1 qt
salt, pepper		
fried bread		

Method

1 Wash and grate carrots, weigh and boil in a little water till tender.
2 Drain well, and sieve or put in blender.
3 Add stock gradually, season, reheat, stirring all the time.
4 Serve hot with cubes of fried bread.

Celery soup

4 persons

	Metric	Imp
2 heads of celery cut in large pieces		
carcass and remnants of a cold roast chicken		
bacon cut up small	50 g	2 oz
flour	25 g	1 oz
white stock (p. 47)	1 l	1 qt
milk	250 ml	½ pt
butter	40 g	1 ½ oz
salt, pepper		

Method

1 Cut up carcass and remnants of chicken into a saucepan; add bacon, celery and stock, and simmer for 1 hr. Strain.
2 Rub celery through a sieve and mix it with the strained liquor.
3 Melt butter in a clean pan, stir in flour and add milk gradually to make a sauce. Add purée gradually.
4 Season and serve.

Note The remnants of chicken may be omitted and 3 pt of stock used.

Chestnut soup

4 persons

	Metric	Imp
chestnuts	800 g	2 lb
white stock (p. 47)	1 ½ l	3 pt
milk	250 ml	½ pt
salt, cayenne		
1 lump of sugar		

Method

1 After removing outer rind from chestnuts, put in hot water and set over moderate heat till the brown skin can be taken off easily.
2 Put in stewpan with half the stock and simmer till quite soft.
3 Press through fine sieve or put in blender.
4 Put purée in pan, add rest of stock, milk, a little salt and cayenne and the sugar. Reheat slowly, stirring occasionally.
5 Serve very hot.

Cucumber soup

4 persons

	Metric	Imp
2 cucumbers		
spinach well washed	400 g	1 lb
white stock (p. 47)	1 l	1 qt
milk	125 ml	¼ pt
butter	50 g	2 oz
2 tsp arrowroot or cornflour		
1 onion sliced		
1 blade mace		
1 bunch herbs		
salt, pepper		
croûtons		

Method

1 Peel cucumbers and cut some balls or dice from one. Boil these in a little water for a few minutes, for garnish.

2 Cut the rest of the cucumber up finely.

3 Melt butter in a pan, add cucumber, spinach, onion, bunch of herbs, mace and seasoning. Cover and cook for 5 min. without browning, stirring occasionally.

4 Add stock and stir till boiling. Simmer till cucumber is soft, about 20 min.

5 Mix arrowroot to a smooth paste with milk, add to soup and stir for 6 min. over slow heat.

6 Rub the soup through a hair sieve, return to pan and heat.

7 Garnish with balls of cucumber and serve with **croûtons** of fried bread.

Haricot soup

4 persons

	Metric	Imp
haricot beans soaked overnight in cold water	200 g	½ lb
vegetable stock (p. 48) or water	1 l	1 qt
milk	125 ml	¼ pt
butter	12·5 g	½ oz
1 turnip sliced		
1 onion sliced		
2 small potatoes sliced		
salt, pepper		

Method

1 Strain beans and put in a pan with the stock. Bring to the boil and skim.

2 In a separate pan, melt butter and **sweat** vegetables for a few minutes with the lid on.

3 Add beans and boiling stock, season, and simmer for 2 hr or until beans are tender.

4 Rub through sieve or blend in liquidizer.

5 Return to pan, add milk, reheat.

6 Adjust seasoning and serve.

Lentil soup

4 persons

	Metric	Imp
lentils	400 g	1 lb
brown stock p. 47	2 l	2 qt
milk	250 ml	½ pt
shredded bacon	50 g	2 oz
1 bunch herbs		
1 tsp celery seeds tied up in muslin		
salt		
dried mint and fried bacon		

Method

1 Soak the lentils for ¼ hr in cold water.

2 Put them into the stock, add celery seeds, herbs and the shredded bacon. Simmer gently for about 2 hr or till lentils are soft.

3 Rub through a sieve or blend in liquidizer.

4 Reheat, add milk, season, and serve hot.

5 Serve with powdered mint and finely shredded fried bacon.

Vegetable marrow soup

6 persons

	Metric	Imp
1 small marrow peeled, seeded and cut in pieces		
croûtons of fried bread		
bacon or ham cut in strips	50 g	2 oz
butter	25 g	1 oz
rice	25 g	1 oz
stock (any kind)	1 ½ l	3 pt
milk	125 ml	1 gill
1 onion chopped		
1 blade mace		
salt, pepper		

Method

1 Melt the butter in a pan, add the onion and bacon and fry gently without browning.

2 Add marrow and stock, bring to the boil and add washed rice, salt, pepper and mace. Simmer for 1 hr.

3 Rub through a sieve or put in blender; return to pan.

4 Add milk, adjust seasoning and stir till boiling.

5 Serve with **croûtons** of fried bread.

Note A richer soup can be made by adding the yolks of two eggs and 2–3 tbsp of cream. This is done by working the yolks and cream together with a wooden spoon in a small bowl and adding, one by one, about 4 spoonfuls of soup to the mixture. When well mixed, return it slowly to the saucepan and stir continuously over a moderate heat till on the point of boil. Serve.

Minestrone

4 persons

	Metric	Imp
small haricot beans soaked overnight	50 g	2 oz
butter or bacon fat	25 g	1 oz
peas	50 g	2 oz
water	1 l	1 qt
vermicelli	50 g	2 oz

1 tomato peeled and sliced
½ cabbage heart shredded
1 large leek shredded
1 potato, 1 carrot diced
3 sticks celery cut small
1 clove garlic crushed
finely chopped gammon or smoked sausage (optional)
grated Parmesan cheese
salt, pepper

Method

1 Heat the fat, fry the onion, leek and garlic gently for 5 min.
2 Add other vegetables, water and gammon if used, and simmer for 1 hr.
3 Add vermicelli, simmer till just soft, about 10 min., correct seasoning.
4 Serve in deep bowls with a dish of finely grated Parmesan cheese offered separately.

Onion soup

4 persons

	Metric	Imp
onions sliced very finely	400 g	1 lb
butter or dripping	25 g	1 oz
white stock (p. 47)	1 l	1 qt
milk	125 ml	¼ pt
breadcrumbs	25 g	1 oz

Method

1 Melt fat in a pan and add onions. Cook gently with the lid on for about 10 min. without browning. Stir occasionally.
2 Add stock and seasoning and simmer for about 1 hr.
3 Rub through a sieve or put in blender.
4 Return purée to pan, sprinkle in breadcrumbs, add milk, stir till boiling, season and serve.

Note 50 g (2 oz) spinach added at Stage 2 greatly improves the flavour of this soup.

Pea soup

6 persons

	Metric	Imp
split peas washed and soaked in enough water to cover them for 24 hr	400 g	1 lb
water or vegetable stock (p. 47)	2 l	2 qt
bacon cut in strips	75 g	3 oz

fresh or dried mint
salt, pepper
toast

Method

1 Put soaked peas into pan with the water in which they were soaked, made up to 2 litres (2 qt) with the stock.
2 Add shredded onions and bacon strips, bring to boil and simmer till soft, about 2 hr.
3 Rub through sieve or put in blender.
4 Return to pan, season to taste and reheat.
5 Put chopped mint in bottom of tureen or soup bowls; pour boiling soup over, and serve with small cubes of toast. If soup thickens too much while cooking, add more stock.

Fresh green pea soup

6 persons

	Metric	Imp
young green peas shelled, with their pods saved	800 g	2 lb
water	2 l	2 qt
butter	40 g	1½ oz
flour	25 g	1 oz

2 hearts lettuce, a handful spinach, washed and finely shredded
1 onion shredded
1 sprig mint
salt, pepper
fried bread

Method

1 Put the washed pods in a pan with the mint and water and boil for about 1 hr.
2 Rub pods through sieve or put in blender.
3 Return pulp and liquor to pan, add shredded lettuce and spinach, peas and shredded onion. Simmer for 2 hr or till vegetables are soft.
4 Knead butter and flour together (**beurre manié**) and add bit by bit, stirring each piece in well before adding next.
5 Season and serve with fried bread.

Potato soup

4 persons

	Metric	Imp
Potatoes peeled and sliced	600 g	1½ lb
rice	50 g	2 oz
butter	25 g	1 oz
white stock (p. 47)	1 l	1 qt
milk	250 ml	½ pt

1 head celery, 3 leeks
and 1 onion, sliced
salt, pepper
fried bread or toast

Method

1 Melt butter in large pan, add sliced vegetables and cook gently without browning for 5 min.
2 Add stock and bring to boil, stirring all the time. Add rice.
3 Simmer for ¾ hr or till vegetables are soft.
4 Rub through sieve or put in blender.
5 Return purée to pan, add milk and seasoning; reheat, stirring all the time.
6 Serve with cubes of fried bread or toast.

Spinach soup

4 persons

	Metric	Imp
spinach well washed	800 g	2 lb
white stock (p. 47)	750 ml	1½ pt
margarine	25 g	1 oz
milk	250 ml	½ pt

1 onion shredded
1 tsp celery seeds (tied in muslin)
salt, pepper, pinch of grated nutmeg
fried bread

Method

1 Put spinach, onion and celery seeds in saucepan and cook slowly without water with lid on till soft (approx. 20 min.).
2 When cooked, remove celery seeds and pass spinach through sieve, or liquidize in blender.
3 Return pulp to pan with the stock, milk and margarine and stir till boiling.
4 Season, add nutmeg and serve with cubes of fried bread.

Tomato soup

4–5 persons

	Metric	Imp
tomatoes sliced **or** 1 large tin (992 g) tomatoes	1 kg	2½ lb
stock (any kind)	1½ l	3 pt
ham cut up small	50 g	2 oz
butter or margarine	40 g	1½ oz
cornflour	25 g	1 oz

1 onion, 1 carrot, 1 turnip,
2 sticks celery, cut up
10 peppercorns
1 blade mace
1 bunch herbs
salt, squeeze of lemon juice
croûtons

Method

1 Melt fat in pan, add ham and all vegetables except tomatoes and stir over low heat for 5 min.
2 Add tomatoes, stock – only 1¼ litres (2½ pt) if tinned tomatoes are used – mace, peppercorns, herbs and salt. Simmer for ¾ hr, or till vegetables are soft.
3 Remove herbs and rub through sieve or put in blender.
4 Return purée to pan, stir till boiling.
5 Blend cornflour with a little cold stock or water and stir into soup; stir till boiling. Boil for 5 min.
6 Add a squeeze of lemon juice, season and serve with fried **croûtons.**

Vegetable mulligatawny soup

4 persons

	Metric	Imp
stock of any kind	1 l	1 qt
fat	50 g	2 oz

2 tbsp flour
1 tbsp curry powder
1 bunch herbs
2 apples, 2 carrots, 2 onions, 1 turnip, 1 leek, sliced
juice of ½ lemon
salt

Method

1 Melt fat in saucepan, add sliced vegetables and fry till brown, stirring often.
2 Add flour and curry powder and fry, then gradually stir in stock and apples.
3 Stir till boiling. Simmer for ¾ hr.
4 Season, add lemon juice and, if too thick, more stock or water.
5 Strain and serve. Hand boiled rice separately.

CEREAL SOUPS

Cream of barley soup   *4–5 persons*

	Metric	Imp
pearl barley washed	50 g	2 oz
white stock (p. 47)	1 l	1 qt
milk	125 ml	1 gill
2 sticks celery cut in lengths		
1 onion sliced		
salt, pepper		
fried bread or toast		

Method

1 Put washed barley in pan with stock, sliced onion and celery. Bring to boil and simmer for 2 hr.
2 Rub through sieve or put in blender.
3 Return purée to pan, adding milk and seasoning and bring to the boil, stirring all the time.
4 Serve with cubes of fried bread or toast.

Macaroni soup   *4 persons*

	Metric	Imp
macaroni	200 g	½ lb
white stock (p. 47)	1 l	1 qt
milk	250 ml	½ pt
grated cheese	50 g	2 oz
croûtons		

Method

1 Boil macaroni in 500 ml (1 pt) of stock till quite tender; take out half the macaroni.
2 Add rest of stock to remainder of macaroni and boil till macaroni is pulpy.
3 Sieve or put in blender.
4 Return purée to pan with milk and stir till boiling.
5 Chop macaroni which was kept back into 2½ cm (1 in.) lengths and add to soup with grated cheese. Reheat but do not allow to boil. Serve with **croûtons**.

COLD SOUPS

Chilled avocado soup   *3 persons*

	Metric	Imp
1 large ripe avocado pear peeled and diced		
rich chicken stock	500 ml	1 pt
1 tsp lemon juice		
generous pinch each of garlic salt and salt		
½ tsp ground nutmeg		
1 tbsp double cream		

Method

1 Put avocado, stock, lemon juice, garlic salt and salt into the blender. Blend at high speed 1 min.
2 Chill thoroughly. Divide into 3 bowls.
3 Just before serving, float 1 tbsp cream on each bowl and sprinkle with nutmeg.

Iced curry soup   *4 persons*

	Metric	Imp
butter	25 g	1 oz
flour	25 g	1 oz
chicken stock	1 l	1 qt
sugar	25 g	1 oz
1 tsp tomato purée		
2 tsp cornflour or arrowroot		
1 tbsp water		
1 tbsp curry powder		
2 medium onions chopped		
grated rind of ½ lemon		
1 bay leaf		
salt, pepper		
4 dssp cream		

Method

1 Melt butter, add onions and curry powder; cook 5 min.
2 Stir in flour, add stock; bringly slowly to boil.
3 Add lemon rind, bay leaf, sugar and tomato purée. Simmer 20 min. with lid on.
4 Strain into clean saucepan. Blend arrowroot or cornflour with water, add to soup and bring to boil, stirring continuously.
5 Chill well, serve with a spoonful of cream in each bowl.

Fruit soup
4 persons

	Metric	Imp
ripe fruit such as raspberries, currants, cherries or plums	400 g	1 lb
vegetable or bone stock (pp. 48, 47)	1 l	1 qt
sago or semolina	25 g	1 oz
1 tsp sugar		
salt, pepper		

Method
1 Stew fruit in stock till soft, then strain.
2 Return liquid to pan; bring to boil and sprinkle in sago or semolina. Stir till cereal is clear.
3 Season with salt, pepper and sugar.
4 When cold, place in refrigerator till well chilled.

Gazpacho
6 persons

	Metric	Imp
tomatoes	1 kg	2½ lb
or tinned tomato juice *plus*		
fresh tomatoes	450 g	1 lb
fresh tomatoes	450 g	1 lb
iced water	about 250 ml	½ pt
dssp red wine vinegar		
3–4 tbsp olive oil		
4 thickish slices stale brown bread		
2 large cloves garlic crushed		
1 large onion grated		
2 tinned red peppers finely chopped		
1 small cucumber grated		
salt, pepper		
cucumber, green pepper, fried bread		

Method
1 Skin and seed tomatoes, chop finely.
2 Cut crusts off bread, crumble and stir in vinegar, garlic and as much oil as crumbs will absorb.
3 Stir in tomato pulp and juice, peppers, cucumber, onion, and season.
4 Dilute to a fine cream with iced water, about 250 ml (½ pt).
5 Chill.
6 Serve with diced cucumber, green pepper and fried bread passed round in separate dishes.

Iced orange soup
6–7 persons

	Metric	Imp
butter	40 g	1½ oz
chicken stock	1 l	1 qt
double cream	250 ml	½ pt
1 large tin carrots		
1 tin concentrated frozen orange juice		
1 medium onion finely chopped		
salt, pepper		
snipped chives		

Method
1 Cook onion in butter till soft but not coloured.
2 Liquidize with drained carrots. Add stock and season.
3 Half an hour before serving, add frozen orange juice and cream. Serve when melted with snipped chives on top of each bowl.

Vichyssoise
4–6 persons

	Metric	Imp
veal stock	1¼ l	2½ pt
milk	250 ml	½ pt
cream	250 ml	½ pt
potatoes peeled and cut up	600 g	1½ lb
8 medium leeks thinly sliced		
chopped chives		
salt, pepper		

Method
1 Simmer potatoes and leeks in stock till soft.
2 Sieve vegetables, return stock to stove and simmer till reduced to half the quantity.
3 Return vegetable purée to the stock, stir in milk and cream, adjust seasoning.
4 Allow to cool and add 8 ice-cubes. When ice has dissolved, serve sprinkled with chives.

Note This soup may also be served hot, sprinkled with chives.

SAUCES, GRAVIES, SAVOURY BUTTERS, BATTERS

Gravies – glaze – thickenings or liaisons – foundation sauces –
hot brown sauces – white sauces – sauces for fish – cold sauces
sweet sauces – savoury butters – batters

A well-made sauce is a very essential part of a good dinner. A badly made sauce will ruin otherwise good cooking, while a good plain sauce, if well made, will improve the most simple dish.

A well-made sauce should be perfectly smooth, neither too thick nor too thin, and should be delicately flavoured. When a sauce is required for coating, it must be thick enough to adhere to the back of a spoon. If required for pouring round a dish, it should be thin enough to flow without being lumpy.

If required to be kept warm for some time, sauces should be put in a **bain-marie**, or if this is not available, the saucepan in which the sauce was made should be placed in another pan of hot water, or in a baking-tin full of hot water. This should be kept on the stove. A **bain-marie** is a large pan containing hot water in which smaller pans, with lids, containing sauces, etc., are placed to keep hot.

The thickest saucepans should be used for sauce-making and only wooden spoons should be used for stirring.

GRAVIES

Plain joints roasted, except lamb, make their own gravy. Made gravies and sauces are necessary for more elaborate, and less homely, cooking.

Two kinds of gravies are made, i.e., brown and white. These are required for making nearly all the other more complicated gravies and sauces, with beef as the foundation of brown or savoury gravies, and veal or fowls that of the white and more delicate gravy. It is not always necessary to use meat or poultry for making a gravy – any kind of stock will do; the trimmings of beef, veal or mutton and the bones of cold joints of meat, or uncooked bones, will all provide materials for it.

Brown gravy
Place the bones, whether beef, mutton or veal, or a mixture of all three, in a stewpan, with a slice or two of bacon or ham, and any bones broken up small. Add a few slices of carrot, an onion, a blade of mace, two or three cloves, black or white peppercorns, and a **bouquet garni**. Cover the stewpan and set it over a slow heat for 6 or 7 minutes, shaking the pan often. Then **dredge** in a little flour, and pour in sufficient water to cover the bones completely. Cover the stewpan and simmer for 3 hours. Season to taste and strain off the gravy. Good gravy can be made from kidney, the skirts of beef, the knuckle of dressed mutton, or any other meat cut into small pieces and fried a nice brown, with onions, a bunch of herbs, and spices. The water in which meat has been boiled improves and adds to the richness of gravy. A cow-heel, also, will yield a good gravy stock. Soak it about 12 hours in cold water, and then boil it for 2 ½ hours. When strained and quite cold, take off the fat carefully. A little gravy browning may be added for extra colour.

White gravy
Simmer the trimmings of veal or fowls with pot vegetables in sufficient water to cover. Do not brown as in previous recipe.

White meats, and all white made dishes, require a smooth, delicately flavoured gravy or sauce; brown made dishes, a more piquant and savoury one.

GLAZE (used for hams, tongue, etc.)

Boil some very strong clear gravy or jellied stock over a quick heat, to the thickness of cream, skimming and stirring constantly until it will adhere like jelly to the spoon. It must then be immediately poured out of the saucepan. The greatest care is required during the time of thickening to prevent it from burning. When required for use, dissolve it by placing the jar (or whatever it may be kept in) in boiling water, and brush it over the meat two or three times, when it will form a clear varnish. Any kind of very rich stock can be boiled down to a **glaze.**

Note A few drops of cold water added occasionally while boiling will help to clear the **glaze.**

How to use glaze
Melt the **glaze** as directed above. Lay it on the meat or cutlets with a pastry brush. It soon becomes firm. When one layer is dry, put on another, till it forms a clear varnish. A ham will take three layers to look really nice, but each layer must be dry before putting on the next.

THICKENINGS OR LIAISONS

A sauce always has some kind of thickening or binding, or **liaison** as it is called.
There are five methods of thickening sauces:

1 **Liaison** with **roux**
2 **Liaison** with butter and cream
3 **Liaison** with eggs
4 **Liaison** with butter and flour (mixed, not cooked, like **roux**)
5 **Liaison** with cornflour, arrowroot, barley, rice or potato flour

To brown flour Put some flour in a pan or dish, and set it in the oven, or over a low heat. Stir it to prevent burning; but let it brown well. Keep it in a sealed jar for browning ordinary gravies.

ROUX

There are three kinds of **roux**: white, blond and brown. These can be made in fairly large quantities and kept in covered jars for use when required.

Brown roux
To be kept for use
200 g (½ lb) butter
200 g (½ lb) flour
Melt the butter over a very slow heat, skim it well, and let it stand to settle. Strain into a small stewpan, **dredge** in the flour and stir it over low heat until it has become a bright brown colour. Keep it in a covered jar.

White roux
200 g (½ lb) butter
200 g (½ lb) flour
Melt the butter over a very slow heat in a clean saucepan, and then stir in the flour; mix it to a firm paste. It must be stirred for ¼ hr, but great care must be taken that it does not in the slightest degree lose its pure white colour. Keep in a covered jar.

Blond roux
100 g (¼ lb) butter
100 g (¼ lb) flour
Melt the butter over a slow fire, stir in the flour and stir over low heat until the mixture becomes pale fawn. Keep in a covered jar.

How to use roux
15 ml (1 tbsp) will thicken 500 ml (1 pt) of liquid. Pour the cold or hot liquid gradually on to the

roux, stirring well. Stir over low heat until boiling. If freshly made hot roux is used, add the hot liquid away from the heat, then stir it over the heat until boiling. Roux must be kept well covered. A smaller quantity may be made, allowing the same proportions of butter and flour.

Liaison with butter and cream

Equal proportions of butter and cream are incorporated gradually into a sauce just before serving it, stirring in small pieces of butter and a little cream alternately. Stir well or whisk, but never let the sauce 'boil' after the butter and cream have been added, or it will be spoilt as the butter may oil. If butter alone is added, never put in a big piece at once, but break it into little bits and add these one by one, beating or whisking each bit in before adding the next.

Egg liaison

For thickening ½ litre (1 pt) liquid, work together 4 egg yolks and 2 or 3 tbsp cream or milk with a wooden spatula in a small bowl. Bring the sauce that is being thickened to the boil, remove from heat, add about 3 tbsp of the hot sauce gradually to the liaison and blend well. Add this mixture to the rest of the sauce and stir until the eggs thicken, but on no account let the mixture boil.

Butter and flour liaison (beurre manié)

Knead as much flour into the butter as is given in the recipe in which it used, and when a soft paste is formed, stir it bit by bit into the hot sauce, whisking until each piece of butter is melted.

Arrowroot, cornflour, etc., liaison

Blend the arrowroot or cornflour with a little cold milk, stock or water; strain it into the boiling liquid and stir until boiling; then simmer for 10 to 15 min.

FOUNDATION SAUCES

The leading foundation sauces are a brown or Espagnole sauce and a white sauce called béchamel. If boiled up daily, these will keep for a week in a refrigerator, and it is useful to have some in reserve.

Béchamel sauce

About 500 ml (1 pt)

	Metric	Imp
milk	500 ml	1 pt
butter	40 g	1½ oz
flour	40 g	1½ oz

3 tbsp top of milk or cream
½ carrot, 1 stick celery, 1 onion, ½ turnip, chopped
1 bay leaf
1 sprig parsley
2 cloves
salt, pepper

Method

1 Put milk in saucepan with vegetables, herbs, cloves and salt. Set it over gentle heat to draw out the flavour of the herbs, bring to the boil, remove from heat and leave for 5 min. to infuse. Strain and cool a little.

2 Melt butter for roux in pan, add flour, mix well and add hot milk slowly, stirring constantly till boiling.
3 Adjust seasoning and simmer uncovered for about 2 or 3 min.
4 Add top of milk or cream and serve.

Brown sauce

About 500 ml (1 pt)

	Metric	Imp
butter	25 g	1 oz
flour	25 g	1 oz
bone stock (p. 47)	500 ml	1 pt

1 carrot, 1 onion, 2 sticks celery, ½ turnip, cut up
1 bunch herbs
10 peppercorns
2 cloves
1 blade mace, salt

Method

1 Melt butter in saucepan. Add onion, stir till brown, add flour and brown also.
2 Draw pan off heat and add stock gradually. When blended smoothly, stir till boiling over heat, simmer 5 min; skim.
3 Add other vegetables, herbs, mace, cloves and seasoning. Simmer ½ hr.
4 Strain. Reheat before using.

Espagnole sauce
1 l (1 qt)

	Metric	Imp
butter	50 g	2 oz
flour	50 g	2 oz
good jellied stock		
(clear and skimmed)	1½ l	3 pt
lean ham	50g	2 oz
1 dssp concentrated tomato purée		
red wine	60 ml	½ gill
sherry	60 ml	½ gill
1 onion, 1 carrot, ½ head celery, cut up		
a few mushroom stalks		
1 bunch herbs, 1 bay leaf		
10 peppercorns		
salt		

Method

1 Melt half the butter in pan, add all vegetables except the mushrooms, and brown.
2 Add ham, herbs and seasoning, stir over heat till light brown; pour off any fat.
3 Add stock, wine, mushrooms and tomato purée. Simmer 1 hr, skimming often. Strain.
4 Melt remaining butter in another pan, stir in flour and brown. Add sauce gradually, stir till boiling and simmer 20 min., skimming occasionally.
5 Add sherry and extra seasoning if necessary before serving.

Melted butter sauce
250 ml (½ pt)

	Metric	Imp
milk and water mixed	250 ml	½ pt
butter	40 g	1½ oz
flour	25 g	1 oz
salt, pepper		

Method

1 Melt butter in pan, add flour and blend well.
2 Add water and milk gradually, stir till boiling.
3 Simmer for 5 min.; season and serve.

Melted butter
(Oiled butter)
About 60 ml (½ gill)

	Metric	Imp
fresh butter	75 ml	3 oz
salt, pepper		

Method

1 Melt butter in a small, very clean pan and stir over low heat till melted; do not let it boil.
2 Add seasoning and serve in a hot sauce boat. This is used with asparagus, sea kale, globe artichokes, and sometimes with poached fish.

White sauce made with stock *(velouté)*
500 ml (1 pt)

	Metric	Imp
butter	50 g	2 oz
flour	40 g	1½ oz
veal or chicken stock	500 ml	1 pt
squeeze of lemon juice		
salt, pepper		

Method

1 Melt butter in a pan, add flour and blend well. Cook over low heat without browning for 5 min., stirring all the time. Remove from heat.
2 Add stock gradually, returning to heat and stirring till boiling, simmer 10 min.
3 Add lemon juice and season to taste.

HOT BROWN SAUCES

Black butter sauce

60 ml (½ gill)

	Metric	Imp
fresh butter	50 g	2 oz
1 tbsp wine vinegar		
1 dssp chopped parsley		
salt, pepper		

Method

1 Put butter in small pan and heat till golden brown. Cool slightly.
2 Add vinegar off the heat, and reheat very slowly, but do not boil.
3 Add parsley and seasoning.

Note This is served with skate or brains.

Curry sauce

500 ml (1 pt)

	Metric	Imp
stock (any kind, according to dish the sauce is to accompany, e.g. use fish stock for fish.)	500 ml	1 pt
1 tbsp curry powder		
butter	50 g	2 oz
flour	25 g	1 oz
½ tsp vinegar		
1 onion chopped		
1 apple chopped		
2 sprigs thyme		
4 peppercorns		
salt		

Method

1 Melt the butter in a pan, add onion, peppercorns and thyme and brown very lightly over gentle heat.
2 Add flour and curry powder and brown.
3 Add vinegar and stir in stock gradually.
4 Stir till boiling, add the apple, simmer till thick, stirring occasionally, about 20 min.
5 Season, strain and use.

Demi-glace (half-glaze) sauce

250 ml (½ pt)

	Metric	Imp
Espagnole sauce (p. 65)	250 ml	½ pt
meat glaze (p. 62)	15 ml	½ oz

	Metric	Imp
madeira or red wine	60 ml	½ gill

Method

1 Put the sauce in a pan and reduce it by boiling for 20 min.
2 Add the glaze and stir till it has dissolved.
3 Add the wine, bring to the boil and serve.

Sauce for hare or venison

500 ml (1 pt)

	Metric	Imp
brown sauce (p. 64)	375 ml	¾ pt
butter	40 g	1 ½ oz
stock or gravy (any kind)	125 ml	1 gill
vinegar	60 ml	½ gill
2 tbsp redcurrant jelly		
1 onion, 1 carrot, sliced		
1 blade mace, 1 clove		
1 sprig thyme		
a little horseradish		
salt, pepper		

Method

1 Melt butter in a pan, add vegetables, mace, clove and thyme. Brown lightly.
2 Stir in vinegar, stock, brown sauce and horseradish. Season to taste and simmer for 40 min.
3 Add redcurrant jelly, strain and serve.

Indian devil sauce

185 ml (1 ½ gills)

	Metric	Imp
butter	50 g	2 oz
4 tbsp cold gravy		
1 tbsp vinegar		
1 tbsp chutney		
1 tbsp tomato ketchup		
1 tsp salt		
2 tsp made mustard		

Method

Mix all the ingredients smoothly in a shallow bowl with the butter just melted. This sauce is useful for cold meat, game and poultry which is to be reheated – in other words 'devilled'.

Italian sauce

250 ml (½ pt)

	Metric	Imp
beef or veal stock	250 ml	½ pt
white wine	60 ml	½ gill
2 lumps of sugar		
juice of ½ lemon		
2 mushrooms sliced		
1 sprig parsley		
salt, pepper		

Method

1 Put stock in a pan with mushrooms and wine, and simmer for ¼ hr.
2 Squeeze in lemon juice, add parsley, sugar, salt and pepper. Bring gently to boil. This may be thickened with 10 ml (1 dssp) of brown **roux** (p. 63).

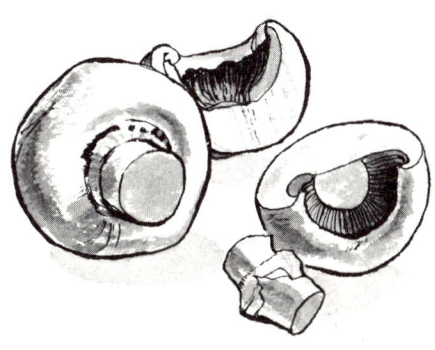

Brown mushroom sauce

	Metric	Imp
mushrooms wiped and sliced	200 g	½ lb
butter	25 g	1 oz
brown gravy or stock	250 ml	½ pt
flour	25 g	1 oz
rind and juice of ½ lemon		
salt, pepper		

Method

1 Put mushroom in pan with gravy and thinly peeled lemon rind, salt and pepper; simmer till tender (approx. 10 min.).
2 Melt butter in another pan, add the flour and brown.

3 Gradually stir in mushroom mixture, and simmer 5 min., stirring all the time. Add lemon juice, remove peel and serve.

Robert sauce

250 ml (½ pt)

	Metric	Imp
butter	12·5 g	½ oz
Espagnole sauce (p. 65)	250 ml	½ pt
2 tbsp vinegar		
1 tsp anchovy essence		
1 tsp French mustard		
1 Spanish onion finely chopped		
salt, pepper		

Method

1 Brown onion lightly in butter, add vinegar, mustard and a little pepper and salt.
2 Reduce to half quantity, add the Espagnole sauce and anchovy sauce and simmer for 10 min.
3 Strain and use.

Note This sauce is served with chops or steaks, pork or goose.

Tomato sauce

250 ml (½ pt)

	Metric	Imp
stock (any kind)	250 ml	½ pt
bacon cut in strips	25 g	1 oz
cornflour	25 g	1 oz
butter	25 g	1 oz
½ tsp celery seeds		
6 tomatoes wiped		
1 onion sliced		
thyme, a bay leaf		
salt, pepper and cayenne		

Method

1 Melt butter in pan; add tomatoes, onion, bacon, herbs and seasonings, and cook gently for 5 min.
2 Add stock and simmer till tomatoes are soft.
3 Pass through sieve to remove skin and pips, return to pan.
4 Blend cornflour with a little cold stock or water and stir into the sauce. Stir till boiling, simmer for 5 min. and serve.

WHITE SAUCES

Apple sauce

About 500 ml (1 pt)

	Metric	Imp
apples peeled, cored and sliced	600 g	1½ lb
butter	25 g	1 oz
sugar	25 g	1 oz
water	100 ml	¾ gill

Method

1 Boil apples in water till sufficiently tender to pulp.
2 Beat up smoothly with butter and sugar.

Bread sauce

250 ml (½ pt)

	Metric	Imp
milk	250 ml	½ pt
fresh white breadcrumbs	100 g	4 oz
butter	12·5 g	½ oz
1 peeled onion stuck with 2 cloves		
salt, pepper		

Method

1 Put onion with cloves into a pan with milk, cover and set over very low heat for at least 10 min. Remove onion.
2 Add breadcrumbs and simmer 3 or 4 min.
3 Remove from heat and add seasoning and butter. If too thick, add a little more milk or some cream.
4 Reheat and serve at once.

Caper sauce

	Metric	Imp
béchamel sauce (p. 64)	250 ml	½ pt
1 tbsp capers chopped		
1 dssp caper vinegar		
salt, pepper		

Method

1 Add capers to hot sauce, boil for 2 or 3 min.
2 Season, add vinegar and serve.

White celery sauce

375 ml (¾ pt)

	Metric	Imp
white stock	250 ml	½ pt
milk or single cream	125 ml	1 gill
butter	25 g	1 oz
flour	25 g	1 oz
1 head celery cooked and sieved		
salt, nutmeg		

Method

1 Melt butter, add flour and stir well.
2 Add stock and nutmeg. Stir till boiling.
3 Add celery purée and milk or cream; bring gently to just below boiling point.
4 Season and serve.

Cheese sauce (Sauce Mornay)

250 ml (½ pt)

	Metric	Imp
melted butter or béchamel sauce (pp. 65, 64)	250 ml	½ pt
grated cheese	50 g	2 oz
½ tsp made mustard		
salt, pepper and cayenne		

Method

1 Add mustard to a spoonful of sauce; blend well. Stir into rest of sauce.
2 Add cheese and stir over gentle heat till cheese has melted.
3 Season and serve.

Note A richer sauce is made by adding 1 tbsp chopped cooked mushrooms to the sauce before adding the cheese. Strain, add the cheese and finish as above.

Chestnut sauce

250 ml (½ pt)

	Metric	Imp
white stock	250 ml	½ pt
milk or single cream	125 ml	1 gill
chestnuts peeled	200 g	½ lb
peel of ½ lemon		
salt, cayenne		

Method

1 Put chestnuts in pan with stock, lemon peel cut very thin, and a very little cayenne and salt.

2 Simmer till chestnuts are quite soft.
3 Rub through a sieve or put in blender.
4 Return purée to pan, adjust seasoning and add cream, and simmer for a few minutes, stirring constantly, but do not allow to boil.

Egg sauce   *250 ml (½ pt)*

	Metric	Imp
melted butter or béchamel sauce (pp. 65, 64)	250 ml	½ pt
butter	12·5 g	½ oz
1 or 2 hard-boiled eggs, chopped finely		
salt, pepper		

Method
1 Add chopped eggs to hot sauce.
2 Whisk in butter bit by bit.
3 Season and serve.

Note If used for fish, make sauce of half milk and half fish stock.

Fennel sauce   *250 ml (½ pt)*

	Metric	Imp
melted butter or béchamel sauce (pp. 65, 64)	250 ml	½ pt
1 tbsp fennel		
salt, pepper		

Method
1 Wash the fennel, pick it from the stalks and cook in boiling water until tender. Drain very well and chop finely.
2 Add fennel to hot sauce, simmer for 2 min.
3 Season and serve.

Note The sauce can be made with half fish stock when used for fish.

Onion sauce   *250 ml (½ pt)*

	Metric	Imp
melted butter or béchamel sauce (pp. 65, 64)	250 ml	½ pt
4 onions chopped		
salt, pepper		

Method
1 Boil onions in salted water till tender. Drain well.
2 Make the sauce hot, add the onions.
3 Reheat and season. Serve.

Orange sauce for wild fowl *(Sauce Bigarade)*   *250 ml (½ pt)*

	Metric	Imp
Espagnole or brown sauce (pp. 65, 64)	250 ml	½ pt
red wine	125 ml	1 gill
2 dssp fresh orange juice		
rind of ½ orange		
juice of ½ lemon		
a strip of lemon peel		
a little cayenne pepper		

Method
1 Boil the orange and lemon peel in the sauce for 10 to 15 min.
2 Strain and add the orange and lemon juice and wine.
3 Warm it and season with cayenne. Serve.

Note A Seville orange can be used for this recipe, in which case a lump of sugar should be added at Stage 1.

Parsley sauce *(Maître d'Hôtel)*   *250 ml (½ pt)*

	Metric	Imp
melted butter or béchamel sauce (pp. 65, 64)	250 ml	½ pt
1 dssp chopped parsley		
squeeze of lemon juice		
salt, pepper		

Method
Add parsley and lemon juice to hot sauce. Check seasoning and serve.

Sauce for binding rissoles, etc.   *125 ml (1 gill)*

	Metric	Imp
flour	25 g	1 oz
butter	25 g	1 oz
milk and water	125 ml	1 gill

Method
1 Melt butter, add flour and blend well. Cook for 3 min., stirring all the time.
2 Add milk and water and stir till boiling; season.
3 Simmer for 5 min., stirring all the time or it will burn.

Soubise sauce

250 ml (½ pt)

	Metric	Imp
béchamel sauce (p. 64)	250 ml	½ pt
2 tbsp cream		
3 large onions		
salt, cayenne pepper		

Method
1 Peel and stew onions slowly to a pulp over a slow heat for 1 hr or until tender.
2 Drain well and press through a sieve.
3 Put onion purée into a pan with the béchamel sauce, and stir till boiling.
4 Season, add the cream, reheat the sauce and use.

Note The béchamel sauce must be fairly thick as the onion purée thins it down.

SAUCES FOR FISH

Anchovy sauce

250 ml (½ pt)

	Metric	Imp
melted butter or béchamel sauce (pp. 65, 64)	250 ml	½ pt
2 tsp anchovy essence		

Method
Add the essence to the sauce and boil for a minute or two.

Note Make the melted butter sauce with fish stock or half milk and half fish stock.

Green gooseberry sauce for boiled mackerel

125 ml (1 gill)

	Metric	Imp
green gooseberries	200 g	½ lb
butter	25 g	1 oz
sugar	25 g	1 oz
water	125 ml	1 gill
handful of sorrel leaves (spinach will do)		
salt, pepper, nutmeg		

Method
1 Wash sorrel or spinach, stew gently without water till soft. Press out juice to extract a wineglassful.
2 Stew gooseberries in the water, drain and rub through a sieve.

3 Combine gooseberry purée and sorrel juice in a pan. Add butter, sugar, salt, pepper, nutmeg. Serve very hot.

Hollandaise sauce

250 ml (½ pt)

	Metric	Imp
butter	50 g	2 oz
3 tbsp velouté sauce (p. 65)		
1 tsp Tarragon vinegar		
4 egg yolks		
salt, pepper		

Method
1 Put the well-beaten egg yolks into a small pan with the velouté sauce and the butter.
2 Stir over a very low heat until it has a thick creamy appearance. Take care not to let it boil or it will curdle.
3 When creamy, remove from heat, add vinegar slowly and season to taste. Keep warm in a **bain-marie.**

Mustard sauce

250 ml (½ pt)

	Metric	Imp
white stock	125 ml	1 gill
vinegar	60 ml	½ gill
milk	60 ml	½ gill
butter	25 g	1 oz

	Metric	Imp
cornflour	25 g	1 oz
1 dssp mustard		
salt, pepper		

Method

1 Melt butter in pan, add cornflour and blend well.

2 Add stock and stir till boiling.

3 Mix the mustard with the vinegar, stir into the sauce, add milk, boil up again and season. Serve with herrings and mackerel.

Oyster sauce *250 ml (½ pt)*

(economical)

	Metric	Imp
clear gravy or white stock	125 ml	1 gill
melted butter	200 g	8 oz
12 oysters (tinned will do)		

Method

1 Stew the beards of the oysters in their own juice with the stock or gravy.

2 Strain juice into the melted butter in another pan, put in oysters and simmer for 3 min.

Piquante sauce *100 ml (¾ gill)*

	Metric	Imp
made mustard	30 ml	2 tbsp
vinegar	100 ml	¾ gill
2 tbsp soft brown sugar		
salt, pepper		

Method

1 Mix the brown sugar and made mustard, mix in salt, pepper and vinegar.

2 Stir over low heat till the sugar has melted, serve in a sauce boat. This is an excellent sauce to serve with fresh herrings as it counteracts the richness of that fish.

Shrimp sauce *250 ml (½ pt)*

	Metric	Imp
melted butter	200 g	8 oz
peeled shrimps	100 g	4 oz
salt, pepper		

Method

Add shrimps to melted butter. Season and serve.

COLD SAUCES

All cold sauces should be more highly seasoned than hot ones.

A **chaudfroid** sauce is a well flavoured, nicely seasoned cold sauce, used for coating fish, meat or poultry and occasionally vegetables.

Brown chaudfroid sauce *250 ml (½ pt)*

	Metric	Imp
Espagnole or brown sauce (p.65)	250 ml	½ pt
aspic jelly	60 ml	½ gill
sherry	60 ml	½ gill
water	60 ml	½ gill
dssp gelatine		
salt, pepper		

Method

1 Heat the sauce.

2 Melt gelatine in the water and strain into sauce. Add aspic and sherry and heat gently till all is dissolved.

3 Season and allow to cool, stirring often.

Note This is used for coating dark meat, game cutlets or duck and should be used when on the point of setting, i.e. just thick enough to pour over the article to be coated without slipping off.

White chaudfroid sauce *500 ml (1 pt)*

	Metric	Imp
béchamel sauce (p. 64)	500 ml	1 pt
water	60 ml	½ gill
3 dssp gelatine		
1 tbsp cream		
cayenne, salt		

Method
1 Heat the sauce.
2 Melt gelatine in the water, strain into sauce.
3 Add cream, season, strain and stir often till cold.

Note This is used when cold and nearly setting to coat chicken, fish eggs or timbale moulds, and allowed to set.

Horse-radish sauce   *100 ml (¾ gill)*
(cold)

	Metric	Imp
cream	60 ml	1½ gill
1 tbsp vinegar		
1 tsp mustard		
salt		
a stick of grated horse-radish		

Method
1 Mix horse-radish with the cream.
2 Add mustard and salt and stir in vinegar very carefully.
3 Serve in a sauceboat to accompany roast beef, smoked trout or smoked eels.

Mayonnaise sauce   *250 ml (½ pt)*
(traditional method)

	Metric	Imp
olive oil	250 ml	½ pt
2 tsp white wine vinegar		
2 egg yolks (room temperature)		
salt, pepper		
pinch of sugar		
a few drops lemon juice		

Method
1 Mix egg yolks with seasoning, sugar and lemon juice for a few minutes with a wooden spoon or sauce whisk.
2 Add 2–3 tbsp of oil a drop at a time, stirring vigorously in the same direction the whole time.
3 When thick and creamy, add a little vinegar, then continue with oil drop by drop till half oil is used, adding vinegar at intervals when mixture is too thick.
4 The second half of oil can be added more quickly, and finally poured in a steady stream till all is used. Adjust seasoning.

Note Should the sauce curdle, put another egg yolk into a fresh basin, and stir the sauce very slowly into it.

Mayonnaise sauce   *250 ml (½ pt)*
(quick blender method)

	Metric	Imp
olive oil	250 ml	½ pt
2 tsp white wine vinegar		
1 tbsp cold water		
1 tbsp lemon juice		
1 egg		
salt, pepper		

Method
1 Put egg, water, lemon juice and 7 tbsp oil into blender and whisk at top speed till thick and emulsified (about 1 min.)
2 Add remains of oil and the vinegar and whisk again at full speed till fully blended.
3 Season to taste.

Mint sauce   *125 ml (1 gill)*

	Metric	Imp
wine vinegar	125 ml	1 gill
sugar	10 ml	½ oz
2 tbsp water		
2 tbsp chopped mint		

Method
1 Mix all ingredients together and serve in sauce boat with roast lamb.

Salad dressing   *About 60 ml (½ gill)*
(French dressing)

3 tbsp salad oil
3 dssp wine vinegar
1 clove garlic crushed (optional)
½ tsp made mustard (optional)
salt, pepper

Method
1 Put mustard, salt, pepper and garlic in a bowl, gradually stir in oil and add vinegar.
2 Mix all well. This is easily blended if put in a screw-top jar and shaken vigorously.

Tartare sauce
250 ml (½ pt)

	Metric	Imp
mayonnaise sauce (p. 72)	250 ml	½ pt
1 tbsp chopped parsley		
1 tbsp chopped gherkins		
1 dssp chopped capers		
1 tsp chopped tarragon		
½ tsp chervil		

Method
Stir the chopped ingredients and chervil into the mayonnaise and serve with fish.

SWEET SAUCES

Brandy sauce
see **Sweet Melted Butter** (p. 74)

Caramel sauce
250 ml (½ pt)

	Metric	Imp
sweet melted butter sauce (p. 74) or custard	250 ml	½ pt
loaf sugar	40 g	1½ oz
2 tbsp water		
vanilla essence to taste		

Method
1 Put sugar in a small pan; stir over low heat till melted and browned.
2 Add water and bring to boil.
3 Stir into melted butter sauce or custard and reheat.
4 Flavour with vanilla and serve.

Chocolate sauce
250 ml (½ pt)

	Metric	Imp
grated plain chocolate	50 g	2 oz
arrowroot or cornflour	10 ml	½ oz
castor sugar	25 g	1 oz
water	250 ml	½ pt
a few drops vanilla essence		

Method
1 Put chocolate, sugar and ¾ of the water into a saucepan; stir till chocolate melts and mixture boils.
2 Blend the arrowroot or cornflour with the rest of the water, add to the chocolate and simmer 5 min., stirring well.
3 Strain into a clean pan, add vanilla and serve hot.

Cranberry sauce
125 ml (1 gill)

	Metric	Imp
cranberries	200 g	8 oz
water	125 ml	1 gill
soft brown sugar	75 g	3 oz

Method
1 Put washed fruit into a pan, bruise with a fork, add water and simmer gently till soft.
2 Rub through a sieve.
3 Add sugar and stir over heat till dissolved.

Note This can be served hot or left for 12 hr and served as a jelly.

Custard sauce
500 ml (1 pt)

	Metric	Imp
hot milk	500 ml	1 pt
sugar	10 ml	½ oz
2 eggs		
a few drops of any flavour essence		

Method
1 Beat up eggs and sugar.
2 Stir in hot milk and cook over boiling water, stirring constantly till it thickens. Add flavouring. Do not allow mixture to boil.

German sauce (Sabayon)
125 ml (1 gill)

	Metric	Imp
Madeira	125 ml	1 gill
castor sugar	50 g	2 oz
2 egg yolks		

Method
Put all ingredients in a double saucepan

containing boiling water and whisk over a low heat till thick and frothy. Do not let this boil or the eggs will curdle. Serve immediately.

Hard sauce for plum pudding

	Metric	Imp
butter	50 g	2 oz
castor, icing or soft brown sugar	100 g	4 oz
1 tbsp rum or brandy		

Method
Beat the butter with the sugar to a froth, then beat in the brandy or rum gradually. Leave the sauce in a cold place to harden. Serve in a small glass dish.

Jam sauce   *125 ml (1 gill)*

	Metric	Imp
water	250 ml	½ pt
loaf sugar	50 g	2 oz
4 tbsp raspberry or strawberry jam		
½ tsp lemon juice		
cochineal		

Method
1 Put sugar, water and jam into a pan and boil for 5 min.
2 Add lemon juice and 2 or 3 drops cochineal.
3 Strain and serve.

Sweet melted butter   *250 ml (½ pt)*

	Metric	Imp
butter	25 g	1 oz
castor sugar	10 ml	½ oz
flour	25 g	1 oz
milk	250 ml	½ pt
flavouring to taste		

Method
1 Melt butter, add flour and blend well.
2 Add milk and sugar and stir till boiling. Simmer 10 min.
3 Add any flavour liked, e.g. vanilla, almond, lemon, a spoonful of brandy, strong coffee, rum or maraschino.

Note The sauce takes its name from the flavouring.

Treacle sauce   *125 ml (1 gill)*

	Metric	Imp
golden syrup or treacle	60 ml	½ gill
water	125 ml	1 gill
juice of 1 lemon strained		

Method
Boil all ingredients together for 10 min. Serve hot.

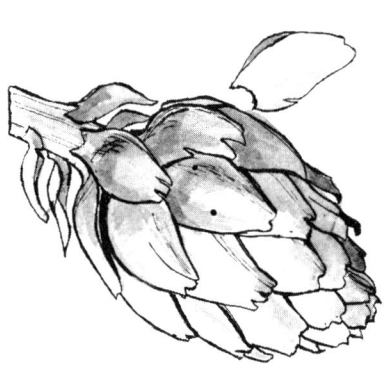

SAVOURY BUTTERS

Savoury butters are useful for serving with grills or for making hors d'oeuvres, savouries and sandwiches.

Anchovy butter

	Metric	Imp
butter	75 g	3 oz
8–10 anchovy fillets		

Method
Pound anchovies in a mortar with the butter and rub through a sieve. Make into a pat on a plate and leave in a cold place.

Note Use with boiled, grilled, fried and poached fish.

Lobster butter

lobster coral or spawn cooked
and dried in a cool oven
butter
salt, pepper

Method
Pound lobster spawn with double its quantity of butter in a mortar, season to taste and rub through a hair sieve. Keep in a cool place.

Curry butter

	Metric	Imp
butter	75 g	3 oz
1 tsp curry powder		
¼ tsp black pepper		
pinch of cayenne		

Method
Mix butter with all other ingredients, working them well together. Keep in a cold place. Serve with grills.

Maître d'hôtel butter

	Metric	Imp
butter	50 g	2 oz
4 tbsp finely chopped parsley		
a few drops of lemon juice		
salt, pepper		

Method
Mix butter very smoothly with lemon juice, chopped parsley and seasoning. Leave to set and mould into small pats to place on top of meat or fish before serving.

Garlic butter

	Metric	Imp
4 crushed garlic cloves		
2 tbsp chopped parsley		
salted butter	100 g	4 oz

Method
Cream all the ingredients together with a wooden spoon or in a blender.

Note The garlic should either be crushed very thoroughly with the tip of a knife or in a garlic press before mixing with the other ingredients.

Prawn or shrimp butter

	Metric	Imp
butter	50 g	2 oz
peeled shrimps or prawns chopped	100 g	4 oz
½ tsp anchovy paste		
cayenne		

Method
Pound shrimps or prawns, butter and paste together; add a little cayenne, and salt if necessary. Rub through a hair sieve, and put on a plate in a cold place.

Ravigote butter

	Metric	Imp
butter	50 g	2 oz
Tarragon, chervil,	10 ml	½ oz
cress, parsley	each	each
1 shallot, chopped		
salt, pepper		

Method
1 Put herbs into boiling water for 2 min., drain and lay on a cloth to dry.
2 Pound in a mortar with other ingredients.
3 Pass through a hair sieve. The butter should be a good green colour. If too dark, add more butter.
4 Harden in refrigerator.

Watercress butter

	Metric	Imp
butter	50 g	2 oz
1 tbsp finely minced watercress		
salt, pepper		

Method
Squeeze watercress dry in a cloth, pound it with the butter, season and put it on a plate in a cold place.

BATTERS

Coating batter

	Metric	Imp
flour	100 g	4 oz
milk or water	up to 125 ml	up to ¼ pt
1 tbsp oil		
1 egg white		
pinch of salt		

Method
1 Sieve flour and salt into a basin and make a hollow in the centre.
2 Mix oil and tepid water or milk and stir in a little at a time. Beat well till smooth and creamy. Stand for 1 to 2 hr.
3 Just before using, beat egg white stiffly and fold into batter.

Frying batter (for pancakes)

	Metric	Imp
flour	100 g	4 oz
milk	250 ml	½ pt
1 egg		
salt		

Method
1 Beat egg thoroughly into milk. (This may be done in the blender.)
2 Sieve flour and salt together into a bowl. Make a well in the centre and stir in the milk and egg mixture gradually. (If using the blender, pour flour and salt mixture into egg and milk and blend at medium speed for 2 min.). Beat for several minutes with a wooden spoon.
3 Allow to stand for 2 hr before using.

STUFFINGS AND GARNISHES

Stuffings – forcemeats – dumplings – garnishes

STUFFINGS

Apple stuffing

	Metric	Imp
cooking apples peeled, cored and sliced	600 g	1½ lb
boiled rice	100 g	4 oz
sugar	25 g	1 oz
butter or margarine	25 g	1 oz
1 egg		
pinch of nutmeg		

Method

1 Put apples in a pan with just enough water to keep them from burning, add butter and simmer till tender.

2 Add the sugar and nutmeg and stir in the rice, which should be boiled very soft. Mix thoroughly.

3 **Bind** with beaten egg.

Note Use for stuffing pork or goose.

Chestnut stuffing

	Metric	Imp
chestnuts shelled and peeled	400 g	1 lb
breadcrumbs	75 g	3 oz
melted butter	50 g	2 oz
1 egg		
water or stock		
salt, pepper		

Method

1 Simmer chestnuts in enough water or stock to cover them, till soft.

2 Strain off liquor and rub through a sieve or put in blender.

3 Add breadcrumbs and butter; season well.

4 Beat up egg and add, mix well and use. If too dry, add a little milk.

Note This is used for stuffing poultry. Tinned chestnut purée may be used, in which case only stages 3 and 4 are followed.

Nut stuffing

	Metric	Imp
shelled nuts (any variety)	50 g	2 oz
shelled almonds	50 g	2 oz
soft breadcrumbs or boiled rice	50 g	2 oz
butter or margarine	40 g	1½ oz
1 tbsp milk or evaporated milk		
1 shallot minced		
1 egg		
salt, pepper		

Method

1 **Blanch** and chop nuts finely.

2 Melt butter in a pan, add nuts and shallot, and fry till lightly browned.

3 Add breadcrumbs, beaten egg, milk and seasoning to taste, and mix well.

Note Use for stuffing game, poultry, peppers, cabbages, marrows, etc.

Sage and onion stuffing

	Metric	Imp
soft breadcrumbs	125 g	5 oz
melted butter	25 g	1 oz
3 onions peeled		
8 sage leaves or 1 tsp dried sage		
Salt, pepper		

Method

1 Boil onions in two waters to extract strong flavour. **Scald** sage leaves for a few minutes.

2 Drain onions and press as dry as possible. Chop them with sage.

3 Mix with breadcrumbs; season; add melted butter. Use for duck, goose or pork.

FORCEMEATS

Oyster forcemeat

	Metric	Imp
12 oysters		
soft breadcrumbs	125 g	5 oz
melted butter	25 g	1 oz
1 tsp chopped parsley		
peel of ½ lemon grated		
salt, nutmeg, a little cayenne		
1 egg yolk		

Method
1 Beard the oysters, wash well in own liquor, chop finely.
2 Mix well with lemon peel, parsley, seasonings and butter.
3 Add breadcrumbs and **bind** with egg yolk and some of the oyster liquor.

Note To make the oyster liquor, put the beards and existing liquor and a little water into a pan, simmer for 5 min. and strain.

Panada (Used as the basis of forcemeats, soufflés, etc.)

	Metric	Imp
water	250 ml	½ pt
butter	25 g	1 oz
flour	100 g	4 oz
salt		

Method
1 Put butter and water in a pan to boil.
2 Sprinkle in flour and salt and stir vigorously over heat with a wooden spoon till the mixture thickens and forms a ball, leaving the sides of the pan clean.

Liver Farce (Farce de Foie de Veau)

	Metric	Imp
calves liver	200 g	½ lb
fat bacon	25 g	1 oz
potatoes mashed	200 g	½ lb
stock	60 ml	½ gill
2 egg yolks		
1 shallot		
bunch of mixed herbs		
pinch of nutmeg		
salt, pepper		

Method
1 Wash and dry liver and cut into small pieces, removing all skin.
2 Chop bacon and fry in pan for a few minutes.
3 Add liver and brown a little on both sides.
4 Chop shallot finely and add to pan with herbs tied together.
5 Moisten with the stock and simmer until liver is well cooked. Remove herbs, and pound the cooked ingredients in a mortar.
6 Add mashed potatoes, nutmeg, salt and pepper and bind the mixture with the beaten egg yolks.
7 Rub mixture through a fine sieve and use for pigeons, game etc. as directed.

Sausage forcemeat

	Metric	Imp
sausage meat	200 g	½ lb
soft breadcrumbs	100 g	4 oz
melted butter or margarine	25 g	1 oz
1 dssp chopped parsley		
1 egg or milk to **bind**		
Salt, pepper		

Method
Mix all ingredients together and use for stuffing poultry or veal.

Forcemeat balls for poultry, veal, hare, fish, etc.

	Metric	Imp
lean bacon shredded finely	75 g	3 oz
soft breadcrumbs	150 g	6 oz
chopped suet	100 g	4 oz
1 tsp chopped parsley		
½ tsp thyme and marjoram, mixed and chopped		
grated rind of ½ lemon		
2 eggs		
Salt, pepper, nutmeg		

Method
1 Stir bacon, suet, lemon peel and herbs into breadcrumbs. Mix well.
2 Season well, add a pinch of nutmeg.
3 Beat eggs and **bind** mixture with them.
4 Divide into balls; coat with flour and fry light brown. May also be used as stuffing.

DUMPLINGS

Suet dumplings

	Metric	Imp
flour	100 g	4 oz
suet	50 g	2 oz
salt, pepper		
water to mix		

Method
1 Sieve flour with a pinch each of salt and pepper.
2 Add suet and mix to a stiffish paste with water.
3 Shape into balls with a little flour.
4 Put into boiling water or stock or the gravy of stews.
5 Simmer for 10 min.

GARNISHES

The appearance of a dish is as important as the taste – as important, but not more so. One should never risk a hot dish losing its heat through too much time being spent on its decoration, and however beautifully food is presented, it will never make up for poor flavour. Garnishes should both look good and taste good; they should provide a contrast or a complement to the dish they decorate and always be edible.

Always choose a dish of a suitable size; if too small, it looks overcrowded; if too large, the food is lost in it. Wipe all splashes or drops of gravy or sauce or any crumbs from the edges.

The principal garnishes for either hot or cold dishes are vegetables, cooked or uncooked, used whole, or cut into fancy shapes. Several vegetables may be mixed and are then called a *macédoine*. Forcemeats or farce made into quenelles or balls; bread and pastry cut into various shapes; eggs; parsley, cresses, endive and so on.

Fish dishes are decorated with fish quenelles, oysters, crayfish, prawns, shrimps, cockles, scallops, fried smelts, mussels, eggs, cucumber, parsley, chervil and lemon, truffles, aspic or any savoury jellies and so on.

Sauces hot or cold, plain or coloured are also used as garnish.

Sweet dishes are garnished with crystallized or glacé fruits and flowers, fresh fruit, whipped cream, meringue, coloured sugars, icing of various kinds, coconut, whole, chopped or shredded nuts of different kinds, sweet jelly.

Aspic jelly for ordinary garnishing

	Metric	Imp
good jellied white stock	750 ml	1½ pt
gelatine	40 g	1½ oz
water	125 ml	1 gill
sherry	125 ml	1 gill
2 tbsp Tarragon vinegar		
2 egg whites		
crushed egg shells		
1 bay leaf		
salt		

Method
1 Melt stock, but do not heat it more than necessary. Add vinegar, bay leaf, sherry, water, gelatine and salt.
2 Whip egg whites slightly and add to mixture with crushed egg shells.
3 Whisk over low heat till just on boiling point. Boil up quickly, remove from heat and let stand to settle.
4 Pour through jelly bag or a clean cloth tied to inverted legs of chair.

Note Aspic jelly may be coloured by adding some tomato juice strained through muslin; use more gelatine if adding much tomato juice. Aspic is often chopped or cut into fancy shapes and used for decorating dishes.

Egg garnish

Boil the eggs hard, separate the whites from the yolks, rub the yolks through a sieve and use them for decorating. The whites are chopped or cut into slices and fancy shapes, and also used for decorating.

BREAD GARNISHES

Browned breadcrumbs

Any stale bread, crust or crumbs, may be used for these. Dry the bread in a cool oven, crush it with a rolling pin or mince it. Keep the crumbs in tins or bottles with well-fitting lids or corks.

White breadcrumbs for keeping

Rub the crumbs of some stale bread through a sieve, place it on a piece of paper in a very cool oven and dry without browning.

CROÛTONS

Croûtons for garnishing

Cut some thin slices of bread. Remove the crusts and cut the slices into triangles, rounds, hearts, diamonds, crescents, dice, and so on. Fry in hot fat, drain well. A 'croûte' is a large piece of fried bread on which entrées are served.

Pastry croûtons

Scraps of good pastry, puff or otherwise, rolled out thinly and cut into match-like shreds about an inch long or into fancy shapes called 'fleurons'.

VEGETABLE GARNISHES

Celery

Cut into strips or small dice and use in soups.
To curl: wash the celery well, trim, and with a sharp knife cut the tops in fine strips to a depth of 5 cm (2 in). Place the celery in cold water and the strips gradually curl.

Cucumber

Choose a straight, firm cucumber for garnishing. Wipe it and cut it into blocks about 5 cm (2 in.) long. **Score** the skin down in narrow strips, remove each alternate strip and cut each piece of cucumber into very thin slices. Scallops are formed by cutting each block of cucumber in halves after removing the strips. Slice each half finely and arrange the pieces round the dish.

Macédoine of vegetables

Carrots, turnips, cucumber, peas and French beans, cut into small balls, dice, strips and fancy shapes and boiled until soft in water or stock.

Olives

Olives are often used as a garnish, either plain or stuffed. They must be stoned as follows: cut a small piece from the stalk end of each to enable them to stand firmly, then with a sharp penknife peel or 'turn' them. Begin at the thick end and cut to the stone, then keeping the knife pressed against the stone, peel round and round as if peeling an apple. The stone should come out quite clean and the olive form a coil which falls back into its original shape.

Parsley

Parsley can be used for decorating, either raw or fried. Used raw, it is either chopped finely and sprinkled over the dish, or broken into sprigs and arranged round it. Fried dishes should be decorated with fried parsley. To fry, wash the parsley, pick off any stalks which are too long, squeeze very dry in a cloth. Put it into the fat after frying the article the parsley is to decorate. The fat should not be over the heat when putting in the parsley, and a few seconds in the hot fat is enough.

To chop parsley, wash it well, remove the stalks, squeeze it dry in a clean cloth, then chop very finely on a board, using a sharp knife; or use a parsley mill.

To prepare potatoes for garnishing

	Metric	Imp
potatoes	800 g	2 lb
butter	60 g	2½ oz
milk	60 ml	½ gill
breadcrumbs	25 g	1 oz
2 dssp chopped parsley		
2 eggs		
salt, pepper		

Method

1 Boil potatoes and sieve.

2 Melt butter in a pan, add potatoes, seasoning, parsley, and one egg beaten up in milk; leave till cold.

3 Roll potatoes in balls or shapes, coat with egg and breadcrumbs.

4 Fry in hot fat; drain lightly and use as garnish.

HORS D'OEUVRES

Hors d'oeuvres is the name given to small appetizing dishes served at the beginning of a meal – usually cold. They generally take the place of soup.

Many different foods are used for making hors d'oeuvre: meat, fish, vegetables or fruit; they may be served raw or cooked or made into dishes with aspic or mayonnaise or into pâtés and mousses.

Avocado pear   *2 persons*

Method

1 Cut a ripe avocado in half lengthways and remove the stone. Sprinkle the flesh with a little lemon juice.

2 The cavity may be filled with a little French dressing (p. 72) or with prawns or shellfish in mayonnaise; or mayonnaise which has been flavoured with a little curry powder and into which snippets of crisply fried bacon have been folded.

Note The test for ripeness of an avocado pear is to press it gently between the palms of the hands. If ripe, it should yield. If unripe when bought, store in a plastic bag at room temperature for about 3 days.

BOUCHÉES

Chicken patties   *8 patties*

	Metric	Imp
8 small puff pastry cases		
cooked chicken chopped finely	100 g	4 oz
cooked ham or tongue chopped	50 g	2 oz
velouté or béchamel sauce (pp. 65, 64)	250 ml	½ pt
1 tsp chopped parsley		
2 mushrooms chopped		
a little butter		
salt, pepper		

Method

1 Cook the mushrooms in a little butter. Drain.

2 Mix chicken, ham, and mushrooms with the sauce, season and heat.

3 Fill the pastry cases with the mixture, sprinkle with chopped parsley.

Note Game may be used in place of chicken for game patties.

Haddock patties   *6 patties*

	Metric	Imp
6 vol-au-vent cases		
smoked haddock fillet	200 g	8 oz
milk	125 ml	1 gill
butter	25 g	1 oz
flour	25 g	1 oz
1 small glass sherry or a squeeze of lemon juice		
3 tbsp cream		
1 tsp chopped parsley		
salt, pepper, cayenne		

Method

1 Simmer haddock in the milk for 10 to 15 min. Remove from milk.

2 Separate flesh from skin and bone, and **flake.**

3 Melt butter in a pan, add flour and stir a few minutes over low heat without browning. Add gradually the milk in which the fish cooked, stirring continuously.

4 Bring to the boil and simmer for 5 min.

5 Add **flaked** fish, heat up mixture, then remove from heat and add cream and sherry or lemon juice. Season and add parsley.

6 Warm patty cases and fill with the mixture; put on the lids and serve hot or cold.

Note Shrimp or prawn patties are made like haddock patties, substituting cooked shrimps or prawns for haddock, and milk in place of cream.

Cold cheese creams

6 persons

	Metric	Imp
grated Parmesan cheese	40 g	1½ oz
grated Roquefort cheese	40 g	1½ oz
aspic jelly	125 ml	1 gill
cream	125 ml	1 gill
1 tsp gelatine		
salt, mustard and cayenne		
chopped parsley		

Method

1 Melt the gelatine in a small quantity of water.
2 Melt the aspic and strain the gelatine into it.
3 Whip the cream and stir the grated cheese into it.
4 Mix the mustard gradually into the aspic and when all blended in, whip till frothy. **Fold in** cheese mixture.
5 Season well and put into small china or paper soufflé cases round which a band of stiff paper has been fastened, reaching 5 cm (2 in.) above the case. Leave in a cool place to set.
6 Remove paper bands from the cases and serve with a little chopped parsley sprinkled on top.

Mock Crab savoury

3 persons

	Metric	Imp
grated cheese	50 g	2 oz
1 tsp vinegar or beer		
1 tsp made mustard		
1 tsp cream		
pepper, cayenne		
6 small croûtes of fried bread or toast		
parsley		

Method

1 Mix the cheese, mustard, vinegar or beer and seasoning.
2 Stir in the cream, mix well.
3 Pile on small round croûtes and garnish with parsley.

Corn on the cob

There are two methods of boiling corn on the cob. The outer husks are removed and the silk stripped off in a downwards direction. The cobs are then either plunged into cold salted water and brought to the boil for 3–4 min., or put straight into boiling water for 20 min. The corn is then served with little holders stuck in either end, and pats of butter are offered for spreading on at table.

Grapefruit salad

Allow half a grapefruit per person. Cut the grapefruits in halves, remove all the pips, and with a sharp knife loosen the pulp from the rind. Cut a hole in the centre of each half. Fill in the centre with a spoonful of kirsch or maraschino, and if liked, a pinch of ground ginger. Place a glacé cherry on top and serve on individual plates.

Another method of preparing the fruit is to remove the pulp and juice with a teaspoon and put into a basin. Mix a little maraschino or kirsch with the grapefruit, add some halved glacé cherries, or if fresh cherries are in season, stone and add them. Clear out all the pith from the fruit and fill the fruit cups with the prepared pulp. Keep the grapefruit on ice or in a very cold place until required.

Melon salad

Melon is a favourite hors d'oeuvre and may be served plain, with castor sugar and powdered ginger handed separately. Cantaloup and Honeydew melons are served in segments, about ¼ to ⅙ of a melon, depending on the size. Charentais and Ogen melons are served in half and are sometimes filled with port or liqueurs. Melons should be just ripe, but not over-ripe, and must be very cold.

Another method of serving the melon is to cut a piece out of the top, remove the seeds and scoop out the interior, leaving the rind intact. Cut the pulp into cubes, mix with salt, pepper, and a pinch of powdered ginger and pour over a dressing of 30 ml (2 tbsp) white wine mixed with 30 ml (2 tbsp) tarragon vinegar. Return the mixture to the interior of the melon and serve very cold.

Oysters au naturel
4–6 per person

Oysters are usually served raw as hors d'oeuvre. They must be very fresh, and should not be opened long before they are required. Allow 4 to 6 per person. Wash, scrub and dry the shells, open the oysters, (see p. 108). Arrange four to six on each plate in the deep shells, with the valve sides of the shells meeting in the centre of the plate. Put a quarter of cut lemon in the centre, and garnish with small sprays of parsley. Serve with brown bread and butter, and cayenne or tabasco sauce.

Chicken liver pâté
4 persons

	Metric	Imp
chicken livers	200 g	8 oz
butter	75 g	3 oz
1 dssp brandy		
1 medium onion chopped		
1 clove garlic crushed		
pinch of mixed herbs		
salt, pepper		

Method
1 Melt 25 g (1 oz) butter, cook onion and garlic gently for 5 min.
2 Add chicken livers and cook a further 3 min., stirring well. Add herbs and seasoning, cook 1 more min. Cool.
3 Chop and pound, or put in blender.
4 Stir in remaining butter, melted, and brandy.
5 Put into a mould, chill.
6 Turn out and serve with hot toast, and butter separately.

Pork pâté
8–10 persons

	Metric	Imp
pig's liver trimmed and cut in large pieces	300 g	12 oz
streaky bacon with rind removed	200 g	8 oz
pork sausagemeat	300 g	12 oz
stuffed green olives	40 g	1½ oz
1 tsp Worcestershire sauce		
2 good pinches of garlic salt		
salt, pepper		

Method
1 Mince liver and half the bacon.
2 Mix very well with sausagemeat, garlic salt, seasoning, Worcestershire sauce.
3 Line a 750 ml (1½ pt) pudding basin with remaining rashers of bacon which have been spread out thin with a knife. Fill with pâté mixture, press in stuffed olives at varying depths, and smooth top.
4 Stand basin in a tin of cold water and bake on middle shelf of a warm oven (160°C, 325°F, Mark 5) for 1¾ hr.
5 Leave pâté overnight with a saucer held down by a heavy weight on top, to press pâté down.
6 Turn out and serve with hot toast, and butter separately.

Potted shrimps
4 persons

	Metric	Imp
peeled shrimps	500 ml	1 pt
butter	50 g	2 oz
½ tsp ground mace		
salt, pepper		

Method
1 Heat a third of the butter in a pan, add seasoning and mace.
2 When hot, add shrimps and stir well. Heat thoroughly.
3 Place in little pots. Allow remaining butter to melt and pour over shrimps just to cover. Leave to cool.

4 Serve with brown bread and butter or hot fresh dry toast and butter.

Note Potted shrimps are also bought in small pots or small cartons, and served straight from the pot or they may be turned out.

Prawn cocktail   *4 persons*

	Metric	Imp
peeled prawns	200 g	8 oz
mayonnaise (p. 72)	250 ml	½ pt
½ tsp concentrated tomato purée		
a little paprika		
shredded lettuce		

Method

1 Mix the mayonnaise thoroughly with the tomato purée and paprika.
2 **Fold in** prawns.
3 Put some lettuce in the bottom of 4 large glasses, add the prawns and chill.
4 Serve with a lemon slice and thin brown bread and butter.

Hors d'oeuvres variés are a mixture of several small dishes which should present a contrast in texture, colour and taste. If no proper hors d'oeuvre dish with separate compartments is available, from which people can help themselves, a selection can be arranged attractively on individual plates for each person. Suggestions for mixed hors d'oeuvres are: slices of cooked meats such as salami, liver sausage or ham rolled into cornets; tinned fish such as sardines or anchovies, drained from their oil and sprinkled with chopped parsley; smoked fish (eels and salmon), roll-mop herrings, cooked vegetable salads (p. 200) and raw salads.

Very small sandwiches filled with some savoury mixture make an excellent hors d'oeuvre.

Smoked sausages are cut into very thin slices, the skin removed, and the slices neatly arranged in an hors d'oeuvre dish, garnished with parsley. Sometimes slices of sausage are used in conjunction with other ingredients.

Herrings and **mackerel** can be bought pickled, in which case they are generally drained, cut into fillets or strips and served, nicely arranged on glass dishes, garnished with capers and parsley.

Tunny fish, and **fillets of sour herrings** are generally served drained from the oil in which they are preserved and cut into thin slices, fresh oil and vinegar dressing being poured over them. They may be garnished with chopped parsley, chervil, tarragon or chopped gherkins.

Prawns and **shrimps** make excellent savouries, and are usually served *au naturel*. They may be dished on individual hors d'oeuvre dishes, allowing about 8 to 12 prawns or shrimps per person. They are cooked but not shelled and should stand up round half a cut lemon, which should be turned cut side down upon a plate. The heads should point towards the top of the lemon, the tails being caught underneath it. Fill the centre with well-washed and dried parsley.

Salted almonds

Blanch almonds and dry them. Melt some butter in a very clean baking tin, add the almonds and put them into a moderate oven (175°C, 350°F, Mark 4) until pale brown (about 10 min.). Turn them frequently so that they brown evenly all over. Turn the almonds on to a piece of white kitchen paper and sprinkle with table salt. When quite cold, shake off any loose salt and arrange the almonds in small glass or silver dishes. Salted almonds remain on the table throughout the dinner. Any nuts may be salted in this manner – peanuts, filberts, hazel nuts and so on. They will keep good for some time if kept in a tightly corked bottle.

Devilled almonds or other nuts are made in the same way, a little cayenne pepper being sprinkled over them with the salt.

Devilled chestnuts

Chestnuts
oil or butter for frying
salt, cayenne

Method

1 Boil the chestnuts (p. 213) for about 30 min.
2 Remove both skins and fry about 8 min; drain well.
3 Sprinkle at once with a mixture of salt and cayenne. Coat well, then shake any surplus off and serve nuts in small paper cases.

Devilled prunes

18 prunes
2 tbsp thick mayonnaise (p. 72)
1 dssp chutney
cayenne, salt, pepper
chopped parsley

Method

1 Stew the prunes carefully without breaking (20–30 min.). Cool.
2 Remove the stones.
3 Mix the mayonnaise and chutney. Season very well. Fill the prunes with the mixture.
4 Sprinkle with parsley and serve on cocktail sticks.

Olives

Olives can be plain green, black or stuffed. The green ones should be a good green colour. Steep the olives in cold water for a short while before serving them and put a few drops of water in the dishes. Any that are left over should be put at once into a bottle with salt water, or they turn black. It should be remembered that metal should not touch the olives as it turns them black; therefore, when preparing them, use a wooden fork or skewer.

Cornets

Pastry of any kind may be rolled out very thinly and cut into thin strips, which are placed round a cornet mould or twisted round a well-washed and scraped carrot. Begin at the pointed end of the carrot and roll round and round it, letting each strip of pastry overlap the one that preceded it. Bake these in a hot oven. Remove the pastry from the mould or carrot, and fill it with any savoury mixture in sauce. Very small cornets should be made for hors d'oeuvre.

Small cases may also be made out of bread. Cut a slice of bread about 5 cm (2 in.) thick. Out of this, cut rounds 5 cm (2 in.) in diameter. With a smaller cutter, stamp a round in the centre of each croûte of bread, not pressing right through to the bottom of it. Remove the centre, shake off any loose crumbs and fry these cases in hot fat. Drain well and fill with any savoury mixture liked.

Little cups cut from cooked cucumber, cooked beetroot, the whites of hard-boiled eggs, and tomatoes also form cases in which to serve savoury mixtures, hot or cold.

Very small moulds coated with aspic jelly may be filled with prawns or shrimps, green peas, *macédoine* of vegetables, small cubes of chicken or game and peas, chopped hard-boiled eggs and so on, filled in with more liquid aspic and left in a cold place to set. These make good cold hors d'oeuvre. Turn them out on to a hors d'oeuvre dish and garnish with a little chervil, a few sprays of watercress, or some chopped aspic.

Canapés

Cut some slices of bread about 1 cm (½ in.) thick. Stamp them out into small rounds or ovals, and fry in hot fat; drain well. These can be covered with any mixture of fish, chicken, game, ham or tongue paste, egg, fancy butters or cheese. Garnish with salads, and use as hors d'oeuvre.

Radishes may be used with hors d'oeuvres variés. They should be washed, trimmed and soaked in cold water for a few minutes, then placed in a glass dish with very little water at the bottom. The outside skins are sometimes cut into sections like petals, which makes them look like small flowers.

Small portions of various vegetable salads make good additions to hors d'oeuvres variés. In France a tomato salad is often served on its own as a first course.

Beetroot salad

Peel and wash a cooked beet, cut it into very small dice, add one finely minced raw onion, arrange on an hors d'oeuvre dish. Sprinkle with salt and cayenne and pour over a good salad dressing.

Cauliflower salad

Break up the sprigs of a cold cooked califlower; arrange them in an hors d'oeuvre dish, sprinkle a few chopped capers over, and coat with mustard sauce (p. 70).

Celery salad

Cut the best parts of 2 or 3 heads of celery in thin strips. Mix with mayonnaise sauce and serve in an hors d'oeuvre dish.

Tomato salad

Wipe and slice tomatoes thinly with a very sharp knife. Arrange slices neatly in an hors d'oeuvre dish and sprinkle over a little minced raw onion and chopped parsley. Pour over it some French dressing (p. 72).

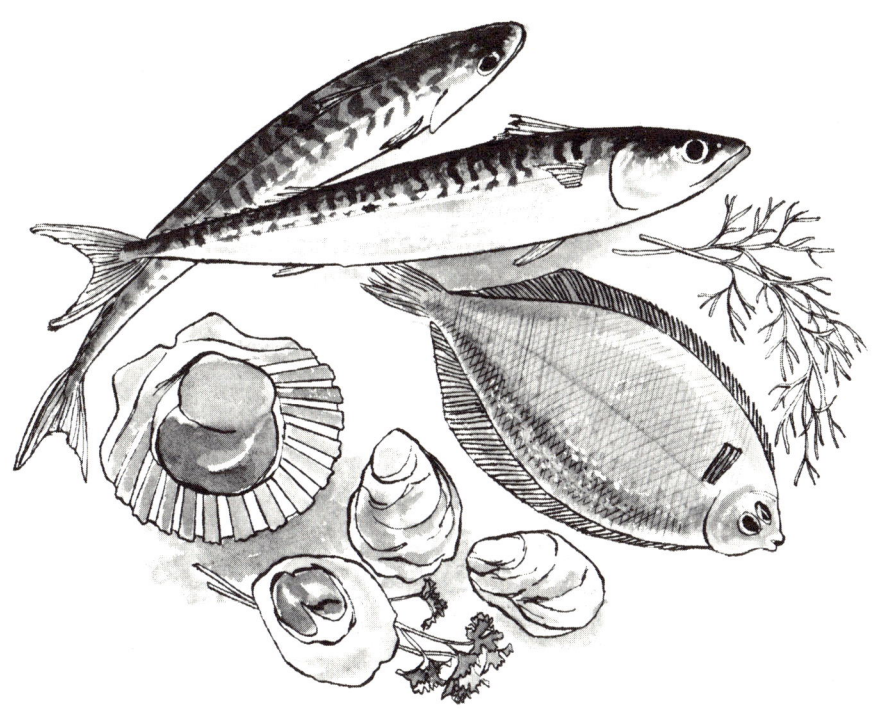

FISH

*Cleaning – skinning and filleting – basic preparations used for
cooking fish – principles of cooking fish – recipes for hot and
cold fish dishes – made-up fish dishes*

CLEANING FISH

Fish will normally be cleaned, scaled, and filleted, if required, by the fishmonger. It may be necessary, however, to deal with freshly caught fish, in which case it should be washed well in cold water, using salt if the fish is at all slimy. Check that all the blood is removed from the backbone, and remove any black skin in the cavity of the fish by rubbing it with salt.

The scales on a fish should be scraped off with a knife; if very difficult to remove, plunge the fish into boiling water for a minute or two. Lay the fish on a board, and holding the tail towards you, scrape from the tail towards the head. Cut off the head, unless it is to be cooked with the head on; in which case, remove the eyes by cutting the skin covering them with scissors and pushing them out from the inside. Trim the tail and cut off the fins with a pair of scissors. With a sharp knife, slit the middle of the underside of the fish and scoop out the intestines with the fingers or with a spoon.

Freshwater fish is the only fish which requires soaking to remove the muddy flavour. All other fish should be rinsed under the tap and not left lying in the water.

Fish freezes very satisfactorily and can be used while still frozen or when just thawed. The following instructions and recipes for fish assume that the fish is thawed if it was originally frozen.

SKINNING FISH

Flat fish, such as sole, plaice and so on, are skinned from the tail to the head. Clean and wash the fish, dry it with a cloth, cut off the fins, make a cut across the skin, on the dark side of the fish, just above the tail. Raise the skin gently with the tip of a knife, then with finger and thumb dipped in salt, work the skin away from the flesh with the thumb, first up the right side of the fish, then up the left. Hold the tail down on the board and pull the loosened skin sharply towards the head. Turn the fish over and remove the skin on the other side in the same manner.

Round fish, such as haddock, whiting, and so on, are skinned from the head to the tail. Wash the fish, dry and cut it across the skin just under the head, using a sharp-pointed knife. Care must be taken when skinning round fish, as the flesh is less compact than that of flat fish and breaks more easily. Loosen the skin carefully, pulling it gently towards the tail. Turn and remove the skin from the other half of the fish also.

When skinning fish, the skin may be held by a cloth, or the fingers may be dipped in coarse salt, to prevent them from slipping.

FILLETING FISH

Flat fish With a sharp-pointed knife, cut through the middle of the fish along the faint line on the skin right down to the backbone, then cut down each side of the fins, where the flesh ends in the fin bones: do this on both sides of the fish, then begin on the black side. Lay the fish on a board and begin at the left-hand side, working from the head to the tail. Insert the knife into the incision at the back nearest the head, and work the flesh from the bone, keeping the knife pressed against the bone and giving long sweeping strokes under the flesh. Raise this with the other hand. The flesh should come off entire from one half of the fish. Turn the fish so that the tail is farthest away, and begin the filleting from the tail, raising the flesh from the bone in the same manner. When the fillets have been removed from one side, turn the fish over and remove them from the other side in the same way. The fillets are left whole or are cut in halves as desired.

Round fish Wash and dry the fish, cut off the head, trim the tail and fins, and with a sharp knife make an incision down the dark line on the ridge of the back, cutting down to the bone. Make another incision down the cut side of the fish. Work the flesh from the bones, beginning at the open side of the fish, at the head end. When the fillet is removed from one side, turn the fish round then remove the second fillet. Round fish have only two fillets. These may, however, be cut into two or three pieces each as desired. The cuts should be made in a slanting direction.

BASIC PREPARATIONS USED FOR COOKING FISH

Simple court-bouillon

A **court-bouillon** is a liquor prepared in advance and used for poaching fish (p. 94). This will give added flavour to the dish.

	Metric	Imp
water	2 l	2 qt
cider or wine vinegar	125 ml	¼ pt
carrots sliced	400 g	1 lb
onions	200 g	½ lb
salt	40 g	1½ oz
1 bay leaf, 1 sprig each thyme and parsley		
10 peppercorns		

Method

Simmer all ingredients together for 1 hr; strain and cool.

Court-bouillon for salmon and trout

	Metric	Imp
water	2 l	2 qt
white wine	250 ml	½ pt
tarragon vinegar	60 ml	½ gill
shallots minced	50 g	2 oz
salt	25 g	1 oz
1 blade mace and 1 bay leaf		
10 peppercorns		

Method

Simmer all ingredients for ½ hr. Strain and cool.

A pickle for sousing or collaring fish

	Metric	Imp
vinegar	2 l	2 qt
salt	50 g	2 oz
12 peppercorns		
6 cloves		
3 bay leaves and 3 blades mace		
large pinch each of ground allspice and ground nutmeg		

Method

Boil up all ingredients for a few minutes, then simmer the fish in the liquor very slowly for ¾ hr, with a lid on the dish. Leave to get cold before uncovering.

A marinade for fish

A **marinade** is a cooked or uncooked liquid which is highly flavoured and which imparts its flavour to the fish or meat which is soaked in it. Usually the quantity of **marinade** is quite small, so the fish or meat is turned several times in the liquid, to become well impregnated.

2 tbsp lemon juice
2 tbsp olive oil
2 tbsp chopped shallot
2 tsp chopped parsley
salt, pepper
a pinch of mixed herbs chopped

Method

Mix together and soak fish in it for at least ½ hour.

PRINCIPLES OF COOKING FISH

Fish may be baked, poached, steamed, fried, grilled, or stewed.

To poach   This is the best method of cooking large whole fish or large pieces of fish such as salmon, cod, hake, and so on. Fish should never be boiled.

The French always poach fish in a **'court-bouillon'** in preference to water, a fashion we should do well to follow, as it enhances the flavour of the fish.

A **court-bouillon** may be a simple stock made of water flavoured with onion, carrot, celery, herbs and spices, or it may contain white wine, vinegar or lemon juice (p. 93).

If not using a **court-bouillon**, fish may be poached in water, to which approximately 5 ml (a good teaspoonful) of salt and 15 ml (a tablespoonful) of vinegar or lemon juice have been added to each litre (1 quart) of water. This helps to keep the flesh of the fish firm. Parsley, mace and peppercorns give added flavour.

If poaching fish for invalids, use half milk and half water; this makes the fish very mellow. Milk added to the water also helps to mellow salt fish.

To prepare for poaching   Wash the fish, wipe with a cloth, trim and weigh. Sprinkle the fish with salt, pepper and lemon juice. Wrap it in a piece of muslin and, if possible, cook it in a fish-kettle with a strainer. This enables it to be lifted out of the water without breaking it. Should no fish-kettle be available, put the fish on a plate that will fit into the saucepan to be used. Put a piece of thin cloth or thick muslin under the plate and tie it over the top of the fish. When the fish is cooked, the plate can then be easily lifted out of the water by the cloth.

All fish, with the exception of small fish, must be put into water or court-bouillon that is just warm. Bring to the boil, skim and then simmer very gently. Small fish and sliced fish is put straight into boiling liquid.

Never let fish cook fast. It must simmer very gently. The time is calculated at about 10 minutes to 450 g (1 lb) and 10 minutes over, but it is not possible to give the exact time, as a very thick fish will take longer to cook than a thin fish of the same weight. If the fish weighs a good many pounds, it is customary to allow 6 minutes to 450 g (1 lb) for the whole. A fish of 4 kg (10 lb) will take about an hour to cook.

The cooking can be tested by running a wooden skewer into the fish near the bone, and if it parts easily from the bone, the fish is done.

Never leave fish in the water after it has been cooked, or it will become woolly.

Poached fish should be drained very thoroughly and served with plain boiled or steamed potatoes and garnished with sprigs of fresh parsley. The sauce should be handed separately.

To steam   Steaming is a very excellent method of cooking fish, but takes a little longer than poaching. Small pieces may be steamed as well as large.

Prepare the fish as for poaching, wrap it in muslin and place it in a steamer over a saucepan of boiling water. Dish and garnish as for poached fish and hand the same sauces.

A very good method of steaming small fish, fillets or fish steaks, which is especially suitable for invalids, is to grease two plates; prepare and sprinkle the fish with salt, pepper and lemon juice, place it on one plate, cover with the other, and put the plates over a saucepan of boiling water. The fish takes from 20 to 30 minutes to cook, according to its size and thickness. Fish cooked in this manner is generally served on a hot dish with the liquor which has oozed from it poured round. Garnish with a little parsley.

To bake   Fish may be baked whole, or in fillets or steaks. Whole fish is often stuffed with some savoury mixture, or coated with a seasoning of chopped parsley, shallot, onion, mushrooms and breadcrumbs, and a few pieces of butter placed over the top. This should then be wrapped in foil and placed on a baking tray in the oven, or it should be baked in a fireproof dish rubbed over with butter or margarine. Sometimes a little white wine or milk is poured round the fish, but fat of some sort should be placed over the fish when baking, otherwise it will be too dry. When cooked, it may be dished on a hot dish or served in the dish in which it was baked.

To stew   Fillets, or small pieces of fish, stew the best and should be stewed in fish stock (p. 48), fish stock and wine, milk, or cider.

The fish must be prepared according to the recipe and then simmered very gently in the liquid. When cooked, lift it out on to a hot dish and thicken the liquid with a little flour. Boil this for 5 or 6 minutes and pour it over the fish. Garnish with parsley or cut lemon, fancy **croûtons** of fried bread, or pastry.

To fry   There are two methods of frying fish – deep and shallow frying. For both methods, the fish must be quite dry and coated in a suitable substance.

Deep frying   The best medium for deep frying is oil, which should be hot enough to seal the coating immediately and so keep in the flavour and juices of the fish. The temperature of the oil can be roughly judged by faint blue smoke rising from the pan, and a cube of bread taking a minute to brown in it. There should be enough fat to cover the fish; immersing the fish in the oil will reduce the temperature of it, so this must be counteracted by raising the heat under the pan to raise the temperature again. Fat used for frying fish should be kept only for that purpose, as the flavour of the fish will linger. Always strain any oil before re-using it, as it will contain particles of flour and breadcrumbs from the previous frying.

Coatings for deep frying are:

Egg and breadcrumbs
Milk and flour
Batter

Fish for frying should not be too thick. When it is cooked, it should rise to the surface. It should then be drained thoroughly on kitchen paper and served with fried parsley. Sauce is handed separately.

Shallow frying   This may be done as for deep frying, simply cooking the fish on both sides with less oil, or it can be done more gently in butter, which is most suitable for delicately flavoured fish like sole and plaice. The fish is lightly covered in seasoned flour and fried in melted butter which has been heated to foaming point, but has not changed colour. There should be enough butter to cover the bottom of the pan. Cook gently on one side till golden brown, then turn with a fish slice and cook on the other side. It will take 5 to 10 minutes on each side depending on the thickness of the fish. Serve at once.

To grill   Grilling is a good method of cooking small fish, thick slices or steaks of large fish. Herring, trout, haddock, mackerel, red mullet, salmon steaks and so on are all excellent grilled.

To prepare fish for grilling   Cut off the head and fins, wash and skin the fish and dry it in a cloth. If whole fish is to be used, it is customary to **score** it diagonally on both sides to prevent it from cracking. Sometimes the fish is opened and the bone removed.

To grill   Heat the grill well before starting to cook the fish. It takes 7 to 10 minutes to cook, according to the thickness and size of the fish. Turn it once, taking care not to break the skin or to over-cook it, or it will break.

Grilled fish should be served with pats of Maître d'Hôtel butter (p. 75) on the top, or some sharp sauce such as mustard, tartare or piquante sauce (pp. 70, 73, 71). It may be garnished with watercress or parsley, sometimes lemon. Should there be any roes, these are usually grilled and served as a garnish.

HOT AND COLD FISH DISHES

BASS

The bass is a fish of a beautiful silvery appearance, and is very popular in some localities. It has been called the white salmon, as it is similar in shape and firmness of flesh to the salmon.

Bass, cut in slices, may be poached, fried or grilled, according to any recipe given for dressing salmon. It may be poached whole, or, if small, cut open and fried, with breadcrumbs, seasoning and mixed herbs, following the directions given for frying herrings (p. 99).

FRESHWATER BREAM

A flat fish, but not often eaten, as it is dry and bony and rather tasteless. It is poached according to the directions on p. 94, and requires a well-flavoured sauce.

SEA BREAM

May be baked, grilled, poached or fried according to any recipe used for cod.

BRILL

A large brill can only be distinguished with difficulty from a small turbot when very well cooked, but it is longer than, and not so round as turbot. It may be cooked according to any recipe for turbot.

COD

Cod is one of the most useful, nourishing and wholesome fish obtainable. It is at its best from October to Christmas, though it is obtainable nearly all the year round, but from February to July it is not so good. The ling is even larger than the cod, but is inferior in quality. Cod should have a small head and a thick neck. It is better cooked in slices than poached whole.

Baked cod

4 persons

	Metric	Imp
4 cod cutlets		
shrimps	200 g	8 oz
butter	25 g	1 oz
flour	25 g	1 oz
milk and water mixed	500 ml	1 pt
1 tbsp anchovy essence		
1 bunch herbs		
salt, pepper		
lemon, fried parsley		

Method

1 Butter a shallow fireproof dish thickly and lay in it the cutlets, seasoned with salt and pepper.

2 Pour in the milk and water to just cover the fish and add the herbs. Place in moderate oven (175°C, 350°F, Mark 4) for about 40 min.

3 Remove cod cutlets carefully on to a hot dish.

4 Melt butter, stir in flour, then add 250 ml (½ pt) fish liquor. Stir till boiling, simmer a few minutes, stir in anchovy essence.

5 Add the shrimps, pour a little round the fish; serve the rest separately. Garnish with lemon and fried parsley.

Cold cod

Cooked cod may be used up in many ways. Divided into flakes and nicely seasoned with pepper, salt and fragrant herbs, dished on salad and coated with mayonnaise, it makes a good fish salad for luncheon or supper.

Mixed with a thick sauce and seasoned well, made into balls or enclosed in pastry, egged, crumbed and fried, it makes rissoles or croquettes. It may also be made into fish cakes or pudding and so on.

Poached cod

Cod is usually poached in water, though it can be cooked in a **court-bouillon**. It should be served with a caper or Hollandaise sauce (pp. 68, 70), or with melted butter and served with boiled potatoes. It may also be placed in a shallow fireproof dish between layers of cheese sauce (p. 68), sprinkled with grated cheese and browned under the grill.

Salt Cod

Salt cod should be soaked in lukewarm water for 12–24 hours, changing the water once or twice. Wash, put into a pan or fish kettle with milk and water to cover. Bring slowly to the boil and simmer for about 30 minutes, till cooked. Skim, drain, remove the skin and large bones and put the fish on to a hot dish. Coat with egg sauce and serve hot. Boiled or mashed potatoes may be used as garnish or may be handed separately.

COLEY

Coley is also known by various other names: saithe and coalfish being the two most often used. It is an inexpensive fish with a rather dingy flesh, but this becomes whiter with cooking, and can be treated in the same way as cod. Poached coley needs a fairly strong sauce to accompany it, such as a curry sauce, in which case the fish should be served with boiled rice.

THE CONGER

The conger eel is plentiful on the south coast of England and Ireland and round the Channel Isles. It grows to a great size, but the flesh on the larger ones is tasteless and rather coarse. The smaller fish are the more delicate.

Fried conger

For frying, conger should be cut into slices 2–4 cm (1½–2 in.) thick, coated in egg and breadcrumbs and fried in deep fat for 20 to 25 min. It should be served with melted butter or anchovy sauce (pp. 65, 70).

Stuffed conger

6–8 persons

	Metric	Imp
Stuffing:		
breadcrumbs	75 g	3 oz
chopped suet	40 g	1½ oz
grated peel of ½ lemon		
a pinch of mixed herbs		
salt, pepper, nutmeg		
beaten egg to **bind**		
Fish:		
conger eel cut in a piece		
about 30 cm (1 ft)		
from the head and boned	800 g	2 lb
water	500 ml	1 pt
butter	25 g	1 oz
salt, pepper		

Method

1 Mix stuffing ingredients to a firm consistency.

2 Wash and wipe fish dry. Stuff and sew up.

3 Place in a buttered fireproof dish, add water, butter and seasoning. Bake in a moderate oven (175°C, 350°F, Mark 4) till cooked (about ½ hr from the time it reaches simmering point.)

4 Lift fish gently out of water and drain well.

5 Serve with parsley or tomato sauce (pp. 69, 67).

EELS

Both fresh- and salt-water eels are obtainable all the year round, but are at their best in the autumn and winter. They should be eaten very fresh and should be soaked in salt water for some time before cooking. They may be baked or fried, like conger eel.

Smoked eel can be bought ready for use, either whole or in fillets. Serve in small pieces and hand horse-radish sauce with it.

Collared eels

5–8 persons

	Metric	Imp
1 large eel washed		
vinegar	500 ml	1 pt
a sprig each of parsley, thyme and marjoram minced		
2 sage leaves minced		
2 blades mace		
2 cloves		
12 peppercorns		
1 tsp salt		
a pinch of allspice		
parsley		

Method

1 Cut off the head and tail of the fish, remove skin and backbone without tearing the flesh. Spread out flat on a board.

2 Pound the spices and mix with salt and herbs. Spread over the eel and roll it up from head to tail end. Tie with tape.

3 Put backbone, head and tail into a pan with salt, pepper, mace and vinegar. Bring to the boil, skim.

4 Add the eel and simmer gently for about ¾ hr or till tender.

5 Put fish into a deep dish, boil up liquor with a little more vinegar and spice, cool and strain over fish.

6 Serve cut in pieces or whole garnished with parsley.

GURNARDS

There are several species of this fish, but the red is generally considered the best. They are a well-flavoured, but rather dry fish, and may be cooked according to any recipe given for cooking haddock.

HADDOCKS

The haddock is a delicate fish with a fine flavour. It may be filleted and fried like sole, or baked whole.

Baked haddock

4 persons

	Metric	Imp
1 haddock	800 g	2 lb
butter	25 g	1 oz
veal stuffing (p. 79)	75 g	3 oz
1 egg beaten		
breadcrumbs		
salt, pepper		

Method

1 Thoroughly clean and dry the haddock.

2 Fill with veal stuffing and sew up.

3 Brush it with the egg and sprinkle with breadcrumbs. Dot with pieces of butter, season and bake in a moderate oven (175°C, 350°F, Mark 4) ½–1 hr, depending on the thickness of the fish. Baste frequently.

4 Lift out carefully with a fish slice and put it on to a dish. Hand anchovy sauce separately.

Poached haddock

4 persons

	Metric	Imp
haddock fillets or steaks	600 g	1½ lb
court-bouillon (p. 93)	1 l	1 qt
butter	25 g	1 oz
1 chopped shallot		
salt, pepper		

Method

1 Poach haddock in **court-bouillon** for 15–20 min.
2 Dish up fish and keep warm.
3 Add shallot to cooking liquor and reduce to 120 ml (1 gill)

4 Add butter, and as soon as it boils, remove from heat. Season if necessary.
5 Strain into a sauceboat.
6 Serve the fish on a hot dish with boiled potatoes and hand sauce separately.

Smoked haddock

This is poached in water without the addition of seasoning; or water with a little milk added. Simmer in a large frying pan with just enough liquid to cover, about 10 min. to 450 g (1 lb). Serve with a pat of butter on the top.

Smoked haddock is excellent for kedgeree (p. 110).

HAKE

A common west-country fish, somewhat resembling cod, and much eaten on the coast of Devonshire. It should always be cooked very fresh and can be done according to any recipe for cod or halibut and is excellent stuffed and baked like fresh haddock.

HALIBUT

Halibut is a large flat fish, being sometimes five or six feet long, and weighing up to 88 kg (200 lb). Being so large, it is cut up before being sold. The flesh is delicate and palatable, and may be cooked according to recipes for turbot, cod, brill and sole.

HERRINGS

Herrings are the most abundant of our British fish and are nutritious and wholesome, though some find them difficult to digest, owing to their oily nature. Herrings are dried and cured in many ways, the most familiar methods in this country being the split, flattened herrings, called kippers, which are slightly salted, dried and smoked, and are intended to be eaten soon afterwards. Other dried herrings are red herrings, herrings pickled in salt, often called white herrings, and bloaters.

Fried herrings

Herrings may be fried whole, or boned and opened out flat. Sprinkle them with salt and pepper and coat thoroughly in coarse oatmeal. Fry in hot fat till brown on both sides, about 10 min. Garnish with lemon and parsley. Serve with boiled potatoes.

Grilled herrings

Herrings may be grilled whole or filleted. If grilled whole, **score** the fish two or three times on either side to allow the heat to reach the centre. No fat is needed for grilling herrings as they are oily. Cook gently until brown on one side, turn and cook on the other side. This will take approximately 5 min. on either side, according to the thickness of the fish. The fish is done when the flesh comes away from the bone easily.

To fillet herrings   Cut off the head, leaving the innards attached to the head. These should then come away also. Cut the fish open along the back and prise the fish open with a finger. Hold the fish by the tail and slip a knife under the backbone from the tail end and pull it out.

Soused herrings

Clean and wash the herrings, place in an ovenproof dish, cover with **marinade** (p. 112) and cover. Cook in a slow oven (130°C, 275°F, Mark 1), till fish are cooked, about 1½ hr. (The liquid must not boil). To serve, strain the liquid over the fish and leave till quite cold.

Stuffed and baked herrings

Herrings that have been split open and boned are laid skin-side down and spread with veal stuffing (p. 79). The fish is then rolled up and tied with string and put into a greased baking tin and dotted with butter or dripping. Bake in a moderate oven for (175°C, 350°F, Mark 4) about 20 min., **basting** often. Remove string and serve with parsley and a sharp sauce.

Kippers

Kippers may be grilled or steeped in boiling water. To grill a kipper, place the fish on the grill, skin-side down and dot with a little butter. Cook for 5–7 min.

They may also be cooked by immersing them completely in a jug of boiling water and leaving them to plump out without further cooking for 5 min. Drain very well.

JOHN DORY

A fish much esteemed by epicures. It should be eaten very fresh. It is nearly always cooked in fillets, which can be treated in the same ways as sole.

MACKEREL

Mackerel is a nourishing fish but requires to be eaten quite fresh, within 12 hours if possible, as it is liable to become poisonous when kept. It is not so easily digested as white fish, and disagrees with many people. It may be cooked like herring.

Boiled mackerel

Mackerel is the exception to the rule regarding no boiling of fish. It should be cleaned, the head and fins cut off and put into a pan or fish-kettle with just enough cold water to cover it. Add salt and a bunch of herbs, a carrot and an onion sliced, bring to the boil quickly and allow to boil for a few seconds. Reduce the heat and poach gently for about 15 min. Drain well, skin and serve on a hot dish. Serve fennel or gooseberry sauce separately.

Note Mackerel is put into cold water, as hot water would crack the delicate skin.

Collared mackerel or herrings

4 persons

	Metric	Imp
4 mackerel or herrings		
vinegar and water	250 ml	½ pt
1 tbsp chopped parsley		
1 tsp powdered mace		
1 bay leaf		
pinch of grated nutmeg		
8 peppercorns		
salt		

Method

1 Wash and clean the mackerel, cut off the heads and tails and split them carefully down the back, remove the bones and season the insides with salt and spices.

2 Roll the fish up, skin outside, and tie with tape. Simmer gently in vinegar and water to which a little salt, peppercorns, bay leaf and parsley have been added, till fish is tender, about 20 min.

3 Lift out fish into a deep dish, pour vinegar mixture over when quite cold. It should cover the fish. If there is not enough boil up extra vinegar and add when cold. Leave overnight.
4 Serve on a flat dish, garnished with sprigs of fennel.

Note Smoked mackerel which are very similar to smoked trout, but much less expensive can be bought in delicatessens and fishmongers. Serve them cold without further preparation, and hand horse-radish sauce separately.

Grilled stuffed mackerel   *4 persons*

	Metric	Imp
4 cleaned mackerel, with heads removed		
soft breadcrumbs	50 g	2 oz
1 egg yolk		
grated peel of ½ lemon		
1 tsp chopped parsley		
½ tsp chopped fennel		
a little flour		
cooking oil		
salt, pepper		

Method
1 Take out the roes and simmer till cooked.
2 Mash them, mix with beaten egg yolk, add salt, pepper, lemon peel, fennel, parsley and enough breadcrumbs to make a soft but firm consistency.
3 Stuff the mackerel, coat with flour and brush with oil. Grill about 10 min., turning carefully half-way through.
4 Serve with melted butter.

MULLET

Red mullet is a very delicate fish, and has been justly called the woodcock of the seas. It is superior in flavour to the grey mullet. It should be very red, rather short, and firm to the touch. Care must be taken when cleaning it. Scrape lightly, pull out the gills, with which will come all the inside that need be removed. The liver is considered a great delicacy and is always left in the fish. Red mullet should never be boiled; it is best grilled or baked.

Baked red mullet   *3 persons*

	Metric	Imp
2 red mullets		
butter	25 g	1 oz
juice of ½ lemon		
1 tbsp chopped parsley		
browned breadcrumbs		
salt, pepper		

Method
1 Prepare the fish, score on both sides.
2 Grease a fireproof dish and sprinkle with some of the parsley and breadcrumbs. Place the fish on top, cover with the rest of the breadcrumbs, dot with butter.
3 Bake in a moderate oven (175°C, 350°F, Mark 4) 15–20 min., or till fish is cooked.
4 Serve in the dish in which it was cooked.

Red mullet en papillote   *2 persons*

(See note on papillote p. 37)

	Metric	Imp
1 red mullet		
Italian or mushroom sauce (p. 67)	250 ml	½ pt
2 tbsp olive oil		
2 tbsp lemon juice		
2 tbsp chopped parsley		
2 tbsp chopped shallot		
salt, pepper		

Method
1 Clean mullet, cut off fins, wash and **score** two or three times.
2 Mix all other ingredients.
3 Place fish in a dish, pour mixture over and leave for at least ½ hr. Turn occasionally.

4 Wrap in well-oiled greaseproof paper or kitchen foil, twisting up the edges of the paper to seal the parcel.

5 Cook in a moderate oven (175°C, 350°F, Mark 4) for 20–25 min., according to the size of the fish.

6 Serve on a hot dish and hand Italian or mushroom sauce.

Note Red mullet may be grilled without wrapping it in paper. Soak in the **marinade** as above and grill, turning once. Serve with a pat of Maître d'Hôtel butter (p. 75), or with tartare sauce (p. 73).

PERCH

Perch is a freshwater fish, which has a pleasant flavour. It is rather difficult to scale, so should be dipped in boiling water for 2 or 3 min, when the scales may be scraped off. Perch may be grilled, fried, boiled or stewed.

PIKE

This river fish is best for eating at a weight of 1 kg–1600 g (2 ½–4 lb). The flesh is inclined to be dry, so it should be served with a good sauce. It is usually baked or braised. The fins are usually cut off and the fish must be very carefully scraped and cleaned.

BAKED PIKE

Skin and clean a medium-size pike, stuff it with veal forcemeat (p. 79) and curl it round with its tail in its mouth. Fasten with a skewer, season and place in a greased baking tin. Dot with pieces of butter and wrap lightly in oiled greaseproof paper or kitchen foil. Bake for ¾–1 hr (175°C, 350°F, Mark 4). 10 min before serving, remove paper and scatter breadcrumbs over fish. **Baste** well. Serve on a hot dish garnished with lemon. Serve anchovy sauce or tomato sauce separately (pp. 70, 67).

PLAICE

Plaice is one of the commonest of the flat fish. It lacks the delicacy and flavour of sole, but, if carefully cooked, may replace sole in many dishes. The upper side is dark, with bright orange spots. If these spots are dark, it is a sign that the fish is not fresh. It may be cooked according to any recipe given for sole.

SALMON

Salmon is the king of fish, and is always considered a delicacy. It should be stiff, and red in the gills; the flesh should be of a bright full colour, and the scales bright and silvery. Connoisseurs prefer those which are small in the head and thick in the neck. Before cooking the fish, scale it carefully, and clean it thoroughly, scraping away the blood and impurities with a knife and washing it as little as possible. Salmon fishing is regulated by special laws and it is illegal to sell it out of season. Dutch and Canadian salmon may, however, be bought all the year round. Salmon should be cooked as soon as possible after it is caught, as there is then a creamy curd between the flakes which disappears later. It will, however, keep good for three or four days if kept in a cold place.

Baked salmon

Whole salmon, if not too large, or a piece from the middle can be baked in foil, Cover the fish first with slices of streaky bacon, then wrap it all in a piece of lightly oiled kitchen foil. Bake in a moderate oven (175°C, 350°F, Mark 4) allowing 10 min. to 450 g (1 lb). This method will give the fish a smoky flavour and it will be beautifully moist and will need no sauce with it. Serve with boiled potatoes.

Grilled salmon

Slices of salmon about 1 cm (½ in.) thick should be seasoned with salt and cayenne pepper and brushed with oil. They should be cooked under a hot grill for about 5 min. on both sides and served with the centre bone removed after cooking. Grilled salmon is accompanied by piquante sauce or tartare sauce (pp. 71, 73) or with Maître d'Hôtel butter (p. 75).

Poached salmon

Salmon may be poached whole, if not too large; in a piece taken from the middle of the fish or in cutlets about 3–4 cm (1 ½ in.) thick.

A whole salmon or a large piece should be simmered in a **court-bouillon** (p. 93), allowing 8 min. to 450 g (1 lb). The fish is put into warm liquid and brought up to the point where it is just heaving, and the time counted from then.

Cutlets of salmon should be cooked in a **court-bouillon** without vinegar, as this tends to spoil the colour. Allow 6–10 min. cooking time according to the thickness of the cutlet.

To dish   Lift out the fish carefully, drain well and dish on a hot folded napkin. Serve with boiled or steamed potatoes and hand shrimp or Hollandaise sauce (pp. 71, 70) and dressed cucumber. Poached cutlets may be served with pats of Maître d'Hôtel butter (p. 75).

SKATE

Skate is sold by the wing, either whole, which can weigh about 1 kg (2 lb) or in pieces. A 1 kg wing will serve 3–4 persons. It must be eaten very fresh and only in season, and steeped in cold water for a couple of hours before cooking, and scrubbed with a stiff brush. It must always be skinned after cooking.

Skate with black butter

Cut the wing of skate into strips about 8 cm (3 in.) wide, and remove the fringe of gristly bone from the edge. Poach in **court-bouillon** or milk or well salted water for 25–30 min. Lift the fish out of the liquid carefully, skin it and keep it hot. Make the black butter sauce (p. 66), sprinkle the fish with a few capers and serve with the sauce poured over it.

SMELTS

A delicate little fish which has a singular perfume of violets or syringa. It requires great care in cleaning. Pull the gills out, and the inside will come out with them. Wipe and dry gently. Smelts should not be washed more than is necessary just to clean them.

Fried smelts

Wash, cut off the fins, dry the fish in a cloth, and **dredge** a little flour over them. Beat up an egg and dip the smelts into it, then into breadcrumbs, and plunge them into a pan of boiling fat; let them fry gently for a few minutes until a bright brown.

To dish   When cooked, dish the fish on a napkin, garnish with fried parsley, and hand anchovy or shrimp sauce (pp. 70, 71).

SOLES

The black Dover sole is the finest variety of sole and may be cooked whole or filleted. A black sole of under 200 g (½ lb) in weight is called a slip sole. When a sole has roes, it should only be used filleted, as the flavour is then very inferior.

Lemon sole is rounder than the Dover sole, with a smoother reddish-brown upper skin. It is inferior in quality to the Dover sole and is therefore cheaper, but is still a very delicate fish. There are well over a hundred classical recipes for cooking sole, but it is a fish which, when absolutely fresh, is equally delicious cooked simply and without a sauce.

When cooking a sole whole, cut off the head and the end of the tail. Pull off the black skin on the back, by getting hold of it at one end and tearing it off. If the sole is soaked in cold water for 15 min. the skin will pull off much more easily. Clean the inside of the sole.

To fillet a sole, skin it on both sides from the tail end, then proceed as on p. 92.

Fillets of sole au gratin

Skin and fillet the sole, spread veal stuffing (p. 79) on each fillet and roll it up. Put a ring of mashed potatoes on a fireproof dish, arrange the fillets in a circle, sprinkle with breadcrumbs and put a small piece of butter on each. Cook in a moderate oven (175°C, 350°F, Mark 4) for about 20 min. Fill the centre with baked forcemeat balls and pour round a little good brown or Espagnole sauce (p. 65).

Fried sole à la meunière

Sole can be cooked in this manner either whole or filleted. Flour the fish in seasoned flour and fry on both sides in foaming butter. When golden brown, lay the fish on a hot dish. Melt 25 g (1 oz) of butter in a clean pan and allow to brown lightly. Add a teaspoonful of lemon juice. Pour over the fish and serve with slices of lemon.

SPRATS

Clean a number of sprats well, allowing 450 g (1 lb) for 3 persons, draw them through the gills, wipe dry and dip in flour. Fasten them in rows by a skewer run through their gills, place them under a hot grill, and cook them to a nice brown. Draw out the skewer and serve them very hot. Garnish with cut lemon and parsley, and hand thin brown bread and butter.

TROUT

There are several species of trout: the sea trout, the brown trout and the rainbow trout are the most important. Lake trout are usually a little larger than river trout. Brown trout probably have the best flavour but all trout are delicious if cooked really fresh.

Fresh trout are best fried or grilled in butter.

Smoked trout can be bought at delicatessens or from deep-freeze stockists. They do not lose any flavour from being frozen provided they are thoroughly defrosted before being eaten. Serve them cold with horse-radish sauce.

Fried trout

Thoroughly clean the trout, remove the gills, but leave the head on. Melt enough butter to cover the bottom of a large frying pan. When the butter is hot, put the fish in and cook for half a min. on one side, then turn to the other side. This will prevent the fish curling up. Continue cooking for 3–4 min., then turn back to the first side and cook for a further 3–4 min. Lift out the fish carefully on to a heated dish and sprinkle 50 g (2 oz) of flaked almonds per fish into the remaining melted butter in the pan and brown lightly. Pour the almonds and butter over the fish and serve with slices of lemon.

TURBOT

Turbot is one of the finest of the flat fish, its usual weight being from 2–8 kg (5–20 lb). A good fish should be thick; the flesh is firm, and the fish stiff when it is fresh. It may be baked, filleted and fried, grilled, stewed and made into various dishes.

Poached turbot

Put a **court-bouillon** (p. 93) or water to which salt and vinegar or lemon juice have been added into a fish-kettle and bring nearly to the boil. Make an incision in the skin of the back of the turbot nearly to the bone, to prevent the skin of the white side from cracking. Do not cut off the fins; these are considered a delicacy. Place the cleaned and washed turbot on the strainer of the fish-kettle on a cloth or piece of muslin and put it into the water, which should quite cover it. Let it simmer slowly and skim the water very carefully. Calculate the time of cooking according to the weight, a fish weighing 8 kg (10 lb) should take an hour to cook. If only 1½–2 kg (3 or 4 lb) of turbot are being cooked, allow 8–10 min. to 450 g (1 lb), according to whether the thick or thin part of the fish is being cooked.

When it is done, lift up the strainer and let the turbot drain; keep it very hot.

To dish　Slide the fish gently on to a hot dish, on which a folded napkin or a dish paper has been placed. It is usual to serve the under or white part of the turbot uppermost. Garnish the fish with lobster coral rubbed through a sieve and the dish with sprigs of curled parsley and slices of lemon. Hand lobster, shrimp or anchovy sauce (pp. 265, 71, 70) separately.

WHITEBAIT

Fried whitebait

Allow 450 g (1 lb) whitebait for 4 persons.

Wash and drain the whitebait in a colander, dry in a cloth. Put a little flour in another cloth or on a large sheet of paper, add a few of the whitebait and toss them in the flour. Put them into a frying basket and place this in a deep pan of lard, from which a faint blue smoke should begin to rise. Fry for 2 min., shaking the basket gently all the time. Turn the fish on to a paper to drain, and then coat a few more whitebait with the flour. Re-heat the fat and fry. Continue this until the fish has all been fried. Re-heat the fat and put as many whitebait as possible into the basket and fry a second time until crisp, about 2 min. Drain on paper, sprinkle with salt and dish on a folded napkin. Garnish with cut lemon and hand thin brown bread and butter. Serve as hot as possible.

WHITING

Whiting should not be too large. They are in season all the year round and are very delicate, easily digested fish, therefore especially suitable for invalids. Whiting may be cooked according to any recipe given for cooking fresh haddock.

Baked whiting

Butter a dish and sprinkle with chopped parsley and shallots. Lay the fish, either whole or filleted, on them, season and moisten with white wine. Bake in a moderate oven (175°C, 350°F, Mark 4), **basting** frequently, allowing about 20 min. for fillets, and a little longer for whole fish. Dish the whiting, thicken the liquor with a little **beurre manié** (p. 64), pour over the fish and brown quickly.

SHELLFISH

CRABS

The medium to heavy crabs are usually considered the best, the light ones being watery. The shell, whether the crab is alive or dead, should be of a bright red colour, and the joints of the legs stiff. Crabs are stale when the eyes look dull.

They may be killed by running a skewer between the eyes or by plunging them into absolutely boiling water.

Crabs are boiled in the same manner as lobsters.

To dress crab

Twist off the large and small claws, pull off the flaps or 'aprons' and separate the upper shell from the lower one. Remove the intestines, the stomach, which is a little bag near the head, and the 'fingers' from the sides. Pick out all the meat and free it from pieces of shell, remove the meat from the claws also, chop it finely, mix with oil, vinegar, salt, pepper and cayenne. Wash and dry the shell and fill it with the mixture. Arrange on a dish and garnish with some of the small claws and chopped parsley. Garnish the dish with dressed watercress.

Note Mayonnaise sauce (p. 72) may be used in place of oil and vinegar.

Devilled crab

3–4 persons

	Metric	Imp
1 cooked crab	25 cm (across)	10 in.

brown sauce (p. 64)
1 tsp vinegar
1 tsp chutney
1 tsp chopped gherkins
1 tsp Worcestershire sauce
1 tbsp breadcrumbs
½ tsp made mustard
salt, cayenne pepper

Method

1 Remove meat from body and claws of crab.

2 Heat the sauce, add all ingredients (except breadcrumbs) and the crab meat and stir over heat till hot.

3 Wash and dry the shell of the crab, fill with mixture, sprinkle with breadcrumbs and bake in moderate oven for 8–10 min.

4 Serve on a hot dish with fried parsley and fried bananas cut lengthwise if desired.

CRAWFISH

The crawfish resembles a lobster without the large claws. It has not the delicate flavour of the lobster, but may be cooked according to any recipe used for lobster.

CRAYFISH

Crayfish are a freshwater shellfish, much like a lobster, only considerably smaller. They are delicate little fish, usually imported into this country and much used as a garnish for salmon and other fish dishes. They also make a good soup and hors-d'oeuvre.

LOBSTER

Medium-sized lobsters are the best; they should be chosen by weight, the heaviest being the best. Very often a good small-sized lobster will weigh more than a large one.

The male is the better for boiling as the flesh is firmer and the shell of a brighter red; but the hen lobsters are valuable on account of their spawn or coral, which gives such a beautiful colour to sauces and is so useful for decorations. They make excellent sauces, salads, and made-up dishes.

The hen is usually distinguished by its broader tail, the two uppermost fins within the tail being less stiff and hard than those of the male lobster.

To kill a lobster

There are two methods of boiling a lobster; it can either be plunged head downwards into boiling salted water or **court-bouillon**, in which case it is killed instantly, and the cooking time is then calculated at 15 min. to 450 g (1 lb), or it can be placed in cold water and brought gradually to the boil, which some believe is more humane, but possibly results in a loss of flavour.

For baked and grilled lobster dishes, it is necessary to kill them by plunging the point of a sharp knife through the cross marked on the head, under which the brain lies; this will kill them instantly.

To dress a lobster

Break off the claws and crack them carefully with nutcrackers, removing the flesh in one piece. Keep any spawn or coral that is under the tail for decorating the dish. Split the body and tail lengthwise down the middle and remove the grey intestinal line down the tail and the bag in the head, which is the stomach. Remove the flesh, wash and dry the shells and use them for holding the lobster meat for serving. A French dressing or mayonnaise is served with cold lobster, the claws arranged on either side.

Grilled lobster

Kill the lobster with a knife as described above and split it lengthwise. Remove the stomach (bag in the head) and the intestine running down the tail, and brush each half all over with oil, including the shell. Sprinkle with pepper and grill, cut side uppermost for 10 min. turn and grill shell side for 5–10 min.

To dish Arrange the shells on a hot dish, crack the claws and put them between the shells. Hand melted butter.

MUSSELS AND COCKLES

Clean the shells with repeated washings, scrubbing them to get rid of sand and impurities. Discard any that are open. Scrape away the filament at the joint of the shell and put the mussels in a large pan with a chopped onion, shallot, clove of garlic, sprig of parsley, small glass of white wine, 40 g (1½ oz) butter, salt and pepper, and cook all together over a fairly strong heat for about 5 min., shaking the pan frequently. The mussels will open when cooked.

Moules marinière

The mussels are prepared and cooked as above. When they are open, they are removed from the liquor, one shell is taken away leaving them attached to the other and they are served in a hot bowl with the liquor strained over them. This liquor may be thickened with a little **beurre manié** if desired.

OYSTERS

Oysters should be eaten very fresh and should be plump and firm. They are at their best *au naturel* – that is, opened and served raw in the deep shell with thin brown bread and butter and cut lemon (p. 86).

Sometimes the oysters are served on a bed of shaved ice on individual plates.

To open oysters

Scrub the shell, hold the oyster in a cloth in the left hand, with the deep shell downwards. Insert a sharp oyster knife between the edges of the shells at the valve side and cut through the hinge.

Grilled oysters
6 per person

Wash the shells clean and open the oysters, leaving them in the half shell. Place them in the grill pan. Melt 25 g (1 oz) of butter and mix with 1 tsp Worcestershire sauce. Pour a small quantity over each oyster, season and place under a hot grill for about 5 minutes. The oysters will curl at the edges when done. Serve with lemon juice and brown bread and butter.

Oyster fritters
2–3 fritters per person

Open the oysters and remove the beards, **scald** in their own liquor, by putting them into a pan with the liquor and bringing it to the boil, then drain the oysters through a fine sieve. Dip them one by one into frying batter (p. 76) and put them into a pan of boiling fat, and fry a light brown. Take them out carefully with a perforated spoon, drain on soft paper and serve as a garnish for poached fish, or use as an hors d'oeuvre.

PRAWNS OR SHRIMPS

If these are freshly caught, they should be boiled in salted water for about 4 min., cooled in the liquid and then drained very well.

Cooked prawns and shrimps may be used for salads and hors d'oeuvre or for garnishing fish dishes. They may be mixed with a béchamel sauce (p. 64) and served in vol-au-vent cases, or with rice to make a pilaff; they may be curried and shrimps will make a good sauce for serving with fish (p. 71).

SCALLOPS

Scallops are always opened by the fishmonger, and it is possible to use both the white and the orange parts of the flesh. Scallops are usually cut up and poached and served in a sauce in their shell; one should allow two scallops per person unless they are very large, in which case three will do between two people, especially if they are to be served as a first course.

Scallops in cheese sauce *(Mornay)*

Cut the scallops in cubes and poach them in a little white wine for about 10 minutes. cover the scallop shells with cheese (*mornay*) sauce (p. 68) and place the well-drained scallops on it. Cover with more sauce, sprinkle with grated cheese and brown under the grill.

MADE-UP FISH DISHES

Cod au gratin   *4 persons*

	Metric	Imp
cooked cod or other white fish flaked	400 g	1 lb
shrimp or cheese sauce (pp. 71, 68)	250 ml	½ pt
butter or margarine	25 g	1 oz
breadcrumbs	100 g	4 oz
salt, pepper, nutmeg		

Method

1 Grease a fireproof dish and put in some of the sauce, then half the fish. Season with salt, pepper and nutmeg.
2 Repeat the process, ending up with a layer of sauce.
3 Cover completely with breadcrumbs, dot with butter or margarine.
4 Bake in a moderate oven (175°C, 350°F, Mark 4) for ½ hr.

Curried fish   *4 persons*

	Metric	Imp
uncooked white fish skinned, filleted and cut into pieces, or peeled prawns	200 g	8 oz
butter or margarine	25 g	1 oz
flour	25 g	1 oz
milk	125 ml	1 gill
water or fish stock	250 ml	½ pt
rice	200 g	8 oz
1 dssp curry powder		
1 onion, 1 apple, chopped		
salt		

Method

1 Melt fat in a pan, add onion and stir over low heat for 5 min. without browning.
2 Add curry powder and flour and stir a few more minutes.
3 Add stock and milk gradually, stir till boiling.
4 Add chopped apple and fish and a good pinch of salt.
5 Simmer till fish is cooked, about 20 min.
6 Serve with boiled rice and hand chutney separately.

Note Cooked fish may be used, but in this case, simmer the sauce for 10 min. before adding the fish, which is then heated in the sauce for 10 min.

Fish in batter   *4 persons*

	Metric	Imp
cooked fish, any kind, **flaked**	400 g	1 lb
flour	100 g	4 oz
milk	500 ml	1 pt
butter	25 g	1 oz
1 egg		
1 tsp mixed herbs		
1 dssp chopped parsley		
salt, pepper		

Method

1 Make a batter with milk, egg, flour and a little salt. Let it stand for ½ hr.
2 Grease a pie-dish, and put in the **flaked** fish. Sprinkle with herbs and seasoning.
3 Melt the butter, pour over fish, then pour on the batter.
4 Bake in a moderate oven (175°C, 350°F, Mark 4) till the batter is firm and pale brown (about 30 min.). Serve immediately in the pie-dish.

Fish cakes   *4 persons*

	Metric	Imp
cooked fish **flaked**	300 g	¾ lb
mashed potatoes (p. 196)	300 g	¾ lb
2 tbsp chopped parsley		
2 eggs		
breadcrumbs		
oil for frying		
salt, pepper		

Method

1 Mix the fish with the potato and season to taste.
2 Add chopped parsley and 1 beaten egg to **bind**. Leave mixture till quite cold.
3 Divide mixture into 8 portions, and roll each into a ball on a floured board. Flatten into cakes.

4 Coat in egg and breadcrumbs and fry in hot oil.
5 Drain well on kitchen paper and serve on a hot dish. Hand a sauce separately (anchovy, tomato, shrimp or parsley (pp. 70, 67, 71, 69)).

Fish croquettes

4 persons

	Metric	Imp
cooked fish **flaked** finely	200 g	½ lb
sauce for binding (p. 69)	125 g	1 gill
1 egg plus 1 egg yolk		
dried breadcrumbs		
oil for frying		
salt, pepper		

Method
1 Mix the fish with the sauce over gentle heat, stirring continuously for 2 or 3 min. Season.
2 Remove from heat and stir in beaten egg yolk.
3 Spread mixture on a butter dish about 1 cm (½ in.) thick. Leave till quite cold.
4 Divide into equal portions, roll and shape on a floured board.
5 Dip in egg and coat very thoroughly in breadcrumbs, and fry in deep fat in a frying basket till golden brown.
6 Drain on kitchen paper, serve on a hot dish and hand tomato or piquante sauce (pp. 67, 71).

Note If preferred, this mixture may be made into rissoles, by enclosing it in pastry. Roll out some shortcrust pastry (p. 218) very thinly and stamp it into rounds the size of the top of a tumbler. Put a little of the fish mixture in the centre of each. Moisten the edges well together, brush them with beaten egg, dip in crushed vermicelli and fry in deep fat. Drain on kitchen paper and serve like croquettes. Eat hot or cold. These are excellent for picnics.

Fish kedgeree

4 persons

	Metric	Imp
rice	200 g	8 oz
cooked flaked fish (white fish; salmon, fresh or tinned; smoked fish)	200 g	8 oz
butter	100 g	4 oz
1 tbsp chopped parsley		
2 hard-boiled eggs		
1 onion (optional)		
salt, pepper, ground mace		

Method
1 Boil the rice and make sure it is really dry.
2 Chop the onion finely, soften in the butter, add fish and chopped hard-boiled eggs.
3 Season and mix well.
4 Heat the mixture and serve piled on a hot dish sprinkled with chopped parsley.

Fish pie

4 persons

A fish pie may be made by mixing 400 g (1 lb) cooked, flaked fish with 250 ml (½ pt) Béchamel sauce, chopped parsley and seasoning, put into a greased pie-dish and covered with mashed potatoes. It is then baked in a moderate oven (175°C, 350°F, Mark 4) till hot and brown (about ½ hr).

MEAT

Preparing meat (boning, larding, barding, marinading – methods of cooking meat – spicing and potting meat – recipes for meat dishes – offal dishes

PRELIMINARY PREPARATIONS

To prepare meat for cooking   Wipe all meat with a clean cloth wrung out in hot water. If there is any sign of taint in the meat, wash it in a solution of vinegar and water; cut off any badly tainted portions. Trim off all unsightly portions and superfluous fat which can be kept for **clarifying**, and remove any cartilage and all piping. See that the butcher chops the joints of the necks and loins of animals, so that they are easily carved when served. The butcher also skewers the meat in shape for cooking.

Frozen meat must be thawed before using by keeping it in a warm kitchen for two or three hours.

BONING

It is sometimes an economy to bone a joint before cooking it. It is more easily carved, and may be stuffed which will make the joint go further and enhance the flavour. The butcher will generally bone a joint if asked, and the best way of learning to bone is to watch him doing it.

Use a sharp-pointed knife for boning, cut round the bones, keeping the knife pressed well against the bone, and working the flesh gradually from it. If a joint is reached, divide it and remove the bone from which the flesh has been taken. Then continue to work the flesh from the remaining portion of bone.

Ribs of beef are comparatively easy to bone, as is breast of veal or mutton. These three joints after boning are laid skin side down on a board, a savoury forcemeat spread over, and the joint then rolled and tied with tape or string.

If boning a leg of lamb or mutton, cut off the first joint and use the meat on it for a stew. Next begin at the thick end and insert the knife against the bone and work away all the flesh, following the bone with the knife until the joint is reached. This may be jointed and the first bone removed. The next joint is removed in the same manner, working from both the thick and the thin end of the joint. Wipe the meat, insert the stuffing in the cavity and sew up the skin, shaping the joint as well as possible.

LARDING

Strips of fat are threaded into the meat with a special **larding** needle. Cut small smooth strips of the required length off the firmest part of a piece of bacon fat. Special fat bacon is sold for this purpose, cured without saltpetre, called **larding** bacon. Put these strips or lardons of bacon into a larding needle. Pierce the skin, and a very little of the flesh of the meat, fowl, sweetbread, etc., you may wish to **lard**, with the needle and draw it through, leaving the bacon in, and the two ends at equal lengths outwards. These punctures for lardons are made in rows at any desired distance from each other.

Lardons should be 5 cm (2 in.) in length and 3 mm (⅛ in.) in width, for larding poultry and game; for fillets of beef and loin of veal they should be rather thicker.

BARDING

Cut a slice of fat bacon sufficiently large to cover the breast of any bird. Slit the bacon in two or three places to prevent it curling up and tie it over the breast with string or tape.

MARINADING

A **marinade** is a liquid in which fish or meat is soaked before cooking. There is usually only a small quantity of this liquid so the fish or meat must be turned in it at intervals. The object of **marinading** is to add extra flavour to the food, and to tenderize the fibres. A **marinade** may be cooked or uncooked. An uncooked **marinade** may consist of wine or brandy or lemon juice mixed with oil and herbs and possibly onion or garlic. A cooked **marinade** is used for large joints, and after being boiled up, is used when cold.

Marinade for meat

	Metric	Imp
wine or cider	500 ml	1 pt
wine vinegar	125 ml	¼ pt
carrot, onion, celery, chopped	50 g each	2 oz
olive oil	60 ml	½ gill
1 clove garlic crushed		
1 bay leaf		
4 peppercorns		

1 sprig each parsley and rosemary, chopped
salt, pepper

Method
1 Brown the vegetables in oil.
2 Add all other ingredients and simmer ½ hr.
3 Allow to get quite cold, then pour over the meat.
4 **Baste** twice a day, and keep meat in **marinade** for one or two days.

DIFFERENT METHODS OF COOKING MEAT

The methods of cooking meat are: roasting, boiling, stewing, braising, frying and **sautéing**, and grilling.

Time-table for cooking meat

The usual time allowed for roasting is:

15 minutes to 450 g (1 lb) and 15 minutes over for thin pieces of mutton, lamb or beef.

20 minutes to 450 g (1 lb) and 20 minutes over for thick joints, with little or no bone.

25 minutes to 450 g (1 lb) and 25 minutes over for pork and veal.

25 minutes to 450 g (1 lb) and 25 minutes over for salt beef (boiled).

These times apply also to boiled meat.

A little longer should be allowed for boned and rolled meat than for a joint with a bone; the weight of the stuffing should be added to that of a joint when calculating the cooking time of a stuffed one.

ROASTING

The most usual method of roasting meat is to pre-heat the oven to the required temperature 190°C (375°F, Mark 5) and to calculate the time according to the time-table above.

Roast beef, however, is often seared at a higher temperature for about 10 minutes to seal in the juices, then cooked for the remaining time at the usual temperature.

It is inclined to be dry, and must be **basted** very frequently. If this is not possible, the joint should be **barded**, or cooked in foil and only unwrapped for the last 20 minutes.

Lamb and *mutton* are excellent roasted, and need very little extra fat. A little seasoned flour rubbed into the surface of the meat will help produce a crisp coating, and the joint should be cooked on a rack in the baking tin to allow the surplus fat to drain away.

Leg of lamb or *mutton* may be cooked by putting it into a cold oven set at 180°C (350°F, Mark 4) and cooking it for 30–35 minutes to 450 g (1 lb).

Veal is also dry when roasted, and needs a really moist stuffing when cooked this way.

Pork needs only rubbing with a little oil before roasting. To get crisp crackling, **score** the fat across in stripes 1 cm (½ in.) apart with a sharp knife and rub with olive oil and a little salt. Stand the meat on a rack.

When the roast meat has been taken up, the fat which has dripped from it into the pan should be poured into a basin and cold water poured over it. When cold, the fat will have formed a cake of dripping at the top, under which will be found a meat jelly fit for gravies, etc.

Veal, pork and *lamb* should be thoroughly done, not retaining any red gravy; at the same time, care should be taken not to dry the meat up, or roast till the flesh parts from the bones.

To serve a roast joint   Lift the meat on to a hot dish, remove all skewers and string and keep it hot while making the gravy. Garnish according to the direction on pp. 80 and 81 and serve the gravy separately.

Gravy for roast beef   Strain off the fat from the dripping tin into a basin or jar, pour a little hot water or stock into the tin, add salt and stir over the fire until boiling, skim off all fat and serve in a hot gravy boat.

Thickened gravy is served with roast game, veal or rabbit. To make it, strain nearly all the fat from the dripping tin, add 1 dssp flour; mix this with a spoon over the heat until brown. Draw the tin to the side of the heat and stir in 250 ml (½ pt) of stock or water. Stir over the heat until boiling; season and simmer for five minutes, then serve in a hot gravy boat.

POT ROASTING

This is an excellent method of cooking a joint or bird without using the oven.

Prepare the joint as for roasting. Melt 25–50 g (1–2 oz) of dripping in an iron stewpan or a casserole, put in the meat or bird, **baste** it well, cover the pan and cook over low, steady heat until ready. Baste often and turn the meat once or twice. It is advisable to brown the meat on both sides when first putting it into the pan, and to lessen the heat under the pan later. Finish and dish as for roast beef. The gravy may be thickened according to the directions on p. 114.

BOILING

1 Fresh meat is put into boiling salted water which is kept boiling for the first five minutes for the heat to form a coating on the surface of the meat. The heat is then lessened under the pan as the contents must never boil later, only simmer, or the meat becomes tough.

2 Remove all scum as it rises.

3 Keep the lid on the pan and see that the meat is covered with water the whole time it is cooking. If the water evaporates add more boiling water.

4 Pot vegetables – carrots, turnips, parsnips, onions or leeks – may be cooked with the meat.

5 The length of time for boiling depends upon the size and kind of joint (see time-table for roasting, p. 143).

Lean meat is more suitable for boiling than fat meat. Small joints should not be boiled.

To dish   Lift the meat from the pan, remove all skewers and string and serve on a hot dish. To garnish, see pp. 80 and 81. The liquor in which the meat was cooked is generally served as gravy, but a sauce is often preferred such as caper, parsley, etc. (pp. 68, 69).

To boil salt meat   Salt meat requires longer boiling than fresh meat. When smoked and dried it takes longer still. Pickled or salted meat should be soaked in cold water before boiling to soften it and draw out any excess of salt. The time for soaking depends upon the size and saltness of the joint. Put it into tepid water, bring slowly to the boil, skim, then simmer gently for the length of time indicated in the time-table on p. 143. Keep it well skimmed.

Pot vegetables are generally added to salt beef, as are suet dumplings. The vegetables are added when the water comes to the boil after removing the scum. The dumplings only take 20–30 minutes to cook, so are added in the last half hour.

To dish   Lift the meat on to a hot dish, remove all skewers and string, pour round a very little of the liquor in which it was cooked and garnish with the vegetables and dumplings. Hand more of the liquor in a sauce boat.

STEWING

Stewing, being a slow method of cooking, is suitable for the tougher, cheaper cuts of meat. Vegetables are cooked with the meat, making an economical meal. Stewing must always be done over slow heat and the stewpan lid should fit well. The meat should be kept at a gentle simmer without letting it boil, and it must cook for several hours, tough cuts of beef taking from 3–5 hours and mutton about 2.

The meat and vegetables are fried lightly first, the liquid is then added, hot. The meat may be dusted lightly in seasoned flour before frying or not. This will affect the final thickness of the gravy. If this is too thin, either cook a little more briskly with the lid off for the last few minutes, or thicken with arrowroot blended with cold water, or with **beurre manié.** If too thick, add more hot liquid. Dumplings may be added in the last 20 minutes. Remember that evaporation will take place with stewing, so that salt will be more concentrated. It is best to adjust the seasoning just before serving.

BRAISING

Braising is another slow method of cooking. This is done in a heavy casserole with a well fitting lid, in the oven, so that the heat reaches the food from above as well as below. Meat for braising is browned in fat then placed on a bed of vegetables that have been fried lightly first, and liquid (wine or stock) is added to about quarter of the thickness of the meat. It is then cooked slowly for about 2 hours.

FRYING AND SAUTÉING

Frying is the quickest method of cooking, which should only be used for small and tender cuts of meat and is much used for cooking small pieces of meat and made-up dishes. There are two kinds of frying, dry frying (**sautéing**), and deep or wet frying.

Dry frying or **sautéing** is cooking in a shallow frying pan in a small quantity of fat. The fat must be made quite hot; when a faint smoke rises from the fat, the meat is placed in it and cooked on both sides. The heat under the pan should be lessened after a coating is formed on both sides. This method is used for chops, steaks, liver, kidneys, sausages, and so on. Butter, good dripping, lard or oil may be used for frying in this way.

Deep frying means cooking in sufficient fat to cover the article to be fried. It is used for fritters, rissoles, croquettes, and other made-up dishes. The articles to be fried are usually coated with batter, egg and crumbs or pastry. Oil, lard and **clarified** fat are used for deep frying, never butter or margarine.

GRILLING

Many kinds of steaks, chops and cutlets are far better grilled than fried.

The usual practice is first to place the food under a fierce heat, to seal in the juices, and then to lower the heat in order that the food may cook right through, without risk of burning the outside.

Meat should be turned constantly during grilling, but never spear it with a fork, as this will puncture it and allow the juices to escape. Turning is best done with tongs, or with flat utensils such as a spatula or a fish-slice.

Most people prefer grilled mutton chops or beefsteaks rather lightly done, but lamb and pork chops should be thoroughly cooked. Everything grilled should be served very hot, the moment it is cooked.

For cooking on a spit, see p. 17.

SPICING AND POTTING MEAT

These recipes are for large dishes that would be suitable for a buffet party, and some need several days' preparation. They are quite easy to do so long as they are prepared in plenty of time.

Pressed beef

Start 2 weeks before needed

	Metric	Imp
thick brisket of beef	3½–4½ kg	8–10 lb
salt	800 g	2 lb
moist brown sugar	200 g	½ lb
saltpetre	25 g	1 oz
½ tsp allspice		
bouquet garni		
1 onion stuck with cloves		

Method

1 Rub beef well with half the salt; leave for 24 hr.
2 Mix all the other ingredients except herbs and onion together, rub into beef and turn it every day, rubbing it well, for 2 weeks.
3 Wash well, put in a pan of tepid water, bring to the boil. Skim.
4 Add herbs and onion. Simmer 4–5 hr or till bones will slip out easily.
5 Remove from the pan, take out the bones and press meat between two dishes with a weight on top, till cold.
6 Brush with **glaze** and use.

Brawn

Start 3 days before needed

	Metric	Imp
a pig's head	2½–3 kg	6–7 lb
saltpetre	25 g	1 oz
salt	50 g	2 oz
1 bunch herbs		
4 or 5 cloves		
20 peppercorns		
2 onions peeled		
½ tsp ground allspice		
pinch each of pepper and cayenne		

Method

1 Cut off ears, remove brains, gristle and soft part of nostrils. Wash head in warm water and rinse in cold water.
2 Rub in saltpetre and salt and leave for 3 days.
3 Wash, put in a pan, cover with cold water and bring to the boil.
4 Throw away water, repeat stage 3, add herbs, onions and spices and simmer till bones come away easily (2½–3 hr), skimming frequently.
5 Strain liquor, remove skin from head and tongue, cut up meat into small pieces, discarding all superfluous fat and gristle. Season with salt, pepper and cayenne.
6 Skim fat from liquor and boil till **reduced** by half.
7 Put meat in a mould, pour over some of the liquor, put a weight on and leave till cold and set.

Potted beef

	Metric	Imp
lean beef	1 kg	2½ lb
clarified butter	125 g	5 oz
salt, pepper, mace		

Method

1 Remove all skin and gristle from meat.
2 Put in a stone jar with 3 dssp hot water and stand in a deep pan of boiling water to boil slowly for 3½ hr.
3 When done, mince meat fine and pound with salt, pepper and mace. This may be put into the blender in batches.
4 When smooth and like a thick paste, mix in some **clarified** butter and a little of the gravy from the jar.
5 Press into pots, pour butter over the tops and tie down for use.

Potted chicken and ham

	Metric	Imp
cold roast chicken, without skin or bones, shredded	200 g	½ lb
lean ham	100 g	¼ lb
butter	150 g	6 oz
a little grated lemon peel		
salt, pepper		
pinch each of nutmeg and cayenne		
clarified butter		

Method

1 Pound all the ingredients except **clarified** butter together in a mortar or put in a blender.

2 Put into pots, pour over a thick layer of **clarified** butter. Tie over a layer of grease-proof paper.

Note This will keep for some time if kept in a dry place. Tongue, veal or rabbit may be potted in the same way.

BEEF DISHES

Boiled fresh beef
6 persons

	Metric	Imp
silverside, brisket or topside	1600 g	4 lb with bone
2 carrots, 2 turnips, 2 onions, chopped		
1 bunch herbs		
4 cloves		
8 peppercorns		
salt		
water to cover		
1 head celery chopped (optional)		

Method

1 Put the meat in a heavy pan and cover with cold water. Salt and bring to the boil. Skim.

2 Simmer gently for about an hour.

3 Add herbs, vegetables and spices and simmer till meat is tender (about ¾ hr.).

4 Place on a hot dish, remove any string or skewers; serve garnished with vegetables and a very little of the liquid.

5 Skim off all fat from the rest of the liquid and serve in a sauce boat.

Note This meat may be eaten cold, in which case boil some of the cooking liquid to a **glaze** and brush over the meat. Garnish with parsley or watercress and serve with a green salad.

Boiled salt beef
6 persons

	Metric	Imp
salt silverside, brisket or topside	1600 g	4 lb

3 each carrots, leeks, turnips, chopped
2 onions chopped
suet dumplings (p. 80)

Method

1 Soak meat in cold water to cover for a few hours or overnight.

2 Tie into a round; put in a pan of cold water and bring slowly to the boil.

3 Remove the scum. Simmer very gently for an hour, remove scum again.

4 Add vegetables and continue to cook very slowly till meat is cooked, about 2 more hours. The last half-hour, add the dumplings.

5 Serve on a hot dish, garnish with the vegetables and dumplings and serve the liquor separately.

Note If this is to be eaten cold, omit the dumplings and garnish with watercress or parsley and serve with Russian or green salad.

Beef goulash
4 persons

	Metric	Imp
lean beef (leg, thin flank, chuck or skirt) cut in pieces	400 g	1 lb
dripping	25 g	1 oz
onions sliced	200 g	½ lb
potatoes	400 g	1 lb
tomatoes	200 g	½ lb
stock (brown)	125 ml	1 gill
red wine	125 ml	1 gill
1 tbsp flour		
1 tbsp paprika		
1 tbsp tomato purée		
salt, cayenne pepper		

Method

1 Cook onions till transparent in fat, remove to a plate.
2 Add meat to fat and brown.
3 **Dredge** the meat with flour, paprika, cayenne and salt.
4 Return onions to meat, add all the other ingredients except the potatoes and simmer gently 2½ hr.
5 Add potatoes, peeled and sliced, and cook for another ½ hr.
6 Adjust seasoning, remove any surplus fat, and serve.

Beef à la mode   8–10 persons
Start the day before it is needed

	Metric	Imp
fillet or topside of beef	1600 g	4 lb
larding bacon	50 g	2 oz
brown sauce (p. 64)	125 ml	¼ pt
dripping	25 g	1 oz
stock (brown)	750 ml	1½ pt

2 onions chopped
½ tsp each allspice, cloves, cinnamon, ginger mixed together
1 bunch herbs
1 wineglass red wine
salt, pepper
juice of ½ lemon
2 carrots scraped and chopped
3 or 4 sticks of celery chopped

Method
The day before cooking:
Wipe meat, trim it and rub in the mixed spices. Place in deep dish, strain lemon juice over and leave for 12 to 24 hr.

The next day:
1 **Lard** meat (p. 112) and tie in shape.
2 Brown meat on both sides in hot, melted dripping. Remove meat.
3 Brown onions and carrots. Add celery, herbs and stock, bring to boil.
4 Return meat to pan, cover with greased paper and lid; simmer for approximately 3 hr. till tender. **Baste** frequently.
5 Put meat on hot dish, **larded** side up and keep hot.
6 Strain stock into small pan and stir in brown sauce. Stir till boiling, **reduce**, add wine and season well.

7 Serve meat on hot dish with some sauce strained round it and rest handed in sauce boat. Garnish with carrots.

Note Beef à la mode is excellent cold. The liquid should be skimmed as it cools, and strained over the meat when cold.

Pot roasted beef   4 persons

	Metric	Imp
round or topside of beef	800 g	2 lb
dripping	25 g	1 oz
stock (brown)	125 ml	1 gill

1 onion finely chopped
salt, pepper

Method
1 Melt the fat and cook onion gently till soft, in a casserole.
2 Add meat and brown on both sides.
3 Add stock and seasoning, and cook with a tight lid on, in a low oven (130°C, 275°F, Mark 1) or over a low heat, so that it is just simmering, for 3 hr.
4 Serve with grilled tomatoes or mushrooms.

Braised ribs of beef   5–6 persons

	Metric	Imp
back or top ribs of beef, chined and tied with string	1200 g	3 lb
flour	25 g	1 oz
dripping	50 g	2 oz
larding bacon	50 g	2 oz
carrots sliced	200 g	½ lb
turnips sliced	150 g	6 oz
stock (brown)	500 ml	1 pt

6 button onions peeled
1 bunch herbs
salt, pepper

Method
1 **Lard** the meat (p. 112).
2 Melt 25 g (1 oz) dripping in pan, put in meat, cover and cook very slowly for 10 min.
3 Add stock, bring to boil and skim.
4 Add vegetables and herbs, cover and cook in a medium oven (175°C, 350°C, Mark 4) for 2 hr.

5 Lift out meat on to a hot dish and keep it warm. Skim fat from liquor and strain it.
6 Melt 25 g (1 oz) dripping in another pan, add flour and brown, gradually add liquor, stirring continuously. Simmer for 5 min., season and, if necessary, add a little browning. Pour a little of this gravy round the meat and hand the rest in a tureen. Garnish with the vegetables.

Roast ribs of beef

Back and top ribs are best braised as above, but fore ribs may be roasted. Remove the **chine** bone and upper part of the rib bones. Fasten the flap bones under the joint with small skewers and then cook and serve the joint as for sirloin (see below).

Ribs of beef may be boned and rolled before roasting, and are sometimes stuffed with veal forcemeat (p. 79) before rolling.

Roast sirloin

6 persons

	Metric	**Imp**
sirloin	1200 g	3 lb
water or brown stock	375 ml	¾ pt
dripping		
horseradish sauce (p. 72)		
salt, pepper		

Method
1 Rub the dripping well into the meat, place in a roasting pan and place in a hot oven (230°C, 445°F, Mark 7) for ¼ hr.
2 Reduce the temperature to 195°C (380°F, Mark 5), and allow 15 min. to 450 g (1 lb) and 15 min. over. **Baste** frequently. Season.
3 When cooked, put the meat on to a hot dish and keep it warm. Strain the fat from the dripping tin, put in about 375 ml (¾ pt) of water or stock, season with salt and pepper and stir over the fire until boiling.

Note If liked, a very little of this gravy may be poured round the meat, but it is better to serve it all in a sauce boat, as the meat is then easier to carve. Garnish the meat with finely grated horse-radish and serve Yorkshire pudding (p. 236) separately. Baked potatoes and any vegetable in season may be served with the meat. Hand horse-radish sauce.

Grilled steak

Allow 150–200 g (6–8 oz) rump steak per person

The steak should be 1·5–2 cm (¾–1 in.) thick. Brush it over with melted fat or oil, and smear with a little crushed garlic if liked. Have the grill really hot, and cook about 4 to 5 min. on either side, depending on the thickness of the steak.

To dish Put 25 g (1 oz) of butter and 1 tbsp mushroom ketchup on a hot dish, rub the steaks lightly with butter, put them on the dish, sprinkle with salt and pepper and serve immediately. Grilled steak may be served with oyster sauce (p. 71).

Fried steak

Allow 150–200 g (6–8 oz) per person

The steak should be cut a little thinner than for grilling, and some of the fat may be left on it. Trim it neatly and heat a little dripping or oil in a pan till a faint blue smoke begins to rise. Put the steak in and brown quickly on either side. Reduce the heat slightly, and continue cooking, turning several times, for about 10 to 15 min.

Fillets of beef

A fillet really is the undercut of the sirloin and is supposed to be the best cut of beef. It is often served whole, when it is called by the French 'entrecôte', braised or roasted and generally **larded**; or it may be cut into small portions, which are called fillets, *tournedos, filets mignons, médaillons*, according to the size and thickness of the fillets. *Château-briand* steak is generally cut from the thickest part of the undercut of the sirloin and is served in various entrées which take their name from the garnish and sauce used. Mashed potatoes, potato straws or *pommes soufflées* may be served with any of these dishes.

Fillet of steak à la châteaubriand

4–5 persons

	Metric	Imp
2 fillets of sirloin steak, about 4 cm (1¾ in.) thick		
Maître d'Hôtel butter (p. 75)	50 g	2 oz
salt, pepper		
olive oil		

Method

1 Trim fillets, remove all sinewy parts.
2 Season with salt and pepper. Brush over with olive oil.
3 Cook under a hot grill about 15 to 20 min., turning once.
4 Serve on a hot dish with a pat of Maître d'Hôtel butter on each fillet, and **sauté** potatoes.

Various garnishes for grilled châteaubriand

Baked stuffed tomatoes and Espagnole sauce (pp. 198, 65).

Artichoke bottoms filled with green peas, asparagus points, or braised and **glazed** chestnuts, with demi-glace sauce (p. 66).

Quarters of fried sausage and tomato sauce (p. 67).

Cooked mushrooms with demi-glace or mushroom sauce (pp. 66, 67).

Glazed carrots and button onions with a good brown sauce (p. 65).

Fillets of beef à la pompadour

4–5 persons

	Metric	Imp
fillet of beef	600 g	1½ lb
Maître d'Hôtel butter (p. 75)	25 g	1 oz
dripping or butter	50 g	2 oz
demi-glace sauce (p. 66)	250 ml	½ pt
2 tomatoes sliced		
grated horse-radish		
salt, pepper		
mashed potatoes		

Method

1 Cut 6 or 8 fillets from the beef and sprinkle with salt and pepper.

2 ·Grill or fry for about 8 min. in the dripping, with the tomatoes.
3 Arrange a thin line of mashed potatoes on a hot dish and place the fillets of beef with a slice of tomato between each on this, leaning up against each other.
4 Place a small pat of Maître d'Hôtel butter on each fillet, pour round the demi-glace sauce and garnish with grated horse-radish.

Fillets of beef à la viennoise

4 persons

	Metric	Imp
lean beef minced	400 g	1 lb
dripping or butter	50 g	2 oz
flour	25 g	1 oz
brown or demi-glace sauce (pp. 64, 66)	250 ml	½ pt
1 tsp mixed herbs		
1 tsp chopped parsley		
1 egg		
pinch of grated nutmeg		
salt, pepper		
1 croûte of fried bread		

Method

1 Mix the minced beef, mixed herbs, seasoning and beaten egg, and shape into round cakes on a floured board.
2 Coat cakes with flour and fry in hot dripping for about 10 min., turning often.
3 Drain well and serve on a croûte of fried bread or on a bed of mashed potatoes.
4 Decorate with parsley, pour the sauce round and serve.

Note If liked, these may be decorated with fried onion rings. To make these, the onions are sliced and the rings carefully divided. Dip them in flour, then in the beaten white of egg, then back into the flour and fry in dripping or butter until golden brown. Drain well and arrange over the fillets.

Porterhouse steak

4 persons

2 sirloin steaks
a little butter or margarine
salad oil or oiled butter
6 tomatoes cut in halves
salt, pepper

Method

1 Cut 2 steaks about 2·5 cm (1 in.) thick from the sirloin. Each steak should have the undercut left but should be cut from the **chine** bone portion. The steak should look like a large chop.
2 Trim these and flatten them with a cutlet bat.
3 Sprinkle with salt and pepper, brush over with oiled butter or salad oil.
4 Grill under a brisk heat, turning several times. They take about 10 to 15 min. to grill and should be rather underdone.
5 Melt the butter in a pan and put the tomatoes skin-side down in this and cook gently for about 5 min.
6 Serve the steaks neatly on a hot entrée dish and place the tomatoes round. Sprinkle the steaks with salt and pepper.

Note Porterhouse steaks may be **larded** with larding bacon before grilling (p. 115) and they can also be served with grilled mushrooms in place of the tomatoes. The steak may be baked after **larding** it, and is then served with gravy and garnished with cooked vegetables.

Tournedos are steaks cut from the heart of the fillet. They should not be less than 2.5–3 cm (1–1½ in.) thick, and tied round with a piece of string to keep in shape. When grilled or fried, they should only be turned once, and cooked for about five minutes on either side with strong heat, so that the flesh inside is a medium pink colour.

Tournedos of beef with chestnut purée

8 persons

	Metric	Imp
fillet of beef	1200 g	3 lb
Italian sauce (p. 67)	250 ml	½ pt
clarified dripping	100 g	4 oz

chestnut purée made with 800 g (2 lb) chestnuts (p. 213) or 1 tin of unsweetened purée
salt, pepper

Method

1 Cut the beef into neat rounds about 7·5 cm in diameter (3 in.) and 2·5–3 cm (1–1½ in.) thick.

2 Melt dripping in a pan, and when hot, put in fillets and cook for 8 to 10 min., turning once.
3 Drain well and **glaze.**
4 Arrange a thin ring of chestnut purée on a hot dish and put the tournedos on this in a circle; fill the centre with more purée and strain the sauce round.

Boiled marrow bones

½ marrow bone per person
paste of flour and water
salt, pepper
toast

Saw the bones to any size desired, cover the end with a paste of flour and water. Tie each in a cloth and place it in boiling water. Simmer gently for about 2 hr.

To dish Serve the bones upright on a folded napkin on a hot dish and hand toast, salt, pepper and cayenne. A special fork or spoon should be given to each person for removing the marrow from the bones. Another method of serving is to take the marrow from the bones, and spread it on to small squares of toast, sprinkle with salt, pepper and cayenne, and serve at once. As the marrow chills quickly, it should be served directly it is spread on the toast. Some people use hot water plates or dishes on which to serve the marrow.

Ox tail, stewed

4 persons

	Metric	Imp
1 large ox tail jointed		
butter	25 g	1 oz
flour	25 g	1 oz
1 tbsp chopped parsley		
2 small onions peeled		
2 large carrots sliced		
4 cloves		
salt, pepper, cayenne		

Method

1 Put the washed ox tail into a large pan and cover with cold water. Bring to the boil, skim.
2 Add onions stuck with cloves, carrots, parsley and seasoning, and simmer gently for about 3 hr.

3 Dish up the pieces of tail and keep warm.
4 Thicken the gravy with **beurre manié** (p. 64) made from the butter and flour. Season and pour over the ox tail.
5 Serve with **croûtons** of fried bread, or in a ring of mashed potatoes with green peas in the middle.

Boiled ox tongue
8 persons

Choose a plump tongue with a smooth skin. A rough skin indicates age. If bought already salted and dried, soak the tongue in cold water for at least 12 hours, changing the water once or twice. If fresh from the pickle, the tongue only requires soaking for 3 or 4 hours. Wash it well, trim the root and skewer it into shape. Put a smoked tongue into cold water, a freshly pickled tongue into luke-warm water to cover. Bring it very slowly to the boil. Smoked tongues should take an hour to reach boiling point. Skim and simmer very gently for 2½ hours. If liked, a bunch of herbs and flavouring vegetables may be added to the water after it comes to the boil. Skim when necessary. When the tip of the tongue is tender, put it at once into cold water for a minute or two, as this enables the skin to be removed easily. If eaten hot, cover the tongue with greased paper after skinning it and re-heat it in the oven for about 10–15 minutes. Brush it over with **glaze** (p. 62).

To dish Place the tongue on a hot dish, garnish with slices of lemon or parsley or with little heaps of any cooked vegetables in season. Hand espagnole or tomato sauce (pp. 65, 67) and potatoes, or boiled macaroni.

Ox tongue to serve cold

Cook the tongue as above, and after removing the skin truss it into shape on a board by sticking a fork through the root, then bending it into a nice shape and fastening it down by the tip with a skewer or fork. When cold, trim some of the fat from the root and brush the tongue over with glaze. Fasten a paper frill round the root.

To dish Place the tongue on a dish sufficiently large to hold it comfortably and garnish with parsley, or pipe a design round it with butter put through a forcer. Very often the tongue is decorated with leaves of aspic jelly and the dish garnished with a little chopped aspic. A small unsmoked tongue takes from 2 to 2½ hours to cook, a large one an hour longer. A small smoked tongue takes 3 hours to cook, and a large one 4 or 5 hours. Ox tongue is sometimes pressed and served in a solid round instead of being dished as above. To do this, after skinning the tongue, while still hot, trim the roots, removing any small bones there may be and the superfluous fat. Roll the tongue round and press it into a round tin (a cake tin would do), previously rinsed out in cold water. Press the tongue well into this, place a board on it with a weight on the top and leave until cold, for about 12 hours. Turn it out on to a dish and garnish with parsley. The tongue will be found to be covered with a coating of jelly when pressed in this manner, and it is very easy to carve without any waste.

Stewed shin of beef
4–6 persons

	Metric	Imp
shin of beef trimmed and cut in pieces	600 g	1½ lb
dripping	25 g	1 oz
flour	25 g	1 oz
hot water or brown stock	500 ml	1 pt
carrots cut in strips	400 g	1 lb
small onions peeled	400 g	1 lb
½ clove crushed garlic (optional)		
bouquet garni		
salt, pepper		

Method
1 Melt dripping in a flame-proof casserole. Fry onions and garlic gently till transparent.
2 Remove and fry meat till well browned.
3 Sprinkle in flour. Mix well, then add liquid. Stir till boiling.
4 Add remaining ingredients, and simmer in a slow oven (130°C, 275°F, Mark 1) for 2½ to 3 hr. Dumplings may be added in the last ¼ hour.
5 Serve with boiled or mashed potatoes.

LAMB DISHES

Lamb, like all young meat, should be well cooked. It is at its best when about 2 months old. The forequarter is cooked as soon as possible without hanging, but the hindquarter should hang for a short while. When lamb is large, it is cut up and used in much the same way as mutton, but when quite small it is cut into quarters. The forequarter consists of the neck, shoulder and breast; the hindquarter, the leg and loin. The saddle is the double loin from both sides of the animal. Frozen lamb may be cooked according to any recipe for fresh meat, but should always be thawed before being cooked. Never put the meat in front of the fire to thaw, it is quite sufficient to let it remain in a warm kitchen for about two or three hours. Lamb should never be allowed to become high. The saddle, forequarter or hindquarter, shoulder, or any joint of lamb may be braised, roasted or baked in the oven, and may be varied by the different garnishes and accompaniments which are served with it. The joint may be covered with a thick layer of soubise sauce and coated with oiled butter, and then browned in the oven, and tomato sauce handed, or it may be garnished with small potato cassolettes filled with a ragoût of lamb's sweetbread or mushrooms. Other accompaniments are: small stuffed tomatoes, potato balls, forcemeat balls, small stuffed spring cabbages, braised lettuce, stuffed aubergines, fried bananas, stuffed mushrooms and mixed spring vegetables. Various sauces may be handed, such as piquante, tomato, brown or soubise.

Grilled breast of lamb

6–8 persons

	Metric	Imp
1 breast of lamb		
butter	50 g	2 oz
stock (any kind)	½–1 l	1–2 pt
breadcrumbs		
1 onion peeled		
1 bunch herbs		
salt, pepper		
2 cloves		
1 egg		
thickened gravy		
mint sauce (p. 72)		

Method

1 Wipe and trim the meat, put it into a pan with stock to cover, add the peeled onion stuck with cloves, the herbs, salt and pepper.

2 Simmer very gently for about 1½ hr, or until sufficiently tender for the bones to be easily removed.

3 Take out the bones, sprinkle the meat with salt and pepper, brush over with beaten egg and coat with breadcrumbs, brush with melted butter, then grill under a fairly hot grill. When nicely browned on one side, turn and brown the other.

4 Serve on a hot dish and hand thickened gravy and mint sauce.

Note Shoulder of lamb may be cooked in the same manner. After it has simmered it is not boned, but the skin is **scored** in small chequers, brushed over with egg and coated with breadcrumbs mixed with herbs, parsley and seasoning. Grill, and serve with gravy flavoured with mushroom ketchup.

To trim cutlets

Cutlets are always taken from the best end of the neck or loin of mutton or lamb. They are expensive to buy ready cut at the butchers, but can be quite easily trimmed at home. The meat on the loin being larger, it is more generally used for chops, navarins and noisettes.

To trim the cutlets at home, the butcher should be asked to saw off the **chine** bone so that the cutlets can be easily divided. With a very sharp knife, divide the cutlets, allowing a bone to each. Sometimes, if very big, it is possible to take two cutlets from one bone, in which case one would be without bone. Trim off the fat, leaving only a very narrow rim round the meat and scrape the bone perfectly clean for about 2·5 cm (1 in.). Remove the skin as far as possible from the inner side of the bone. Should the bones be found too long, chop a piece off each, but keep the cutlets as much the same size as possible. Beat them out a little with a rolling pin or a cutlet bat. Any fat removed from the cutlets can be used for **clarifying**, and any trimmings of meat may be used for mince or some such dish.

Lamb cutlets with asparagus

4 persons

	Metric	Imp
4 lamb cutlets		
brown sauce (p. 64)	250 ml	½ pt
squeeze of lemon juice		
cooked asparagus points		
salad oil or oiled butter		
salt, pepper		
mashed potatoes		

Method

1 Prepare and trim the cutlets as directed above. Sprinkle with salt and pepper.
2 Dip them in salad oil or oiled butter, and grill under a hot grill, turning often. They take about 10 min. to grill.
3 Arrange the potatoes in two lines on a hot dish and put the cutlets on these, leaning up against each other, with the bones all turning one way. Place a paper frill on each cutlet and garnish the dish with small heaps of asparagus points. Pour round some brown sauce to which a few drops of lemon juice have been added.

Note Mutton cutlets may be cooked in the same manner.

Lamb cutlets en papillote

4 persons

	Metric	Imp
4 lamb cutlets		
cooked ham minced	50 g	2 oz
margarine or butter	25 g	1 oz
chopped shallot	25 g	1 oz
chopped parsley	25 g	1 oz
chopped mushrooms	25 g	1 oz
piquante, brown or tomato		
sauce (p. 71, 64, 67)	125 ml	1 gill
salt, pepper		

Method

1 Trim cutlets according to directions above.

2 Melt fat in pan, add shallot and fry for a few minutes till transparent.
3 Add mushrooms and cook 5 more min. Add ham, parsley and seasoning. Mix well and cool.
4 Take squares of kitchen foil or strong white paper large enough to enfold each cutlet, brush with oil.
5 Coat cutlets on each side with ham mixture, place on each piece of paper; fold paper over and turn up edges firmly.
6 Put on greased baking sheet and bake in moderate oven (175°C, 350°F, Mark 4) for ¼ hr. Serve in papers and hot dish and hand sauce separately.

Note The classic papillote consists of 2 heart-shaped pieces of greaseproof paper for each piece of meat or fish to be enclosed. The heart shape should be 5 cm (2 in.) longer at the top and bottom of the heart than the food enclosed. This is placed on one piece of paper, covered with the second, and the 2 pleated together at the edges so that the packet is made airtight.

Lamb fillets

4 persons

	Metric	Imp
4 loin chops		
mushrooms chopped	100 g	¼ lb
stock (any kind)	60 ml	½ gill
dripping	25 g	1 oz
demi-glace sauce (p. 66)	250 ml	½ pt
1 tsp chopped parsley		
juice of ½ lemon		
4 artichoke bottoms		
4 leaves tarragon		
glaze (p. 62)		
salt, pepper		

Method

1 Remove meat in one piece from each bone and trim into a fillet, taking off all surplus fat, making 4 noisettes.

2 Melt dripping in a pan, cook noisettes 3 to 4 min. on each side. Sprinkle with salt and pepper. Dish and keep warm.

3 Warm artichoke bottoms in stock.

4 Cook mushrooms in noisette pan; drain off fat, add a squeeze of lemon juice, a spoonful of **glaze** or meat extract, parsley and tarragon. Season and heat. Fill artichoke bottoms with this mixture.

5 Serve the noisettes with an artichoke on top of each and pour round the demi-glace sauce.

MUTTON DISHES

Mutton comes from sheep over a year old, and in some districts is difficult to obtain. The meat is tough unless hung and has a great deal of fat distributed through the meat. Any fat that can be trimmed before cooking should be removed, as it has a rather strong flavour. Well-hung meat will have a brownish, even purplish tinge, and New Zealand mutton will be labelled New Zealand lamb.

Mutton will be cheaper than lamb, and carefully cooked, will provide some succulent dishes.

Boiled leg of mutton

	Metric	Imp
Leg of mutton washed and dried		
caper sauce (p. 68)	250 ml	½ pt
1 onion stuck with cloves		
1 bunch herbs		
salt, pepper		
turnips and carrots		

Method

1 Cut off shank bone and trim knuckle.

2 Place in a pan of boiling water with just enough to cover.

3 Bring to boiling point. Skim.

4 Add onion, herbs and seasoning.

5 Simmer with the lid on, skimming occasionally, till the joint is cooked (20 min. per 450 g (1 lb) and 20 min. over).

6 Serve on a hot dish and garnish with turnips and carrots.

7 Hand mashed potatoes and caper sauce separately.

Note The shoulder, neck or breast of mutton may be boiled in the same way, as may the leg or shoulder of lamb.

Braised leg of mutton

	Metric	Imp
leg of mutton wiped		
rindless bacon rashers	200 g	8 oz
stock (any kind)	375 ml	¾ pt
2 onions sliced		
4 carrots sliced		
glaze (p. 62)		
1 bay leaf		
1 bunch herbs		
salt, pepper		
any available bones		
carrots, turnips		

Method

1 Cut off the shank bone and trim knuckle.

2 Put half the bacon at the bottom of a braising pan, add the carrots, onions, bay leaf, herbs, bones and then the mutton. Cover with rest of bacon, pour stock round and season.

3 Cover pan and cook very slowly for 4 hr.

4 Remove mutton and brush with **glaze**.

5 Serve on a hot dish. Skim fat from gravy, strain round and garnish with carrots and turnips.

Roast leg of mutton
Method

1 Wipe mutton dry and dust with a little flour and pepper.

2 Cut off knuckle and remove thick skin.

3 Put a little salt and water in a dripping pan, place meat on a grid in the pan, put in a hot oven (220°C, 425°F, Mark 7) for 20 min., basting with the water. Reduce heat gradually to 175°C (350°F, Mark 4) and **baste** frequently until joint is cooked (20 min. per 450 g (1 lb) and 20 min. over).

4 Serve mutton on a hot dish, make gravy according to p. 62 and hand it separately in a sauce boat. Serve redcurrant jelly.

Note Wether leg of mutton is best for roasting. If liked, the knuckle may be cut off and boiled separately, or, if preferred, the cut end can be covered with a paste of flour and water and roasted, in which case two roast dinners can be had from the one joint.

Loin, neck and shoulder of mutton may be roasted in this manner, as may be the leg, forequarters and shoulder of lamb. The mutton may also be boned and stuffed with veal forcemeat before roasting it.

Arabian stew

4 persons

	Metric	Imp
neck of mutton jointed	800 g	2 lb
rice	50 g	2 oz
tomatoes skinned and sliced	200 g	½ lb
2 onions sliced		
1 small vegetable marrow peeled and cut in small pieces		
water		
salt, pepper		

Method

1 Remove all skin, superfluous fat and piping from meat and place it in a stewpan or casserole, cover with water, season and bring slowly to the boil.

2 Remove all scum, add onions, tomatoes and marrow and bring again to the boil. Cover the pan, and simmer for ½ hr.

3 Sprinkle in rice and continue to cook for another ½ hr, or until meat is tender and rice cooked. Season again to taste.

4 Serve in casserole or on a hot dish with meat in a circle and vegetables in the centre with gravy around.

Note If boneless stewing mutton is used, allow 150 g (6 oz) per person and 200 g (8 oz) of meat with bone per person.

Haricot of mutton

4 persons

	Metric	Imp
middle neck of mutton	1200 g	3 lb
dripping	50 g	2 oz
3 carrots, 3 turnips, sliced		
2 onions sliced		
1 dssp walnut ketchup		
salt, pepper		
water		

Method

1 Trim off the surplus fat and divide the chops.

2 Fry lightly in dripping; remove from pan.

3 Fry vegetables gently for a few minutes, stirring occasionally.

4 Put mutton in stewpan, vegetables on top, season and just cover with hot water. Bring to boil and simmer till chops are tender, about 1¾ hr.

5 Add walnut ketchup and more seasoning if necessary. Allow to cool.

6 Take off all fat very carefully.

7 Reheat and serve on a hot dish with meat surrounded by vegetables and gravy.

Irish stew

4 persons

	Metric	Imp
scrag or middle neck of mutton	800 g	2 lb
onions sliced	400 g	1 lb
potatoes peeled	1 mg	2½ lb
water		
salt, pepper		

Method

1 Wipe meat; trim away skin, fat and piping; joint and cut long ends of bones into neat joints, allowing two bones to a joint.

2 Put meat in a pan, sprinkle with salt and pepper and cover with cold water. Bring to boil.

3 Remove scum; add onions and half the potatoes, sliced. Bring to boil again.

4 Cover pan and simmer till meat is tender, 1 to 1½ hr, adding remainder of potatoes, cut in halves, for the last ½ hr.

5 Serve on a hot dish with meat surrounding vegetables and gravy poured round.

Note This stew must cook very gently, the

pan shaken occasionally to prevent sticking, but it should not be stirred. More boiling water may be added if the liquid boils away, but the stew must not be watery.

Lancashire hot-pot

4 persons

	Metric	Imp
neck of mutton trimmed and jointed as on p. 177	800 g	2 lb
mushrooms sliced	200 g	½ lb
potatoes sliced	800 g	2 lb
water	250 ml	½ pt
3 mutton kidneys sliced		
3 onions sliced		
a few oysters (optional)		
a little fat		
salt, pepper		

Method
1 Brown chops on both sides in hot fat and place a layer at the bottom of hot-pot dish.
2 On this, place a layer of kidneys, onions, potatoes and mushrooms, and a few oysters, if used.
3 Season, and continue these layers till ingredients are used up, ending in potatoes.
4 Cover with water, and oyster liquor, if any; cover and simmer very slowly in oven (120°C, 250°F, Mark ½) for 2 hr.
5 Remove lid, and brown potatoes for another ½ hr.
6 Serve in casserole.

Grilled mutton cutlets

Mutton cutlets should be trimmed in the same way as lamb (p. 177). Brush the cutlets on both sides with oil, season and coat with breadcrumbs. Cook under a hot grill 8 to 10 min. turning once. Put a thin line of mashed potato on a hot dish and arrange the cutlets in a line, leaning against each other on this. See that the bones all turn one way and put a cutlet frill on each. Garnish with watercress. Cutlets grilled in this manner may be served with small baked tomatoes, stuffed cucumbers, green peas, halves of hard-boiled whites of eggs filled with peas or some savoury mixture. Tomato or brown sauce (pp. 67, 64) may be served as well.

Note The cutlets may be served on a purée of green peas, or cooked macaroni or spaghetti with a little sauce poured round. The name of the dish is usually taken from the garnish or accompaniments.

Mutton cutlets à la milanaise

Mutton cutlets are grilled as above and served on a pyramid of spaghetti which has been cooked with tomatoes and mushrooms. They are then sprinkled with grated cheese.

Noisettes of mutton à l'Espagnole

A noisette is the meat removed from the cutlet bone all in one piece, which makes a small fillet and is cooked in various ways.

4 persons

	Metric	Imp
4 cutlets from best end of neck or loin of mutton		
chopped ham	25 g	1 oz
dripping	25 g	1 oz
Espagnole sauce (p. 65)	500 ml	1 pt
2 tbsp salad oil		
1 tbsp wine vinegar		
1 shallot chopped		
1 bay leaf		
2 tsp chopped parsley		
2 tomatoes		
egg, breadcrumbs		
salt, pepper		

Method
1 Cut meat from bone of cutlet in one piece.
2 Mix oil, vinegar, shallot, bay leaf and parsley in a deep dish and **marinade** meat in this mixture for 5–6 hr.
3 Wipe on a cloth, dip in breadcrumbs, then beaten egg, then crumbs again.
4 Halve the tomatoes and remove seeds. Mix ham with a little Espagnole sauce and fill tomatoes with mixture.
5 Place tomatoes on greased baking sheet and bake in moderate oven (175°C, 350°F, Mark 4) 5 min.
6 Add dripping to pan and when hot, put in noisettes. Brown quickly on both sides, then cook gently for 10 to 15 min.

7 Serve on a hot dish against a line of mashed potato or spinach. Pour Espagnole sauce round and garnish with the halves of tomato.

Boiled sheep's head *2–3 persons*

	Metric	Imp
1 sheep's head		
white sauce (p. 68)	250 ml	½ pt
2 onions stuck with cloves		
2 carrots		
2 turnips		
2 sticks celery chopped		
1 bunch herbs		
salt		
lemon, fried bacon		

Method

1 Split the head in halves, take out the brains and tongue, wash and scrape the head well, take out the eyes and shorten the jaw bones where there is no flesh, and be careful to remove all the gristle from inside the nose, chopping off everything that should be removed. Put the head into cold water for ½ hr, then rinse well. Replace the tongue, tie the two halves of the head together, and put it into a saucepan of boiling water to cover.
2 Bring to the boil, skim well, add onions and herbs.
3 Skim again, add a little salt and simmer for 2 hr.
4 Add vegetables, chopped. Simmer 1 more hr.
5 Lift out head; remove all meat from bones and cut in slices.
6 Skin tongue and cut in slices.
7 Add chopped, cooked brains (p. 136) to 250 ml (½ pt) white sauce, and pour over sliced meat.
8 Garnish with lemon and rolls of fried bacon. Serve the broth separately as gravy.

Note The liquor in which the head has been cooked makes excellent soup with the addition of barley and vegetables. Sometimes a gang of trotters are cooked and served with the head. Italian sauce (p. 67) may be handed. The brains may be served with the head, or saved and used for some other dish. Lamb's head may be cooked in the same manner, but takes only about 1½ hr to cook.

Sheep's tongues, stewed *4 persons*
allow 1 sheep's tongue per person

Sheep's tongues may be bought uncooked or partly cooked. If uncooked, they should be soaked for 3 hours in cold water, then rinsed. If partly cooked they only need washing.

	Metric	Imp
4 sheep's tongues		
mushrooms chopped	100 g	4 oz
good stock (any kind)	750 ml	1½ pt
butter	50 g	2 oz
flour	25 g	1 oz
2 shallots chopped		
1 tbsp chopped parsley		
salt, pepper		
croûtons of fried bread		

Method

1 Soften the mushrooms and shallots in half the butter. Set aside.
2 Cover the tongues with stock, bring to the boil and simmer for 2 hr or ¾ hr according to whether they are uncooked or partly cooked.
3 When tender, remove the tongues, skin them and cut them in two, lengthwise.
4 Melt the rest of the butter in the pan, stir in the flour, cook gently till brown, then add slowly 500 ml (1 pt) of the cooking liquor. Stir till boiling, add shallots and mushrooms and parsley.
5 Season and put in slices of tongue and simmer for 10 min.
6 Arrange slices of tongue on a hot dish and pour sauce over. Garnish with **croûtons** of fried bread.

Note If liked, the tongues can be served in a border of mashed potatoes, macaroni or cooked spinach.

Sheep's trotters, stewed

2–3 persons

	Metric	Imp
1 set sheep's trotters skinned		
stock (any kind)	750 ml	1½ pt
milk	125 ml	1 gill
1 tbsp flour		
1 tbsp chopped parsley		
1 onion stuck with cloves		
1 blade mace		
1 bunch herbs		
salt, pepper		
toast or fried bread		

Method

1 Wash trotters well, put in a pan with cold water to cover, bring to the boil and drain.
2 Put in a pan with the stock, onion, herbs, mace and salt. Cover the pan and simmer gently till meat parts from the bones (1½–2 hr). Strain.
3 Remove meat from bones, dice.
4 Return 125 ml (1 gill) liquor to the saucepan, blend flour and milk smoothly, add to liquor and stir over heat till thick.
5 Season, add parsley and meat and heat gently for 10 min.
6 Arrange pieces of meat on a hot dish, pour sauce over and garnish with snippets of toast or fried bread.

Note Sheep's trotters may be cooked according to any recipe for calves' feet, and may be cooked in tomato, brown or Italian sauce (pp. 67, 64, 67).

PORK DISHES

Great care should be exercised in buying pork, as the meat is easily tainted. Pork should always be very well cooked, allowing from 20 to 25 minutes per 450 g (1 lb) and 25 minutes over. A pig for boiling or roasting should not be more than 6 months old. Larger and older pigs are usually salted and pickled.

Boiled leg of pork

8–10 persons

1 leg of pickled pork
turnips or parsnips
salt
water

Method

1 Choose a nice small compact leg of pickled pork. Soak it for ½ hr in cold water, wash and then put it into a saucepan of boiling water, bring to the boil, skim and then simmer very gently until cooked, calculating the time according to the weight of the meat. Great care must be taken not to let the pork cook fast, or the meat becomes hard and the knuckle end becomes cooked before the thicker part.
2 When half done, washed and peeled parsnips or turnips may be added to the pan and cooked until soft.
3 Put the pork on to a hot dish, garnish with turnips or parsnips. Pour round a very little of the liquor in which the pork was boiled, and hand the rest in a tureen. Pease pudding (p. 208) should be served with boiled pork, and green vegetables such as cabbage, sprouts or kale.

Note The water in which pork has been boiled makes an excellent stock for haricot, pea or lentil soup. The **chine** is salted and boiled in the same manner.

Roast leg of pork

8–10 persons

	Metric	Imp
leg of pork		
apple sauce (p. 68)	500 ml	1 pt
brown gravy		
salad oil		

Method

1 The leg to be roasted should not weigh more than 3 kg (6–7 lb).

2 Score the rind or skin with a sharp knife all round the joint, brush it over with salad oil and cook in a hot oven (220°C, 425°F, Mark 7) for the first 20 min., lessening the heat later (190°C, 375°F, Mark 5). **Baste** often. It will yield sufficient dripping to **baste** itself without butter.

3 Place the pork on a hot dish and hand brown gravy and apple sauce. Other accompaniments are tomato sauce, sauce Robert (p. 67) and baked apples, or stewed prunes or plums.

Note The leg may be stuffed with sage and onion stuffing (p. 78), which is inserted in a slit cut in the knuckle. Loin, spare rib and saddle of pork may also be roasted in this manner.

Chine of pork

This joint is usually served with turkey. It should be salted for about 60 to 70 hours and then roasted. Chine may be boiled, but roasting is usually preferred. In roasting pork, the skin should be **scored** lengthways in small strips, not deep enough to reach the meat.

Chine, roasted

6–8 persons

	Metric	Imp
chine of pork salted	1600 g–2 kg	4–5 lb
sage and onion stuffing (p. 78)	200 g	½ lb
apple sauce (p. 68)	250 ml	½ pt
salad oil		
thickened gravy		

Method
1 Wash well, then **score** the skin deeply lengthways.
2 Make an incision to hold the stuffing, insert it, brush the skin over with salad oil and roast gently (190°C, 375°F, Mark 5) in the oven. **Baste** often.
3 Put the pork on a hot dish and hand thickened gravy and apple sauce.

Baked ham

10–12 persons

Method
1 Take a medium-sized ham and place it to soak for 10–12 hr.
2 Cut away the rusty part from underneath, wipe it dry and cover it rather thickly with a paste of flour and water.
3 Put it into an earthenware dish or fireproof casserole and bake in a moderately hot oven (175°C, 350°F, Mark 4), allowing 25 min. to 450 g (1 lb) up to 6 kg (12 lb), and 15 min. for every 450 g (1 lb) over.
4 When cooked, remove the paste carefully and pull off the skin. Strew the surface with bread raspings, or brush it over with **glaze.**
5 Serve the ham on a hot dish and garnish with cut vegetables.

Boiled ham

12 or more persons

1 ham
1 sprig thyme
1 blade mace
2 bay leaves
a few cloves
bread raspings or **glaze** (p. 62)
parsley

Method
1 Soak the ham in several waters for 24 hr, if hard and salt, changing the water 2 or 3 times. If the ham is not very salt, 12 hours' soaking is usually sufficient.
2 Trim and scrape the ham very clean and put it into a large saucepan with cold water to cover.
3 Bring slowly to the boil, skim carefully, add the mace, cloves, thyme and bay leaves and, if liked, 1 or 2 scraped carrots and an onion.
4 Simmer gently for 4 or 5 hr, according to the weight of the ham. A new ham requires 25 min. to 450 g (1 lb), and old one, 28 min., counting the time from when the water boils.
5 When cooked, let the ham remain in the water until cold, then remove the rind carefully, press a cloth over the ham to absorb as much grease as possible, and stew the fat with bread raspings or brush it over with **glaze.**

6 Put the ham on a dish and garnish it with parsley or aspic jelly. Put a paper frill round the knuckle or ornament it with vegetable flowers.

To serve a ham hot

Soak and boil the ham as above. When cooked, remove the skin, sprinkle the ham with breadcrumbs, put a paper frill round the knuckle and serve on a hot dish. Garnish with parsley.

Ham soufflé   *4 persons*

	Metric	Imp
minced lean ham	200 g	½ lb
milk	125 ml	1 gill
butter	50 g	2 oz
flour	25 g	1 oz
3 separated eggs		
salt, pepper, nutmeg		

Method

1 Melt butter in a pan, stir in flour and cook a few minutes without browning. Add milk gradually, then stir with a wooden spoon very fast till mixture leaves the side of the pan. Cool a little.
2 Stir in ham, seasoning and egg yolks one by one.
3 If too dry, add about 30 ml (¼ gill) milk.
4 Beat whites of egg stiffly and fold in to ham mixture, adjusting seasoning if necessary.
5 Bake in a moderately hot oven (175°C, 350°F, Mark 4) for 20 to 25 min., on the middle shelf.

Note This soufflé may also be steamed very gently for about an hour, which gives a firmer texture than a baked soufflé, in which case it should be served with a white sauce.

Boiled bacon

Should the bacon be very salt, soak it in cold water for 2 hours before cooking, rinse and put into a saucepan with plenty of boiling water. Bring to the boil, skim and then simmer very gently, allowing 20 min. per 450 g (1 lb) and 20 min. over. A large piece of gammon of bacon when cooked should be skinned like a ham and powdered over with breadcrumbs.

Broad beans are excellent with bacon and should be added when the bacon has cooked for an hour. The bacon may be dished on the beans and coated with parsley sauce, or the beans may be served separately.

It is far better really to steam bacon than to boil it. There is no waste as to quantity, the flavour is better preserved and the bacon much more tender, as there is no danger of letting it boil too fast. Prepare the bacon as for boiling and put it into a steamer over boiling water. Steam according to the weight, allowing 25 minutes per 450 g (1 lb) and 25 minutes over. Boiled or steamed bacon makes a good accompaniment to veal and poultry, or it may be served alone with greens. Cabbage may be added to the bacon when partially cooked and is served with it.

Pork chops with sauce Robert   *4 persons*
Marinaded overnight

	Metric	Imp
loin of pork	800 g	2 lb
sauce Robert (p. 67)	250 ml	½ pt
white wine	125 ml	1 gill
wine vinegar	60 ml	½ gill
breadcrumbs	50 g	2 oz
1 onion and 2 shallots, minced		
1 tsp chopped herbs		
2 bay leaves		
1 egg yolk		
pinch each of allspice and mace		
1 bunch herbs		
salt, pepper		

Method

1 Remove the skin from the pork, divide into chops and trim.
2 Boil up the wine, vinegar, bunch of herbs, minced onion and shallots, bay leaves and spices in a pan, then let **marinade** cool.
3 When cold, pour over chops; turn them frequently and leave in liquid overnight.

4 When required, remove chops from **marinade**, dry them, brush over with egg yolk, dip in breadcrumbs mixed with chopped herbs.

5 Grill for 15 to 20 min., turning several times.

6 Serve on a hot dish with sauce Robert poured round.

VEAL DISHES

Veal should be obtained from a calf about 2 or 3 months' old when wanted for very delicate dishes. Always remove the piping from the veal and skirt from the breast in hot weather directly it arrives from the butcher. The best joints for roasting are the fillet and the loin.

Blanquette of veal

4 persons

	Metric	Imp
breast of veal cut into pieces and sprinkled with salt and pepper	800 g	2 lb
butter	50 g	2 oz
flour	25 g	1 oz
milk	60 ml	½ gill
white stock	375 ml	¾ pt
2 egg yolks		
1 tsp lemon juice		
salt, pepper		
1 bunch herbs		

Method

1 Blanch veal by covering with boiling water and steeping for ½ hr.

2 Melt butter in a pan, add veal and cook for 5 min. without browning, turning once or twice.

3 Remove veal and add flour. Stir for 2 or 3 min. over heat, then add stock. Stir till boiling.

4 Season, add bunch of herbs, and return meat to pan.

5 Cover and simmer gently for an hour.

6 Remove pan from heat, beat up egg yolks with milk and add.

7 Stir over gentle heat till mixture thickens, but do not allow to boil. Season and add lemon juice.

8 Dish veal on a hot dish and pour sauce over.

Veal cutlets

4 persons

	Metric	Imp
cutlets from best end of neck of veal	800 g	2 lb
butter	75 g	3 oz
sliced bacon or ham	100 g	4 oz
Espagnole sauce (p. 65)	250 ml	½ pt
1 tbsp minced herbs		
1 egg		
breadcrumbs		
salt, cayenne, nutmeg		
grated peel of ½ lemon		

Method

1 Divide cutlets and cut meat carefully from the bone, retaining shape.

2 Mix breadcrumbs and herbs, lemon peel, seasoning and nutmeg.

3 Brush cutlets with beaten egg and dip in breadcrumbs.

4 Melt butter in pan, and when hot, fry cutlets about 15 min., turning often.

5 Roll up slices of bacon or ham and grill till brown.

6 Serve cutlets on a bed of mashed potatoes, garnish with bacon rolls and pour round Espagnole sauce.

Escalopes are slices cut from a lean piece of veal. These used to be taken from the noix, the tender part down the length of a leg of veal. This is now so prohibitive in price that substitutes are cut from the loin or across the grain of the leg. Escalopes should be cut about 6 mm (¼ in.) thick and beaten thinner with the flat of a heavy knife. They are then often coated in egg and breadcrumbs and fried lightly in butter and garnished with lemon, anchovies, egg or capers according to the dish.

Smaller pieces of veal left over from cutting escalopes may be used for dishes cooked with a little liquid, either wine or stock, and cream.

Veal escalopes à l'Italienne

4 persons

	Metric	Imp
escalope pieces, 6 mm (¼″) thick and 3–4 cm (1½″) square	about 400 g	about 1 lb
butter	50 g	2 oz

1 tbsp stock (any kind) or *bouillon*
1 clove garlic
1 bay leaf
10 mushrooms sliced
juice of ½ lemon
salt, pepper

Method

1 Melt half the butter in a frying pan with the garlic and bay leaf.
2 Season veal and fry for a few minutes, turning the pieces frequently.
3 Add the rest of the butter and the mushrooms and cook a further few minutes, stirring occasionally.
4 Remove the garlic and bay leaf, place meat on a hot dish and cover with mushrooms.
5 Pour bouillon and lemon juice into pan and boil for a minute, stirring all the time.
6 Pour over the meat and serve.

Veal olives

4 persons

	Metric	Imp
fillet of veal cut in 4 thin slices about 10 × 8 cm (4 × 3 in.)	400 g	1 lb
veal forcemeat (p. 79)	100 g	4 oz
fat bacon rashers	100 g	4 oz
butter	40 g	1½ oz
brown sauce or gravy	250 ml	½ pt

1 shallot minced finely
salt, pepper, cayenne
chopped parsley
carrots and turnips

Method

1 Place a thin slice of bacon on each slice of veal; spread a layer of forcemeat over and a pinch of shallot; sprinkle with salt, pepper and cayenne and roll up slices and tie with string.
2 Melt butter in a pan and when hot, brown olives all over.
3 Add gravy or sauce and simmer with lid on for about 1 hr or till olives are tender.
4 Remove string and serve on a bed of mashed potatoes. Skim all fat from sauce and pour round dish. Sprinkle chopped parsley down each olive. Garnish with fancy shapes of cooked carrots and turnips.

Note Beef or chicken olives may be made in the same way.

Haricot of veal

4 persons

	Metric	Imp
middle neck of veal	1 kg	2½ lb
shelled peas	200 g	½ lb
fat	50 g	2 oz
white stock	750 ml	1½ pt

2 tbsp flour
4 carrots, 4 turnips, sliced
1 cucumber peeled and sliced
salt, pepper

Method

1 Shorten bones on veal and remove piping, gristle and surplus fat and cut into joints.
2 Melt fat in a flameproof casserole, and brown veal on both sides. Sprinkle with flour and cook till golden.
3 Add stock and seasoning and simmer for about 1 hr.
4 Add vegetables and simmer for a further ½ hr.
5 Dish the chops on a hot dish, lift out the vegetables with a perforated spoon and place round meat, and serve gravy in sauce boat.

Stewed breast of veal

4 persons

	Metric	Imp
breast of veal boned	800 g	2 lb
butter	25 g	1 oz
veal stuffing (p. 79)		
green peas	800 g	2 lb
dripping	25 g	1 oz

peel and juice of ½ lemon
4 small onions
1 bunch herbs
1½ blades mace
¼ tsp ground allspice

2 cloves
1 small glass sherry
1 tbsp flour
3 dssp mushroom ketchup
3 dssp mushroom sauce (p. 67)
salt, pepper
water
bacon rolls
forcemeat balls

Method

1 Lay the stuffing on the veal, roll up and tie with string.
2 Melt dripping in a pan and brown meat all over.
3 Drain off the fat; add herbs, mace, cloves, allspice, peeled onions, thinly sliced lemon peel, salt and pepper. Cover with boiling water and simmer with a tight lid on for 2 hr.
4 Strain the gravy and to 500 ml (1 pt) add the sherry, tomato sauce, lemon juice and ketchup. Thicken with butter rolled into the flour and simmer 15 min., skimming well.
5 Serve meat in a border of green peas boiled separately and garnish with bacon rolls and forcemeat balls.

Roast fillet of veal

6 persons

	Metric	Imp
fillet of veal boned	2 kg	5 lb
veal forcemeat (p. 79)	100 g	4 oz
1 lemon		
dripping		
parsley		

Method

1 Stuff the veal and tie into a round and fasten with string or skewers. Rub dripping well in.
2 Wrap in foil and cook in a hot oven (220°C, 425°F, Mark 7) for the first 20 min., lowering the temperature a little for the next 1 hr 20 min.
3 Remove foil and cook a further 20 min., **basting** frequently.
4 Remove string or skewers and serve on a hot dish with parsley and wedges of lemon. Hand gravy separately.

Note It is usual to serve ham, bacon or pickled pork with veal. If liked, the veal may

be garnished with potato balls shaped like pears with stalks of parsley.

Loin, breast and shoulder of veal may be roasted in this manner. They may be boned and stuffed with veal forcemeat before roasting, if desired. These joints may also be boiled and served coated with white sauce. Sometimes rice, pearl barley or macaroni are cooked with the veal and served round the dish.

Minced veal and macaroni

4 persons

	Metric	Imp
minced veal	400 g	1 lb
minced ham	100 g	4 oz
breadcrumbs	100 g	4 oz
white stock	60 ml	½ gill
tomato or brown sauce (p. 64)	250 ml	½ pt
2 eggs		
grated rind of ½ lemon		
salt, pepper		
fried bread or cooked turnip		

Method

1 Mix minced meats with breadcrumbs and lemon rind. Bind with stock and well beaten eggs, season to taste.
2 Grease a pudding basin and line it with the macaroni. Fill the centre with the veal mixture.
3 Cover with greased paper and steam for ¾ hr.
4 Turn out on to a hot dish and pour round tomato or brown sauce or a good gravy. Garnish with cubes of cooked turnip or fried bread.

Boiled calves' feet

4–5 persons

	Metric	Imp
2 calves' feet		
parsley sauce (p. 69)	500 ml	1 pt
white stock or water		
salt		

Method

1 To prepare the feet, bone them as far as the first joint, wash and scrape the feet, put them into a pan with cold water to cover, bring to the boil, drain and wash again.

2 Put them into a pan with stock or water and salt, and simmer very gently for about 2 hr.

3 When tender, take out the feet and put them on a hot dish and coat with parsley sauce.

Calf's head, boiled

3–4 persons

	Metric	Imp
1 calf's head		
parsley sauce (p. 69)	500 ml	1 pt
2 carrots		
1 turnip		
1 onion		
1 bunch herbs		
salt		
1 lemon		
parsley		

Method

1 Calves' heads are sold either skinned or unskinned. If unskinned, put the head into boiling water and let it remain for a few moments.

2 Then take it up and scrape off the hair with a blunt knife.

3 Cut the head in half, take out the eyes brains and tongue and wash the head most carefully, paying particular attention to the ears and nostrils. Clear out any cavities with the fingers, then put the head in cold salted water to cover and leave it for 2–3 hr.

4 Turn and drain the head, wrap it in a piece of muslin and tie it in shape.

5 Put it into a pan with cold water to cover and bring very slowly to the boil. Skim well.

6 Then add the vegetables cut into pieces, the herbs and salt. Cover the pan and simmer very gently until the head is cooked, about 2 hr.

7 When cooked, drain and remove the bones from the head, skin the tongue and cut it into slices and cut the ear into a fringe with a pair of scissors. Arrange the pieces of the head on a hot dish and garnish with the slices of tongue. Pour over the parsley sauce and garnish with cut lemon and parsley. Boiled ham or bacon is usually served with calf's head. Brain sauce may be used instead of parsley sauce. Remove the brains from the head, boil, chop and mix with 500 ml (1 pt) of white sauce (p. 68).

Note Half a calf's head is more usually served than a whole one. If this is the case it should be prepared in the same manner, but it takes a shorter time to reach boiling point. The time varies according to the size of the head, but it must not be overcooked, or the flesh falls to pieces and becomes tasteless. Should the liquor boil away, replenish the pan with more boiling water, as the head must be covered. The tongue should be cooked with the head.

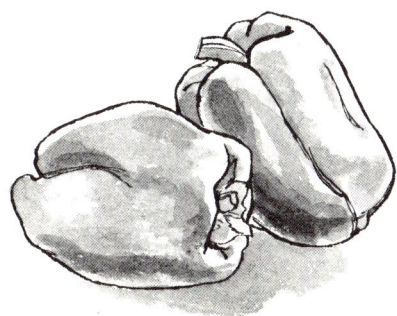

OFFAL DISHES

Calves' brains

Before cooking brains, they should be soaked for 15 min. in cold water to which a little vinegar is added. Then, under the cold tap, remove any clots and the membrane. Leave to soak in cold, salted water for another hour.

Calves' brains à la Maître d'Hôtel

4 persons

	Metric	Imp
2 calves' brains cleaned		
parsley sauce	250 ml	½ pt
frying fat		
1 chopped onion		
1 bay leaf		
4 thin slices of bread cut in the shape of a scallop shell		
parsley		

Method

1 Poach the cleaned brains in boiling salted water, to which a chopped onion and a bay leaf have been added, for about 10 min. till tender. Drain and keep warm.
2 Meanwhile, fry the slices of bread in deep fat till pale brown and drain well.
3 To serve, cut each brain in half and place each half on a piece of fried bread and coat with parsley sauce. Garnish with parsley.

Note If liked, brains cooked in this manner may be heated in the parsley sauce and put into scallop shells, sprinkled with bread-crumbs and browned under the grill.

Roasted ox heart

4–5 persons

	Metric	Imp
1 ox heart		
veal forcemeat (p. 79)	100–150 g	4–6 oz

Method

1 Cut off the flaps or the lobes from the heart and remove all pieces of gristle and cartilage.
2 Wash thoroughly in several waters, then soak in lukewarm water for 1 hr and rinse again. Wipe well with a cloth and stuff the cavity with the forcemeat.

3 Tie the heart up in greased foil, put it on a greased baking tin and roast in a moderate oven (175°F, 350°F, Mark 4) for about 2 hr, or more if the heart is very large.
4 When ready, remove the paper and brown the heart for a few minutes.
5 Serve on a hot dish and make gravy as for roast beef (p. 62). Hand redcurrant jelly.

Note This may be served on a croûte of fried bread and garnished with carrots.

Kidneys on toast

4 persons

	Metric	Imp
4 sheep's kidneys skinned		
butter	40 g	1½ oz
stock or gravy (any kind)	125 g	1 gill
1 tbsp flour		
squeeze of lemon juice		
salt, pepper		
toast		

Method

1 Cut kidneys across, remove core and slice.
2 Melt butter in pan, add flour, brown a little; add stock or gravy, stirring till boiling.
3 Put in kidneys, season and add a squeeze of lemon juice. Simmer 12 to 15 min. till cooked.
4 Serve on hot buttered toast.

Grilled lamb's kidneys

2 persons

	Metric	Imp
4 kidneys skinned		
butter	25 g	1 oz
Maître d'Hôtel butter (p. 75)	40 g	1½ oz
4 thin rashers streaky bacon		
4 small tomatoes		
salt, pepper		

Method

1 Cut kidneys in halves without separating them. Remove core. Insert a small skewer in each to keep them open.

2 Melt the butter and dip kidneys in this. Put them, cut side down, on well-greased grill pan, and cook under a hot grill 6 to 8 min., turning once or twice.

3 Fry the bacon, and for the last 3 min., the tomatoes.

4 Serve each kidney on a rasher of bacon, fill centre with Maître d'Hôtel butter and garnish with tomatoes.

Note Devilled kidneys are served on fried bread with curry butter in place of the Maître d'Hôtel butter.

Calf's liver à la Française

4 persons

	Metric	Imp
calf's liver	400 g	1 lb
wine vinegar	125 ml	1 gill
breadcrumbs	50 g	2 oz
butter broken in small pieces	25 g	1 oz
rindless slices of streaky bacon	100 g	4 oz
brown sauce (p. 64)	250 ml	½ pt
½ tsp chopped mixed herbs		
1 tsp chopped parsley		
1 egg yolk		
salt, pepper, cayenne		
fried bread		
lemon and parsley		

Method

1 Soak liver for 4 hr in vinegar to render it firm. Rinse in cold water and wipe dry.

2 Cut into slices about 6 mm to 1 cm (¼ to ½ in.) thick.

3 Mix breadcrumbs, butter, parsley, herbs and seasoning and bind with yolk of egg.

4 Spread mixture on each piece of liver and cover with bacon slice.

5 Place on greased baking sheet and bake in moderate oven (175°C, 350°F, Mark 4) for ¾ hr.

6 Dish each piece on a small piece of fried bread, garnish with cut lemon or parsley and hand round brown sauce.

Liver and bacon

4 persons

	Metric	Imp
calf's, lamb's or pig's liver cut in 1 cm (½ in.) thick slices	400 g	1 lb
streaky bacon rashers	100 g	4 oz
stock (any kind)	250 ml	½ pt
dripping	25 g	1 oz
1 tbsp flour		
1 onion sliced		
salt, pepper		

Method

1 Mix flour and seasoning on a plate and dip the slices of liver in the mixture.

2 Put bacon in pan with dripping and fry lightly.

3 Remove bacon and put in liver. Fry brown on both sides, add onion and fry a little.

4 Shake in any remaining flour, brown slightly, then add stock and stir till boiling.

5 Simmer very gently about 20 min., or till liver is cooked. Just before serving, return bacon to pan and reheat.

6 Serve liver on a hot dish, check seasoning of sauce, boil it up quickly and pour round liver. Garnish with the pieces of bacon rolled up.

Mock goose

4 persons

	Metric	Imp
calf's, lamb's or pig's liver cut in slices 1 cm (½ in.) thick	400 g	1 lb
potatoes sliced	800 g	2 lb
boiling water or stock	250 ml	¾ pt
1 tbsp flour		
salt and pepper		
1 tsp sage		
2 onions chopped finely		
1 apple peeled, cored and chopped		

Method

1 Mix flour and seasoning on a plate and dip liver in this.

2 Mix onion, apple and sage.

3 Put a layer of liver in a greased casserole, then a good sprinkling of onion mixture, season well and cover with a layer of potatoes. Repeat this till dish is full, ending with potatoes.

4 Pour over hot water or stock and bake in moderate oven (175°C, 350°F, Mark 4) for about 1½ hr with the lid on. A short time before serving, remove lid to let potatoes brown. Serve at once.

Pig's fry
4 persons

Pig's fry is not easily obtainable these days, but when it is, it provides an economical and nourishing dish. It consists of pig's offal which is sold as a mixture of liver, heart, sweetbreads, chitterlings, etc. and is cooked all together, either fried or in the following way:

	Metric	Imp
pig's fry washed and scalded	600 g	1½ lb
potatoes sliced	1 mg	2½ lb
water	375 ml	¾ pt
1 large boiled onion chopped		
1 tsp chopped sage leaves		
salt, pepper		

Method

1 Put half the pig's fry into the bottom of a pie-dish. Sprinkle over a thin layer of the sage, onion, salt and pepper.

2 Add a layer of sliced potatoes, then repeat layers of fry, onions and potatoes, ending in potatoes.

3 Add the water and put into a moderate oven (175°C, 350°F, Mark 4) and cook for 2½ hr. Serve hot.

SWEETBREADS

Either lambs' or calves' sweetbreads may be used. They are very delicate and easily digested, so are very suitable for invalids. There are two kinds of sweetbread, called the heart and the throat, the former being considered the better. The throat sweetbread is longer in shape and is better for dishes where the sweetbread is minced in some manner. The heart sweetbread is firmer in texture and whiter in colour and should be chosen for dishes where the sweetbread is to be used whole.

Sweetbreads should always be used very fresh, and the preliminary preparation must be undertaken directly they arrive from the butcher.

To prepare Wash the sweetbreads, then soak them in cold water for 1 hour. Rinse and **blanch** by putting them into a saucepan with water to cover; add a few drops of lemon juice to whiten them, bring slowly to the boil, cook gently for about 5 minutes, drain, put the sweetbreads into a basin of cold water and take away all the fat, veins and any membranes there may be, but do not destroy the shape. Put them between two dishes with a light weight on the top. Press until cold. They may then be used as desired.

Sweetbreads à la poulette
4 persons

	Metric	Imp
4 sweetbreads		
flour	25 g	1 oz
white stock (p. 47)	250 ml	½ pt
cream	60 ml	½ gill
butter	25 g	1 oz
1 dssp chopped parsley		
2 egg yolks		
1 blade mace		
a grate of nutmeg		
salt, pepper		

Method

1 Prepare the sweetbreads according to the directions above.

2 Melt the butter in a pan, add flour, blend well, add stock. Stir till boiling.

3 Add sweetbreads, mace and seasoning; simmer 20 min.

4 Remove sweetbreads and keep hot. Remove pan from heat.

5 Beat egg yolks with cream, stir into sauce over low heat, add parsley and nutmeg. Whisk till sauce thickens; do not let it boil.

6 Serve sweetbreads in a ring of mashed potatoes; pour sauce over and round. Serve green peas separately.

Baked sweetbreads

4 persons

	Metric	Imp
2 calves' sweetbreads prepared as on p. 138		
veal forcemeat (p. 79)	100 g	4 oz
brown gravy	375 ml	¾ pt
1 tsp chopped parsley		
1 tbsp mushroom ketchup		
1 tsp finely chopped thyme and marjoram mixed		
1 egg		
breadcrumbs		
1 lemon		
salt, pepper		

Method

1 Mix parsley, herbs, salt, pepper and breadcrumbs together and dip the prepared sweetbreads into beaten egg and then breadcrumb mixture.
2 Shape forcemeat into a shape like the sweetbreads and wrap it in kitchen foil.
3 Put sweetbreads and forcemeat on to a greased baking sheet and bake in a moderate oven (175°C, 350°F, Mark 4) for 30 to 40 min. Remove foil.

4 Heat the gravy and add mushroom ketchup and a squeeze of lemon juice to it.
5 Place sweetbreads on either side of the forcemeat on a hot dish and pour gravy round. Garnish with slices of lemon.

Fricassée of sweetbreads

4 persons

	Metric	Imp
2 calves' sweetbreads prepared as on p. 138 and sliced		
flour	25 g	1 oz
butter	25 g	1 oz
veal stock	750 ml	1½ pt
mushrooms chopped	100 g	4 oz
milk or cream	125 ml	1 gill
grated peel of ½ lemon		
salt, pepper, nutmeg		

Method

1 Melt butter in a pan, add mushrooms and cook gently for 5 min.
2 Add flour and blend well, then stock, and stir till boiling.
3 Season with salt, pepper, nutmeg; add lemon peel and sweetbreads and simmer for 30 min.
4 Add cream and stir for 1 min. without boiling.
5 Serve with slices of lemon.

TRIPE

To prepare   Tripe is the inner lining of the stomach of the cow or ox and is very easily digested, but requires careful preparation. There are various kinds of tripe, such as 'blanket', 'honeycomb', and so on, according to the part of the animal from which it is taken, but the 'blanket' and 'honeycomb' are the kinds usually offered for sale.

Tripe is usually prepared beforehand by the butcher, in which case it simply requires washing and **blanching**.

To blanch   Put the tripe into a saucepan with cold water to cover, bring to the boil and then strain. Again cover with water, or half water and half milk, and simmer gently for about 2 hours, when it may be used as desired.

If, however, the butcher has not prepared the tripe, it requires a great deal of preparation. Wash it well in tepid water, scrape with a knife, and then rinse very thoroughly. Put it into a pan with cold water to cover, bring to the boil and pour the water away. Again wash and continue this washing and **blanching** until it loses its unpleasant smell. When cold, return to the pan with fresh cold water, bring to the boil, and simmer gently for 6 or 7 hours, or until quite tender. See that the tripe is always covered with water, adding more if necessary as it boils. When cooked, put the tripe with the liquid in which it was cooked into a basin and leave until the following day, when it can be used as desired.

Fricassée of tripe
4–5 persons

	Metric	Imp
tripe cooked as above and cut into small squares	800 g	2 lb
mushrooms sliced	200 g	½ lb
margarine	40 g	1½ oz
breadcrumbs	50 g	2 oz
tomato sauce (p. 67)	125 g	1 gill
stock (white or vegetable)	500 ml	1 pt
salt, pepper		

Method

1 Melt margarine in a pan; add prepared tripe and mushrooms, and simmer very gently for 10 min.

2 Pour in enough stock to cover. Put lid on and simmer till mushrooms are tender.

3 Add tomato sauce and heat.

4 Place in a fireproof dish and add seasoning; sprinkle with breadcrumbs and brown under grill.

Note Tripe may be curried by warming the cooked tripe in curry sauce (p. 66). Serve in a border of cooked rice.

Tripe and onions
4–5 persons

	Metric	Imp
tripe prepared as on p. 139 and cut into small squares	800 g	2 lb
flour	25 g	1 oz
milk and water	500 ml	1 pt
4 onions sliced		
salt, pepper		
fried bread or toast		

Method

1 Dip the pieces of prepared tripe into flour and put in a pan with the milk and water and seasoning.

2 Bring to the boil and simmer 15 min.

3 Meanwhile, simmer sliced onions in salt water for 10 min. Strain.

4 Add onions to tripe and continue simmering for a further 15 min. Season well.

5 Serve on a hot dish with snippets of fried bread or toast.

POULTRY AND GAME

Drawing, trussing and jointing a chicken – time-table for roasting poultry and game – recipes for poultry – recipes for game

POULTRY

Poultry can be bought frozen, chilled or fresh and is usually prepared ready for the oven.

Frozen birds are always of good quality, but lack the flavour of a fresh bird, and consequently should be cooked with a good amount of seasoning, a spicy stuffing or an interesting sauce. A frozen bird must always be completely thawed before cooking. This is because bacteria will not be destroyed if the flesh is not throughly cooked and incomplete defrosting may result in the centre of the bird remaining uncooked.

A whole chicken will need 8 to 12 hours according to size to thaw out from being completely frozen. A turkey will need 2 to 3 days at room temperature, again according to size. In an emergency, a bird can be thawed by immersing it in tepid water, but this is not very satisfactory.

Chilled poultry needs about an hour to bring it to room temperature before cooking.

To choose fresh poultry see p. 26.

In the event of having to pluck, draw and truss a bird, it is always easier to do the plucking while the bird is still warm. Plunging the bird briefly into very hot water will make the cold bird easier to pluck. Pull the feathers out a few at a time, holding the skin down with the other hand to avoid tearing it. If there are any hairs or down left after plucking, these can be singed off with a taper or over a gas flame.

To draw a chicken   Cut off the head, slip the skin back from the neck, and cut off the neck close to the body leaving a flap of skin to fold over the back. Remove the windpipe and the crop, which is a little bag of skin lying close to the neck. Insert the first finger inside the neck and loosen all the inside, breaking the ligaments that can be felt with the finger. Turn the bird round, make a slit across the skin between the tail and the vent. Insert the finger at this end and loosen everything from this side. Grasp the gizzard and draw everything out. Hold the bird up to the light and see that no part of the internal organs has been left behind. The lungs must be removed also, and any soft fat. Cut away the oil bag at the back of the rump or parson's nose. Hold the bird under the tap and let cold water run through it, then wipe it both outside and in with a damp cloth. Remove the bag of stones from the gizzard and the gall bladder from the liver. Wash the neck, liver and gizzard and use them for making stock.

To truss a chicken for roasting   Cut through the skin 5 cm (2 in.) below the leg joint, bend the leg at the cut and crack the bone, then pull out the tendons, twisting the legs to make them draw out easily. There should be seven sinews. Care must be taken not to cut through these when cutting the skin, or they cannot be removed. **Scald** the piece of leg left on the chicken, and peel off the skin. If the bird is to be stuffed, insert the stuffing next, in the breast. Place the bird on its breast, pull down the flap of skin from the neck over the back, and cross the ends of the wings over this. Turn the bird over, and push the rump through the slit in the skin. Push the legs forward towards the wings. Thread the trussing needle with fine string, pass it through the right wing and the top of the leg, right through the body and catch the leg and the wing on the other side. Turn the bird over, catch the points of the wings and the skin of the neck with the needle. Tie the ends of the string together, leaving both ends at least 11–13 cm (4–5 in.) long. Bring these ends of string down and tie them round the rump of the chicken. Bring the two legs close together and tie them, making the shanks stand up.

To truss a chicken for boiling   Choose white-legged chickens for boiling, as their flesh is usually whiter than that of a chicken with black legs. Pluck and draw the bird, cut the skin round the leg at the knee joint, crack the joint, twist the shank and pull it off, bringing the sinews with it. Insert the finger in the hole made for drawing the bird, raise the skin from the flesh of the legs, then press the leg joints inside, and draw the loosened skin over them. Push the rump inside, and draw the skin of the neck over the back and cross the ends of the wings over this. Truss as for a roast chicken, but twist the string twice round the narrow end of the bird instead of tying it round the rump. Tie it tightly to prevent the legs from slipping and breaking through the skin.

To joint a whole bird Cut each leg through the skin, close to the body and then press the leg outwards till the joint cracks. A large joint will be divided again at the knuckle. With the neck of the bird towards you, cut off the pinions with kitchen scissors and cut the breast meat along the breast-bone to the wing joint which is divided and cracked like the legs. This will make one piece which, in a large bird, can be divided into two. Cut down the back from neck to vent to make two more portions.

To bone a turkey or chicken Singe the bird and remove the legs at the knee joint or drumsticks; withdraw the sinews or tendons at the same time. The bird should not be drawn. Cut through the skin down the centre of the back and raise the flesh carefully on either side until the sockets of the wings and thighs are reached. Disjoint the legs and wings from the body, when it is easy to separate the flesh from the whole body, and take out the entire carcass.

Next bone the legs. Remove as much of the wing bones as possible. Some leave the first bone in the wing. Remove all sinew and gristle and cut off any discoloured portions of the neck and tail. The bird, thus prepared, may be restored to its original form by filling the legs and wings with forcemeat and the body with the livers of two or three chickens mixed with alternate layers of sausage meat or veal forcemeat, or thin slices of bacon. It may then be sewn into shape as usual. If preferred, the skin can be cut right down after boning the bird. It is then laid skin downwards on a board and flattened out, the stuffing spread all over and the bird rolled. Tie with tape to keep it in shape.

General Time-table for Roasting Poultry and Game

Spring chicken	20–30 min.	Pigeon	20–30 min.
Medium sized chicken	45 min.	Hare	1¼–2 hr
Large chicken	1 hr	Leveret	1 hr
Capon	1¼ hr	Rabbit	1–1½ hr
Duck	¾–1 hr	Pheasant (large)	45 min.
Duckling	25–35 min.	Pheasant (small)	30 min.
Goose	15–18 min. per 450 g (1 lb)	Partridge	20–30 min.
		Grouse	30–45 min.
		Black game	¾–1 hr
Turkey, up to 4½ kg (10 lb)	20 min. per 450 g (1 lb)	Woodcock	20–25 min.
		Teal and widgeon	20–25 min.
Turkey, 4½ kg–7 kg (10–16 lb)	15 min. per 450 g (1 lb)	Wild duck	20–25 min.
		Quails	12–15 min.
Turkey, over 7 kg (16 lb)	12 min. per 450 g (1 lb)	Snipe	15–20 min.
		Plover	20–25 min.
Guinea fowl	¾–1 hr	Ptarmigan	30–35 min.

CHICKEN

Boiled chicken
4–5 persons

	Metric	Imp
1 boiling chicken		
parsley, oyster, celery or		
béchamel sauce (pp. 69, 71		
68, 64)	500 ml	1 pt
water or white stock	1 l	1 qt
1 onion		
3 sticks celery		

Method
1 Truss the bird for boiling (see p. 142). Wrap in greased paper.
2 Place it breast down in boiling salted water or stock. Boil for 3 min. Skim.
3 Add peeled onion and celery and simmer gently till bird is cooked (2–3 hr according to size).
4 Take bird out, remove paper and put on a hot dish.
5 Remove string and skewers and coat with parsley, oyster, celery or béchamel sauce. Serve more sauce separately.

Note Boiled ham, tongue or bacon usually accompanies boiled chicken. Garnish with boiled broccoli, baked or grilled tomatoes, or mushrooms.

Braised chicken
3–4 persons

	Metric	Imp
1 young chicken		
stock	500 ml	1 pt
sherry or white wine	125 ml	1 gill
mushrooms	200 g	½ lb
butter	25 g	1 oz
mushroom sauce (p. 67)	250 ml	½ pt
veal forcemeat	200 g	½ lb
veal bones and trimmings		
1 onion stuck with cloves		
1 blade mace		
1 scraped carrot		
a few slices of bacon		
bouquet garni		
salt, pepper		

Method
1 Stuff the bird with forcemeat and truss as for roasting (see p. 142).

2 Put any bones of poultry, plus veal bones or trimmings, herbs, mace, onion, carrot, sherry, stock and seasoning in a large pan.
3 Cover breast of chicken with bacon slices and place chicken on vegetables in pan. Cover with lid and simmer for 1 hr.
4 Peel and wash the mushrooms, place them in a fireproof dish and dot with butter. Season with salt and pepper.
5 Remove bird and put in oven to brown. Put mushrooms in to bake.
6 Strain stock from pan into a smaller one and boil to a glaze. Brush bird over with **glaze.**
7 Serve on a hot dish, garnish with mushrooms and watercress and serve mushroom sauce separately.

Casseroled chicken
4 persons

	Metric	Imp
4 chicken joints		
fat bacon cut in chunks	100 g	4 oz
stock or water	250 ml	½ pt
1 onion sliced		
4 peppercorns		
a piece of lemon peel		
1 bunch herbs		
salt, pepper, mace		

Method
1 Sprinkle joints with salt, pepper and a hint of mace.
2 Fry bacon in casserole, add chicken and brown lightly.
3 Add onion, stock, peppercorns, lemon peel and herbs. Cover and simmer for 1 hr.
4 Serve in the casserole.

Roast chicken
6 persons

	Metric	Imp
1 roasting chicken	2 kg	4–5 lb
stuffing (veal, chestnut or		
sausage, pp. 79, 78, 79)	200–400 g	½–1 lb
butter, margarine or dripping		
a little flour		
fat bacon slices		
salt, pepper		

Method

1 Stuff the chicken and truss for roasting (see p. 142).
2 Cover the breast with fat bacon and greased paper. Add fat.
3 Roast in a hot oven (220°C, 425°F, Mark 7) for 1–1¼ hr, **basting** frequently. Just before it is done, remove paper, **dredge** lightly with flour and **baste** with warmed butter till browned.
4 Place on a hot dish, remove all trussing string and skewers.
5 Serve brown gravy, made in the dripping tin, and bread sauce (p. 68).

Note If liked, garnish with bacon rolls or chipolata sausages.

Chicken boudins

4 persons

	Metric	Imp
raw chicken flesh minced	200 g	½ lb
white sauce	250 ml	½ pt
butter or margarine	25 g	1 oz
flour	25 g	1 oz
chicken stock or milk	60 ml	½ gill

1 egg
a little extra stock for cooking
salt, pepper

Method

1 Put the stock and butter in a pan and heat. Stir in the flour and cook, stirring rapidly till mixture forms a ball or panada in the centre of the pan. Let it cool.
2 Pound minced chicken in a mortar till smooth; add panada and beaten egg gradually. Season well and rub through sieve.
3 Roll mixture into very small sausage shapes.
4 Put them in a buttered frying pan and pour over just enough stock or water to keep them from burning. Cover with buttered paper and cook over low heat till set.
5 Dish boudins on mashed potato, and coat with a good white sauce.

Note These boudins may be made in the same manner with game, veal, rabbit, hare, pigeons, sweetbreads or poultry. Dark game should be coated with brown sauce. Some-times the boudins are cooked in the oven in a greased pan with sufficient water or stock to steam them.

Chicken à la Bourgeoise

4 persons

	Metric	Imp
1 jointed roasting chicken or 4		about
chicken joints	1 kg	2½ lb
dripping	100 g	4 oz
white stock	750 ml	1½ pt
flour	2 oz	50 g
mushrooms	200 g	½ lb

1 onion, 1 carrot, shredded
1 tbsp chopped parsley
4 tomatoes cut in quarters
salt, pepper

Method

1 Melt dripping in a pan, add onion and carrot and cook gently for 5 min., stirring all the time.
2 Add chicken joints and seasoning, and cook 5 more min., stirring continuously.
3 Stir in flour, then gradually add stock. Stir till boiling, add tomatoes and simmer for 30 min. with lid on.
4 Peel, wash and trim the mushrooms and add them to the pan with the parsley and simmer 10 more min. Check seasoning.
5 Put chicken on a hot dish, pour sauce over and garnish with mushrooms.

Entrée of chicken legs

4 persons

	Metric	Imp
4 chicken legs boned		
stock	250 ml	½ pt

4 rindless slices of streaky bacon
1 tbsp sherry
1 shallot, 1 carrot, sliced
1 bunch herbs
salt, pepper

Method

1 Place bacon at bottom of a casserole. Add herbs, shallot, carrot, stock and sherry. Place the chicken legs on top, cover with buttered paper and lid, and cook in a fairly hot oven (205°C, 400°F, Mark 6) for 30 min.

2 Remove legs and press under a weight till cold.

3 Wrap each leg in a slice of bacon, season and wrap in kitchen foil. Bake for 15 min.

4 Serve with brown sauce made from the liquor in which the chicken was braised.

Fricassée of chicken   *6 persons*

	Metric	Imp
1 boiling chicken jointed and skinned		
butter or margarine	50 g	2 oz
flour	25 g	1 oz
milk	125 ml	1 gill
1 peeled onion stuck with cloves		
1 sprig parsley		
1 bay leaf		
½ blade mace		
1 egg yolk		
salt, pepper		

Method

1 Blanch chicken joints in boiling water for 2 or 3 min; remove from water and rinse under cold tap.

2 Put carcass, giblets, herbs and seasoning into the water used for **blanching** and simmer for ¾ hr.

3 Melt butter in pan, add flour and blend well, then 250 ml (½ pt) of the strained stock. Stir till boiling.

4 Add pieces of chicken and simmer for ¾ hr.

5 Remove pieces of chicken and arrange in a line on a hot dish and keep hot.

6 Beat up yolk of egg with milk, stir into sauce. Re-heat, season and pour over chicken. Garnish with a little parsley.

Grilled chicken or spatchcock   *2–3 persons*

	Metric	Imp
1 spring chicken	800 g	2 lb
melted butter or olive oil	75 g	3 oz
brown or tomato sauce (pp. 64, 67)		
breadcrumbs		
1 lemon		
salt, pepper		
watercress		

Method

1 Split the bird down the back, not cutting right through.

2 Flatten it, skewer it open and season with salt and pepper.

3 Brush on both sides with melted butter or oil and sprinkle with breadcrumbs.

4 Grill for 7 min., skin side uppermost, taking care not to have the chicken too close to the heat. Add more butter halfway through.

5 Turn and brush again with melted butter and grill a further 7 min.

6 Turn once again, brush with butter and grill the skin side for a final 5 min. till the chicken is crisp and golden.

7 Serve very hot on a good sized croûte of fried bread. Garnish with watercress and cut lemon. Hand brown or tomato sauce.

Note Any young game bird can be cooked in this manner, but it is not a suitable way of cooking old birds.

DUCK

To truss a duck   Ducks are trussed in the same manner as chickens (p. 142) except that the feet must be left on and turned close to the legs, first **scalding** them and removing the skin.

Roast duck   *3–4 persons*

Ducks should always hang for one day and even longer if the weather is cold enough to allow it.

	Metric	Imp
1 duck	1300–1600 g	3½–4 lb
sage and onion stuffing (p. 78)	200 g	½ lb
butter	1·25 g	½ oz
brown sauce or gravy	250 ml	½ pt
dripping		
flour		
watercress		

Method

1 Place the stuffing in the lower end of the bird, truss the duck as above.

2 Cover the breast with greased paper and place bird in a greased baking tin with the dripping and roast in a moderately hot oven (175°C, 350°F, Mark 7) 40 to 50 min., **basting** well.

3 Remove paper, **dredge** the breast with flour and pour over a little liquid butter to brown breast.

4 Put duck on a hot dish, remove trussing string and skewers, and hand a brown sauce made from the giblets and flavoured with orange juice, or a clear brown gravy. Garnish with watercress.

Green peas, and potato straws or chips, form a good accompaniment to roast duck. Other stuffings may be used in place of sage and onion, such as apple, or chestnut (p. 78). Apple, cranberry and tomato sauce (pp. 68, 73, 67) may be handed also. Roast duck may be jointed after cooking, and dished neatly, garnished with watercress and quarters of orange.

Grilled duckling   *4 persons*

	Metric	Imp
1 duckling		
butter	50 g	2 oz
orange sauce (p. 69)	250 ml	½ pt
salt, pepper		
watercress		

Method

1 Cut duckling down the back, open out, flatten it well and skewer it open.

2 Sprinkle with salt and pepper, brush with melted butter and bake in a fairly hot oven (205°C, 400°F, Mark 6) for 10 min.

3 Remove from the oven, brush with more butter and grill for about 10 min., turning several times, until it is cooked.

4 Cut into 4 joints and serve on a large croûte of fried bread. Pour orange sauce round and garnish with watercress.

Duck with young turnips   *4 persons*

	Metric	Imp
1 duckling jointed		
butter	50 g	2 oz
young turnips peeled	400 g	1 lb
stock	125 ml	1 gill
white wine	125 ml	1 gill
2 tsp chopped parsley		
1 small onion chopped finely		
a little thyme		
salt, pepper		

Method

1 Melt half the butter in a pan and brown duck and onion together.

2 Add wine and stock, seasoning and herbs and simmer with the lid on for 50–60 min.

3 Meanwhile, boil turnips in salted water till just tender, then drain and fry lightly in remaining butter.

4 Dish duck on a hot plate with turnips round, sprinkle with chopped parsley and pour sauce over.

Salmis of duck

4 persons

	Metric	Imp
1 duck trussed for roasting	1400 g	about 3½ lb
diced bacon	75 g	3 oz
whole bacon rashers	75 g	3 oz
stock	375 ml	¾ pt
dripping	50 g	2 oz
flour	25 g	1 oz
1 shallot sliced		
1 bunch herbs		
salt, pepper		

Method

1 Melt 25 g (1 oz) of dripping in a baking tin, add diced bacon and bake in moderate oven (175°C, 350°F, Mark 4) till crisp.

2 Add the shallot, place the duck on top and cook in a moderate oven for 20 min.

3 Untruss the duck and joint it.

4 Melt remainder of dripping in a pan, add flour and brown, gradually add stock, bring to the boil and skim.

5 Stir the sauce till boiling, season well, add joints of duck and herbs and simmer for 30 min.

6 Skim off all fat; remove herbs. Bake rest of bacon in rolls for garnish.

7 Serve duck on a large croûte of fried bread, pour sauce round and garnish with rolls of fried bacon and watercress.

Note Wild duck may be cooked in the same manner, but a little claret and 2 or 3 cloves should be added to the sauce. Just before serving, squeeze in the juice of half a lemon. Widgeon and teal may also be cooked in the same manner, adding the juice of an orange to the sauce, and, if liked, some mushroom trimmings or chopped mushrooms.

GOOSE

To draw and truss a goose Draw and truss it in the same way as a chicken (p. 142), except that the wings are not crossed over at the back and the legs are stuck close down by the side of the body.

Roast goose

6–8 persons

	Metric	Imp
1 goose	4½ kg	10 lb
sage and onion stuffing (p. 78)	200 g	½ lb
dripping	50 g	2 oz
butter	25 g	1 oz
1 tbsp flour		
apple sauce (p. 68)		

Method

1 Truss the goose (see p. 142). Fill with stuffing and fasten at both ends by tying the skin of the neck over the back of the bird, and passing the rump through the slit made in the skin.

2 Cover the breast with greased paper, bake in a hot oven (220°C, 425°F, Mark 7) for the first ¼ hr, then lessen the heat of the oven to 190°C (375°F, Mark 5) and cook for about 2 hr. **Baste** often with dripping.

3 A short time before serving, remove paper, **dredge** the breast with flour and **baste** with a little butter till brown.

4 Serve on a hot dish; remove all **basting** string and skewers, pour a little gravy round and hand more in a tureen. Serve apple sauce separately.

GUINEA FOWL

Guinea fowls are often served in place of game when the latter is out of season. When a guinea fowl is roasted plain, it is trussed like a turkey (p. 142); when it is **larded**, it is trussed like a chicken (p. 142). Cook it according to any recipe for roast turkey or pheasant, for ¾–1 hr.

If roasted, hand bread, celery or oyster sauce (pp. 68, 68, 71) and brown gravy. Garnish with watercress.

PIGEONS

To truss pigeons   A pigeon should be carefully cleaned, drawn, and trussed like a chicken (p. 142), washed thoroughly and dried with a cloth. Pigeons should not be kept long, as they lose their flavour. Draw them directly they are killed, and cut off the toes at their first joint. Pigeons may be plainly roasted with 25 g (1 oz) butter and seasoning placed inside the bodies of the birds. Hand brown gravy and bread sauce (p. 68). Pigeons may also be stuffed with liver farce (p. 79) to which the liver of the birds have been added. A little port may be added to the gravy or sauce, if desired. Pigeons may also be stewed or braised in a casserole.

TURKEY

Directions for choosing a turkey will be found on p. 26. Break the leg bones close to the feet, cut through the skin 5 cm (2 in.) below the leg bone, but on no account cut through the tendons. Bend the leg at the joint, and cut the bone. Hang the turkey on a hook, and then pull and twist the leg to get the tendons out. The tendons of a turkey leg are more difficult to draw than those of a chicken, therefore by hanging the bird on a hook it is easier to apply more power when pulling. For drawing, trussing and preparing the bird, see directions for drawing a chicken (p. 142).

Roast turkey   *Allow 300 g (¾ lb) per person*

Ideally, turkey for roasting should be **larded** to counteract the dryness of the flesh of the bird. Slices (lardons) of fat bacon each about ½ cm (¼ in.) thick and 7 cm (3 in.) long are cut from a piece of fat bacon and one at a time threaded into the end of a larding needle (obtainable from good kitchen stores).

Method
1 Draw the lardons through the flesh of the bird so that both ends are left sticking out quite close to each other. In cooking, the ends of the lardons melt away adding to the flavour of the bird.
2 Stuff the breast with chestnut stuffing (p. 78) and the cavity with forcemeat, or place a little butter in the cavity and cook the stuffing in a separate dish.
3 Wrap the bird in foil and place in a hot oven (220°C, 425°F, Mark 7) for ¼ hr then gradually lessen the heat of the oven to 175°C (350°F, Mark 4). See roasting time-table on p. 143 for cooking time.
4 Half an hour before it is due to finish cooking, remove the foil, **dredge** the breast with flour, then with a little butter to froth and brown it.

5 Serve turkey on a hot dish, remove all strings and skewers.
6 Make gravy in dripping tin as for roast beef (p. 114), pour a little round bird and serve rest in sauce boat.
7 Garnish with forcemeat balls and fried sausages, and hand bread sauce and cranberry jelly or sauce. Chestnut, celery or mushroom sauce may be served with turkey instead of gravy.

Braised turkey wings   *2 persons*

	Metric	Imp
wings of a turkey		
veal or nut forcemeat		
(pp. 79, 78)	200 g	½ lb
tomato sauce (p. 67)	250 ml	½ pt
salt, pepper		
creamed spinach		
straw potatoes		

Method
1 Bone wings of turkey and stuff with forcemeat.
2 Season and wrap in greased foil.
3 Bake in fairly hot oven (205°C, 400°F, Mark 6) for 15–20 min.

4 Serve with creamed spinach and potato straws, and hand tomato sauce.

Note Chicken wings may be cooked in the same manner.

GAME

GROUSE

Grouse is in season from August 12 to December 10. Young birds can be recognized by their downy breast feathers and are suitable for roasting or grilling. Older birds should be casseroled. Hang them for three to six days by the legs before plucking and drawing them.

Roast grouse

1–2 persons

Pluck and draw the bird according to the directions for a chicken (p. 142), wipe it inside and out with a damp cloth. Mix a piece of butter the size of a walnut with salt, pepper and lemon juice, and put it inside the bird with the liver. Then truss as for a roast chicken, using, however, a finer trussing needle and fine string. Tie a piece of fat bacon over the breast and roast the bird in a hot oven (220°C, 425°F, Mark 7). **Baste** it often with dripping, bacon fat or butter. A few minutes before serving, remove the slice of bacon and **dredge** (i.e. sprinkle lightly) the breast with flour, **baste** it with a little oiled butter and brown. A young bird takes from 25 to 30 minutes.

To dish Put the grouse on a hot dish, remove the trussing strings and skewers. Make gravy in the dripping tin as for roast beef (p. 114), pour a very little round, and garnish with watercress. Hand the rest of the gravy in a tureen. Chip potatoes, breadcrumbs and a green salad should accompany grouse.

In Scotland grouse are often wrapped in slices of fat bacon and washed sprigs of fresh heather before roasting them.

Blackcock is roasted in the same manner.

Salmis of grouse

4 persons

	Metric	Imp
2 grouse prepared and trussed as for roasting		
butter or dripping	50 g	2 oz
mushrooms sliced	200 g	½ lb
brown sauce (p 64)	250 ml	½ pt
1 tbsp sherry or white wine		
1 tbsp tomato purée		
1 bunch herbs		
12 stoned olives		
1 large onion sliced		
a croûte of fried bread		
salt, pepper, cayenne		

Method

1 Put grouse in a baking tin, dot well with butter or dripping and bake in a hot oven (220°C, 425°F, Mark 7) for 10 min., **basting** frequently.

2 Remove from oven, untruss and joint them.

3 Cut up remaining carcasses, and fry in fat left from roasting. Then place carcasses, wine, sauce, herbs and tomato purée in a pan and bring to the boil.

4 Skim, then simmer for 10 min. Strain into a clean pan and season.

5 Add joints of grouse, onion, mushrooms and olives. Simmer for 20 min.

6 Place fried bread in centre of a hot dish, arrange pieces of grouse on it and pour sauce over.

Note Any game may be cooked in this manner.

HARE

Hare is a very solid meat and an adult hare will serve up to 10 people. A leveret, or young hare, will serve about 6. Hares must be hung head down for 8 to 10 days. They are then drawn and skinned, taking great care to reserve the blood which has collected under a membrane by the ribs. This blood is used in jugged hare and for the gravy of roast hare. Never wash a hare after skinning, only wipe it.

To joint a hare Cut off the hind legs, then the front legs, and cut all in two. The back can be cut into 6 pieces.

To truss a hare for roasting Follow the directions for trussing a rabbit (p. 155), but curl up the tail and fasten it to the back with a small skewer.

Roast hare

6–8 persons

	Metric	Imp
1 hare		
veal stuffing well seasoned		
(p. 79)	200 g	½ lb
butter		
milk		
flour		
gravy		
1 glass port wine		
redcurrant jelly	fat bacon	
salt, pepper	1 lemon	

Method

1 After the hare is prepared, wipe it dry with a clean cloth, fill the inside with well-seasoned veal stuffing, and sew it up.
2 Truss as directed for rabbit (p. 155).
3 Tie some pieces of fat bacon over the body and cover it, head and all, with greased paper and roast it in a hot oven (220°C, 425°F, Mark 7) for 1½–2 hr.
4 **Baste** well, with milk at first, and later with butter or dripping.
5 When nearly cooked remove the paper and bacon, **dredge** a little flour over the hare, and **baste** it well with butter to make it froth and brown.
6 Serve the hare on a hot dish, remove all string and trussing skewers. Make some gravy thickened with flour in the dripping tin, add the port wine and redcurrant jelly and boil up. Season and strain a little of the sauce round the hare and hand the remainder in a sauce boat. Garnish the dish with rolls of fried bacon and cut lemon, and serve redcurrant, rowanberry or gooseberry jelly.

Note Hare is sometimes **basted** with a thin batter made with 50 g (2 oz) of flour, 1 tbsp salad oil and 500 ml (1 pt) of milk.
     A **leveret** is trussed and roasted like a hare, but is more usually served without stuffing. It may be **larded**, if desired. The saddle (back and sides of the hare) is often stuffed, **larded** and roasted or braised, the remainder of the hare being jugged.

Jugged hare

8–10 persons

	Metric	Imp
1 hare cut into pieces		
streaky bacon cut in strips		
5 cm (2 in.) long	100 g	4 oz
brown stock	1 l	1 qt
Espagnole sauce (p. 65)	500 ml	1 pt
dripping	50 g	2 oz
wine vinegar	125 ml	1 gill
claret or port	125 ml	1 gill
2 onions, 2 carrots, shredded		
2 leeks, ½ head celery, shredded		
24 button onions peeled		
12 forcemeat balls		
1 tbsp redcurrant jelly		
beurre manié (p. 64)		
1 bunch herbs		
salt, pepper		

Method

1 Put bacon in a pan and fry a little, add shredded vegetables and herbs and brown, add vinegar and simmer till **reduced** to half.
2 Add stock, wine and joints of hare, salt and pepper to taste. Bring to the boil, stirring occasionally, then simmer with lid on for 2 hr.

3 Meanwhile, melt dripping in a pan and fry button onions till golden brown. Remove and simmer them gently in Espagnole sauce till sauce is **reduced** to a **glaze.**

4 Fry forcemeat balls till brown and put aside.

5 When hare is cooked, strain off the liquor into a clean pan, keeping hare and bacon pieces warm.

6 Reduce sauce by boiling. Skim well. Stir in **beurre manié** to thicken to a thin cream, boil for a minute then draw aside.

7 If blood is to be used, add several spoonfuls of gravy to the blood, mix well, then pour back into gravy.

8 Add redcurrant jelly, stir well and add button onions and forcemeat balls to warm in gravy.

9 Serve hare on a hot dish and pour sauce over, arranging onions and forcemeat balls round meat. Garnish with half-moons of fried bread.

Note Rabbit may be jugged in the same way, leaving out the wine if desired.

Leveret chasseur

6 persons

	Metric	Imp
1 leveret cut in pieces		
brown stock	500 ml	1 pt
small mushrooms	200 g	8 oz
dripping	50 g	2 oz
1 tbsp finely chopped shallot		
1 tbsp chopped parsley		
1 tbsp glaze (p. 62)		
juice of ½ lemon		
salt, pepper, nutmeg		
triangles of fried bread		

Method

1 Melt dripping, fry leveret till brown all over.

2 Add shallot and parsley and simmer with a lid on for 10 min.

3 Drain fat off. Add stock, mushrooms, glaze, salt, pepper and nutmeg to taste. Cover pan and simmer for ½ hr.

4 Add lemon juice.

5 Serve leveret on a hot dish, strain sauce over and garnish with mushrooms and pieces of fried bread.

Note Rabbit may be cooked in the same manner.

PARTRIDGE

Partridge is in season from September 1 to February 1. Only young birds should be roasted, the older ones may be casseroled or braised. A young bird is distinguished by its pointed wing feathers; in the older bird this is rounded and the beak will be yellow and the legs dark. Hang partridge for about 7 days.

Roast partridge

2–3 persons

Partridge is trussed, roasted and served according to the directions for roast grouse (p. 150). Grilled mushrooms make a good accompaniment to partridges. Young partridges may be dished on a croûte of fried bread, if desired.

Fillets of partridge

4 persons

	Metric	Imp
2 partridges		
2 egg yolks		
rather stiff Espagnole sauce		
(p. 65)	60 ml	½ gill
panada (p. 79)	50 g	2 oz
boiled rice	100 g	4 oz
tomato sauce (p. 67)	250 ml	½ pt

1 egg and breadcrumbs for frying
frying fat
salt, pepper

Method

1 Remove breasts from the birds. Take off skin and flatten by beating with the flat of a large knife.

2 Take off the meat from legs and wings, mince and pound in a mortar, add egg yolks and Espagnole sauce, season and rub through a sieve.

3 Spread this forcemeat over each fillet of partridge; dip in egg and breadcrumbs.

4 Heat some fat in a deep pan; when a faint blue smoke rises, fry fillets pale brown, lowering the temperature after immersion.

5 Drain well on paper.

6 Mix boiled rice and tomato sauce; serve on centre of a hot dish and place fillets round.

Partridge with cabbage

4 persons

	Metric	Imp
2 partridges cut in half		
butter	50 g	2 oz
bacon cut in strips	100 g	4 oz
brown stock	250 ml	½ pt
brown sauce (p. 64)	250 ml	½ pt
pork sausages	250 g	½ lb
1 medium hard cabbage		
1 carrot, 1 onion, sliced		
1 bunch herbs		
salt, pepper, nutmeg		

Method

1 Trim cabbage and cut in quarters. Cook in boiling, salted water for 5 min., strain and press out water.

2 Melt butter in a casserole and brown partridges slowly. Remove from casserole.

3 Brown onions and carrots lightly and remove from casserole.

4 Line casserole with bacon slices, lay on half the cabbage, the onion and carrot, sprinkle with salt, pepper and a little nutmeg, then put in the partridge halves topped with the rest of the cabbage. Pour the stock over, add the herbs, cover tightly and simmer gently over low heat or in the oven (130°C, 275°F, Mark 1) till partridges are cooked, about 1½ hr.

5 Add sausages and simmer a further ½ hr.

6 Serve cabbage, onion and carrots on a hot dish with the partridge on top and surrounded by the bacon strips and sausages cut in pieces. Hand brown sauce separately.

Note If preferred, the sausages may be fried separately and placed round the partridge, cut in neat pieces.

Partridge hot-pot

4 persons

	Metric	Imp
2 partridges boned and cut into neat joints		
stock (any kind)	125 ml	1 gill
rindless bacon rashers	200 g	8 oz
calf's liver sliced	100 g	4 oz
butter	25 g	1 oz
potatoes peeled and sliced thinly	200 g	8 oz
6 oysters with beards removed		
1 shallot chopped		
browned breadcrumbs		
salt, pepper, cayenne		

Method

1 Rub a casserole with butter and put in a layer of partridge covered with a layer of bacon, liver, 2 or 3 oysters, shallots, potatoes and seasoning.

2 Repeat these layers till all ingredients are used up, reserving enough potatoes to cover top completely.

3 Before putting on last potatoes, add stock, then cover with potatoes. Dot with butter, sprinkle with breadcrumbs.

4 Cover with greased paper, put on lid and bake in a moderate oven (175°C, 350°F, Mark 4) for 2 hr.

5 Serve in the casserole.

Salmis of partridge

4 persons

	Metric	Imp
2 young partridges		
stock (any kind)	125 ml	¼ pt
red wine	125 ml	¼ pt
button mushrooms	100 g	4 oz
flour	10 g	½ oz
butter	50 g	2 oz
1 tsp chopped thyme and parsley		
1 tbsp finely chopped shallots		
2 slices fat bacon		
juice of ½ lemon		
salt, pepper		
croûtes of fried bread		

Method

1 Draw the partridges, replace the heart and liver and truss for roasting.

2 Cover breasts with bacon and bake in a fairly hot oven (205°C, 400°F, Mark 6) for about 15 min.

3 Meanwhile melt butter in a pan, soften shallots, stir in flour, cook for 2 min., stirring. Add wine and stock, herbs and seasoning and simmer with lid on for 10 min.

4 Cook mushrooms for 5 min. in a little water and the lemon juice.

5 Carve the breasts from the partridges and place in a pan with the drained mushrooms.

6 Pound the remains of the partridges, including heart and liver and add to stock with mushroom liquor. Simmer 3 min.

7 Strain over partridge breasts and mushrooms and reheat these gently without boiling.

8 Serve partridge breasts on croûtes on a hot dish and pour sauce over.

PHEASANT

Pheasant is in season from October to February. A cock bird will feed about 4 people, a hen is usually smaller but more succulent. Pheasant should be hung by the neck for about a week before drawing and plucking.

Roast pheasant is trussed, roasted and served according to the directions for roast fowl (p. 142). The flesh of pheasant is rather dry, so the bird needs to be covered liberally with bacon and **basted** frequently with butter or oil.

When plucking a pheasant, it is customary to reserve the best of the tail feathers for garnish, and when the bird is dished, to put the tail feathers in place.

Roast pheasant may be served with bread sauce, clear gravy, potato crisps, fried breadcrumbs, redcurrant jelly and forcemeat balls.

Roast for about ¾ hr. in a hot oven (220°C, 425°F, Mark 7).

Casseroled pheasant

4 persons

	Metric	Imp
1 pheasant jointed		
butter	50 g	2 oz
stock (any kind)	250 ml	½ pt
white wine	125 ml	¼ pt
flour	50 g	2 oz
mushrooms, sliced	100 g	4 oz
juice and peel of 1 orange		
salt, pepper		

Method

1 Melt butter in a pan and fry pheasant gently on both sides till golden brown. Take out pieces and put in casserole.

2 Fry mushrooms gently for 5 min., add to casserole.

3 Add flour to fat, stir and cook for 3 min., add stock, wine and orange juice slowly, stirring till it thickens. Season.

4 Pour over pheasant, cover casserole and put in moderate oven (175°C, 350°F, Mark 4) for about 1½ hr.

5 Meanwhile, remove pith from skin of orange, cut in small strips and simmer in water till soft. Drain.

6 Serve pheasant in casserole with orange strips sprinkled over.

PTARMIGAN

Ptarmigan is in season from August 12 to December 12. It is one of the smallest of the grouse tribe and is found in mountainous districts. The plumage turns white in winter, hence ptarmigan are often called 'white grouse'. They are imported from Russia and Norway in large quantities. The flesh of the older birds has a bitter flavour. They are trussed, roasted and served like grouse (p. 150).

QUAILS

Quails are members of the partridge family. They are sometimes raised on farms and sold direct for eating.

To truss a quail

A quail must be plucked, singed and drawn from the neck end. The droppings or trail may be left in if liked. Remove the head and neck and cut off the wings at the first joint. Truss like a fowl.

Roast quail

4 persons

4 quails
bacon
a little gravy
butter
vine leaves
fried bread or toast
watercress
fried breadcrumbs

Method

1 Pluck, draw and truss the birds, cover the breasts with vine leaves, and wrap each in a slice of fat bacon.

2 Roast them for 12 or 15 min. in a hot oven (220°C, 425°F, Mark 7), **basting** constantly with butter.

3 Take up the quails, remove the trussing strings, but not the bacon and vine leaves. Dish each bird on a croûte of fried bread or toast. Garnish with watercress, and hand good gravy and fried breadcrumbs.

RABBIT

To joint a rabbit

Chop off the legs and cut the 'wings' away from the ribs. Cut the body straight across into three sections. Remove the head and neck and use these for stock.

To truss a rabbit for roasting

Wash and wipe the rabbit dry with a cloth, stuff it with forcemeat and sew it up. Bend the hind legs forwards and the forelegs backwards, cutting the sinews to enable the legs to lie close to the body. Fix them in place with a trussing needle and string or with skewers. Raise the head and skewer it into position by passing a skewer through the mouth and down the back between the shoulders. **Dredge** the rabbit with flour and tie some slices of fat bacon over the back.

Roast rabbit

5 persons

	Metric	Imp
1 rabbit	1¼ kg	about 2½ lb
veal forcemeat (p. 79)	100 g	4 oz
fat bacon rashers	100 g	4 oz
dripping or butter	50 g	2 oz
brown gravy	500 ml	1 pt
1 tbsp flour		
redcurrant jelly		
salt, pepper		

Method

1 Stuff rabbit with forcemeat, sew it up and truss it as directed above.

2 **Dredge** it with flour, pepper and salt. Tie bacon over the back.

3 Roast in a fairly hot oven (205°C, 400°F, Mark 6) for 50 min., **basting** frequently with dripping or butter.

4 Remove bacon and let rabbit brown for a further 10 min.

5 Put on a hot dish. Remove all thread and skewers. Pour a very little brown gravy round and hand more in a tureen. Garnish with forcemeat balls or cut lemon; serve redcurrant jelly separately.

Note If desired, the body of the rabbit may be lined with sausage meat and then with veal forcemeat; sometimes bread sauce is served with roast rabbit.

Fricassée of rabbit

4–5 persons

	Metric	Imp
1 rabbit jointed and soaked in cold water for 15 min.		
butter or dripping	25 g	1 oz
rice or pearl barley	50 g	2 oz
flour	25 g	1 oz
stock (any kind)	250 ml	½ pt
streaky bacon cut in strips	75 g	3 oz
12 button onions peeled		
salt, pepper		
parsley		

Method

1 Melt fat in a pan or casserole, brown bacon and onions lightly in it, then remove from pan.
2 Put in rabbit joints and brown.
3 Add flour and brown, add the stock gradually, stirring till boiling.
4 Season well, add onions and bacon. Cover and bring to the boil.
5 Add barley and simmer 1 hr. If rice is used, simmer rabbit first for ½ hr, then add rice and simmer a further ½ hr.
6 When tender, dish rabbit in a circle on a hot dish, strain gravy round and over. Fill centre with rice, onions and bacon. Garnish with sprays of parsley.

Note If barley is soaked overnight, it cooks more quickly.

Rabbit à la poulette

5 persons

Soak rabbit overnight in vinegar and water

	Metric	Imp
1 rabbit jointed	1¼ kg	about 2½ lb
vinegar	125 ml	1 gill
butter	25 g	1 oz
white stock or milk and water	500 ml	1 pt
flour	25 g	1 oz
½ head celery cut in pieces		

1 carrot sliced
1 bunch herbs
3 onions stuck with cloves
1 small tin mushrooms
2 egg yolks
salt, pepper
croûtons of fried bread

Method

1 Dry rabbit joints which have soaked overnight. Put in pan with onions, celery, carrot, herbs, vinegar and water to cover. Season, put on lid and simmer for 1 hr.
2 Melt butter, stir in flour and make a sauce with the white stock or milk and water, stirring continuously till it thickens.
3 Remove from heat, add mushrooms and beaten egg yolks and stir well.
4 Return to very low heat, stir continuously till yolks thicken. Do not let mixture boil. Season.
5 Dish rabbit pieces on a hot dish and pour sauce over. Garnish with **croûtons** of fried bread.

Rabbit à la provençale

5 persons

Soak rabbit overnight in vinegar and water

	Metric	Imp
1 rabbit cut in small pieces	1 kg	2½ lb
stock (any kind)	500 ml	1 pt
olive oil	125 ml	1 gill
tomato sauce (p. 67)	250 ml	½ pt
1 tbsp chopped parsley		
1 clove garlic crushed		
6 tomatoes skinned		
salt, pepper		

Method

1 Dry rabbit pieces.
2 Heat oil in a large saucepan, add rabbit and fry brown all over.
3 Drain off oil, add stock, tomato sauce, garlic and tomatoes. Season with salt and pepper. Cover and simmer for ½ hr.
4 Serve rabbit on a hot dish, pour sauce over and garnish with chopped parsley.

TEAL AND WIDGEON

Pluck, truss and roast according to the directions for Wild Duck (p. 157).

WOODCOCK AND SNIPE

Woodcock is in season from October 1 to January 31 in England, and in Scotland from September 1 to January 31. It is best eaten after hanging for 2 days.

Snipe is in season from August 12 to January 31. It can be eaten hung or unhung.

To truss woodcock and snipe

Pluck and wipe the outside of the birds very clean. Do not draw them, but remove the gizzards. Skin the heads and necks, but leave them on. Remove the eyes. Twist the joints of the legs to enable the feet to be brought back upon the thighs. Press the legs and wings together, draw the heads round and run the beak through the wings and legs. Tie a string round the legs and breast and pass it round the head and tip of the bill.

Roast woodcock or snipe

1 bird per person
butter
toast
fat
bacon
lemon
watercress

Method

1 Pluck and truss the birds, brush each over with oiled butter and place a piece of fat bacon over the breast.
2 Place them on a baking tin in a fairly hot oven (205°C, 400°F, Mark 6) and cook from 15 to 20 min. **Baste** often.

3 Put some toast buttered on both sides under the birds to catch the droppings or trail.
4 Remove the bacon a few minutes before serving, flour the birds, **baste** them with butter and brown them.
5 Dish each bird on a piece of toast, remove all strings, garnish with watercress and cut lemon, and serve gravy made in the roasting tin.

Note Snipe should never be over-roasted and must be served very hot. The trails must always be preserved and spread on the toast.

WILD DUCK

Wild duck is in season from September 1 to January 31. It can have a fishy taste and to neutralize this, a raw carrot placed inside before trussing will help absorb the flavour.

To truss wild duck

Prepare and truss the birds in the same way as fowls (p. 142), except that the feet are left on and twisted backwards close to the thighs.

Roast wild ducks

	Metric	Imp
2 wild ducks		
brown sauce of bigarade		
sauce (pp. 64, 69)	250 ml	½ pt
watercress		

4–5 persons

butter
1 lemon
1 orange
flour
orange salad

Method

1 Prepare, truss and cook the wild ducks in the same way as fowls (p. 142).
2 Put the birds on to a hot dish, garnish with watercress and cut lemon. Hand a brown sauce to which strained juice of an orange has been added, or hand bigarade sauce and orange salad.

Note Wild duck may be braised, jointed and served on a large croûte of fried bread, coated with bigarade sauce and garnished with orange sections.

VENISON ·

There are three kinds of venison in Great Britain – the red deer, the fallow deer, and the roebuck deer – the latter peculiar to Scotland as the red deer now is to Ireland. The flesh of the fallow deer is the best. Venison should be dark, finely grained, and firm, with a good coating of fat. It requires to be well hung in a cold dry larder. The finest parts of venison for roasting are the haunch and saddle; the loin and neck also roast well. The shoulder and breast are better for ragoûts or stews. Chops are cut from the loin or neck. Buck venison is superior in quality to doe and is in season from the end of July to the end of February, while doe is in season from the end of October to the end of February, in England and Wales; whereas in Scotland the dates vary according to the type of deer.

Roast haunch of venison

10–18 persons

	Metric	Imp
1 haunch of venison		
butter or dripping	50 g	2 oz
brown sauce (p. 64)	250 ml	½ pt
flour and water paste		
redcurrant, cranberry or rowanberry jelly		
parsley or watercress		

Method

1 Choose a moderate-sized haunch, trim off the chine bone and the end of the knuckle.
2 Wipe the meat over with a damp cloth, dry with a clean cloth, then brush it over with melted butter or dripping and wrap it in a sheet of greased paper.
3 Over this, place a paste of flour and water and cover the paste with another sheet of greased paper. Great care is required when cooking venison, as the fat burns very easily before the lean is ready, and the fat of venison is considered a great delicacy; also the fat gets cold very quickly, therefore the joint must be dished as soon as possible after cooking, and it is advisable to use a hot water dish when serving venison.
4 Roast the venison in a hot oven (220°C, 425°F, Mark 7), judging the time by the weight (20 min. to 450 g (1 lb) and 20 min. over); **baste** often.
5 About 20 min. before it is cooked, remove the paste and paper, **dredge** the meat with flour and **baste** it with a little butter to froth it, and allow it to brown.
6 Put the venison on a hot water dish, if possible, or on a very hot dish and hand brown sauce flavoured with claret or port, and redcurrant, cranberry or rowanberry jelly. Garnish the venison with parsley or watercress.

Note Green salad very often accompanies venison. French beans also make a good accompaniment to this dish. Saddle and neck of venison are roasted in the same manner. The saddle may be **larded**, if desired.

DISHES USING COOKED MEAT, POULTRY AND GAME; CURRIES

Entrées – family dishes – curries

Cooked meat, poultry and game may be used for making simple, homely dishes such as hash and cottage pie, or for more sophisticated ones that will provide a course for a formal menu. This course used to be, and often still is, called an entrée and precedes the main course. Entrées may be hot or cold and are generally light. They may consist of dishes such as soufflés, vol-au-vents, rissoles, croquettes, fritters and so on, and are made of cooked or uncooked meat, game or poultry. Recipes for entrées using uncooked meat, poultry or game will be found in the section concerned with the main ingredient.

Cold entrées are usually elaborate and artistically decorated; these are dealt with in the section on buffet dishes.

Sauces form an important part of entrées as nearly all are served with a sauce of some kind.

Quenelles, fritters, bouchées, vol-au-vents, crêpes, cassolettes, croustades, scallops, coquilles, croquettes, cutlets and rissoles are all suitable for light entrées.

Quenelles are pounded meats mixed with a panada.

Bouchées and vol-au-vents are usually made of small puff pastry cases, filled with various savoury preparations of fish, meat, poultry or game, called salpicon, a bouchée being smaller than a vol-au-vent.

A boudin is usually a mixture something like a quenelle, called a farce, made of fish, meat or poultry, which is generally steamed or poached and served with sauce.

Crêpes or pancakes can be filled with any savoury meat, poultry or game mixtures.

Cassolettes or croustades are baked or fried pastry, bread, potato or fried batter shapes filled with a salpicon of fish, meat, poultry or game.

Scallops or coquilles are usually small shells of silver, china or the natural scallop shell, filled with minced meat, poultry or game mixed with sauce.

Croquettes, cutlets and rissoles are excellent methods of using up cooked meat, poultry, game, ham or tongue, or a mixture of two kinds. The mixture may be kept quite plain or may be made richer in flavour according to the various ingredients employed. The plain mixture can be made from any cooked beef, mutton, kidney, liver, veal, poultry or game with the addition of about half the quantity of meat in breadcrumbs, mashed potatoes, rice or cooked macaroni, with sufficient stiff, thick white or brown sauce to **bind**, with or without eggs, according to the richness desired.

Plain rissoles or croquettes are usually flavoured with chopped parsley or chopped herbs and a suspicion of chopped onion; more elaborate ones with chopped cooked mushrooms, shallots, chives and sometimes hard-boiled eggs. Cream may also be added for a very rich mixture, and a pinch of powdered mace or nutmeg enhances the flavour for those who like these spices.

Croquettes are usually rolled into balls or cork shapes, cutlets are pear-shaped, and rissoles are generally a savoury mixture enclosed in a thin pastry covering. These are brushed over with egg, dipped in breadcrumbs or crushed vermicelli and fried in hot fat.

ENTRÉES

Potato bouchées

4 persons

	Metric	Imp
mashed potatoes (p. 196)	400 g	1 lb
cooked game, chicken or		
veal, minced	200 g	½ lb
béchamel sauce (p. 64)	375 ml	¾ pt
mushrooms chopped	50 g	2 oz
1 egg yolk		
browned breadcrumbs		
salt, pepper		

Method

1 Beat egg yolk and add to mashed potato. Season well.

2 Mix mince with enough sauce to moisten, add mushrooms, season well and stir over heat till hot.

3 Grease some small moulds and sprinkle with browned breadcrumbs. Line with some potato purée. Fill with mince mixture and cover with more potato. Smooth lid.

4 Bake in a moderate oven (175°C, 350°F, Mark 4) for 20 min.

5 Turn out bouchées on to a hot dish and pour round the remainder of the béchamel sauce.

Cassolettes of game

4 persons

	Metric	Imp
short or puff pastry (p. 217)	200 g	½ lb
brown sauce (p. 64)	125 ml	1 gill
cooked game minced	200 g	½ lb
cooked ham minced	100 g	4 oz
butter	25 g	1 oz
mushrooms sliced	100 g	4 oz
1 shallot chopped		
mashed potatoes		
salt, pepper		
parsley		

Method

1 Roll out pastry very thinly, line small greased moulds or patty pans with it.

2 Fill with greased paper and raw rice and **bake blind** in moderate oven (175°C, 350°F, Mark 4) till pale brown. Remove rice and paper.

3 Melt butter in a pan, add chopped shallot and fry a little, add mushrooms and fry 5 min.

4 Add meat, sauce and seasoning and cook gently 5 more min.

5 Pour mixture into pastry cases, top with mashed potatoes and bake for 10 min. at 175°C (350°F, Mark 4).

6 Turn out carefully and serve hot. Garnish with parsley.

Croquettes

4 persons

	Metric	Imp
cold beef or mutton minced	200 g	½ lb
breadcrumbs	100 g	4 oz
brown sauce or **binding**		
sauce (pp. 64, 69)	125 ml	1 gill
1 tsp chopped parsley		
1 tsp chopped herbs		
1 egg		
grated rind of ½ lemon		
egg and breadcrumbs for coating		
deep fat for frying		
salt, pepper		
fried parsley		

Method

1 Combine meat, herbs, lemon rind, and seasoning with soft breadcrumbs in a saucepan. Add sauce and stir over gentle heat till hot.

2 Remove from heat and add beaten egg. Stir well. Turn on to a plate and shape into a cake 1 cm (½ in.) thick. Allow to get quite cold.

3 Divide into equal portions. Roll into balls or cork shapes, brush with beaten egg and coat very thoroughly in browned breadcrumbs.

4 Heat fat in a deep pan; when smoking, add croquettes in a frying basket and fry till golden brown.

5 Drain on kitchen paper.

6 Serve on a hot dish garnished with fried parsley. Hand brown, tomato (pp. 64, 67) or any sauce liked.

Note Any kind of meat, poultry or game may be used for these either alone or mixed with ham. Cooked rice or potatoes may be used in place of the soft breadcrumbs.

Dresden patties or croustades

4 persons

	Metric	Imp
4 slices of stale bread		
cold meat minced	100 g	¼ lb
white or brown sauce		
(pp. 65, 64)	125 ml	1 gill
herbs (optional)		
egg and breadcrumbs for coating		
salt, pepper		
deep fat for frying		
fried parsley		

Method

1 Cut slices of bread into rounds about 7 cm (3 in.) in diameter. With a smaller cutter mark a hole in the centre. Keep the top of this for a lid, scoop out the centre, leaving a thin layer of bread at the bottom.
2 Brush with beaten egg and roll in breadcrumbs.
3 Heat a pan of deep fat till a faint blue haze rises, and fry both cases and lids till a good brown. Drain upside down on soft paper.
4 Fill the cases with a mixture of mince and sauce, flavoured with herbs as desired, seasoned and heated. Place the lids on.
5 Serve on a hot dish, garnished with fried parsley. Serve hot.

Chicken kromeskis

4 persons

	Metric	Imp
cooked chicken minced	100 g	4 oz
frying batter (p. 76)	125 ml	1 gill
white sauce (p. 65)	125 ml	1 gill
minced ham or tongue		
(optional)	50 g	2 oz
4 slices streaky bacon		
deep fat for frying		
salt, pepper		
fried parsley		

Method

1 Mix chicken and ham or tongue, if used, with white sauce. Season well and make hot, stirring all the time. Turn on to a plate to cool.
2 When cold, shape into cork-like croquettes.
3 Remove rind from bacon; wrap each roll in a slice of bacon.

4 Heat a pan of deep fat. When really hot, dip each roll in batter and fry at once till pale brown. Drain well on soft paper.
5 Serve on a hot dish, garnished with fried parsley.

Note Mince of any kind of meat, game or poultry may be used this way. Kromeskis are nearly always wrapped in bacon or sometimes in very fine pancakes before dipping them in the batter.

Beef rissoles

4 persons

	Metric	Imp
cooked beef minced	100 g	¼ lb
sauce for **binding** (p. 69)	60 ml	½ gill
cooked ham minced	25 g	1 oz
short pastry (p. 218)	200 g	½ lb
1 tsp mixed herbs		
1 tsp chopped parsley		
2 egg yolks		
browned breadcrumbs		
oil for frying		
salt, pepper, nutmeg		
fried parsley		

Method

1 Mix meats, herbs and sauce together in a pan over gentle heat. Stir well and season. When hot, stir in one egg yolk. Turn on to plate to cool.
2 Roll out pastry as thinly as possible. Cut into 7 cm (3 in.) rounds.
3 Put a little of the mixture in the centre of each, brush round the edges with water, double over and press edges together.
4 Brush with egg and dip in breadcrumbs or crushed vermicelli.
5 Heat oil in a deep saucepan. When a faint blue smoke rises, put in rissoles, lowering the heat a little and fry.
6 Drain on soft paper. Serve on a hot dish garnished with fried parsley.

Note Rissoles may be made with any of the croquette mixtures or any mixture liked enclosed in pastry and fried in deep fat. Smaller rissoles may be made for buffet refreshments.

Meat sanders

4 persons

	Metric	Imp
cooked beef or mutton minced	200 g	½ lb
gravy	250 ml	½ pt
butter	25 g	1 oz
creamed potatoes	400 g	1 lb
1 medium onion minced		
salt, pepper		

Method
1 Mix meat and onion, season well, add gravy and make hot. Simmer 10 min.
2 Divide mixture into 4 greased scallop shells.
3 Top with creamed potato, dot with butter.
4 Grill for 5 min. till potato is golden brown.

Note Any kind of poultry or game mixed with suitable sauce may be made into scallops.

Partridge soufflé

4 persons

	Metric	Imp
cooked partridge	200 g	½ lb
brown stock	125 ml	1 gill
Espagnole sauce (p. 65)	500 ml	1 pt
butter	25 g	1 oz
flour	25 g	1 oz
cream	60 ml	½ gill
3 separated eggs		
salt, pepper		

Method
1 Remove skin from flesh. Mince partridge finely.
2 Melt butter in a pan, stir in flour, brown a little, stir in stock, boil quickly till mixture leaves the sides of the pan. Cool.
3 Beat in egg yolks and mince. Season well. Rub through a sieve.
4 Whip cream slightly. Whip egg whites stiff, **fold** both lightly **into** mixture.
5 Fill a buttered soufflé case with the mixture and cover lightly with a piece of greased paper.
6 Steam gently for 40 min. or till the mixture is firm when pressed.

7 Turn out on to a hot dish and pour Espagnole sauce round.

Note This soufflé may also be baked in a moderate oven (175°C, 350°F, mark 4) for 25 to 30 min. The texture will be less firm, and a sauce is not necessary. A baked soufflé is served in the soufflé case.

Timbales of game or poultry

4 persons

	Metric	Imp
cooked game or poultry minced	300 g	¾ lb
stock or gravy made from bones of the bird	250 ml	½ pt
butter	25 g	1 oz
brown sauce (p. 64)	500 ml	1 pt
1 egg		
2 tbsp cream		
salt, pepper, nutmeg		
cut lemon		

Method
1 Combine mince with butter; pound together and season with salt, pepper and nutmeg.
2 Add a little stock and rub through a sieve or blend in a liquidizer.
3 Add rest of stock, cream and beaten egg, mix well.
4 Grease 4 small moulds or 1 large pudding basin, and nearly fill with the mixture.
5 Twist a piece of greaseproof paper over basin and steam for ½ hr.
6 Turn moulds out on to a hot dish and coat with brown sauce. Garnish with cut lemon.

Note Any kind of meat, ham, tongue, rabbit or sweetbread, or two kinds mixed, may be made into timbales.

FAMILY DISHES

Beef bubble and squeak
4 persons

	Metric	Imp
cooked beef	300 g	¾ lb
cooked cabbage or other greens chopped	300 g	¾ lb
cooked potato sliced	300 g	¾ lb
dripping	75 g	3 oz
salt, pepper		

Method

1 Remove skin, gristle, fat from meat and cut into thin slices.

2 Heat dripping in a large frying pan, add beef and fry gently on both sides till browned. Remove from fat and keep warm.

3 Fry cabbage and potato together, stirring occasionally till brown. Season.

4 Serve cabbage mixture on a hot dish and arrange meat slices on top.

Note This is an excellent way of using up corned beef, and any small pieces of ham or tongue may be mixed in with the beef.

Beef fritters
4 persons

	Metric	Imp
cold roast beef	400 g	1 lb
frying batter (p. 76)	125 ml	1 gill
tomato or Espagnole sauce (pp. 67, 65)	500 ml	1 pt
frying fat		
salt, pepper		
parsley		

Method

1 Trim all fat and gristle from beef, cut into strips.

2 Sprinkle with salt and pepper, dip in batter.

3 Heat a pan of deep fat till a faint blue smoke rises. Fry pale brown, drain on soft paper.

4 Garnish with parsley. Hand tomato or Espagnole sauce separately.

Note Any kind of meat, poultry or game may be cooked in this manner.

Blanquette of chicken
4 persons

	Metric	Imp
cooked chicken cut in small pieces	400 g	1 lb
tongue cut in thin slices	100 g	4 oz
white sauce	500 ml	1 pt
stock (any kind)	125 ml	1 gill
juice of ½ lemon		
salt, pepper		

Method

1 Add stock to white sauce.

2 Mix chicken and tongue and add to sauce.

3 Season well, strain in lemon juice and stir over heat till thoroughly hot.

4 Dish pieces of chicken on a hot dish, pour sauce over and garnish with tongue.

Cannelon of cold beef
4 persons

	Metric	Imp
cooked beef minced	200 g	½ lb
ham, tongue or corned beef minced	100 g	4 oz
soft breadcrumbs	100 g	4 oz
2 tbsp brown or tomato sauce (pp. 64, 67)		
1 tbsp chopped parsley		
1 tsp mixed herbs		
1 egg		
a little flour		
salt, pepper		
cooked macaroni or boiled rice		

Method

1 Mix minced meats together, add breadcrumbs, parsley, herbs and season to taste. Mix well.

2 Add beaten egg and sauce together to mixture.

3 Shape into a roll with a little flour and wrap in greased foil.

4 Bake in a fairly hot oven (205°C, 400°F, Mark 6) ½ hr.

5 Remove foil, serve on a hot dish, coat with brown sauce, and surround with cooked macaroni or boiled rice.

Note Any kind of meat, game, poultry or rabbit may be made into a cannelon in this fashion. White meat should be coated with white sauce and decorated as desired.

Chicken cutlets

6 persons

	Metric	Imp
1 cold roasted chicken jointed		
butter	40 g	1½ oz
white stock	250 ml	½ pt
white sauce (p. 65)		
1 bunch herbs		
6 slices of bread		
1 egg		
½ carrot sliced		
grated rind of ½ lemon		
breadcrumbs		
frying oil		
salt, pepper, powdered mace		
fried parsley		

Method

To make the gravy:

1 Melt butter, fry carrot and herbs gently for 10 min. Add stock and simmer 15 min. Strain and keep warm.

Meanwhile:

2 Trim bread slices to the same size as the chicken pieces. Fry in hot oil. Drain well.
3 Add beaten egg to white sauce and stir over low heat till egg thickens.
4 Dip chicken pieces into this. Coat them in a mixture of breadcrumbs, lemon rind, mace, salt and pepper.
5 Fry for 8 to 10 min. in hot fat. Drain well.
6 Serve each cutlet on a piece of fried bread. Garnish with fried parsley. Hand gravy separately.

Cottage or shepherd's pie

4 persons

	Metric	Imp
cooked beef minced	400 g	1 lb
butter or margarine	25 g	1 oz
flour	25 g	1 oz
brown stock	250 ml	½ pt
mashed potatoes (p. 196)	600 g	1½ lb
1 onion sliced		
salt, pepper		

Method

1 Melt fat in a pan, add onion and brown; add flour and brown and gradually stir in stock. Stir till boiling, simmer for 5 min.

2 Add the meat and seasoning, and turn mixture into a greased pie dish. Cover with mashed potatoes.
3 Bake in a fairly hot oven (205°C, 400°F, Mark 6) about 20 min. or till the potato is brown on top.
4 Serve hot in the pie dish.

Note This may also be made with cooked lamb. Raw minced beef can also be used for making this pie. In this case, the mince should be browned with the onion and simmered in the stock for about ½ hr before turning into the pie dish.

Duck with green peas

	Metric	Imp
the remains of cold roast duck		
gravy	375 ml	¾ pt
butter	25 g	1 oz
flour	25 g	1 oz
shelled peas	400 g	1 lb
grated peel of ½ lemon		
salt, pepper, cayenne		

Method

1 Cut duck into neat pieces, remove skin, sprinkle with salt, pepper, cayenne and lemon peel.
2 Put meat in a pan, pour gravy over, bring to boil and simmer 15 min.
3 Boil peas in salted water with a sprig of mint; drain well and stir in the butter rolled in flour. Season well and stir till hot.
4 Arrange duck on a hot dish with peas round and pour gravy over.

Goose à la bourgeoise

6 persons

	Metric	Imp
cooked goose jointed	800 g	2 lb
haricot beans soaked overnight	200 g	½ lb
tomato sauce (p. 67)	125 ml	1 gill
cooked ham chopped small	200 g	½ lb
dripping or goose fat	25 g	1 oz
2 onions chopped		
browned breadcrumbs		
salt, pepper		

Method
1 Boil haricot beans in the water in which they soaked and simmer for 1 hr.
2 Melt fat in a pan, and brown onions in it.
3 Add tomato sauce, strained beans, 250 ml (½ pt) of the water they cooked in and seasoning. Simmer 5 min.
4 Put half haricot mixture into a greased casserole, add ham and goose, cover with remaining mixture. Sprinkle with bread-crumbs and dot with fat.
5 Bake in moderate oven (175°C, 350°F, Mark 4) 30 min.
6 Serve in the casserole.

Hash

4 persons

	Metric	Imp
cooked beef or meat		
of any kind	400 g	1 lb
flour	25 g	1 oz
dripping	25 g	1 oz
stock (any kind)	500 ml	1 pt
1 onion sliced		
salt, pepper		
toast		

Method
1 Remove all skin, fat and gristle from meat and cut into thin slices.
2 Melt dripping in a pan, and when hot, add onion and brown, add flour and brown, stir in stock off the heat.
3 Return to heat, stir till boiling, skim, season and put in pieces of meat.
4 Cover pan and simmer extremely slowly for 15 min.
5 Arrange pieces of meat on a hot dish and pour sauce over. Garnish with snippets of toast.

Note Any kind of meat, poultry, game or rabbit may be used for this. The hash may be served in a circle of creamed spinach, a green pea purée, haricot beans tossed in tomato purée, cooked macaroni or rice.

Meat in batter

4 persons

(Toad-in-the-hole)

	Metric	Imp
cooked meat of any kind		
sliced thinly	300 g	¾ lb
Yorkshire pudding batter		
(p. 236)	250 ml	½ pt
¼ tsp powdered herbs		
1 tsp chopped parsley		
salt, pepper		

Method
1 Make batter and let it stand for an hour before using.
2 Heat oil or dripping in a Yorkshire pudding tin in a very hot oven (240°C, 475°F, Mark 9) for 5 min.
3 Quickly place meat over the bottom, sprinkle with herbs and parsley, season, and pour over the batter. Replace at once in oven.
4 Bake for 10 min., then reduce tempera-ture to hot (220°C, 425°F, Mark 7) for another 30 min. Batter should be well-risen and brown.
5 Cut the batter in slices and place on a hot dish or serve in the tin.

Note Sausages may be used for this dish in which case they are put into the tin at the same time as the dripping or oil.

Meat and rice cake

4 persons

	Metric	Imp
cooked meat minced	200 g	½ lb
rice	60 g	2½ oz
stock (any kind)	250 ml	½ pt
dripping	25 g	1 oz
browned breadcrumbs	150 g	6 oz
brown or tomato sauce		
(pp. 64, 67)		
1 dssp chopped parsley		
1 egg		
salt, pepper		

Method
1 Boil rice for 5 min. in a large pan of salted water. Drain well.
2 Melt dripping in a pan, add rice and stir well; add stock and simmer gently till rice is soft and all stock absorbed.

3 Stir in meat, beaten egg, parsley and seasoning.

4 Line a greased pudding basin with breadcrumbs, put in mixture, cover with greased paper and steam for about ½ hr or till firm to the touch.

5 Turn out on to a hot dish and pour round a little brown or tomato sauce.

Note Any kind of meat, poultry or game may be used this way; serve white sauce with white meats and mushroom sauce with game. Cooked macaroni, chopped small, may be added instead of rice.

Minced beef

4 persons

	Metric	Imp
cooked beef minced	400 g	1 lb
stock (any kind)	250 ml	½ pt
dripping	25 g	1 oz
flour	25 g	1 oz
1 onion chopped finely		
mashed potatoes, cooked rice, macaroni or spinach purée		
salt, pepper		
triangles of fried bread		

Method

1 Heat dripping, brown onion lightly, add flour and stir till browned.

2 Add stock gradually, stirring over moderate heat till boiling. Season, add the meat and simmer very gently for 15 min.

3 Serve inside a border of mashed potatoes, cooked rice, cooked macaroni or cooked spinach. Arrange triangles of fried bread round the mince.

Note Any kind of meat, poultry or game may be used this way, adding a little minced ham or tongue if possible. White meats should be mixed with white sauce, and sometimes tomato sauce is used instead of brown for dark meats.

Moussaka

4 persons

	Metric	Imp
cooked lamb minced	400 g	1 lb
aubergines unpeeled and sliced thickly	300 g	¾ lb
stock or gravy (any kind)	250 ml	½ pt
milk	375 ml	¾ pt
3 egg yolks		
2 large onions sliced		
3 tbsp tomato purée		
olive oil for frying		
salt, black pepper		

Method

1 Beat egg yolks and milk together, season and put in the top of a double boiler over simmering water. Stir occasionally. Do not allow water to boil or mixture will curdle. The mixture will take up to an hour to thicken.

2 Heat olive oil and fry aubergine slices till transparent, not brown. Remove from pan.

3 Fry onions till brown.

4 Place some aubergine slices at the bottom of a greased casserole, cover with half the mince, then the onions, the rest of the aubergines and top with mince. Press firmly.

5 Heat the stock, mix in the tomato purée, season and pour over the meat.

6 Cover with the custard and bake in a moderate oven (175°C, 350°F, Mark 4) for 1 hr.

7 Serve in the casserole.

Rechauffé of chicken

	Metric	Imp
remains of cooked chicken		
flour	25 g	1 oz
gravy or stock	250 ml	½ pt
butter	25 g	1 oz
dripping	50 g	2 oz
breadcrumbs	100 g	4 oz
1 egg		
1 tbsp minced parsley		
1 tbsp walnut or mushroom ketchup		
1 lemon		
salt, pepper, nutmeg		

Method

1 Cut chicken into neat joints, and remove skin.

2 Mix salt, pepper, nutmeg and parsley with breadcrumbs.

3 Brush chicken with egg, dip in breadcrumbs. Fry in hot dripping. Drain and keep warm.

4 Melt butter in a pan, add flour, blend well and brown.

5 Remove from heat, add stock gradually, stirring. Return to heat and stir till boiling. Add ketchup, stir for 5 min. Season well.

6 Arrange pieces of chicken on a hot dish, strain gravy round. Garnish with slices of lemon.

Note Cold turkey, pigeons or rabbit may be reheated in this way.

Rechauffé of mutton

4 persons

	Metric	Imp
the remains of a leg of mutton		
mashed potatoes	400 g	1 lb
dripping	75 g	3 oz
salt, pepper		
gravy		

Method

1 Remove the knuckle bone and cover the cut surface of the meat thickly with mashed potatoes seasoned to taste.

2 Melt some dripping in a baking tin, put in leg of mutton and pour more dripping over.

3 Bake in a fairly hot oven (205°C, 400°F, Mark 6) for ½ hr, **basting** frequently. The potato should form a brown crust.

4 Serve on a hot dish and hand gravy separately.

Rechauffé of ox tongue

4 persons

	Metric	Imp
cooked ox tongue	300 ml	¾ lb
brown or Espagnole sauce (pp. 64, 65)	500 ml	1 pt
1 tbsp capers		
2 tomatoes		

Method

1 Cut the tongue into neat slices.

2 Heat the sauce, and when boiling, put in the tongue.

3 Cover the pan and simmer very gently for 15 min.

4 Arrange the slices on a hot dish, and pour the sauce over and round.

5 Garnish with capers and slices of tomato and serve hot.

Note If liked, the tongue may be served in the centre of a ring of mashed potatoes or creamed spinach, cooked rice or macaroni.

Salmis of cold game

4 persons

	Metric	Imp
any cold game cut in neat pieces	800 g	2 lb
good stock (brown or game)	375 ml	¾ pt
butter	25 g	1 oz
flour	25 g	1 oz
port or red wine	60 ml	½ gill
1 bunch herbs		
1 small onion sliced		
salt, pepper, cayenne		

Method

1 Melt butter in a pan, add flour, stir till brown; add stock, stir till boiling.

2 Add wine, onion and herbs. Simmer gently for ½ hr, skimming often.

3 Sprinkle game with salt, pepper and cayenne. Put in the sauce and heat without boiling.

4 Serve on a hot dish, season the sauce and strain over.

Devilled turkey legs

4 persons

	Metric	Imp
the legs of a cold turkey		
brown or mustard sauce (pp. 64, 70)	250 ml	½ pt
curry butter (p. 75)		
olive oil		
a little meat extract		
salt, pepper, cayenne		
parsley		

Method

1 Remove the skin, cut each leg in half at the joint, cut deep gashes in each portion.

2 Rub the legs with a little meat extract and fill the gashes with curry butter; sprinkle with salt, pepper and cayenne.

3 Brush all over with oil and put under a grill which is not too hot for 10–15 min.
4 Serve on a croûte of fried bread and garnish with parsley. Hand brown or mustard sauce and chutney.

Note The legs of a chicken, goose or guinea-fowl may be devilled in the same way.

Fried turkey

4 persons

	Metric	Imp
cooked turkey	800 g	2 lb
1 egg		
browned breadcrumbs		
frying fat		
brown or tomato sauce (pp. 64, 67)		
salt, pepper		
fried parsley		

Method
1 Cut the turkey into large pieces. Remove the skin.
2 Sprinkle the joints with salt and pepper, brush with beaten egg and dip in bread-crumbs.
3 Heat some fat in a deep pan, and fry the turkey for about 10 min. Drain on soft paper.
4 Serve on a hot dish, garnish with fried parsley and hand brown or tomato sauce (pp. 64, 67) separately.

Note Any type of game or poultry may be cooked in this way or the joints may be dipped in frying batter.

CURRIES

The dedicated curry maker will blend her own mixture of spices and make them into a curry powder which will have an individual taste, but for convenience sake, bought curry powder and paste can be excellent, provided a reliable brand is used. The powder and the paste have different ingredients and are sometimes used together in a recipe, so it is advisable to have both in the store cupboard. Buy them in reasonably small quantities as the spices lose their potency with keeping. Variety in flavour can be given to a curry by adding turmeric and chillies which can be bought quite easily. Tamarinds, which are always used in Indian curries, to give the slightly acid taste that helps to bring out the other flavours, can be bought in jars from most of the large stores.

A sour apple or a stick of rhubarb or pickled gherkins may be used in place of tamarinds. No one flavour should predominate in a well-made curry, which really should be delicate in flavour and can vary in strength from mild to very hot.

A curry is always better for being made well in advance. This allows the meat, fish, or whatever is curried to become infused with the spices. A curry can very well be made the day before it is eaten. If cooked meat is to be made into a curry, it should be **marinaded** in the sauce for some hours before being gently heated up. Uncooked meats, of course, require cooking in the sauce.

Curry stimulates the appetite and aids digestion. It should always be served in a deep dish, never on a shallow one. If a proper one is not available, a vegetable dish may be used.

Almost anything may be curried – meat of any kind, poultry, game, eggs, fish and vegetables, cooked or uncooked.

All curries are made in the same way, but are altered by reducing or adding different ingredients. Garlic and green ginger are much used in Indian curries, but may be omitted where the flavour is disliked. Some curries are hotter than others, some are dry – that is, very little liquid is used with them.

Coconut water is added to most curries with stock or milk, or half of each. A spoonful or two of cream or yoghourt improves the more delicate curries. Lemon juice is usually added, but vinegar or chilli vinegar may replace it.

In India and Ceylon, a vegetable curry is always handed with the meat curry. Curry powder is not used with it, but saffron or turmeric and coconut water and milk and onions give flavour.

The more oily fish, such as mackerel and herring, and salted or smoked fish do not curry well.

Fat should not be added to curry, as sufficient is used in the form of dripping or butter when making the sauce.

Boiled rice is always served with curries and various adjuncts are handed, such as chutney, Bombay ducks and coconut, and in India a 'sambal'. A 'sambal' is usually made of dried or green chillies, Maldive fish (dried shark from the Maldive Islands), onions, coconut milk and so on. These ingredients are pounded and shaped into moulds on a small glass or china dish, and handed with the curry.

To make **Coconut Water**, either grate ¼ of a fresh coconut finely or use desiccated coconut. Cover 75 g (3 oz) of grated coconut with 125–200 ml (1 or 1 ½ gills) of boiling water and leave until cold. Strain and use.

Note Fresh coconut makes a more milky liquid than the desiccated coconut and, naturally, has a slightly better flavour.

In place of Maldive fish, strips of grilled or fried red herring may be used with good effect in curry.

Bombay ducks can be obtained in most large stores and can be prepared as follows: Flatten them with a rolling pin (unless bought already flattened), brush them over with oiled butter, and grill or bake them in the oven.

Poppadums are bought as flat pancakes, either plain or spiced. When fried in hot oil, they bubble up and become crisp and are served on a wire tray, on the side.

Meats and fish which curry well

Meats	Fish
Beef	All white fish
Mutton	Salmon
Lamb	Lobster
Veal	Prawns
Lean pork	Shrimps
Fowl	Oysters
Pigeon	
Rabbit	
Hare	
Turkey	
Game of any kind	

Geese and ducks do not curry as well as white poultry, as they are inclined to be rather oily.

To boil rice for curry

Patna rice is the best for curry, the next best being Rangoon. Carolina rice is too starchy for curries. Wash the rice in several waters, to remove the loose starch. Drain and put it into a large pan of boiling salted water, and boil fast for 15 to 20 min., or until the rice feels tender if pinched between the finger and thumb. On no account let the rice boil too soft and become mashy. When ready, pour in some cold water, then strain through a fine colander or a sieve, rinse out the pan and return the rice to it. Cover with a clean cloth and put it on the hot plate or at the side of the stove and let it dry and reheat. Stir often with a fork. Each grain should be separate. Serve piled up in a hot vegetable dish.

Some branded rice is sold especially treated so that the result is always dry rice with separate grains. This rice will require little or no washing. Always follow the instructions on the packet carefully, regarding the ratio of water to rice in cooking.

Curried meat balls

4 persons

	Metric	Imp
lean minced beef	400 g	1 lb
stock (any kind)	250 ml	½ pt
dripping	60 g	2½ oz
coconut water (p. 170)	125 ml	1 gill
flour	25 g	1 oz

1 tbsp curry powder
1 onion minced
1 clove garlic chopped finely
½ tsp green ginger chopped finely
1 egg
1 apple peeled and chopped
1 tbsp cream
1 tsp lemon juice
salt
rice
chutney

Method

1 Mix meat, ginger and garlic, season well, **bind** with beaten egg and a spoonful of stock if too dry. Roll into balls the size of a marble.
2 Melt the dripping and fry balls brown. Drain on paper.
3 Brown the onion in the dripping, add flour and curry powder and brown.
4 Stir in stock, coconut water and apple. Stir till boiling. Add beef balls and simmer for 20 min. very gently.
5 Add cream, lemon juice and salt if necessary.
6 Serve in a hot curry or vegetable dish and hand rice and chutney separately.

Note If possible, the beef balls should be allowed to **marinade** in the curry sauce for some hours before the final simmering at stage 4.

Curry of cold roast beef

4 persons

	Metric	Imp
cold beef cut in small squares	400 g	1 lb
flour	25 g	1 oz
stock (any kind)	250 ml	½ pt
coconut water	125 ml	1 gill
butter or margarine	50 g	2 oz

1 onion minced
1 apple cut up small
1 dssp curry powder
juice of ½ lemon
salt
boiled rice, grated coconut, chutney, Bombay duck

Method

1 Fry onion in butter till golden brown. Add flour and curry powder and stir for a few minutes.
2 Add stock and stir till boiling.
3 Add meat, apple, coconut water and salt. If possible, leave to **marinade** for a while.
4 Simmer 10 min., then add lemon juice.
5 Serve in a deep dish. Hand boiled rice, grated coconut, chutney and Bombay duck separately.

Chicken curry

4 persons

	Metric	Imp
1 chicken jointed		
butter	60 g	2½ oz
chicken or vegetable stock	375 ml	¾ pt
coconut water (p. 170)	125 ml	1 gill

1 onion chopped
1 apple chopped
1 tbsp curry powder
1 dssp curry paste
juice of ½ lemon
salt

Method

1 Melt butter in pan, brown chicken joints. Put aside.
2 Add onion, fry brown, add flour and curry powder, fry for 5 min., stirring all the time.
3 Add curry paste and gradually stir in stock and coconut water; stir till boiling.
4 Add chicken, apple and a little salt. Cover pan and simmer for ½ hr, or till chicken is tender.
5 Add lemon juice and serve with boiled rice, chutney and grated coconut.

Vegetable curry

4 persons

	Metric	Imp
mixed vegetables cut up		
small	800 g	2 lb
fat for frying	50 g	2 oz
stock (any kind)	125– 250 ml	¼– ½ pt
1 tbsp flour		
1 tbsp turmeric		
2 onions sliced		
2 apples cut up		
2 tbsp curry powder		
1 small tin tomatoes		
1 tbsp coriander seed		
1 tbsp chutney		
2 tsp salt		
2 tbsp cream		

Method

1 Toss all the vegetables except the onions in the flour and turmeric mixed together.
2 Fry lightly in hot fat for a few minutes and remove from fat.
3 Add onions and apples and fry.
4 Add curry powder and continue cooking a few minutes.
5 Add tomatoes and a little stock. Season, add vegetables, coriander seed and chutney and simmer for 30 min. till vegetables are cooked. Add more stock if necessary.
6 Add cream and serve. Hand boiled rice separately.

Note Cooked vegetables may be curried, in which case they are added to the curry sauce with the tomatoes and merely brought to the boil and served.

Curried eggs

3–4 persons

	Metric	Imp
6 hard-boiled eggs		
ham or corned beef		
chopped	50 g	2 oz
butter	25 g	1 oz
flour	25 g	1 oz
milk	250 ml	½ pt
coconut milk (p. 170)	250 ml	½ pt
1 onion chopped		
1 tbsp curry powder		
6 drops lemon juice		
salt, cayenne		
boiled rice		

Method

1 Fry onion gently in melted butter; add ham or corned beef.
2 Stir in curry powder and flour, cook a few minutes then add milk and coconut water slowly. Simmer for 10 min.
3 Season with salt and cayenne to taste, add lemon juice.
4 Remove shells from eggs and cut in quarters, slicing one for garnish.
5 Heat carefully in the sauce.
6 Serve in a border of boiled rice and garnish with sliced egg.

Curried fish See p. 109

Curried lentils

4 persons

	Metric	Imp
red lentils washed	400 g	1 lb
stock (any kind)	750 ml	1 ½ pt
dripping	75 g	3 oz
coconut water (p. 170)	250 ml	½ pt
2 onions minced		
1 tbsp curry powder		
1 apple chopped		
salt		
boiled rice		

Method

1 Melt fat in a pan, add onions and fry pale brown.
2 Add curry powder and fry for 5 min. Add lentils, stir well over heat; add stock and coconut water.
3 Stir till boiling, add apple and salt and simmer very gently for ¾ hr, or till lentils are soft.
4 Serve in hot curry or vegetable dish and hand boiled rice.

Indian pilau

6 persons

	Metric	Imp
1 boiling chicken	1400 g	3 ½ lb
dripping or butter	75 g	3 oz
rice	300 g	¾ lb
raisins	50 g	2 oz
almonds blanched and		
fried	50 g	2 oz

a small piece of cinnamon
5 cloves
1 onion sliced
2 hard-boiled eggs sliced
2 shallots sliced and fried
salt

Method

1 Simmer the chicken in just enough salted water to cover till cooked (½ hr). Allow to cool, then carve into joints.

2 Melt dripping in a pan, fry onion. Add rice, washed if necessary, and well drained, and stir.

3 Add water the chicken was cooked in and cloves and cinnamon tied together in muslin. Simmer till rice is half cooked (about 10 min.).

4 Add chicken joints, more water if needed, and continue cooking till rice and chicken are cooked (about 15 min.).

5 Dish rice in a pyramid on a hot dish, pile chicken round and garnish with hard-boiled egg slices, fried almonds, raisins and slices of shallot.

CARVING

*Carving meat – carving game and poultry – carving fish –
French cuts of meat*

Carving is not difficult with a little practice, provided one has the right utensils and a knowledge of the positions of the bones of the joint. An expert carver understands how to combine the best cuts of meat with the less choice portions, and to share these out equally.

Meat is always carved across the grain and not with it, except in the case of loin. Cutting with the grain produces long fibres of meat instead of a smooth surface.

The butcher should always be asked to joint the bones in the loin or neck of any animal, so the carver only has to cut the meat between.

Utensils   A very sharp carving knife and a 2-pronged fork with a guard are essential. The dish should be large enough to allow the joint to be turned round. If large game or poultry is served, a pair of carving scissors are a help. In carving fish, a silver fish knife or slice and fork are required, as steel spoils the flavour of fish.

To keep the carving knife sharp   Hold the steel in the left hand, tuck the thumb out of the way, and stroke the blade of the knife at an angle of about 20° to the steel in a circular direction, towards you. Repeat with the other edge of the knife applied to the steel.

If an oilstone is used, again set the knife at an angle of 20° and stroke the knife along the stone several times on one side and then the other.

HOW TO CARVE MEAT

HOW TO CARVE BEEF

Beef is best cut in very thin slices.

Sirloin   If boned and rolled, this is simply carved into slices. If served on the bone, it will be seen to have three different parts, the flank, the fillet and the uppercut. It is best to carve out the flank, then the fillet, and slice these thinly. Then turn the joint so the uppercut is on top and carve in long thin slices from the backbone. Sometimes the fillet is removed from the sirloin and sold separately.

Ribs of beef   These are carved much like the uppercut of the sirloin, beginning at the thick end and cutting slices parallel with the bone, down to the thin end. Then run the point of the knife along the rib bone to loosen the meat. If the ribs of beef are boned and rolled, they are carved in slices like a round of beef.

Round of beef and salt silverside   These are carved in thin slices right across the surface of the joint. A small piece of fat should always be served on each plate. Cut as thinly as possible. The aitch bone is carved in the same way.

Brisket   First remove the rib bones. If the meat is well-cooked, these will slip out easily. Cut the meat in straight slices away from the breast bone.

HOW TO CARVE VEAL

Loin   One of the few joints carved with the grain of the meat and not across it. Trim the base so that the joint stands firm, then carve long slices down the length of the back starting close to the backbone and turning the knife to follow the bone to loosen the meat. Turn the joint round to complete the cut. Turn the joint over to expose the flank, which contains the kidney. Carve this side at an angle down to the bone.

Chump end of leg   Carve the longest possible slices, following the shape of the bone, then turn the joint over and slice in flat layers gradually getting down to the bone.

Neck of veal   If this has been jointed by the butcher and is very small, it can simply be divided into chops; otherwise the chops may be divided into slices of moderate thickness.

Breast of veal   Separate the ribs from the brisket and cut a line horizontally right across the joint, about two or three inches from the bottom of the joint. Then divide the ribs, which should have been previously jointed, from the top to this line. The smaller bones on the bottom of the line are also cut in joints. Some people prefer the small bones to the larger ribs as being the sweetest part of the joint, so it is usual to serve a small portion from them with one of the long ribs. Breast of veal is more generally stuffed and rolled, in which case it is quite easy to cut it into thin slices.

Calf's head   First make long slices from end to end of the cheek, cutting right through the bone. At the fleshy part of the neck end will be found the throat sweetbread, and a small piece of this should be served with the rest of the meat. The eye should be removed with the point of the knife, cutting right round it. Some people consider this a great delicacy. The lower jaw must then be removed, as it contains finely flavoured lean. A portion of the palate, which is under the head, should be offered when carving.

HOW TO CARVE MUTTON OR LAMB AND VENISON

Lamb and mutton are usually cut in fairly thick slices.

Shoulder of mutton or lamb   This is a difficult joint to carve; it should be dished with the skin side uppermost and the knuckle end to the left of the dish. Insert a fork near the knuckle end and raise the joint slightly, then cut as many fairly thin slices as possible from the top of the joint, near the foreleg, down to the bone. This makes wedge-shaped pieces. Good pieces may then be taken from the blade bone, cutting right across the joint from the foreleg to the other end in thin slices; crisp fat should be cut in circular slices from the bottom of the joint. The best portions of the shoulder lie on the underside of the joint and many prefer to cut this side of the joint first. In this case, turn the joint over and begin carving it into wedge-shaped slices from the side nearest to the foreleg. Cut these slices right through to the bone, then take more slices from the blade bone end.

Leg of mutton or lamb   Mutton or lamb should be dished with the knuckle end to the left. Insert a knife about 7–10 cm (3 or 4 in.) from the knuckle end and cut right down to the bone in fairly thick rather slanting slices. Continue cutting up to the thick end of the joint, then turn the joint over and cut the under part in the same manner.

Neck of mutton or lamb   Ask the butcher to **chine** this joint. Remove the **chine** bone then cut down between the ribs, dividing the joint into cutlets.

Loin of mutton or lamb   This is a continuation of the best end. The butcher should chop through the sections of the back bone. The joint is then carved into chops.

Saddle of mutton, lamb or venison   This is the two loins undivided. Carve into slices lengthways from the neck to the tail. Thin slices of fat may be taken from the bottom part of the joint. If preferred, a line may be cut down each side of the vertebrae, that is down the centre of the joint, and then crossways lines carved from this towards the thin end of the joint. A slice of kidney should be given to those who like it.

Haunch of venison   This is the leg and loin undivided. First cut it across lengthways down to the bone, turn the dish with the knuckle end away from you, and then cut slices sufficiently near the knuckle to prevent the escape of any gravy from the centre of either side of the first cut made. The cut should be slanting and fairly thin, and plenty of gravy should be served with each portion. Venison should always be served, if possible, on a hot water dish, as the fat chills very quickly and is most unpleasant when served cold. A little fat should be served with each piece of meat.

Kid, if kept until the age at which lambs are killed, is served like venison. If killed when three or five months old, it is served whole and carved in the kitchen.

HOW TO CARVE PORK

Leg of pork is carved in the same way as a leg of mutton; care should be taken to serve some of the crisp fat or crackling and any stuffing there may be to each person.

Loin of pork is carved like loin of mutton, separating the cutlets. See that the bones are jointed before sending it to table.

Sucking pig　This should be sent to table cut in two down the centre, with the head removed, cut in half and dished on each side of the body. The front and back legs should be first cut away from the carcass and then the ribs separated into chops or cutlets. If stuffed, a little piece of stuffing should be served with each portion.

Ham should be dished with the knuckle end nearest to the carver and the thick portion towards the far side of the dish. Cut through to the bone about 12 to 15 cm (5 to 6 in.) away from the knuckle end, cutting slanting slices as thinly as possible.

HOW TO CARVE TONGUE

Begin cutting across the middle of the tongue in fairly thick slices, cutting the slices alternately from each side. Do not cut right through to the bottom of the tongue, but loosen the slices with a sharp knife from this. A little fat from the root should be served with each portion. If rolled, the tongue must be cut horizontally in thin slices across the top, like a round of beef.

HOW TO CARVE GAME

Pheasants, grouse and large game are carved like chickens. Partridges and small game birds are carved like pigeons, or they may be cut into three as follows: Cut the leg and wing, together with a small portion of the breast from each side, then divide the breast from the carcass and serve it as a third portion, adding to it any trimmings from the back. Very small birds, such as quails and snipe are generally served whole – or cut into two when very small portions are desired.

Wild ducks and widgeon　The breasts are carved in slices, which are removed from the bird.

HOW TO CARVE HARE AND RABBIT

Roast　Cut slices across the back from the head towards the tail. If the hare is young, after removing the shoulder and the legs, the back can be cut across, dividing into several pieces. With a full grown hare this is not practicable unless it is boned first. The shoulder and legs are easily removed by placing a knife between them and turning them back with the point, and the joints can be seen and easily separated. The head is not removed until the last; divide it from the neck, remove the lower jaw and cut through to the division which appears from the nose to the top of the skull and cut it open; a small piece of stuffing should be served with each portion.

Boiled　First remove the legs and shoulders, divide the back into two parts and then cut each part down into joints or slices; a little liver should be helped with each portion.

HOW TO CARVE POULTRY

Chicken　Dish the bird with the legs towards the carver; insert the knife between the carcass and the leg, cut, pull the thigh from the body of the bird and cut through the joint. Separate the thigh from the drumstick by cutting through the joint. Remove the wing portion by cutting right through from the breast to the joint of the wing and press it back as with the leg, then separate the joint. Carve the breast in thin slices. Serve a portion of breast with each wing, thigh or drumstick. Turn the carcass over and remove the oyster or small dark portion which lies at each side of the back bone.

Roast turkey   Loosen the leg from the body, but do not cut if off. Then carve thin slices from each side of the breast, the whole length of the bird. Then remove the legs and divide the thighs from the drumsticks. These joints are very much more easily cut through by the aid of carving scissors. A small piece of forcemeat should be served with each portion of turkey.

Roast goose   Serve the bird with the neck at the left hand side of the dish and carve slices from each side of the breast the whole length of the bird; then separate the legs and wings and divide the drumsticks from the thighs. Stuffing is obtained by making an incision in the apron. Serve a small piece with each portion of the goose.

Ducks are carved in the same way as roast goose.

Pigeons are generally cut right through the middle, into two equal parts, and if too large are then again cut into quarters.

HOW TO CARVE FISH

Turbot and Brill   Make an incision with a silver slice down the backbone, and then cut flat pieces from the backbone to the fins, down to the bone, first on one side of the fish and then on the other.

Flat fish   Plaice if large is carved like turbot, and if small like sole.

Sole   Make an incision right down the backbone and another down the fins and raise a fillet from each side, then remove the bone and cut the bottom portion of the fish into two fillets. Sometimes the sole is divided into 3 or 4 pieces, cutting right through the backbone.

Small fish are served whole or cut into two pieces.

Cod or Salmon   Either of these fish if whole should be placed on the dish with the thin part nearest to the carver; remove the skin from one side, make an incision the whole length of the fish, not exactly in the middle of the fish, but a little nearer to the bottom, then carve from the top of the fish to this line in fairly thick slices, right through to the centre of the backbone. When the top part is finished, remove the bone and carve the lower portion in the same manner.

Mackerel and Herrings are always served head to tail. Divide the meat from the bone by cutting down the back lengthways.

All small fish such as pilchards, smelts, etc., are served whole.

FRENCH CUTS OF MEAT

In order that you may have some understanding of boucherie meat, and also be able to find a substitute for the cut mentioned in a French recipe, we are giving a list of the French cuts most usually sold here and their nearest English equivalents.

The introduction of French cuts, though it is an excellent idea, tends to complicate an already intricate branch of shopping. To add to the confusion, customers often ask for meat by the name of the dish they wish to cook, and butchers are consequently beginning to label meat in this way. You may be offered *boeuf à la mode* or *blanquette de veau*, which could simply be more tempting names for stewing steak or pie veal, though in France *boeuf à la mode* is usually made from topside or top rump, whilst *blanquette* of veal is best if you use meat from the shoulder or the knuckle.

BEEF

French Cut	Nearest English Equivalent
Bavette	Skirt
Côte de boeuf	Wing rib
Entrecôte	Cut from the wing ribs. (Properly from between the ribs)
Faux or contre-filet	Eye of the sirloin
Filet	Fillet
Flanchet	Top rump, or thick flank
Gite à la noix	Roll of silverside
Plat de côte	Forequarter flank
Rumpstek	Rump steak
Tendre de tranche	Best part of the topside. A muscle rimmed with fat, and seamless
Tendron	Brisket

VEAL

French Cut	Nearest English Equivalent
Bas de carré	Scrag
Carré	Best end of neck
Côtelettes	Loin chops
Côtelettes premières	The four cutlets from the best end of neck nearest the loin
Côtelettes secondes	The four cutlets from the best end of neck furthest from the loin
Epaule	Shoulder
Escalope	Fairly thin slice of lean meat cut on the bias, usually from the leg of loin
Fricandeau	A small plump muscle from the leg
Grenadin	A small steak cut from the leg, thicker than a médaillon
Jarret	Knuckle of veal
Longe	Loin
Médaillon	An escalope which is round in shape and often cut from the loin
Noix	Topside of beef
Noix pâtissiere	Thick flank
Quasi	The rump

MUTTON AND LAMB

French Cut	Nearest English Equivalent
Carré	Best end of neck
Collet or collier	Neck or scrag
Côtelettes dans le filet	Loin chops
Côtelettes premières	The four cutlets from the best end of neck nearest the loin
Côtelettes secondes	The four cutlets from the best end of neck furthest from the loin
Filet	Loin
Gigot	Leg
Haut de côtelettes	Between breast and best end of neck

Noisettes	Made by boning and slicing the best end of neck. (Sometimes the adjoining flap is wrapped round the noisettes to keep them in shape)
Poitrine	Breast
Selle	Saddle

PORK

French Cut	**Nearest English Equivalent**
Carré	Best end of neck
Côtelettes	Chops
Echine	Spare ribs
Epaule	Shoulder
Filet	Centre or middle loin
Jambon	Upper part of hind leg
Jambon de devant	Hand and spring
Jambonneau	Hind and fore knuckle
Lard gras or bardière	Back pork fat used for larding and barding
Palette	Blade bone
Pied	Foot
Pointe de filet	Hind loin
Poitrine	Belly
Tête or hure	Head

VEGETABLES AND SALADS

*General remarks on cooking vegetables – recipes for cooking
fresh and dried vegetables – salads*

Shopping for fresh vegetables should be done as frequently as possible and they should be used straight away. The best flavour and food value will be obtained from vegetables straight from the garden. Many cooks have the water ready in the pan before going out to pick their vegetables, so that the latter can be immersed at once and none of the goodness lost.

To boil vegetables

Green leaf vegetables (except spinach, which will be dealt with under its own heading) should be washed in cold water and left soaking in salted water for a short time before cooking, to make sure all insects and grubs have been eliminated. Always drain the vegetables very well before cooking.

There are two methods of boiling green vegetables; it is a matter of personal preference as to which is best. Either immerse them in just enough boiling salted water to cover them, and cook without a lid for the minimum time till they are just *al dente* or crisp but cooked; or heat about 2 cm (1 in.) of water to boiling at the bottom of the pan, add the vegetables and boil gently with a tight lid on so that they are really cooking in the steam. Drain well, add a little butter to the pan and toss the vegetables in it. Serve at once.

Root vegetables are usually put in cold salted water and brought to the boil, then simmered with the pan covered till they are soft but firm.

White root vegetables such as Jerusalem artichokes should have a little lemon juice added to the water, if they are left to soak before boiling, to prevent discoloration.

Certain vegetables, such as turnips, have a rather bitter taste and are best **blanched** first – put into cold water, brought to the boil for 3 minutes, drained, then cooked by the method required.

To braise vegetables

Vegetables may be braised in the oven by putting them in a covered dish with a little butter for ½ to 1 hour, depending on the vegetable and its size. A little stock may be added if desired. Stuffed or unstuffed cabbages, onions, leeks, tomatoes, celery all braise well.

To roast vegetables

Some vegetables such as onions, parsnips, potatoes and pumpkin roast very satisfactorily; they may either be cooked in the hot fat round a joint or cooked in hot fat in a separate pan. They will need **basting** and will take 40 minutes to 1 hour, depending on the size of the pieces.

ARTICHOKES

There are three kinds of artichoke – Jerusalem, Japanese and Globe. The two former are root vegetables, with a slight resemblance to a knobbly potato. The Jerusalem artichoke is a fairly cheap and useful winter vegetable, which may be cooked in various ways, and makes an excellent soup. The Globe artichoke, which has large purple flowers like thistles and grey-green foliage is decorative as well as edible. The bud of the flower is eaten, either the base or *fond*, which is particularly popular in French cooking, and can be bought in tins, or the leafy scales which surround the base, and which are sucked to remove their pulp. Globe artichokes are served hot or cold as a first course.

Boiled globe artichokes

1 artichoke per person
lemon juice
water
salt

Method

1 Young fresh green artichokes should be chosen for boiling. Cut off the stem and remove the large bottom leaves.
2 Wash the artichokes well, and soak them in cold water to which a handful of salt or a few drops of vinegar have been added.
3 Rinse them in fresh water, and drain them.
4 Put the artichokes, head downwards, into a pan three-quarters full of boiling salted water, to which a teaspoonful of lemon juice has been added, and boil them rapidly for 10 min.
5 Reduce the heat, and simmer them gently from ½ to ¾ hr or until the leaves can be easily detached.
6 Turn them upside down to drain well, remove leaves in one piece, scoop out the inedible hairy choke with the handle of a spoon, replace the cap of leaves and serve hot with Hollandaise sauce or cold with French dressing.

Boiled Jerusalem artichokes

4 persons

600 g (1 ½ lb) Jerusalem artichokes
lemon juice or vinegar
salt
water

Method

1 Wash the artichokes very clean, peel and cut them into a round or oval form. As each artichoke is peeled, put it into a basin of cold water to which a few drops of lemon juice or vinegar have been added, as they turn black very quickly when exposed to the air.
2 When all are ready, drain and put them into a pan of boiling salted water.
3 Bring them to the boil, then simmer until the artichokes can be easily pierced with a fork (about 20 min.). The artichokes should be tried frequently after the first ¼ hour, as if over-cooked they become black and lose their flavour.
4 Drain the artichokes well, and put them in a hot vegetable dish. Pour melted butter over them or coat with a white sauce to which a little lemon juice or grated nutmeg has been added.

Other ways of cooking Jerusalem artichokes   They can be simmered in milk; **blanched** and dipped in batter or egg and breadcrumbs for fritters; cooked like potato chips, served parboiled and cold mixed with a little sliced raw leek and boiled potato in a French dressing for a salad, or eaten raw like radishes. They also make a good substitute for water chestnuts in Chinese cooking, or for aubergines in a moussaka. A purée of artichokes is made by rubbing them through a sieve when cooked, and reheating with butter, cream or milk.

ASPARAGUS

The green home-grown asparagus usually has more flavour than the white commercially produced type. The slim stems from the first picking, called sprew, though difficult to eat, are very tender and full of flavour.

Boiled asparagus

100 g (¼ lb) asparagus per person

Method

1 Cut the sticks of asparagus all the same length, removing the wooden parts and scraping the stalks lightly.
2 Tie in bundles and place upright in a pan of boiling, salted water.
3 Boil for 10 min. and if the tips are not in water, lay the bundles flat and cook for another 5 min., or till they are tender.
4 Drain well and untie.
5 Serve on a folded napkin or in a proper asparagus dish. Serve hot with melted butter or Hollandaise sauce, cold with French dressing or mayonnaise.

Note Asparagus can also be steamed, tied in muslin and cooked in a steamer.

AUBERGINE OR EGG-PLANT

Most aubergines are dark purple and shaped like a truncheon, but some varieties are rounder, and some are yellowish-white. The aubergine can be served as an accompanying vegetable or as a separate dish.

If they are to be used whole, they need only be wiped and the stem and calyx removed. They are not peeled. If they are to be sliced, it is usual for them to be sprinkled with salt and left for about 30 minutes before using. This will draw out the liquid, which should be discarded. This process, known as *dégorger*, is said to improve the flavour.

Baked aubergines

4 persons

	Metric	Imp
2 aubergines		
butter or margarine	25 g	1 oz
brown sauce (p. 64)	250 ml	½ pt
water		
salt, pepper		

Method

1 Wipe the aubergines with a cloth, remove the stalks.
2 Put in a pan of boiling salted water and boil for 10 min.
3 Take them out of the water. Leave to cool.
4 Cut in halves, remove the seeds.
5 Melt the fat, brush over aubergines. Put in a greased gratin dish and bake in a hot oven (220°C, 425°F, Mark 7) till soft (about 10 min.).
6 Pour the hot sauce over and serve in the cooking dish.

Note Grated cheese may be mixed with breadcrumbs and sprinkled over the aubergines before baking them. They may be stuffed with any meat mixture and baked.

Other ways of cooking aubergines Sliced, brushed with oil and grilled; dipped in batter and fried in deep fat; baked in the oven in layers alternating with layers of grated cheese in a fireproof dish, the whole covered with tomato sauce and topped with breadcrumbs and melted butter; made into a ratatouille which can be served hot or cold (p. 191) or into a moussaka (p. 167).

BROAD BEANS

Broad beans may be eaten in the pod if they are picked when the flower has just withered. The pod will be only about 7 cm (3 in.) long, and should be cut into two or three pieces before cooking. When the bean is about the size of a large pea, it can be shelled and cooked whole. Once the bean has got larger, the outer skin enclosing it should be removed, so that only the tender green inside is used. Large beans may be cooked in their skin and then sieved to remove this, and made into a purée.

Broad beans with butter

To prepare and boil Shell the beans just before they are to be cooked, as if shelled too long beforehand they become hard. If the beans are old, put them into a basin and cover them with boiling water, let them stand for a few minutes, then remove the skins. This is not necessary with young beans. Drain, and put them into fast boiling, slightly salted water, and allow them to boil gently until tender (from 20–40 minutes). Remove any scum. When they are cooked, drain them well. Melt the butter in a pan, add the beans, and stir them over the heat for a few minutes. Season them with salt and pepper.

To dish Serve them in a hot vegetable dish, and sprinkle them with chopped parsley. If preferred, the beans may be coated with parsley sauce.

Note Broad beans should always be served with boiled bacon or pork.

FRENCH BEANS AND RUNNER BEANS

French beans should be picked young and cooked whole if small, or cut straight across into two or three pieces if larger. Runner beans will need to be topped and tailed and the strings removed from each side. They are then cut into thin slices lengthwise. Cook them rapidly in boiling salted water without a lid for about 10 minutes (French beans) or 15 minutes (Runners). Drain them and stir in a little butter and seasoning. Small French beans are delicious cooked with a little crushed garlic in the water and served tossed in butter and chopped parsley.

BEETROOT

There are two kinds of beetroot, the round turnip-shaped and the long carrot-shaped. Young beetroots should be chosen, as when old they are apt to be tough and fibrous. Beetroots can generally be bought already cooked, and they should be a dark red in colour. If bought uncooked, see that the skin is quite whole and has not been scratched or pierced before cooking, as if the skin is broken before the beet is cooked, the juice runs out, and the rich colour of the beetroot is lost. Beetroots may be served hot as a vegetable, or cold as a salad, with a sharp dressing.

Boiled beetroot

2–3 persons

	Metric	Imp
1 large uncooked beetroot		
melted butter or parsley sauce (pp. 65, 69)	250 ml	½ pt
salt, pepper		
vinegar or lemon juice		
oil		
chopped parsley		

Method

1 Choose a young beetroot, cut off the leaves, and wash it carefully.
2 Put it into a saucepan of boiling water, large enough to hold it without breaking it.

Add 1 dssp salt, and boil gently with the lid on the pan for 1½–2 hr.
3 When cooked, drain and peel it quickly.
4 If the beetroot is to be served hot as a vegetable, put it into a hot dish, season, and pour melted butter or parsley sauce over it. If used cold, peel and cut the beetroot into slices, sprinkle them with salt and pepper, and pour over a little vinegar or lemon juice, and a spoonful of oil if desired. Sprinkle with chopped parsley.

BROCCOLI

There are two kinds of broccoli – the large white or purple, which looks like cauliflower and is cooked in the same way, and the sprouting broccoli, which may be green or purple. Sprouting broccoli is best tied in bundles and cooked like asparagus and served with butter; or **blanched**, dipped in fritter batter and deep fried.

BRUSSELS SPROUTS

Brussels sprouts are more delicately flavoured than cabbage. They should be firm, close and not larger than a walnut. They should be trimmed and washed and cooked in boiling salted water for 10 minutes, or till just tender. Drain very well. Brussels sprouts may be mixed with boiled chestnuts or tossed in butter or cream.

CABBAGE

There are several varieties of cabbage, which are in season at different times of the year, so that some sort of cabbage is obtainable all the year round.

The *Spring cabbage* is in season from May to September. It is rather pointed and does not have much heart, and is best cut in quarters and cooked in salted boiling water for 5 to 10 minutes, drained well and tossed in butter.

Winter cabbage is in season from October to March. This has quite a hard heart, and is best shredded for boiling and needs 10 to 15 minutes. Winter cabbage may be stuffed or braised.

Savoy cabbage is also in season in the winter, it has less heart than the winter variety, and shrinks a good deal in the cooking, but also needs 10 to 15 minutes in boiling water.

The *hard Dutch white cabbage* which is obtainable most of the year round, must be shredded finely before boiling, and needs longer than the green varieties. It is excellent used raw in salads and is used for making Cole-slaw (p. 201).

Red cabbage is in season from November to March. This is shredded and cooked very slowly for about 2 hours in a casserole or on a simmering ring. It makes a good accompaniment for boiled bacon or game. It is also made into red cabbage pickle (p. 310).

Sweet and sour red cabbage

4 persons

1 bay leaf
3 cloves
salt, pepper

	Metric	Imp	Method
1 red cabbage shredded finely	600 g	1½ lb	**1** Melt the fat in a casserole and fry onion gently till transparent. Stir in flour. Cook while stirring 3 min.
flour	25 g	1 oz	
butter or oil	25 g	1 oz	
1 apple chopped			**2** Add all other ingredients and stir well. Bring to the boil.
1 onion chopped			
3 tbsp wine vinegar			**3** Cover casserole tightly and simmer very gently for 2 hr.
3 tbsp water			
1 tbsp soft brown sugar			**4** Serve in the casserole with the juice.

CARROTS

When young and small, carrots need only be washed without scraping, the skin being wiped off with a rough cloth, if necessary, after they are boiled; older carrots should be scraped. Put young carrots into a stewpan with enough boiling water to cover them, and add ½ tsp of salt. Boil them fast for 20 minutes, then take them out, rub off the skins, if necessary, with a clean cloth, and put them whole into the dish. If the carrots are old, scrape or peel them and wash them; if large, cut them in slices, and boil them in plenty of boiling salted water until they are tender.

To dish   Drain the carrots and arrange them neatly on a hot dish. If preferred, the carrots may be cut into dice and pressed into a basin when cooked, and turned out in a mound in a vegetable dish.

Other ways of cooking carrots   They may be made into a purée by mixing them with an equal quantity of mashed potatoes and flavoured with chopped parsley and a little grated orange peel; they may be **glazed** by cutting them into pieces 2 cm (1 in.) long and cooking in a little veal stock, butter and sugar till the liquid is absorbed and the carrots soft (about 25 min.) or they may be served with parsley sauce or melted butter and chopped mint. Grated raw carrot is invaluable in salads.

CAULIFLOWER

Cauliflowers may be cooked whole with the head uppermost in boiling salted water or divided into flowerets and boiled rapidly for ¼ hour. In either case, the cauliflower should be trimmed of most of its stalk and outer leaves, and soaked well in cold, salted water for a time before cooking. It is often served with white sauce, and a pinch of basil in this gives an interesting flavour.

Cauliflower fritters   *4 persons*

1 cooked cauliflower
parsley
frying batter (p. 76)
salt, pepper, cayenne
frying oil

Method
1 Drain cauliflower thoroughly; break off sprays, season with salt, pepper and cayenne.

2 Heat oil in deep saucepan; when faint blue smoke rises, dip cauliflower into prepared batter and drop in hot fat. Fry till pale brown (10 min.).
3 Drain on kitchen paper.
4 Pile fritters on hot dish, sprinkle with fine salt, garnish with parsley. If desired a little grated cheese may be sprinkled over fritters.

Note Brussels sprouts may also be fried in this way.

CELERIAC

Celeriac, or turnip-rooted celery, is much used abroad, though only recently has it become popular in this country. It has the same flavour as ordinary celery, but the root, not the leaf, is edible. It must be peeled and boiled for about ¾ hour according to size and age. It may be made into a purée, mixed with an equal quantity of mashed potato, or parboiled and cut in strips and mixed with a French dressing for a salad. It is also good grated raw.

CELERY

Celery is a very useful vegetable, as it can be eaten either raw or cooked, and it also forms a pretty garnish to various dishes. It is a winter vegetable, and is never at its best until after a touch of frost. The roots, green tops, and outside leaves may be used as flavourings for soups and stews. When fresh celery is out of season, the seeds, tied in muslin, may be used as a flavouring, and the green tops, if dried in the oven and kept in a tin, may be used for the same purpose. Celery will keep for some days if placed in cold water, which should be changed daily.

Celery à la crème

3 persons

	Metric	Imp
1 large head celery washed, trimmed and cut into pieces about 7 cm (3 in.) long		
butter	25 g	1 oz
flour	10 g	½ oz
milk	250 ml	½ pt
1 tbsp cream		
a pinch of grated nutmeg		
salt, pepper		

Method
1 Boil celery pieces in boiling, salted water till tender (about ½ hr).
2 Melt butter in a pan, add flour and blend well. Stir in milk, bring to the boil, season and simmer 5 min.
3 Drain celery well, add to sauce and reheat.
4 Add cream and nutmeg.
5 Serve in a hot dish garnished with sprigs of parsley or celery leaves.

Note A richer sauce may be made by adding the yolks of 1 or 2 eggs to the sauce after it is cooked. Stir over a low heat to thicken, but do not allow it to boil.

Other ways to cook celery Celery hearts may be braised by cooking them in a casserole in the oven on a bed of carrots, onions and bacon, with a little stock, for 1½ to 1¾ hours and serving, drained, in a béchamel sauce (p. 64). They may also be browned in butter and then simmered in stock in a casserole till tender. Celery may also be **blanched** and dipped in fritter batter and fried.

CHICORY

Chicory in England is what is usually called endive on the Continent, whereas endive in England is usually thought of as a curly type of lettuce. Chicory consists of tight, white bud-like plants tipped with pale green which have a slightly bitter taste. **Blanching** in boiling water before cooking will get rid of some of the bitterness. Chicory may be boiled or braised whole in butter; it makes a good supper dish wrapped in ham, braised, and served with a cheese sauce. Raw chicory, sliced, is useful mixed in with a green salad or in a Salade Niçoise (p. 202).

COURGETTES

These are also known as zucchini. They are tiny marrows with dark green skins and are cooked unpeeled, whole if they are small, or sliced if larger. They may be **sautéd** gently in butter till soft, or sliced, floured and fried or made into fritters. They may also be combined with tomatoes and onions into the following dish:

Courgettes provençale

4 persons

	Metric	Imp
2 onions peeled and sliced		
courgettes sliced	400 g	1 lb
tomatoes	200 g	½ lb
butter	25 g	1 oz
1 clove garlic crushed		
4 tbsp olive oil		
2 tbsp browned breadcrumbs		
2 tbsp grated cheese		
salt, pepper		

Method
1 Heat oil in a heavy pan and fry onion, courgettes and garlic for 15 min.
2 Add tomatoes, season and cook till tender, about 10 min.
3 Put in buttered dish, top with a mixture of cheese and crumbs and brown under the grill.

Ratatouille

4 persons

	Metric	Imp
1 medium marrow or 6 courgettes		
tomatoes skinned and quartered	400 g	1 lb
4 small aubergines		
1–2 cloves garlic crushed		
6 tbsp oil		
2 large onions peeled and sliced		

1 red pepper seeded, cored and sliced
salt, pepper

Method
1 Peel and cut marrow into chunks, or wash and slice courgettes thickly.
2 Peel aubergines and cut in chunks.
3 Heat oil in a strong pan, fry onions and garlic till soft.
4 Add rest of vegetables, season, cover and simmer for 30 to 40 min. till tender.

CUCUMBERS

Cucumbers may be served either raw or cooked. When cooked they have a very delicate flavour, and are more digestible than when eaten raw. They may be cooked according to any recipe for vegetable marrow and may be stuffed with a veal or sausage forcemeat or a mince of any cooked meat, poultry or game. Small cucumbers, or gherkins, are usually pickled.

CURLY KALE

Curly kale or curly greens are a species of the cabbage family, and have very curly heads. They must be very fresh and require careful washing and picking over before use. The hard pieces of stalk must be removed, and they may then be cooked according to any recipe for cabbage.

ENDIVE

There are various species of endive, the most generally used looking like a lettuce with a curly, deeply serrated leaf, the inner leaves being a pale greeny white. Endive makes a very decorative salad, but has a slightly bitter flavour, to which some people object.

FENNEL

The chopped leaves are used as a herb to flavour sauces for fish or boiled mutton.
    Florence fennel has a swollen leaf-base which may be served raw in salad, sliced finely across the base; or boiled or braised like celery. Egg, parsley or cheese sauces are good accompaniments.

GARLIC

Each bulb of garlic consists of a number of cloves. A small clove is enough to flavour a stew or a dish for 4 people. Squeeze out the oil with a garlic press or chop it finely on a board and crush it with the flat of a knife with a little salt. For just a hint of garlic in a salad, rub the inside of the bowl with a cut clove.

HORSE-RADISH

Wash, brush and scrape the brown outside from one or two sticks of horse-radish, and lay them in cold water for nearly an hour; then scrape them into very fine shreds with a sharp knife. Use as a garnish to roast beef, or made into a sauce (p. 72).

KOHLRABI

Kohlrabi is the swollen stem base of the plant. Remove the green leaves and stalks and peel thickly. They may be cooked in the same way as turnips: for purées, fritters, or boiled and then **sautéd** in butter. They may also be grated raw and served in a salad.

LEEKS

The leek belongs to the onion tribe, but is very much milder, and more delicate in flavour. Leeks make excellent soup and are often boiled or stewed and served with white sauce.

Leeks should be prepared by removing the roots and coarse outer leaves and washed very carefully. They may be cooked whole or cut in half lengthwise, if very big, or cut in sections across if they are to be boiled and served in a sauce.

Cold cooked leeks may be served whole as an hors d'oeuvre in a French dressing or with mayonnaise.

LETTUCES

There are two main kinds of lettuce, the cos lettuce and the cabbage lettuce, which can be either a crisp and crunchy variety or a softer, tender one. The cos lettuce which is long, comes into season later in the season than the cabbage, which is round with short leaves. Hot-house lettuces, which are of the cabbage variety and without much heart, are obtainable all the year round. Lettuces are one of the most popular of salad vegetables, but they may also be cooked and used as a vegetable, especially when they are too old to use as a salad. Cos lettuce is best braised and cabbage lettuce cooked like spinach.

MUSHROOMS

Field mushrooms are in season from August to September, cultivated mushrooms are in season all the year round. They should be really fresh when cooked. Field mushrooms should be peeled, but cultivated ones may be wiped clean and used whole or sliced. For cooking mushrooms, butter must be used, but they can be sliced and eaten raw as a salad by tossing them in seasoned sour cream to which a little lemon juice has been added.

Baked mushrooms · *4 persons*

	Metric	Imp
20 mushroom flaps		
butter	100 g	4 oz
Maître d'Hôtel sauce		
(p. 75) or mashed potatoes		
and brown sauce (p. 64)	250 ml	½ pt
salt, pepper		

Method
1 Peel mushrooms if necessary, remove stalks, wipe carefully.
2 Put in a greased fireproof dish, a small piece of butter on top of each, season with salt and pepper.
3 Bake in a moderate oven (175°C, 350°F, Mark 4) for 20–30 min.
4 Serve in the cooking dish; hand Maître d'Hôtel sauce or serve on a line of mashed potato with brown sauce poured round.

Grilled mushrooms · *2–3 persons*

	Metric	Imp
6 large mushrooms		
butter	50 g	2 oz
juice of 1 lemon		
salt, pepper		

Method
1 Peel mushrooms if necessary; **score** the under part.
2 Put in a casserole and **baste** well with melted butter.
3 Sprinkle with salt and pepper. Leave to soak 1½ hr.
4 Grill for 10 to 12 min., turning once.
5 Serve on hot buttered toast, sprinkle with salt, pepper and lemon juice.

Note If preferred, they may be served without the toast with a small pat of Maître d'Hôtel butter (p. 75) on each mushroom.

ONIONS

There are various kinds of onions, the larger Spanish ones being milder in flavour than the smaller English ones. Shallots are small and oval, slightly purple in colour and milder than onions. They are usually chopped and used for flavouring.

The small pickling onions are always served whole, either braised or for garnishing dishes or as a vegetable in white sauce, besides for pickling. To eliminate the strong flavour of onions to which some people object, they should be **scalded**, i.e. put into cold water, brought to the boil and drained before using them.

Baked or braised onions (1)

	Metric	Imp
1 Spanish onion per person		
butter	50 g	2 oz
salt, pepper		

Method
1 Peel the onions and cook in boiling water for 15 min. Drain well.
2 Place in a buttered dish, pour over melted butter, season and bake in a moderate oven (175°C, 350°F, Mark 4) till tender (about 1½ hr). **Baste** occasionally.

Baked or braised onions (2)

3 or 4 persons

	Metric	Imp
4 Spanish onions		
milk	250 ml	½ pt
dripping	50 g	2 oz
salt, pepper		

Method
1 Peel the onions, boil them for 5 min. and drain.
2 Put them into a casserole, or fireproof dish, season with salt and pepper.
3 Pour over the milk and add the dripping broken into pieces.
4 Put the lid on the casserole and bake in a moderate oven (175°C, 350°F, Mark 4) until the onions are tender, about 1½ to 2 hr. **Baste** them occasionally.
5 Serve the onions in the casserole.

Other ways of cooking onions Onions may be boiled and served coated with white, brown or tomato sauce (pp. 65, 64, 67); they may also be fried in rings. They can be made crisp by sprinkling the finely sliced rings with salt and leaving them to stand for an hour to draw out the moisture, then tossing them in flour and frying quickly in hot oil.

PARSNIPS

Parsnips are a root vegetable which contain a certain amount of sugar and starch but are inclined to be rather fibrous, which makes them indigestible to some people. They should be peeled and cut in quarters lengthwise, the core removed if it is woody. Parsnips may be boiled and served mashed with a little butter, parboiled and roasted in the dripping round a joint or made into a purée, either alone or mixed with mashed carrots.

PEAS

Allow about 200 g (½ lb) of peas in the pod per person. Shell the peas and cook in boiling salted water, with a sprig of mint and a pinch of sugar, for about 10 minutes. Drain, and toss in a little butter before serving.

Mangetout peas or sugar peas are a special variety of pod containing very small peas which are eaten unshelled. The pods are washed, topped and tailed, **sautéd** in butter for 10 minutes, then with a cup of water added to them, they are simmered for about 20 minutes.

French method of cooking peas

4 persons

	Metric	Imp
peas	800 g	2 lb
butter	25 g	1 oz
flour	10 g	½ oz
a lettuce heart shredded		
6–8 spring onions peeled		
3 tbsp water		
salt, pepper		

Method

1 Put peas, lettuce, spring onions and water in a pan with half the butter.
2 Cook gently till peas are tender, 15 to 20 min.
3 Season. Mix remaining butter and flour together (**beurre manié**) and add to mixture in little pieces to thicken juice.
4 Bring to boil and serve.

PEPPERS

Peppers or capiscum may be green, yellow or red according to the variety and degree of ripeness.

Green peppers may be used raw, sliced up in salads. They are also used cooked in strips for flavouring rice dishes, curries and casseroles. They may be stuffed by **blanching** for a few minutes in boiling water and then baking in the oven for about 1 hour, stuffed with a savoury stuffing and covered in a sauce.

Red peppers have a sweeter flavour and are usually diced and added to omelettes or rice dishes.

The little peppers known as chillies are very hot and are generally used in curries and other peppery dishes.

POTATOES

Baked potatoes

3–6 persons

potatoes
butter
pepper
salt

Method

1 Choose potatoes as much the same size as possible, large ones being the best for baking.
2 Wash and brush them in cold water until they are perfectly clean.
3 Wipe them dry, prick them with a fork and put them into a moderate oven (175°C, 350°F, Mark 4), either on the shelves or on a baking tin, and cook slowly until they are tender (about 1 hr). The oven must not be too cold, or the potatoes will not cook; neither must it be too hot, or the skins become so hard that the steam cannot escape, and the potatoes become sodden, instead of dry and floury. To test when done press them gently between the thumb and finger, when they will feel soft.

4 Place the potatoes on a folded napkin on a hot dish, and hand butter, salt and pepper.

Note Peeled potatoes may be placed under the meat in the dripping tin and roasted with it.

Boiled new potatoes

3–4 persons

	Metric	Imp
new potatoes	600 g	1 ½ lb
a sprig of mint		
salt		
chopped parsley		
butter or margarine		

Method

1 Wash the potatoes, scrape the skins with a knife. If they are very young the skins can be removed by brushing without scraping.
2 Put them into a saucepan with enough boiling water to cover them, add 1 tsp of salt and a sprig of mint.

3 Bring them to the boil, then simmer gently for 15 to 20 min., or until they are soft when tried with a fork.

4 Drain off all the water, and shake them over low heat until they are dry.

5 Turn them into a hot vegetable dish, add some butter, and sprinkle chopped parsley over. New potatoes may be steamed in a steamer.

Boiled old potatoes

4–6 persons

	Metric	Imp
potatoes	800 g	2 lb
salt		
water		

Method

1 Peel some potatoes as nearly the same size as possible.

2 Put them into cold water as they are peeled, then put them into a saucepan, cover them with cold water, add a pinch of salt.

3 When the water boils, simmer the potatoes gently (20–30 min.).

4 When done drain off the water, and sprinkle a little salt over them.

5 Cover them with a cloth, and leave them near the heat to dry.

6 Shake the pan two or three times, and then serve them in a hot vegetable dish.

Note Potatoes may be boiled in their skins if well scrubbed. Serve with the skins on, or peel them after they are cooked.

Potatoes may be steamed over a pan of hot water either peeled or unpeeled. Boiled or steamed potatoes if sieved or put through a vegetable presser are called rice or snowflake potatoes.

Chipped potatoes

4–5 persons

Chipped potatoes should be fried in two stages, in order to get the right degree of crispness and brownness outside while still keeping a soft but cooked centre. The first fry should be in fat of a moderate heat (a piece of bread dropped in will fry at once but only gently); the second frying can be in a shallower pan in hot fat which shows a blue haze.

Do not put too many potatoes in the pan at once or the fat will become chilled and the potatoes be soggy.

Always dry the potatoes well before immersing them in the frying oil. If they are to be straw potatoes (very thin chips), they should be washed in a couple of waters and then dried well to remove the surplus starch in potatoes which is released on the surface with such fine cutting.

	Metric	Imp
potatoes	400 g	1 lb
frying oil or lard		
salt		

Method

1 Wash, peel and cut the potatoes into lengths 1 cm (½ in.) thick and 6 cm (2½ in.) long for ordinary chips, and 3 mm (⅛ in.) thick and 5 cm (2 in.) long for straw potatoes.

2 Dry them in a cloth and leave in the cloth till ready to fry.

3 Heat a saucepan of deep fat or oil till at the moderate temperature mentioned above.

4 Lower the potatoes gently into this, preferably in a basket. Make sure the fat returns to its original temperature and fry for 7 to 8 min., moving the basket occasionally, till chips are soft right through.

5 Remove potatoes, keep warm while frying other batches. Remove them.

6 Heat oil to blue haze. Quickly immerse the soft chips till golden brown and crisp.

7 Remove, drain, salt and serve at once. Do not cover the dish they are in or they will become soggy.

Note Sauté potatoes are cold cooked potatoes, sliced and fried in a small quantity of fat in a shallow frying pan.

Croquette potatoes

4 persons

	Metric	Imp
cooked potatoes sieved	400 g	1 lb
browned breadcrumbs	50 g	2 oz
butter	25 g	1 oz
1 separated egg		
a pinch of nutmeg		
milk if necessary		
1 tsp chopped parsley		
frying fat		
salt, pepper		
fried parsley		

Method

1 Melt butter in a pan, add potatoes, make them hot, season well.
2 Add nutmeg, parsley and beaten yolk of egg. If too dry, add a little milk. Turn mixture on to a plate to cool.
3 Divide into equal portions, flour the hands, roll into balls or any shape desired.
4 Beat up egg white, brush croquettes over, roll in breadcrumbs.
5 Fry in hot fat, drain well on soft paper.
6 Pile on a hot dish and garnish with fried parsley.

Note This mixture may be used as a border on to which to dish cutlets, fillets, quenelles, etc.

Mashed potatoes

4–6 persons

	Metric	Imp
potatoes peeled	600 g	1½ lb
butter	25 g	1 oz
boiling milk	125 ml	1 gill
salt, pepper		

Method

1 Boil potatoes till just soft (20–30 min.), drain and dry over low heat.
2 Sieve them 2 or 3 at a time, keeping rest warm.
3 Put back into the hot saucepan and on to the stove. Add hot milk a little at a time, alternating with the butter. Beat well with a wooden spoon. Continue adding milk till the right degree of creaminess is reached. Season well.
4 Serve in a hot dish, smooth with a knife. If desired, sprinkle with a little paprika for colour, or brown for a short time under the grill.

Note If an egg yolk is beaten into mashed potatoes, they may be piped through a forcing bag round a dish for decoration or into rosettes on a baking tray and browned in the oven. Grated orange peel, chopped chives or a pinch of nutmeg are all flavourings which add interest to mashed potatoes.

Roast potatoes

Potatoes for roasting should be peeled and cut in half, or quartered if very large, so that they are all about the same size, and parboiled for about 7 minutes. They must then be dried thoroughly, and put in the fat in which the joint is cooking or in a separate tin of hot oil and roasted in the oven (220°C, 425°F, Mark 7) for about 1 hour, **basting** frequently.

PUMPKINS

Pumpkins belong to the same family as the vegetable marrow, and are usually cut into wedges and sold by weight, as they grow to a good size. They may be served as a vegetable, cut up like potatoes for roasting, and baked for 50 minutes in a moderate oven (175°C, 350°F, Mark 4), seasoned with salt and pepper and brushed liberally with a mixture of melted butter and brown sugar. They make a pleasant purée, mixed with butter, seasoning, a little nutmeg and a sprinkling of Parmesan cheese. Pumpkins make excellent soup, using the recipe for marrow soup (p. 56), or with cream and brandy can be made into a type of custard tart or pie (p. 225).

RADISHES

There are three kinds of radishes, the long red radish, the small turnip-shaped, and the winter or white radish. Radishes should be freshly gathered, and very tender, to be perfect. Cut off the leaves, leaving about an inch of stalk. Wash them well in cold water, rubbing off all the soil with a brush. Trim neatly, and put them in cold water for an hour. They may be served whole, or cut into thin slices. Arrange them on a plate with the stalk ends downwards. They may also be used as a salad and may be boiled and served with white sauce (p. 65).

SALSIFY

There are two kinds of salsify, the white-skinned one, rather like a parsnip, and the black-skinned one or scorzonera. The latter has the better flavour and should be scrubbed but cooked with the peel on. It should be boiled for 30 to 40 minutes, then peeled and served with black butter or white sauce (p. 65) or parboiled, dipped in batter and fried in deep fat.

SEA-KALE

Sea-kale is a delicate vegetable, somewhat like asparagus in flavour. The stems of the plant are earthed up like celery, to **blanch** them. It may be cooked according to any recipe given for cooking celery, and may be served cold with mayonnaise, or tartare sauce (pp. 72, 73).

Boiled sea-kale

Tie the sea-kale up in bundles, and put it into a stewpan of boiling water, with 1 tsp salt. Boil for about 20 minutes, or until it is tender.

To dish   Drain the sea-kale well. Dish it in a hot vegetable dish, and pour the melted butter over. Cooked sea-kale may be served **au gratin** with a cheese sauce (p. 68).

SPINACH

Boiled spinach   *3–4 persons*

	Metric	Imp
spinach	800 g	2 lb
butter	50 g	2 oz
salt, pepper, nutmeg		
croûtons of fried bread		

Method

1 Remove the stalks and any decayed portions from the spinach, wash it in several waters until no grit remains.
2 Lift it out of the water with the hands, and put it into a pan without drying it.
3 Place it over low heat until the water in the spinach itself begins to ooze out, then cook gently until it is soft (10–15 min.).
4 Drain it well through a colander, then either chop it finely or serve it whole.
5 Melt the butter in a pan, add the spinach, season with salt, pepper and a pinch of grated nutmeg and stir it over the fire until it is hot (4–5 min.).
6 Put the spinach into a hot dish, and garnish with croûtons of fried bread, or press it into a hot mould, and turn it out.

Spinach à la crème is cooked sieved spinach, reheated with butter and cream, and served on toast.

Spinach purée is sieved spinach mixed with white sauce. It must be fairly stiff as it is used as a garnish.

SWEDES

Swedes are cooked like turnips. They are at their best mashed with butter and well seasoned with salt and pepper.

SWEET CORN

Sweet corn is either served on the cob as a first course, or scraped off the cob as an accompanying vegetable. The grains should be pale yellow; once they turn bright yellow, they are dry and hard. Corn should be cooked as soon as possible after it is picked. Remove the husk and the silk and plunge the cobs into boiling salted water for 20 minutes, or immerse in cold salted water, bring to the boil and cook for 3 minutes. Drain and serve with melted butter and salt.

To cook corn off the cob, put the scraped grains into a double saucepan with a little milk, butter and seasoning and cook gently for about 20 minutes.

TOMATOES

Tomatoes lend themselves to such a variety of treatment that they prove a most valuable addition to the menu. They may be eaten raw or cooked, and make excellent pickle, ketchup or jam. They may also be bottled.

To skin tomatoes   Plunge them into boiling water, leave a moment and then put them in a bowl of cold water. The skin can then be peeled off easily.

Stuffed tomatoes

4 persons

	Metric	Imp
4 large tomatoes		
butter	25 g	1 oz
soft breadcrumbs	50 g	2 oz
minced chicken, ham,		
tongue or game, or 2 mixed		
meats	50 g	2 oz
1 tsp chopped parsley		
1 tbsp brown sauce		
a few brown breadcrumbs		
4 **croûtons** of fried bread		
salt, pepper		

Method

1 Wipe tomatoes, remove stalks. Cut a round piece from the top of each. With a spoon handle, scoop out the pulp into a basin, taking care not to break the skin.

2 Sprinkle salt and pepper inside and invert tomatoes to drain.

3 Sieve tomato pulp, mix with meat, sauce, parsley and breadcrumbs. Season well.

4 Melt butter in a pan, stir in mixture over low heat till it swells a little.

5 Fill tomatoes with stuffing, sprinkle a few brown breadcrumbs over and top with a piece of butter.

6 Place on a greased baking tray and cover with greased paper. Cook in a moderate oven (175°C, 350°F, Mark 4) till tender (10–15 min.).

7 Serve on a **croûton** of fried bread, garnish with parsley.

Note Tomatoes may be stuffed with any kind of meat, or with cooked rice or macaroni mixed with sauce and cheese, or with any vegetables mixed with a sauce or with beaten egg. Chopped nuts or nut purée form a nourishing filling for tomatoes.

Tomatoes are also very nice cold, stuffed with any kind of salad vegetable mixed with mayonnaise, especially tinned and drained bean sprouts.

TURNIPS

Baby turnips are delicious **blanched** in boiling water, then fried lightly in butter and served with lemon juice. Older turnips may be used in stews or boiled and mashed with a little top of milk, butter, salt and pepper. This is stirred over heat until thoroughly mixed and hot. It is often served with boiled mutton.

Turnip tops are cooked the same way as cabbage (p. 188).

VEGETABLE MARROW

The tiny ones that are eaten whole are mentioned in the section on courgettes. The larger vegetable marrow tends to be rather insipid if boiled; it is best peeled and cut in pieces, the seeds removed and the pieces cooked gently in butter, seasoning and chopped parsley or chives, in a pan with the lid on, for about 10 minutes, so that it cooks in its own juice. Otherwise it may be stuffed to give it flavour, or made into jam with ginger added.

Stuffed vegetable marrow

4 persons

	Metric	Imp
1 medium-sized marrow		
pork sausage meat or minced beef	400 g	1 lb
white sauce for **binding** rissoles (p. 69)	125 ml	1 gill
soft breadcrumbs	75 g	3 oz
1 large onion chopped		
½ tsp grated lemon rind		
1 tsp chopped parsley		
1 tsp chopped herbs		
salt, pepper		

Method

1 Mix meat, parsley, herbs, breadcrumbs and lemon rind.
2 Mix with the sauce and season well.
3 Peel marrow, cut in half, remove seeds and replace with stuffing.
4 Tie two halves of marrow back in position, wrap in greased paper and place in a well-greased casserole or baking tin.
5 Cover and bake in a moderate oven (175°C, 350°F, Mark 4) ¾ hr.
6 Remove paper and string, serve on a hot dish with brown, white or tomato sauce (pp. 64, 65, 67) poured over.

Note For a vegetarian dish, the marrow may be stuffed with lentils, haricot beans or a nut forcemeat (p. 78).

Vegetable cutlets

5–6 persons

	Metric	Imp
cooked carrots diced	75 g	3 oz
cooked potatoes diced	75 g	3 oz
cooked peas	75 g	3 oz
cooked beetroot diced	75 g	3 oz
cooked cauliflower broken in small pieces	75 g	3 oz
margarine or butter	25 g	1 oz
flour	25 g	1 oz
stock or milk	250 ml	½ pt
1 tsp chopped parsley		
1 tsp chopped mixed herbs		
egg and breadcrumbs		
frying fat		
salt, pepper		
fried parsley		

Method

1 Melt fat in pan, add flour and blend well.
2 Add stock or milk, stir till it boils, simmer for 5 min., stirring.
3 Add vegetables, parsley and herbs, season well. Cook for 5 min.
4 Turn mixture on a plate to cool.
5 When cold, shape into balls or cutlets. Brush over with milk or egg and dip in breadcrumbs.
6 Fry in deep fat till pale brown. Drain well on soft paper.
7 Arrange cutlets on a hot dish and garnish with fried parsley.

Note This may be made with any cooked vegetables in season, provided they are cut small.

Vegetable scallops may be made with this mixture by putting it into greased scallop shells lined with breadcrumbs. Coat with more breadcrumbs mixed with grated cheese and dot with pieces of butter. Brown under the grill.

WATERCRESS

Watercress is very rich in mineral salts, and is used as a salad vegetable. It also makes excellent soup and is used as a garnish for grilled and fried meats.

SALADS

Salads are always in demand and can be made in great variety, from almost any edible material, cooked or uncooked. They may be roughly divided into plain salads which usually accompany some dish, and are mainly composed of salad vegetables, and mixed salads, which form a separate course and are composed of cooked fish or meat, nuts, vegetables and perhaps rice. A real French salad consists of but one kind of vegetable mixed with a few herbs, and plainly dressed with an oil and vinegar or vinaigrette dressing. The French consider that the delicate flavours of the different vegetables become impaired if mixed together. Sharp, rather tart fruits are often introduced into salads nowadays, especially in salads of American origin. The secret of successful salad-making lies in the skilful blending of the different ingredients, which should be of the best quality, and the attractive serving of the same, for a salad must always look cool and inviting. Salads should be served in a deep bowl or on individual side plates.

Preparing salad vegetables

Green vegetables should be young, fresh and crisp. Wash them carefully in cold water and handle as little as possible. Dry them by shaking in a salad basket or on a sieve; toss them lightly in a clean dry cloth, and spread out as much as possible, on the cloth, placed on the sieve, until required. Watercress requires most careful washing and cleaning in several waters. Lettuce is prepared by breaking off the root and any coarse leaves, and washing each leaf separately in two waters. The larger leaves may be torn into small pieces and put into the salad. The smaller leaves and the heart form an attractive decoration or garnish to the salad. Endive is prepared in the same manner as lettuce. Mustard and cress must always be washed carefully in several waters and the small black seeds removed; after washing shake well, and spread on a clean cloth to dry. Radishes should be soaked well in cold water for about 1 hour, dried well, then rubbed with a cloth. Cut off the leaves if they are large, but if the radishes are small and young a few of the leaves may be left on, as they form an effective garnish. Cut off the roots of spring onions, wash well and remove the outer skin. Use whole or cut into thin slices or strips.

Salad dressings

The dressing should never be added to a salad until it is ready to serve, but after it is added the salad should be well mixed, so that the dressing is incorporated with every portion of the vegetables. Use glass, wooden, bone, ivory or composition spoons and forks for mixing and serving salads, as the vinegar in the dressings is apt to discolour silver, and may even cause it to become coated with verdigris. A French dressing is usually served with green salads and with salads that accompany roasts, but meat, fish and cooked vegetable salads and salads which are offered as a separate course are generally served with a mayonnaise or egg dressing of some kind. Always use the best oil and vinegar for salads, as if the oil is at all rancid or the vinegar sour, the flavour of the salad will be completely spoilt. Lemon juice may replace vinegar, and cream or sour cream make good substitutes for oil. Recipes for salad dressings will be found on pp. 201–203.

Chicken salad

the remains of cold chicken minced
1 large lettuce
watercress
1 tsp castor sugar
1 tbsp melted butter or olive oil
2 hard-boiled eggs
2 tsp made mustard
1 tbsp vinegar

Method

1 Wash and dry lettuce. Tear large leaves to pieces and line the bottom of a salad bowl.
2 Place chicken on lettuce, arrange centre leaves round edge, alternating with watercress.
3 Rub yolks into a paste with melted butter or oil; add mustard, sugar and vinegar very gradually; stir well.
4 When ready to serve, pour over the salad dressing and sprinkle with chopped white of egg.

Note Celery may be used instead of lettuce and the salad decorated with green pickles and sliced beetroot.

Cole-slaw

	Metric	Imp
1 small hard white cabbage shredded very fine		
2 medium carrots grated		
sultanas soaked in orange juice till plump	50 g	2 oz
a few chopped nuts (optional)		

Dressing:

	Metric	Imp
salad oil	250 ml	½ pt
castor sugar	25 g	1 oz
1 tsp salt		
½ tsp dry mustard		
1 tsp onion juice		
3 tbsp cider vinegar		
1 tsp celery seeds		
1 tsp paprika		

Method

1 Soak shredded cabbage in ice-cold water for a few hours. Drain and dry very well. Do this while the sultanas are soaking in orange juice.
2 Mix all ingredients for dressing well and leave to chill.
3 Just before serving, mix cabbage, carrots and drained sultanas together with nuts, if used. Pour over dressing and toss well.

Note This makes a good winter accompaniment to cold meats or chicken, when salad greens are in short supply.

Cucumber salad

1 cucumber peeled and sliced thinly
2 tbsp vinegar
2 tbsp olive oil or sour cream
1 tsp chopped parsley
½ tsp chopped shallots
salt, pepper, grated nutmeg

Method

1 Stir vinegar and shallot into cream or oil. Add salt, pepper, nutmeg.
2 Mix in cucumber and put in a shallow dish. Sprinkle with parsley. Keep in a cold place till required.

Note Cucumber may also be cut in small cubes, sprinkled with salt, crushed garlic and chopped mint, left to drain in a strainer for ½ hr, then stirred into plain yoghourt and served very cold. This is particularly good with curry or with a salad in hot weather.

Fish salad

4 persons

	Metric	Imp
cold cooked fish	400 g	1 lb
shrimps	100 g	4 oz
mayonnaise sauce (p. 72)	125 ml	1 gill
1 hard-boiled egg sliced		
1 dssp chopped capers		
1 tsp chopped gherkins		
1 lettuce washed and dried		
salt, pepper		

Method

1 Remove all skin and bone from fish, **flake** it.
2 Mix fish with capers, gherkins and shrimps, sprinkle with salt and pepper.
3 Arrange lettuce leaves at the bottom of

the bowl, pile the fish mixture in it, pour over the mayonnaise sauce and decorate with shredded lettuce and hard-boiled egg.

French lettuce salad
4 persons

2 heads lettuce washed and dried
1 tsp chopped tarragon
a little watercress
French salad dressing (p. 201)
1 hard-boiled egg sliced
1 tbsp chopped parsley
a few small radishes

Method

1 Keep back a few best lettuce leaves and tear the rest to pieces.
2 Arrange in a bowl with a little watercress. Sprinkle over the tarragon and parsley.
3 Pour the dressing over the salad just before it is required and garnish with the best portions of lettuce, watercress, egg and radishes.

Salade niçoise

1 large lettuce
½ head celery chopped
1 large tomato sliced
2 anchovies per person
12 black olives
1 medium-sized onion chopped
1 small cucumber sliced
½ hard-boiled egg per person sliced
1 small tin tuna fish
1 green pepper seeded and sliced
French dressing (p. 201)

Method

1 Line a salad bowl with lettuce leaves, pulled in pieces.
2 Arrange on top celery, tomato, anchovy, olives, onion, cucumber and egg. Put tuna fish on top in large pieces, and scatter finely chopped pepper over.
3 Pour French dressing over, just before serving.

Note This is a substantial salad which is often served as a first course on a summer menu, or even as a main dish for a light luncheon.

Potato salad
4 persons

	Metric	Imp
cooked waxy potatoes diced	400 g	1 lb

1 tbsp mayonnaise sauce
2 tbsp white wine vinegar
3 tbsp olive oil
½ small onion chopped finely
1 dssp chopped parsley

Method

1 Mix oil, vinegar and mayonnaise sauce well and season.
2 Mix potatoes and onion together.
3 Pour dressing over potatoes in a bowl. Sprinkle with parsley.

Note The potatoes may be mixed with cooked beetroot, and cut either in round slices, cubes or dice. Potatoes and tomatoes mixed also make an excellent salad.

Russian salad
5–6 persons

	Metric	Imp
mixed cooked carrots, turnips, peas and French beans	500 ml	1 pt
mayonnaise sauce (p. 72)	125 ml	1 gill

1 tbsp chopped gherkins and capers mixed
1 tbsp chopped parsley
1 tbsp chopped tarragon and chervil mixed
2 tbsp olive oil
1 tbsp vinegar
salt, cayenne

Method

1 Cut carrots and turnips into small dice. Cut beans into diamond shapes.
2 Mix vinegar and oil well together, add cayenne and salt, stir in vegetables, add mayonnaise sauce.
3 Sprinkle in parsley and herbs, garnish with capers and gherkins.

Salad caprice

4 persons

	Metric	Imp
1 lettuce shredded		
1 endive shredded		
watercress		
4 slices tinned pineapple		
pineapple juice	60 ml	½ gill
French salad dressing		
(p. 201)	125 ml	1 gill
salt, pepper		

Method

1 Cut the pineapple into small pieces.

2 Arrange lettuce, watercress and endive in a salad bowl. Sprinkle with salt and pepper.

3 Place pineapple in a mound on top, pour pineapple juice and French dressing on top.

4 Garnish with watercress.

Note This salad is served with roast poultry or game.

Tomato salad (see p. 89)

MEATLESS DISHES

*Dishes made with dried vegetables, pasta, cereals,
nuts and cheese*

Meatless dishes play an important part in cookery nowadays, and can be served as a substitute for meat and fish. They make excellent luncheon and supper dishes.

Meatless dishes are mainly composed of pulse foods – i.e. dried haricot and butter beans, lentils and dried peas; cereals, rice, macaroni and semolina; nuts and various vegetable and cheese dishes.

PULSE DISHES

TO COOK DRIED VEGETABLES OR PULSE FOODS

When cooking dried vegetables, such as haricot and butter beans, green lentils and dried peas of any sort, they should be soaked in cold water from 24 to 36 hours to allow them to absorb the moisture lost in drying. (The red lentil does not need this soaking). Drain and put them into a saucepan of cold water, and bring slowly to the boil. Do not add salt to the water, as it tends to harden the vegetables, but when the water is very hard add a small piece of soda or a pinch of bicarbonate of soda to soften it.

In an emergency, they may be soaked in warm water for 2 to 3 hours.

If the beans are to be made into a purée, they should be cooked in two waters; the first for about an hour, and then drained off; the second should be just sufficient to cover the partly cooked beans so that when they are tender, all liquid has been absorbed. They are then passed through a sieve and butter added. Garlic is a very good flavour to add to dried beans.

HARICOT BEANS

There are two kinds of haricot beans, the red and white. They are the seeds of the kidney or French beans, which are allowed to ripen in the pod and are then dried. They are cheap and nourishing as they, like other pulse vegetables, contain a large percentage of protein, and may be used to replace meat instead of being used with it.

Butter beans are a variety of bean known as the Haricot Beurre, so called from its light yellow pod. Another variety comes from Peru, called Lima beans. They may be cooked according to any recipe for haricots.

Flageolets is the French name for the young green and tender seeds of the finest variety of French bean. They are gathered and shelled and dried before they turn white. They can be used either dried or fresh, but are more often dried in this country.

Haricot bean croquettes

4 persons

	Metric	Imp
cooked haricot beans sieved	200 g	½ lb
melted butter	40 g	1½ oz
brown or tomato sauce (pp. 64, 67)	250 ml	½ pt
2 eggs		
a little flour		
browned breadcrumbs		
frying fat		
salt, pepper		
fried parsley		

Method

1 Mix melted butter and beans and enough beaten egg to **bind**. Season well. Turn on a plate to cool.

2 Shape into balls or cork shapes with a little flour. Brush with beaten egg and dip in breadcrumbs.

3 Fry in hot fat till golden brown (about 10 min.). Drain on kitchen paper.

4 Serve on a hot dish with fried parsley. Hand brown or tomato sauce.

Note These may be shaped like cutlets and, after frying, a small piece of uncooked macaroni should be pressed into the thin end to simulate a bone.

Boiled haricot beans

4 persons

	Metric	Imp
beans washed and soaked in cold water overnight	500 ml	1 pt
butter	50 g	2 oz
water	1 l	1 qt
1 dssp chopped parsley		
juice of ½ lemon		
salt, pepper		

Method

1 Put beans in a large pan of cold water and bring to the boil very slowly.

2 Simmer very gently for 2 hr or longer if necessary.

3 Drain and let stand uncovered till dry.

4 Add butter, salt, pepper and parsley. Shake over heat for a few minutes till hot.

5 Add lemon juice and serve at once.

Note Flageolets and butter beans may be cooked in the same manner.

LENTILS

There are two kinds of lentils, the red or Egyptian lentil and the green lentil. The red lentil does not require soaking like other pulse foods, as it softens much more quickly during the cooking.

Like all pulse foods, lentils are deficient in fat, which should be added in some form, but, like haricot beans, lentils contain a very large amount of protein and so form a good substitute for meat.

Boiled lentils

4 persons

	Metric	Imp
red lentils washed and strained	400 g	1 lb
cold water	500 ml	1 pt
margarine or dripping	40 g	1½ oz
1 onion minced		
1 bunch herbs		
salt, pepper		
a little nutmeg (optional)		
toast or fried bread		

Method

1 Melt fat in a pan, add lentils and onion and stir well till they have absorbed the fat, add cold water.

2 Bring slowly to the boil, stirring all the time, add herbs and cover. Simmer gently for 1½ to 2 hr. Add more water if necessary.

3 Remove herbs and season with salt, pepper, and nutmeg if desired.

4 Pile lentils in the centre of a hot dish, garnish with snippets of toast or fried bread.

Mock duck

4 persons

	Metric	Imp
equal quantity of cooked haricot beans and cooked red lentils drained and sieved	400 g	1 lb
margarine	100 g	4 oz
brown or tomato sauce (pp. 64, 67)	250 ml	½ pt
mashed potatoes	100 g	4 oz
1 tsp chopped parsley		
3 onions minced		
½ tsp powdered sage		
salt, pepper		

Method

1 Melt half the fat in a pan, fry onions gently, mix with beans and lentils.

2 Add potato, sage and parsley and season well.

3 Shape mixture like a duck, put on a greased baking sheet. Pour over the rest of the fat, melted. Bake in a fairly hot oven (205°C, 400°F, Mark 6) till brown (15 min.). **Baste** often.

4 Put duck carefully on a hot dish and strain round the brown or tomato sauce.

DRIED PEAS

There are two kinds of dried peas – the split and the whole peas. They both contain a large amount of nourishment but require soaking for some time before cooking. They are sometimes used as a vegetable in place of fresh peas, and they make excellent purées and soups.

Boiled dried green peas
4 persons

	Metric	Imp
dried green peas washed and soaked overnight	200 g	½ lb
stock (any kind)	60 ml	½ gill
margarine	25 g	1 oz
1 onion peeled and stuck with 2 cloves		
1 bunch herbs		
water to cover		
salt, pepper		

Method

1 Put peas in a large pan, cover with water, bring slowly to the boil.
2 Add onion with cloves and herbs. Cover and simmer very gently till tender (2–3 hr.), stirring often. If necessary, add more boiling water.
3 When soft, drain peas, remove onion and herbs.
4 Melt margarine in a pan. Add peas, mix well. Season to taste.
5 Add stock and re-heat.
6 Serve in a hot vegetable dish.

Note Green pea purée is made by rubbing the peas, after cooking them in this manner, through a wire sieve. Moisten with a little of the water in which they were cooked, and return the purée to a pan with a little margarine or dripping, season well, and if too thick, thin it down with a little stock or milk. This purée is often served with salt beef or salt pork.

Pease pudding
4 persons

	Metric	Imp
Split peas washed and soaked overnight	500 ml	1 pt
margarine or dripping	25 g	1 oz
2 eggs		
water		
salt, pepper		

Method

1 Drain peas and tie loosely in a cloth, leaving room for them to swell.
2 Put them in the cloth in boiling water to cover. Simmer 2 to 2½ hr till peas are soft. Add more boiling water if necessary.
3 When soft, remove peas, drain well, turn out of cloth, rub through a sieve.
4 Add fat and beaten eggs and stir in. Season well.
5 Put mixture in a greased basin, cover with greased paper and steam for 1½ hr.
6 Turn pudding out on a hot plate and serve with boiled leg of pork and boiled beef.

Note This may be made without the eggs, but in this case the pudding will not turn out, but must be served in a gratin dish or casserole. It is a good plan to put a plate at the bottom of the pan under the peas when boiling in the cloth, as there is less danger of the cloth sticking to the bottom of the pan and burning.

PASTAS AND CEREAL DISHES

PASTAS

Pastas may be used as a garnish to soups, as an accompanying vegetable replacing potatoes, as a sweet, or made into dishes which can stand on their own as a first course or main course. They have little individual flavour so need a fairly strong accompanying sauce or stuffing when forming a course on their own.

The pastas which are most easily obtainable in this country are macaroni, which comes in various shapes such as shells as well as the usual tubes; spaghetti, which is thinner; and vermicelli, the thinnest of all, and mostly used in soups and stews. There are flat strips, such as tagliatelli, sold in coils, and noodles; and for stuffing, large tubes or canneloni. Little parcels containing meat called ravioli are usually bought ready stuffed from the delicatessen counter in specialist food stores.

To cook pastas

All pastas should be cooked in plenty of boiling salted water, allowing 2 to 3 litres (2 to 3 qt) for every 200 g (½ lb) of pasta. Do not break up lengths of macaroni or spaghetti, but coil them slowly into a large pan of boiling water, lowering them as they soften. Once in, the water for cooking pastas should be reduced to simmering, and the contents moved about gently every now and again to prevent them sticking together. A little oil added to the water also helps to prevent this. About 20 minutes cooking time is needed. Too long makes them glutinous.

Pasta is cooked when it can be severed with a thumbnail. 200 g (½ lb) of pasta should serve 4 persons.

Macaroni cheese

4 persons

	Metric	Imp
cooked macaroni	200 g	½ lb
milk or ½ milk and ½ water the macaroni was cooked in	500 ml	1 pt
butter	50 g	2 oz
flour	25 g	1 oz
grated cheese	100 g	4 oz
1 tsp made mustard		
browned breadcrumbs		
salt, pepper		

Method

1 Break up cooked macaroni in pieces.

2 Melt ¾ of the butter in a pan, add the mustard and flour and blend well. Take off the heat.

3 Gradually stir in the milk, returning to the heat between additions to thicken. When boiling, stir in ¾ of the cheese, add the macaroni. Mix well and season.

4 Put in a greased fireproof dish. Sprinkle remainder of cheese and some breadcrumbs on top. Melt remaining butter and pour over.

5 Brown in a hot oven (220°C, 425°F, Mark 7) or under the grill for 10 min.

RICE

There are several kinds of rice – Carolina, Patna, Rangoon and Java. Patna rice is the best for curry; it has a long grain and keeps its shape well when cooked. Carolina rice makes the best puddings and moulds. Unpolished rice is really the most nutritious, as polishing the rice removes the greater part of the nutriment. Rice can be made into a large variety of dishes either savoury or sweet. It is one of the most valuable of the starchy foods.

Allow 40 to 50 g (1½ to 2 oz) of uncooked rice per person. Always wash the rice in several waters till the water is clear. This will remove extra starch that is on the surface of the rice and tends to make it sticky.

Boiled rice

Wash the rice in several waters, and remove any black pieces or foreign matter. Have ready a fairly large saucepan three parts full of boiling water. Add salt in the proportion of 1 tsp to 500 ml (1 pt) of water, and sprinkle the rice into this. Stir with a fork for a minute or two until the water boils rapidly again, and then boil fast without a lid from 12 to 15 minutes, or until the grains feel soft when tested between the finger and thumb. Strain through a colander or sieve and allow cold water to run over the rice in order to remove excess starch. Re-heat on a baking tin in a cool oven (130°C, 275°F, Mark 1), turning occasionally with a fork, to free the grains. Rice may be used for any recipe used for macaroni and vice versa.

Note Saffron may be added to boiled rice for flavour and colour. Soak ½ tsp in boiling water for ½ hour and add to the cooking water.

Fried rice

Melt a little dripping or butter in a frying pan. Cook a small chopped onion till transparent. A little garlic may be added, or herbs or turmeric. Add cooked rice, season well, stir and cook till it begins to colour. For Chinese dishes, 1 tbsp of soya sauce beaten up with a raw egg is stirred into the rice mixture just before serving.

Rice croquettes

10–12 croquettes

	Metric	Imp
well washed rice	100 g	4 oz
grated cheese	75 g	3 oz
white stock	250 ml	½ pt
butter or margarine	25 g	1 oz
white sauce	125 ml	1 gill
frying fat		
a little flour		
1 egg		
browned breadcrumbs		
salt, pepper		
fried parsley		

Method
1 Put rice in large saucepan. Cover with cold water. Bring to the boil, cook for 5 min., then drain. Rinse in cold water.
2 Melt fat in a double pan, add rice and stock. Simmer over low heat till rice is cooked and stock absorbed (15–20 min.). Add more stock if necessary.
3 Add cheese and sauce and season well. Spread mixture on to a plate to cool.
4 When cold, divide into 10 or 12 pieces. Shape into balls or cork shapes with a little flour. Brush with beaten egg and dip in breadcrumbs.
5 Fry in hot fat, drain on soft paper.
6 Serve on a hot dish, garnish with fried parsley.

Note The beaten yolk of an egg may be added to the rice mixture if desired. Cooked macaroni cut small may be made into croquettes in the same way.

Risotto

4 persons

	Metric	Imp
washed rice	200 g	½ lb
stock (any kind)	750 ml	1½ pt
butter	50 g	2 oz
grated cheese	75 g	3 oz
2 small onions minced		
salt, pepper, nutmeg		

Method
1 Melt butter in a large pan. Fry onions in it without browning.
2 Dry rice carefully, add to onions and cook a few minutes, stirring continuously.
3 Add boiling stock and a little salt. Bring to the boil and simmer gently till rice is soft and stock nearly absorbed (15–20 min.). Stir occasionally.
4 Season well with salt, pepper and a pinch of nutmeg, add cheese and a little more butter and mix lightly with a fork.
5 Sprinkle with a little extra grated cheese and serve.

Note A few chopped mushrooms or some sliced tomatoes can be added to the rice if liked. They should be cooked with the onions before they are mixed with the rice.

SEMOLINA

Semolina is the germ or the central part of the hard wheats which are rich in gluten. It is largely used in Italy and the south of Europe. It contains about 11 per cent of protein, therefore it is a fairly nourishing food, used for making puddings, savoury dishes and for soups.

Semolina gnocchi

4 persons

	Metric	Imp
semolina	100 g	4 oz
milk	500 ml	1 pt
grated cheese	40 g	1½ oz
butter	10 g	½ oz
1 tsp French mustard		
1 onion		
egg and breadcrumbs for coating		
frying fat		
salt, pepper		

Method

1 Put onion in milk and bring slowly to the boil.
2 Remove onion, sprinkle in semolina and season well. Simmer for about 20 min., stirring frequently.
3 Remove from heat. Stir in mustard, cheese and butter.
4 Spread out 1·5 cm (¾ in.) thick on a plate and allow to cool.
5 When cold, cut into squares and dip in beaten egg and breadcrumbs.
6 Fry in hot fat (deep or shallow).
7 Drain on soft paper, serve on a hot dish and hand brown or tomato sauce (pp. 64, 67).

Note This makes a nourishing starter to a main meal.

NUT DISHES

Nuts are the most nourishing of vegetable foods, as they contain a large amount of protein and fat, and form a good substitute for meat. They are much used by vegetarians. Many people object to nuts on the ground that they are indigestible, but this is often because they are eaten as a dessert after a heavy meal, instead of forming a course of their own to replace meat. As they contain protein in a much more highly concentrated form than meat, serving them with or after meat means that too much protein is being taken at one meal, which can result in indigestion. Where nuts are found to be indigestible when eaten whole, owing to the difficulty of masticating them, they may be ground in a mincer or in a nut mill.

Nut cutlets

4 persons

	Metric	Imp
boiled rice	100 g	4 oz
shelled nuts of any kind minced	100 g	4 oz
stiff brown sauce (p. 64)	250 ml	½ pt
1 separated egg		
1 tsp chopped mixed herbs		
1 tsp chopped parsley		
breadcrumbs		
frying fat		
salt, pepper, nutmeg		

Method

1 Mix the nuts with the sauce and rice. Add herbs, a pinch of nutmeg, parsley and season well. Add beaten egg yolk.
2 Shape into cutlets, brush with beaten egg white. Dip in breadcrumbs.
3 Fry in hot fat. Drain on soft paper.
4 Serve on a hot dish, garnished with parsley.

Note Brazil nuts make excellent cutlets. If preferred, cooked potatoes may be used in the place of rice.

Nut galantine

5–6 persons

	Metric	Imp
cooked potatoes, boiled rice or soft breadcrumbs	400 g	1 lb
shelled nuts of any kind minced	150 g	6 oz
melted margarine	50 g	2 oz
1 tsp chopped parsley		
1 tsp mixed herbs		
1 onion minced		
1 head celery chopped		
1 egg		
a little white sauce		
glaze (p. 62)		
salt, pepper		
watercress or parsley		

Method

1 Mix nuts with potatoes, rice or breadcrumbs. Add onion, celery, herbs and parsley. Season well and mix in beaten egg and margarine. Add a little white sauce if too dry.

2 Shape into a roll, put into a floured, **scalded** cloth, tie the ends, put into boiling water and cook for 1 ½ hr.

3 Take out the roll, tie the ends tighter and put between two dishes with a weight on the top one, and leave till cold.

4 Remove the cloth, trim the ends of the gelatine, and brush with **glaze**.

5 Serve on a dish and garnish with watercress or parsley. Hand green salad separately.

Note This may be served hot, in which case, turn out of the cloth as soon as it is cooked, place on a hot dish and coat with brown or tomato sauce (pp. 64, 67).

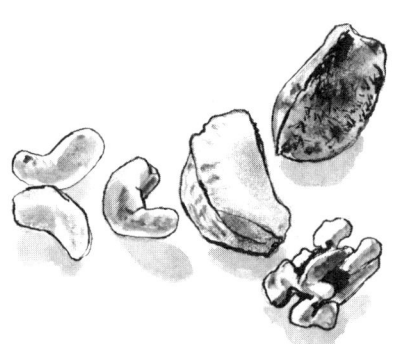

CHESTNUTS

Chestnuts, unlike most nuts, contain a large amount of starch, and in some countries are ground into flour for bread. They form the greater part of the food of the poor in some parts of France and Italy, and may be eaten boiled or roasted, and made into various dishes. The husks and brown skins from the chestnuts may be removed in two ways:

1 Wash the chestnuts and make a slit with a knife in the rounded end of each. Put them into a saucepan with cold water to cover, bring to the boil and boil for 2 or 3 minutes. Draw the pan to the side of the heat, taken out a few chestnuts at a time and remove the skins with a knife.

2 Make a slit in the chestnuts, then put them on a tin in the oven for about 10 minutes or less. Take them out, and while hot remove both the outer and inner skins.

Great care must be taken not to let the chestnuts brown when in the oven, and as it is easier to remove the skins when the nuts are hot, it is advisable not to put too many in the oven at once if a large quantity of chestnuts is being used.

Boiled chestnuts

	Metric	Imp
chestnuts	800 g	2 lb
butter	40–50 g	1½– 2 oz
water		
salt, pepper		

Method
1 Prepare the chestnuts as above, boil for 20 to 30 min. or until tender in salted water, strain.
2 Melt butter in a pan, add chestnuts, sprinkle with salt and pepper and stir till hot.
3 Serve in a hot vegetable dish.

Note The chestnuts may be reheated in parsley sauce or egg sauce (p. 69) or they may be coated in brown sauce (p. 64).

Purée of chestnuts   *4 persons*

	Metric	Imp
chestnuts	800 g	2 lb
butter	50 g	2 oz
milk	375 ml	¾ pt
cream	125 ml	1 gill
salt, pepper		

Method
1 Prepare chestnuts according to the directions on p. 212.
2 Put in a pan with the milk, and simmer gently till soft enough to rub through a sieve (1½ hr).
3 Stir in butter, cream, salt and pepper. Re-heat, stirring all the time.
4 Serve with cutlets or fillets of any kind of meat, poultry or game.

CHEESE

The variety of cheeses available is so great that it is impractical to list them all. On the whole, it is simplest to divide cheeses into three categories: hard, medium and soft. Most English cheeses come into the hard category, except the cream, cottage and curd cheeses. Cream cheese is made from single or double cream, cottage cheese from pasteurized milk and curd cheese from naturally soured unpasteurized milk, sometimes with added cream.

The best cheeses for cooking are Parmesan; a mature, dry Cheddar; Gruyère; and Mozzarella for some special recipes such as lasagne.

Cheese should not be kept in the refrigerator, but put in a loose polythene bag in a cool place. If it has to be stored in a refrigerator for longer periods in hot weather, it must be removed for several hours before using, or it will not have its full flavour. Most cheeses keep well in a freezer, but their texture may be more crumbly when defrosted. Cheese will become stringy and indigestible if over-cooked. It should, therefore, be cooked at a medium temperature, and if put under a hot grill, only for a short time.

Cheese pudding   *4 persons*

	Metric	Imp
fresh breadcrumbs	75 g	3 oz
scalded milk	500 ml	1 pt
grated cheese	100 g	4 oz
2 separated eggs		
salt, pepper		

Method
1 Soak breadcrumbs in the milk for a few minutes.
2 Add cheese, seasoning and beaten egg yolks.
3 Beat egg whites stiffly and fold into mixture.
4 Pour into a well-greased baking dish. Bake in a moderate oven (175°C, 350°F, Mark 4) till risen and set (½–¾ hr).

Cauliflower cheese   *4 persons*

	Metric	Imp
1 cauliflower broken into sprigs and cooked for 15 min. in salted, boiling water	800 g	2 lb

butter	75 g	3 oz
flour	40 g	1½ oz
milk	375 ml	¾ pt
grated Gruyère cheese	40 g	1½ oz
and		
grated Parmesan cheese	40 g	1½ oz
or		
strong Cheddar cheese	75 g	3 oz
2 tbsp fresh white breadcrumbs		
salt, pepper		

Method

1 Melt half the butter in a pan, stir in flour, cook for 1 min.

2 Add milk gradually, to make a sauce. Season with salt and pepper, simmer 2 to 3 mins.

3 Mix a large spoonful each of Gruyère and Parmesan cheese (or 2 large spoonfuls of Cheddar cheese) with the breadcrumbs; set aside.

4 Stir the rest of the cheese into the sauce till melted.

5 Place cooked cauliflower in ovenproof dish. Fold some of the sauce thoroughly into the cauliflower; pour rest of sauce over.

6 Sprinkle with cheese and crumb mixture and dot with remaining butter.

7 Brown in hot oven (220°C, 425°F, Mark 7) 10 min.

For further cheese recipes, see pages 40, 68, 85, 209, 213, 221, 256, 260.

PASTRY AND PASTRY DISHES

*General remarks – different kinds of pastry – meat pies and
puddings – quiches – patties and pasties – sweet pastries*

Hints on pastry making

See that all the required utensils are ready before beginning to make the pastry. A board should be kept specially for pastry-making, or better still a marble slab should be used, as pastry must be kept as cool as possible. Other requisites are a wooden or glass rolling pin, a flour dredger, a knife and a good-sized basin.

The hands must be very clean. Mix the pastry as much as possible with a knife, giving the final **kneading** only with the hands.

Make pastry in as cold a place as possible.

Pastry should be just moist enough to handle easily without sticking to the hands and board.

Avoid incorporating too much loose flour into the pastry, as this makes it hard.

Never rub pieces off the hands into the pastry, but clean them off with a little dry flour before rolling out the pastry.

Flour the board and rolling pin and lift the pastry occasionally to see that it is not sticking to the board. If any pastry has stuck to the board, scrape it off and flour the board again.

The flour should be dry and well sifted. Plain flour is always best for pastry except in the case of short crust pastry where the proportion of fat is less than half that of the flour. In this case, using self-raising flour, or adding baking powder to the flour at the time of sifting will help make the pastry lighter.

For short crust and flaky pastry, a mixture of lard or cooking fat and butter or margarine is best; for puff pastry, all butter should be used.

To bake pastry

To bake pastry successfully, the heat of the oven should be understood, as the hottest part may be either at the top or the bottom, or in some cases uniform all over.

For puff pastries, a bottom heat is best, as this causes the pastry to rise before the outside browns and hardens. The oven should not be hotter on one side than another for puff pastry, or it rises unevenly. If the oven is not hot enough, the butter or fat melts and runs out of the pastry before the starch grains in the flour have burst and absorbed the fat.

For puff pastries, the oven should register about 200°C (400°F, Mark 6) when the pastry is first put in, to be lowered gradually after the pastry has risen.

If pastry becomes too brown before it has finished cooking, cover it with a piece of paper.

Choux pastry

	Metric	Imp
flour	100 g	4 oz
butter	75 g	3 oz
water	125 ml	1 gill
3 eggs		

Method

1 Sieve flour on to a piece of greaseproof paper.

2 Put water, fat and salt into a small saucepan and bring to the boil.

3 Draw pan aside and add flour all at once. Beat till smooth and paste leaves the side of the pan. Leave to cool.

4 Whisk eggs lightly and add by degrees, beating thoroughly.

5 Pipe the mixture on to a greased tin.

6 Bake in a hot oven (220°C, 425°F, Mark 7) for about 30 min. till crisp and light brown. When baked, split the éclairs at one side and cool on a rack.

Flaky pastry

	Metric	Imp
flour	400 g	1 lb
butter or ½ butter, ½ fat	200 g	8 oz
a squeeze of lemon juice		
water		
pinch of salt		

Method

1 Divide the fat into 4 pieces and keep it cool.

2 Sieve together the flour and salt.

3 Rub one quarter of the fat into the flour and mix to a soft dough with enough water and lemon juice to make a smooth but not too moist paste.

4 **Knead** very lightly and roll to a long thin strip on a floured board.

5 Spread another ¼ of the fat in tiny pats over ⅔ of the strip.

6 Fold in three with the plain ⅓ inside, seal the edges and turn the fold to the left-hand side.

7 Roll to a strip and repeat stages 5 and 6 twice. Turn the fold again to the left and roll out. The pastry is now ready for use.

Note This pastry is suitable for covering meat pies and making tarts, tartlets and sausage rolls, etc.

Puff pastry

	Metric	**Imp**
flour	400 g	1 lb
butter	400 g	1 lb
squeeze of lemon juice		
cold water		
pinch of salt		

Method

1 Sieve the flour and salt into a clean basin, make a well in the centre.

2 Strain in lemon juice, add enough very cold water to make a dough. **Knead** till smooth and pliable. Leave to cool for ½ hr.

3 Roll out pastry to a strip twice as long and a little wider than the butter. Place butter in the centre, fold pastry over it and seal the edges.

4 Roll the pastry to a strip, fold in three and set aside in a cold place for 15 min.

5 Turn the fold to the left-hand side and roll out to a thin strip again and fold in three. Repeat this twice more and set it aside again. Repeat until pastry has had seven rolls and seven folds.

6 Roll out to thickness required. Stand half an hour in cold place.

Note Make the pastry in the coldest place available. If possible, use a marble or slate slab. This pastry will keep for several days in cold weather if wrapped in greaseproof paper. It is suitable for vol-au-vents, patties, meat pies, mince pies and various other dishes. If desired, the yolk of an egg may be mixed into the flour with the lemon juice and water.

Rough puff pastry

	Metric	**Imp**
flour	400 g	1 lb
butter	200 g	8 oz
squeeze of lemon juice		
water		
pinch of salt		

Method

1 Sieve flour and salt into a basin.

2 Add butter cut into pieces the size of a walnut.

3 Add lemon juice and water to **bind** to a soft dough, but do not break down the fat.

4 Turn on to a floured board and lightly press pastry together. Do not **knead.**

5 Roll out to a strip, keeping end square and sides even. Do not turn pastry, but roll in short strokes away from you.

6 Fold pastry in three, seal edges with a rolling pin.

7 Turn fold to the left-hand side.

8 Roll out to a strip, avoiding rolling over top and bottom edges as this would expel the air folded in the pastry.

9 Repeat rolling and folding four times. Leave in a cold place. The pastry can then be rolled out and used as desired.

Note In very hot weather it is sometimes necessary, if the pastry becomes very soft, to leave it in a cold place after the second roll. This pastry is suitable for covering meat pies, sausage rolls, mince pies and patties.

Short crust pastry

	Metric	Imp
flour	400 g	1 lb
equal quantities butter and		
fat	150 g	6 oz
cold water		
pinch of salt		

Method
1 Sieve flour and salt into a dry, cool basin.
2 **Rub** fat **into** flour with the tips of the fingers till mixture resembles fine bread-crumbs.
3 Add enough water to form a stiff dough, stirring with a knife.
4 Turn dough out on to a floured board. **Knead** slightly till free of cracks. Roll it out to the size required.

Note When making short crust pastry, the lightest pastry is that rolled first, so when making small tarts, cut out the coverings for the tarts from the pastry which is rolled first, making the bottom of the tarts from the rolled out trimmings. A richer crust can be made by adding the yolk of an egg to the mixture.

Suet crust pastry

	Metric	Imp
flour	200 g	½ lb
shredded suet	100 g	¼ lb
½ tsp baking powder		
pinch of salt		
cold water		

Method
1 Sieve flour, salt and baking powder.
2 Mix suet and flour.
3 Add water very gradually, stirring with a knife till the mixture is a smooth dough which leaves the side of the basin clean.
4 **Knead** lightly till free from cracks, and turn on to a floured board.
5 Flour a rolling pin and roll pastry out to the thickness required.

MEAT PIES

Beefsteak pie
5–6 persons

	Metric	Imp
stewing steak cut in small		
pieces	800 g	2 lb
stock (any kind)	250 ml	½ pt
rough puff pastry (p. 217)	200 g	½ lb
1 tbsp flour		
1 onion chopped		
salt, pepper, cayenne		
1 egg yolk		

Method
1 Mix flour and seasoning, toss meat in it.
2 Put into a pie dish with onion. Add half the stock.
3 Roll pastry out. Wet edge of pie dish, put a border of pastry round it, moisten it with a little water and put on a lid of pastry.
4 Trim the edges, make a hole in the centre and decorate with leaves of pastry.
5 Brush top with beaten egg yolk. Bake in a hot oven (220°C, 425°F, Mark 7) 30 min.
6 Lower the heat to 190°C (375°F, Mark 5), envelop the pie completely in a piece of wet greaseproof paper and continue cooking gently for a further 1½ hr.
7 Add hot stock through the hole before serving.

Note If a cheap cut of meat is used, it is advisable to stew or pressure cook it first and allow it to cool, before covering it with pastry.

Steak and kidney pie is made in the same way, adding 200 g (½ lb) of kidney.

Rabbit pie
4–6 persons

	Metric	Imp
1 rabbit jointed		
bacon or pickled pork diced	300 g	¾ lb
forcemeat balls (p. 79)	300 g	¾ lb
stock made with the rabbit		
giblets	500 ml	1 pt

	Metric	Imp
flaky pastry (p. 216)	300 g	¾ lb
salt, pepper		

Method

1 Pack the meat, bacon and forcemeat balls in a pie dish.
2 Add salt, pepper and stock to fill dish three-quarters full.
3 Cover with pastry and bake in a hot oven (220°C, 425°F, Mark 7) for 15 min.
4 Reduce the heat to moderate (175°C, 350°F, Mark 4), cover pie with damp grease-proof paper and cook for a further 1½ hr. Serve hot or cold.

Roman pie

4–5 persons

	Metric	Imp
cooked meat of any kind		
minced	200 g	½ lb
cooked macaroni cut small	75 g	3 oz
brown sauce (p. 64)	125 ml	1 gill
short crust pastry (p. 218)	400 g	1 lb
1 onion minced		
1 hard-boiled egg sliced		
1 tsp chopped parsley		
pinch chopped marjoram and thyme		
1 egg yolk		
salt, pepper		
parsley		

Method

1 Line a plain round, greased cake tin with pastry, bringing it well up the sides.
2 Mix all other ingredients together, fill pastry case.
3 Wet edges of case and cover with a lid of pastry. Press edges well together, and press into scallops.
4 Make a hole in centre of pie, decorate with leaves of pastry.
5 Brush over with beaten egg yolk. Bake in moderately hot oven (220°C, 425°F, Mark 7) for 1 hr. Remove from oven.

6 Allow pie to stand for a few minutes. Loosen edges with a knife. Turn it out very carefully on to a cloth then back on to a dish right side up. Garnish with parsley and serve hot or cold.

Note This pie may be filled with any kind of cooked meat, poultry or game and cooked rice may replace macaroni.

Veal and ham pie

4–5 persons

	Metric	Imp
flaky pastry (p. 216)	300 g	¾ lb
fillet of veal or veal cutlets	600 g	1½ lb
ham	150 g	6 oz
white stock	125 ml	1 gill
1 or 2 hard-boiled eggs		
1 tsp grated lemon rind		
salt, pepper		

Method

1 Remove all skin, fat, gristle from meat, and cut into small pieces. Cut ham into pieces as well.
2 Sprinkle with salt and pepper and place in layers in a pie dish.
3 Sprinkle over the lemon rind. Arrange sliced eggs over meat. Pour in stock.
4 Roll out pastry and cover the pie.
5 Cook and dish as for beefsteak pie (p. 218).

Note If desired, a little more stock may be poured through the hole in the pastry into the pie when it is cooked. If the pie is to be eaten hot, the stock must be hot. If eaten cold, a little gelatine should be added to the stock. Chicken and ham pie may be made in this manner. The chicken must be jointed and may be boned.

MEAT PUDDINGS

Steak and kidney pudding

5–6 persons

	Metric	Imp
Stewing steak cut in thin squares	400 g	1 lb
beef kidney trimmed and cut in pieces	200 g	½ lb
suet pastry (p. 218)	300 g	¾ lb
4 tbsp stock (any kind) gravy	250 ml	½ pt
salt, pepper		

Method

1 Mix flour and seasoning and coat slices of beef in it.

2 Place a small piece of kidney on each slice of beef and roll up.

3 Grease a pudding basin, roll out paste to about 1 cm (½ in.) thickness and line basin with it. Put in steak and kidney and add stock.

4 Cover with a lid of paste, press edges firmly together. Tie a **scalded** floured cloth over the top (make a pleat in the cloth to allow pudding to rise).

5 Put the pudding in a pan of boiling water. Keep water constantly boiling, adding more boiling water if necessary, and boil 3 hr (4 hr for steaming).

6 Untie the cloth and leave for a minute or two to allow it to shrink. Loosen it round the edges with a knife and serve in the basin with a white napkin tied round. Hand gravy separately.

Note Mushrooms, either whole small ones or larger quartered ones may be added to the pudding. Oysters are also added sometimes.

If the pudding is steamed, allow an extra hour.

Veal, rabbit and **mutton puddings** are made in the same way, adding raw potatoes, onion and parsley or bacon and herbs.

Meat roly-poly

4 persons

	Metric	Imp
cooked meat of any kind minced	200 g	½ lb
suet crust (p. 218)	200 g	½ lb
brown sauce (p. 64)	250 ml	½ pt
1 small onion minced		
1 dssp chopped parsley		
1 tsp mixed herbs		
salt, pepper		

Method

1 Mix meat, onion, parsley and herbs. Season well and add 2 tbsp brown sauce. Mix well.

2 Roll out pastry into a long thin strip about twice as long as it is broad.

3 Spread meat mixture over, roll it up and fasten the ends well together, using a little water to make them stick.

4 Put the roll into a **scalded** floured cloth, tie up the ends and place it in a pan of boiling water with a saucer under the roll, and boil for 2 to 3 hr.

5 Turn the roly-poly out of the cloth on to a hot dish and serve the rest of the brown sauce separately.

QUICHES

Quiches are flans, nearly always savoury, which originated in Alsace and Lorraine. They have become accepted as regular dishes on the British supper table, being suitable either for buffet parties or for light family suppers.

The classic quiche is a savoury custard flan made with cream, butter and eggs, but many variations of the recipe exist.

Quiche lorraine

4 persons

	Metric	Imp
short pastry (p. 218)	200 g	½ lb
butter	50 g	2 oz
single cream	250 ml	½ pt
3 egg yolks		
salt		

Method
1 Line a flan tin or pie plate with pastry.
2 Spread softened butter over the base.
3 Whip egg yolks with cream, season with salt. Pour into flan case.
4 Bake in a hot oven (220°C, 425°F, Mark 7) for 5 min; reduce the temperature to slow (130°C, 275°F, Mark 1) and continue baking till firm to the touch (about 30 min.).
5 Serve cut in wedges, hot, cold or warm, which is best of all.

Note For an economy quiche, substitute milk for cream and use 2 whole eggs plus one extra egg yolk.

Cheese quiche

Cover the buttered surface of the pastry case with thin slices of Gruyère, or grated Cheddar, then cover with the custard and bake as above.

Ham or bacon quiche

Cover the buttered base with finely chopped lean ham, or lean bacon rashers, grilled and broken into pieces. Add the custard to which a little grated nutmeg, dry mustard and cayenne have been added. Bake as above.

Other suggestions for quiche fillings   Onions, softened in butter, drained well and laid on the base with a little grated cheese and 10 chopped anchovy fillets; asparagus; cooked shrimps or prawns; mushrooms, **sweated** in butter and drained well

PATTIES AND PASTIES

To make vol-au-vent cases

Roll out puff pastry very evenly, about 1 cm (½ in.) thick, leave it for a few moments to shrink. Place an oval or round cutter on the pastry about 6 mm (¼ in.) from the edge, with a sharp knife cut round the cutter, holding the knife slantways to make the lower edge of the pastry a little wider than the upper. Remove the cutter and place the cut piece of pastry on a baking tin, brushed over with a little water, placing the under side of the pastry uppermost. This is done because the upper part of the pastry will then shrink a little, making it the same size as the portion which rests on the tin. Brush over vol-au-vents with beaten egg and with a smaller cutter mark an oval or round in the centre. This is afterwards removed to form a lid. Put the tin into a hot oven, about 200°C (400°F, Mark 6), until the pastry has risen well. Cook for about 35 minutes. Should it become too brown, cover with folds of paper and lower the heat of the oven slightly. When cooked, lift the little lid of pastry from the inner circle and scoop out the soft pastry from the centre, being careful not to break the edges. Do not fill the cases until just before using them.

For a very high vol-au-vent, cut out two pieces of pastry the same size and stamp out the middle of one of the pieces completely. Bake separately, then place one on top of the other directly they are taken from the oven, brushing them over with a beaten egg to make them stick properly.

Cornish pasties

4 persons

	Metric	Imp
short crust pastry	400 g	1 lb
raw minced beef	200 g	8 oz
raw diced potatoes	100 g	4 oz
½ onion minced		
2 tbsp cold water		
salt, pepper		
1 egg yolk or milk		

Method

1 Mix the meat, onion and potatoes, add the water, season well.

2 Roll out the pastry rather thinly, stamp into 4 rounds the size of a saucer.

3 Wet the edges of the pastry and put a quarter of the mixture in the centre of each round.

4 Fold the pastry over and press the edges well together at the top. Flute with the fingers.

5 Place pasties on a greased baking tin, brush with a little beaten egg yolk or milk, bake in a hot oven (220°C, 425°F, Mark 7) for 15 min.

6 Lower the temperature to moderate (175°C, 350°F, Mark 4) and cook a further ½ hr, covering pasties with greaseproof paper if they are browning too quickly.

Sausage rolls

Makes 8 rolls

	Metric	Imp
flaky pastry	200 g	½ lb
sausage meat	200 g	½ lb
1 egg yolk or milk		
salt, pepper		

Method

1 Divide meat into 8 sausage-shaped pieces.

2 Roll out pastry to 3 mm (⅛ in.) thick and cut into 8 oblongs about 8 × 10 cm (3 × 4 in.).

3 Lay a piece of sausage meat in the centre of each strip of pastry. Wet round the edges and double the pastry over. Mark the top with three diagonal slits.

4 Place on a greased baking tin, brush with beaten egg yolk or milk and bake in a hot oven (220°C, 425°F, Mark 7) 20 to 30 min.

Veal and ham vol-au-vents

6 persons

	Metric	Imp
cooked veal cut small	150 g	6 oz
cooked ham chopped	50 g	2 oz
white sauce	125 ml	1 gill
cream	60 ml	½ gill
1 tsp grated lemon rind		
1 tsp chopped parsley		
salt, pepper		
6 vol-au-vent cases (p. 221)		

Method

1 Mix veal, ham and sauce and make hot.

2 Add parsley, seasoning and lemon rind.

3 Stir in cream, keep warm but do not allow to boil.

4 Warm pastry cases in the oven and fill with mixture. Put on the lids of pastry. Serve hot.

Note Chicken or rabbit may be used instead of veal.

SWEET PASTRIES

To make a flan case

Grease a plain or fluted flan ring and place it on a greased baking tin. Roll out the pastry to a little less than 6 mm (¼ in.) thick, and line the ring and the tin within the circle with it. Press the pastry well down to the bottom and against the sides of the ring, so that it may take shape well. Cut round the edges of the pastry with a pair of sharp scissors, but leave about 6 mm (¼ in.) of pastry above the ring, to allow for the pastry shrinking. Prick the bottom of the pastry and crimp or scallop the edges, then fill the flan with the fruit or whatever is to be used, and bake it in a fairly hot oven (200°C, 400°F, Mark 6). If it is preferred to bake the flan before filling it, proceed as follows: line the case with greaseproof paper, and fill it with haricot beans, raw rice or crusts of bread. Bake in a fairly hot oven. When cooked, remove the paper, rice or haricot beans and return the tart to the oven for a few minutes in order to dry the inside.

Plain apple pie

4 persons

	Metric	Imp
cooking apples peeled, cored and cut in slices	600 g	1½ lb
brown sugar	100 g	4 oz
water	60 ml	½ gill
short crust pastry	250 g	10 oz
a strip of thinly peeled lemon rind		
a little lemon juice		

Method
1 Put half the apples in a pie dish, add lemon rind and juice, sugar and water. Cover with rest of apples.
2 Roll out pastry thinly, wet edges of dish, put round a band of pastry. Brush this with water and cover with a lid of pastry.
3 Press edges together, scallop them, ornament top with leaves of pastry.
4 Bake on a baking tin in a fairly hot oven (200°C, 400°F, Mark 6) for ½ to ¾ hr.
5 When pastry is cooked, remove pie to cooler part of oven to finish cooking apples. Test these with a skewer inserted under one of the leaves.
6 When ready, sprinkle with castor sugar and serve hot or cold with cream or custard.

Note Rhubarb pie may be made in the same way. Peel and cut the rhubarb into 2 cm (1 in.) lengths.

Blackcurrant plate pie

	Metric	Imp
blackcurrants washed and drained	400 g	1 lb
brown sugar	60 g	2½ oz
shortcrust, flaky or puff pastry	400 g	1 lb
1 tbsp water		

Method
1 Line a deep fireproof plate with pastry.
2 Put in the fruit with the sugar and water.

3 Cover with pastry as with the apple pie (p. 223).
4 Bake for 30 to 40 min. in a fairly hot oven (200°C, 400°F, Mark 6).
5 Sprinkle with castor sugar and serve hot or cold.

Note When making a pie with soft fruit, it should be remembered that the fruit shrinks very much when cooking, so the pie dish should be filled as full as possible.

Redcurrants or redcurrants and raspberries mixed, gooseberries, cherries or blackberries and apples, plums of any kind may be made into a pie in this manner.

Butterscotch flan

4 persons

	Metric	Imp
1 flan case **baked blind** (p. 222)		
milk	250 ml	½ pt
butter	40 g	1½ oz
cornflour	40 g	1½ oz
brown sugar	75–100 g	3–4 oz
castor sugar	50 g	2 oz
salt		
1 separated egg		

Method
Filling
1 Mix together brown sugar, a pinch of salt and the cornflour.
2 Blend in the milk, bring gently to the boil and cook for 3 min., stirring all the time. Remove from heat.
3 Add butter gradually, in small pieces, and the beaten egg yolk. Beat mixture gently with a wooden spoon. Allow to cool slightly.
4 Fill flan case with mixture.

Meringue
5 Beat egg white stiffly, fold in castor sugar, heap on to filling and put in a very slow oven (110°C, 225°F, Mark ¼) for 40 min. or till meringue is set.

Cheese cake

6 *persons*

Case	Metric	Imp
unsalted butter	75 g	3 oz
crushed digestive biscuits	150 g	6 oz
sugar (optional)	25 g	1 oz

Method
1 Melt butter, add sugar, if used.
2 Combine with crumbs, stirring till evenly combined.
3 Spread mixture into a shallow pastry tin.
4 Chill 2 hr before filling.

Filling	Metric	Imp
sieved cottage cheese	200 g	8 oz
cream cheese	100 g	4 oz
gelatine	10 g	½ oz
double cream lightly beaten	125 ml	¼ pt
sugar	100 g	4 oz

3 tbsp water
grated rind and juice of 1 lemon
2 separated eggs
pinch of salt

Method
1 Put gelatine in a small pan in the water. Leave to soak 5 min.
2 Mix sieved cottage cheese and cream cheese together, add lemon rind.
3 Beat egg yolks, 40 g (1 ½ oz) sugar and salt together till creamy and light.
4 Heat gelatine slowly till dissolved; remove from heat and add strained lemon juice.
5 Whisk gelatine into egg yolks, add cheese mixture.
6 Whisk egg whites and remaining sugar till stiff.
7 **Fold into** cheese mixture with cream.
8 Pour into prepared case and chill for 2–3 hr, till firm.

Custard tart

4–6 *persons*

	Metric	Imp
shortcrust pastry (p. 218)	250 ml	½ lb
milk	500 ml	1 pt
castor sugar	75 g	3 oz

2 eggs plus 2 egg yolks
vanilla pod or 2 drops vanilla essence

Method
1 Line a flan tin with pastry.
2 **Scald** milk with vanilla pod or add essence.

3 Whip together eggs, egg yolks and sugar together in a bowl.
4 Pour hot milk over, stir well and pour back and forth between pan and bowl twice more, then pour into uncooked pastry case.
5 Put in hot oven (220°C, 425°F, Mark 7) for 5 min., then lower temperature to low (130°C, 275°F, Mark 1) and continue baking till set, about 30 to 35 min.

Eccles cakes

8–10 *cakes*

	Metric	Imp
flaky pastry (p. 216)	400 g	1 lb
shredded candied peel	50 g	2 oz
melted butter	50 g	2 oz
cleaned currants	300 g	12 oz
castor sugar	100 g	4 oz

1 egg
pinch of nutmeg

Method
1 Roll out pastry into rounds about 10 cm (4 in.) in diameter.
2 Mix currants, butter, peel, nutmeg and sugar.
3 Put a little of this mixture in centre of each round, draw edges together round the top. Turn pastry over so join is at the bottom, work into a round with the hands.
4 Flatten slightly with a rolling pin, slash twice on top, brush with beaten egg.
5 Bake in a hot oven (220°C, 425°F, Mark 7) about 15 min.

Lemon cheese cakes

About 12 cakes

	Metric	Imp
butter	100 g	4 oz
castor sugar	100 g	4 oz
short crust, flaky or rough puff pastry (p. 217)	400 g	1 lb

2 lemons
2 eggs
5 or 6 almonds **blanched** and halved

Method
1 Cream butter and sugar.
2 Add eggs one by one, beating well. Add grated peel of 2 lemons and strained juice of one.

3 Stir over low heat till mixture thickens slightly. Cool.
4 Line patty pans with pastry.
5 Fill with lemon mixture, top with half an almond.
6 Bake in a fairly hot oven (200°C, 400°F, Mark 6) about 15 to 20 min. or till cooked.

Lemon meringue pie   4–6 persons

	Metric	Imp
1 pastry case **baked blind**		
2 ½ tbsp cornflour		
2 separated eggs		
rind and juice of 1 lemon		
castor sugar (for filling)	75 g	3 oz
castor sugar (for meringue)	100 g	4 oz
butter	25 g	1 oz
water	250 ml	½ pt

Method
1 Mix cornflour to a smooth paste with a little of the water.
2 Boil up the rest of the water with grated lemon rind. Pour on to cornflour, mix well, return to pan, boil for 5 min. Remove from heat.
3 Add beaten egg yolks and stir for a few minutes.
4 Add sugar, lemon juice and butter and mix well.
5 Pour into cooked case.
6 Beat egg whites till stiff and dry. Add half sugar and beat again till it stands in peaks. Fold in rest of sugar.
7 Pile on top of filling. Bake in a very slow oven (110°C, 225°F, Mark ¼) for 40 min., or till lightly browned.
8 Serve cold.

Mince pies   About 12 pies

	Metric	Imp
rough puff pastry or puff pastry (p. 217)	400 g	1 lb
mincemeat, bought or home-made (p. 311)		

Method
1 Roll out pastry to just under 6 mm (¼ in.) thick. Cut in rounds a little larger than the patty pans.

2 Roll out trimmings and cut these into rounds to line patty pans.
3 Fill with mincemeat. Wet edges and cover with pastry rounds that were first cut. Press edges well together.
4 Bake in a fairly hot oven (200°C, 400°F, Mark 6) for 25 to 30 min.
5 Brush mince pies with a little stiffly beaten egg white or with water and sift on a little castor sugar. Return to oven for a minute or two.

Pear flan   4–5 persons

	Metric	Imp
1 pastry flan case **baked blind**		
about 8 pear halves, poached in syrup or tinned		
2 egg whites		
castor sugar	100 g	4 oz
a little cochineal		
2 drops vanilla essence		
cherries and angelica		

Method
1 Arrange the half pears in the flan case.
2 Boil up the syrup till thick, colour with cochineal, spoon over the pears.
3 Beat half the sugar into the stiffly beaten egg whites, **fold in** the rest, flavour with vanilla. Pile on top of the pears.
4 Brown quickly in oven, decorate with cherries and angelica.
5 Remove from flan ring. Serve hot or cold.

Note This may be covered with whipped cream in place of the whites of egg, if preferred. Apples, peaches, cherries or any kind of fruit may be made into a flan in the same manner.

Pumpkin pie   6 persons

	Metric	Imp
a large baked flan case made with short crust pastry (p. 218)		
cooked pumpkin purée	200 g	½ lb
milk	150 ml	6 fl oz
soft brown sugar	100 g	4 oz

8 tbsp double cream
3 eggs
½ tsp salt
½ tsp nutmeg or mace
pinch of powdered cloves
2 tbsp brandy or Calvados
whipped cream

Method

1 Blend cream, milk, sugar, salt and spices together and stir well.
2 Add lightly beaten eggs and brandy. Stir in pumpkin purée.
3 Pour into pastry case and bake in a moderate oven (175°C, 350°F, Mark 4) till mixture is firm (about 40–50 min.).
4 Serve warm with whipped cream.

Treacle or syrup tart   *4–5 persons*

	Metric	**Imp**
short crust pastry (p. 218)	200 g	½ lb
4 tbsp golden syrup or treacle		
2 tbsp breadcrumbs		
strained juice and grated rind of 1 lemon		

Method

1 Mix treacle, breadcrumbs, lemon juice and rind together.
2 Roll out pastry and line a flan tin.
3 Put in treacle mixture and cover with any remaining strips of pastry arranged in a lattice pattern.
4 Bake in a hot oven (220°C, 425°F, Mark 7) for 20 min.
5 Serve hot or cold.

PUDDINGS AND HOT SWEETS

Milk puddings – boiled and steamed puddings – baked puddings – soufflés, pancakes and fritters

Puddings may be roughly divided into seven sections:

1 Milk puddings
2 Suet puddings
3 Batters and fritters
4 Soufflés

5 Custards
6 Moulds or cold shapes
7 Cake-like mixtures

MILK PUDDINGS

Rice pudding

4 persons

	Metric	Imp
rice	40–50 g	1½–2 oz
milk	500 ml	1 pt
sugar	25 g	1 oz

flavouring (vanilla, lemon rind, nutmeg, bay leaf or cinnamon, as desired)

Method
1 Wash the rice.
2 Put the rice, sugar, milk and chosen flavouring into a greased pie dish. Stir well.
3 Put into a slow oven (130°C, 275°F, Mark 1) and stir again after 10 min.
4 Cook for about 2 hr, stirring at 10 minute intervals for the first half hour.
5 When cooked, it will be creamy with soft grains of rice and a pale brown skin on top.

Note The same proportions of ingredients may be cooked in a covered saucepan on top of the stove, over very slow heat, stirring occasionally. This will make a creamy pudding without any skin which may be served hot or cold. Tapioca is cooked in the same way.

Semolina pudding

4 persons

	Metric	Imp
semolina	40–50 g	1½ to 2 oz
milk	500 ml	1 pt
sugar	25 g	1 oz

Flavouring (grated lemon rind or orange peel)

Method
1 Heat the milk.
2 Sprinkle in the semolina, stirring well, and add sugar and flavouring.

3 Cook till the grain is clear, stirring all the time.
4 Turn into a greased pie dish and bake in a moderate oven (175°C, 350°F, Mark 4) till brown, or continue simmering in a covered saucepan till thick and creamy, about ½ hr.

Note Sago should be cooked in the same way as semolina.

Baked custard

4–5 persons

	Metric	Imp
4 eggs		
milk	500 ml	1 pt
sugar	50 g	2 oz

few drops vanilla essence
grated nutmeg

Method
1 Beat eggs and sugar together.
2 Heat milk to blood heat.
3 Add to beaten eggs, stirring all the time.
4 Add vanilla essence to taste.
5 Strain into a greased heat-proof dish.
6 Grate a little nutmeg on top.
7 Place dish in a pan of water and bake in a very moderate oven (160°C, 325°F, Mark 3) till set, about 1 hr.

Caramel custard

4–5 persons

	Metric	Imp
Caramel		
granulated or loaf sugar	75 g	3 oz
water	75 ml	3 fl oz
Custard		
4 or 5 eggs		
milk	500 ml	1 pt
sugar	50 g	2 oz

Few drops vanilla essence

Method

1 Put sugar for the caramel and water into a small pan and boil until mixture turns golden brown.

2 Immediately pour into a heated soufflé mould or individual dariole moulds, moving the moulds around so that the caramel coats the bottom and sides. Leave till cold.

3 Beat eggs with rest of the sugar, pour on the heated milk, flavour with vanilla and strain into the mould.

4 Cover with greased paper and steam very slowly for 1 hr or till set, or stand moulds in a baking tin of water and bake in a very moderate oven (160°C, 325°F, Mark 3) for 1 hr.

5 Leave till cold in the mould, refrigerate for a short time if possible, and turn out carefully on to a dish just before serving. The caramel will be partly liquid, so a deep dish is needed.

Note This may also be served hot, in which case it is turned out straight away, and all the caramel will be liquid.

Cornflour, ground rice or arrowroot pudding

3–4 persons

	Metric	Imp
ground rice, cornflour or arrowroot	50 g	2 oz
milk	500 ml	1 pt
sugar	25 g	1 oz
1 separated egg		
strips of lemon rind		
castor sugar		

Method

1 Mix cereal to a smooth paste with a little milk.

2 Boil the rest of the milk and pour on to the blended cereal.

3 Put the mixture into a rinsed pan, bring to boiling point and cook for 10 min. stirring continuously.

4 Remove from heat, add the sugar, lemon rind and egg yolk and mix thoroughly.

5 Fold the stiffly beaten egg white into the cereal mixture.

6 Pour into a greased pie dish and bake in a

moderate oven (175°C, 350°F, Mark 4) for 20 min.

7 Remove rind, **dredge** with castor sugar. Serve hot or cold.

Cornflour custard

3–4 persons

	Metric	Imp
cornflour	25 g	1 oz
castor sugar	25 g	1 oz
milk	500 ml	1 pt
2 egg yolks and 1 egg white		
flavouring to taste		

Method

1 Mix the cornflour to a smooth paste with a little of the milk.

2 Boil the rest of the milk and pour on the blended cornflour, stirring all the time and return to the pan.

3 Stir till boiling, then simmer gently for 10 min., stirring all the time.

4 Remove from heat, cool slightly, then stir in beaten egg yolks and white of 1 egg, sugar and flavouring.

5 Return to the heat and stir for 3 or 4 min. but do not allow to boil.

6 Serve hot or cold in a glass dish or custard cups.

Note Arrowroot or potato flour may be used in place of cornflour for this.

Tapioca pudding with eggs

4 persons

	Metric	Imp
tapioca	50 g	2 oz
milk	750 ml	1½ pt
water	125 ml	1 gill
sugar	50 g	2 oz
1 separated egg		
a pinch of salt		
grated rind of ½ lemon		

Method

1 Wash the tapioca, put in a saucepan with the water and simmer till the water is absorbed.

2 Add the milk, salt and grated lemon rind,

and simmer very gently till tapioca is cooked (approx. 2 hr.), stirring occasionally.

3 Add sugar, cool slightly and stir in the beaten egg yolk.

4 Beat the egg white stiff, **fold into** the mixture and put in a greased pie dish.

5 Bake in a moderate oven (175°C, 350°F, Mark 4) till brown, about 20 min.

BOILED AND STEAMED PUDDINGS

Notes on boiled puddings

First grease a basin with melted margarine, butter or **clarified** fat. The basin must always be quite full, so if the mixture does not absolutely fill the basin, fill it up with crusts of bread. Tie a **scalded** floured cloth over the basin and make a pleat in it before tying on the string, to allow the pudding to rise. Tie the corners of the cloth over the top of the basin. This enables the basin to be lifted easily in and out of the water.

To **scald** a cloth, dip it into boiling water and squeeze it dry and then **dredge** flour over it. Put the basin into a pan containing sufficient boiling water to cover the basin completely and boil for the time given in the recipe. See that the pan does not boil dry, but replenish with more boiling water when necessary. Sometimes puddings are boiled in a cloth and not in a basin. In this case, the cloth must be **scalded** and floured before putting the pudding mixture into it. The cloth should be tied loosely to leave room for the pudding to swell. Place a tin plate or a saucer at the bottom of the saucepan to keep the pudding from sticking. When cooked, if the pudding is to be kept, as in the case of plum puddings, it should be hung up in a dry place until required. If a plum pudding is boiled in a basin, the cloth must be removed from the basin to allow the steam to escape. The cloth must be dried before fastening it on again, or it must be replaced by a fresh dry cloth, otherwise the pudding is liable to become mouldy when kept.

Notes on steamed puddings

There are two methods of steaming puddings:

1 The basin or mould containing the pudding is put into a saucepan on an inverted saucer or dish or something to raise it from the water, and the pan must contain sufficient boiling water to reach halfway up the basin. Bring to the boil again after putting the pudding into the pan and boil gently for the time given in the recipe. The water must not boil too hard or it will bubble up into the pudding and make it heavy. Care must be taken that the pan does not boil dry, and more boiling water must be added when necessary.

2 The pudding is put into a steamer placed over a pan of boiling water. The water under the steamer must be kept boiling rapidly, and should it evaporate more water must be added. It is always necessary to allow ½ hour longer for steaming a pudding than for boiling it.

Very delicate puddings such as soufflés, if steamed according to the first method, must be simmered very slowly, only one or two bubbles showing in the water. The basin should not be quite full for steamed puddings, but should allow room for them to rise. Always cover steamed puddings with greased paper, and when steaming according to the first method, be careful that the water does not touch the paper, as the paper will soak up the water and allow it to penetrate into the pudding.

Suet puddings

There are many varieties of suet puddings. The general proportions and basis of the puddings are usually the same, different ingredients being added to vary and enrich the mixture, such as fresh fruit, dried fruits, candied peel, ginger, spice, various flavourings, eggs, and so on.

A suet pudding mixture should be sufficiently soft to drop heavily from a spoon, but too soft to handle like pastry. It should always be mixed with a wooden spoon. Breadcrumbs, or pieces of bread soaked and squeezed dry, added to the flour, make a lighter pudding than if flour alone is used. The richness of the pudding also depends upon the amount of suet used, a smaller proportion of suet being used for plainer puddings, while to the richer kind, such as plum puddings, more suet is allowed. If shredded suet is used, less is required as there is no waste with it.

To chop suet for puddings Beef suet is usually preferred for puddings, but mutton suet makes a light pudding, while veal suet gives a most delicate flavour. Remove all skin and fibre from the suet, **dredge** it with flour and either grate it on a suet grater and then chop it lightly with a knife or shred it finely with a knife dipped in flour and then chop it. A long pointed very sharp knife should be used. Hold the point of the knife down on the board with one hand, and work the handle end up and down with the other. The more finely it is chopped, the lighter the pudding will be.

To turn out a boiled or steamed pudding Lift the pudding from the saucepan and allow it to stand for a minute or two for the steam to escape a little. Remove the cloth or paper, then loosen the edges of the pudding with a knife and shake the basin to ascertain whether the pudding is loose, then reverse it on a hot dish and remove the basin carefully. If the pudding is boiled in a cloth, lift it out of the water with a fork into a colander and let it drain for a minute or two. Untie the string and draw the cloth carefully away from the sides of the pudding. Turn it on to a hot dish. Should the pudding seem inclined to stick to the cloth, work it off gently with a knife.

Boiled batter pudding
4–5 persons

	Metric	Imp
milk	500 ml	1 pt
melted butter	25 g	1 oz
flour	75 g	3 oz
sweet melted butter (p. 65)	250 ml	½ pt
3 eggs		
pinch of salt		

Method
1 Sieve flour and salt into a basin.
2 Make a well in centre, add 2 eggs and gradually stir the flour from the sides into them, adding the third egg gradually.
3 Stir till smooth, then beat very well for 10 min.
4 Add the milk gradually, beating all the time, and the plain melted butter.
5 Pour mixture at once into a greased basin, cover with a cloth and put in a saucepan of boiling water for 1½ hr. Move the basin about for the first 5 or 10 min., to prevent the flour settling on the bottom.
6 Turn the pudding out on to a hot dish and pour over a little sweet melted butter (p. 65).

Note The success of a boiled batter pudding depends on its being put into the boiling water the moment it is made.

Batter can also be mixed in the blender by putting the milk, melted butter and eggs in and whisking them at top speed for two minutes, then adding the sieved flour and salt spoonful by spoonful at low speed till all is incorporated.

Bread and butter pudding with fruit
4–5 persons

	Metric	Imp
milk	500 ml	1 pt
sugar	50–75 g	2–3 oz
2 eggs		
4 slices of bread and butter		
fresh or bottled fruit		
grated nutmeg		

Method
1 Grease a basin. Line it with bread and butter, cutting a round to fit the bottom exactly.
2 Put in a layer of fresh fruit, prepared as for stewing, or bottled fruit; sprinkle with sugar and cover with more bread and butter. Continue in layers till dish is ¾ full, ending with a layer of bread and butter.
3 Sprinkle nutmeg on top.
4 Beat eggs with milk and pour over.
5 Cover with greased paper, and steam for 1 hr.
6 Turn out very carefully on to a hot dish. Decorate if desired with glacé cherries and angelica.

Note Currants, sultanas and raisins may be used instead of fruit.

Brown Betty pudding

5–6 persons

	Metric	Imp
brown breadcrumbs	150 g	6 oz
shredded suet	100 g	4 oz
shredded candied peel	50 g	2 oz
castor sugar	75 g	3 oz
apples peeled, cored and chopped	400 g	1 lb
sweet melted butter (p. 65)	250 ml	½ pt
3 slices brown bread		
2 beaten eggs		
grated peel of ½ lemon		
a little grated nutmeg and powdered mace		

Method
1 Grease a basin, line it with a slice of bread at the bottom and fingers of bread at the sides.
2 Mix all other ingredients together, except the sweet melted butter, and put into the basin. If the mixture is too dry, moisten with a little milk.
3 Cover with a **scalded** cloth, and boil for 3 hr.
4 Turn out on a hot dish and pour round the sweet melted butter.

Canary pudding

4 persons

	Metric	Imp
3 eggs		
the weight of the eggs in sugar, flour and butter		
chopped almonds	50 g	2 oz
jam sauce (p. 74)	250 ml	½ pt
grated peel of ½ lemon		

Method
1 Cream butter and sugar.
2 Add eggs one by one, beating well.
3 Stir in the flour, grated lemon peel and almonds.
4 Put mixture into a greased basin, cover with greased paper and steam for 1½ hr.
5 Turn out on to a hot dish and pour jam sauce over.

Currant dumplings

5–6 persons

	Metric	Imp
currants	200 g	½ lb
flour	200 g	½ lb
chopped suet	100 g	¼ lb
milk	450 g	1 lb
sweet melted butter (p. 65)	250 ml	½ pt
½ tsp powdered ginger		
2 eggs		
pinch of salt		

Method
1 Sieve flour, ginger and salt into a basin. Add suet and currants.
2 Make a well in the centre, beat up eggs and milk and stir into flour. Mix well.
3 Roll into little balls with a little flour.
4 Put into a saucepan of boiling water, and boil fast for ½ hr. Drain well.
5 Pile on a hot plate and serve with sweet melted butter.

Note This mixture may be made into a roll, tied in a **scalded**, floured cloth and boiled like a roly-poly pudding for 1½ to 2 hr.

Fig pudding

6 persons

	Metric	Imp
soft breadcrumbs	200 g	½ lb
flour	100 g	4 oz
shredded suet	100 g	4 oz
brown sugar	100 g	4 oz
milk	125 ml	1 gill
dried figs chopped small	100 g	4 oz
1 tsp baking powder		
2 eggs		
½ tsp grated nutmeg		
pinch of salt		

Method

1 Sieve the flour, baking powder, nutmeg and salt into a basin.
2 Add the rest of the dry ingredients.
3 Beat up the eggs with the milk and beat into the mixture.
4 Put into a greased basin, cover with greased paper and steam for 4 hr.
5 Turn out on to a hot plate and serve with sweet melted butter or jam sauce (p. 74).

Note This may be made with stoned dates for date pudding.

Fruit pudding

6 persons

	Metric	Imp
suet crust (p. 218)	300 g	¾ lb
fruit in season prepared as		
for stewing	600 g	1½ lb
sugar	100 g	4 oz
water	60 ml	½ gill
a little lemon juice		

Method

1 Grease a pudding basin. Put aside enough suet crust for the lid, roll out the remainder and line the basin with it.
2 Half fill with the fruit, add the sugar and lemon juice and put in the remainder of the fruit.
3 Roll out the suet for the lid, wet the edges of the pudding, put on the lid and press down edges.
4 Cover with a **scalded** floured cloth, put in a pan of boiling water and boil for 1½ hr, or cover with greased paper and steam for 2 to 2½ hr.
5 Turn out on to a hot dish.

Note If apples are used, they may be flavoured with cinnamon, nutmeg or cloves.

Ginger pudding

6 persons

	Metric	Imp
flour	100 g	¼ lb
shredded suet	150 g	6 oz
soft breadcrumbs	300 g	¾ lb
Demerara sugar	100 g	4 oz
golden syrup or treacle	125 ml	1 gill
milk	125 ml	1 gill
sweet melted butter or		
treacle sauce (pp. 65, 74)	250 ml	½ pt
1 tsp baking powder		
2 tsp ground ginger		
1 egg		
pinch of salt		

Method

1 Sieve the flour, baking powder, ginger and salt into a basin.
2 Mix with breadcrumbs and suet.
3 Put syrup, milk and sugar into a pan and stir over low heat till sugar has melted; stir into the flour mixture.
4 Add beaten egg and mix well.
5 Put into a greased basin, cover with greased paper and steam for 3 hr.
6 Turn out on to a hot dish and serve with sweet melted butter or treacle sauce.

Jam roly-poly

4 persons

	Metric	Imp
suet crust	200 g	½ lb
jam	100 g	4 oz
sweet melted butter (p. 65)	250 ml	½ pt

Method

1 Roll out suet crust into a strip twice as long as it is broad.
2 Spread the jam over it to within 2·5 cm (1 in.) of the edges.
3 Roll it up, seal the edges well and put into a **scalded** floured cloth. Tie up the ends.
4 Put a saucer in the bottom of a pan of water and bring to the boil. Put in the pudding and boil for 2 hr.
5 Turn the pudding out of the cloth on to a hot dish and serve with sweet melted butter.

Norfolk dumplings

12 dumplings

	Metric	Imp
bread dough (p. 290)	400 g	1 lb
German sauce or sweet melted butter (pp. 73, 65)	250 ml	½ pt

Method

1 Divide the dough into small pieces, shape into rounds and drop into a pan of boiling water.
2 Boil quickly for ¼ hr. Drain well.
3 Serve on a folded napkin on a hot dish with German sauce or sweet melted butter.

Christmas pudding

2 puddings for 4 persons
1 pudding for 8 persons

	Metric	Imp
raisins	400 g	1 lb
sultanas	200 g	½ lb
currants	200 g	½ lb
chopped mixed peel	200 g	½ lb
brown sugar	100 g	4 oz
breadcrumbs	300 g	¾ lb
flour	200 g	½ lb
shredded suet	300 g	¾ lb
brandy	60 ml	½ gill
6 eggs		
1 tsp ground ginger		
1 tsp nutmeg		
pinch of salt		

blanched chopped almonds, grated lemon peel or 2 apples, cored, peeled and chopped, may be added if desired.

Method

1 Sieve the flour, ginger, nutmeg and salt into a large basin.
2 Mix with it the breadcrumbs, suet and sugar.
3 Add the cleaned dried fruit and peel.
4 Beat up the eggs with the brandy and stir well into the mixture. Cover the basin and leave it for 12 hours.
5 Stir again. Divide mixture into two portions if desired, and put into greased basins. Alternatively, the mixture may be tied into **scalded** floured cloths.
6 Steam or boil puddings for 6 hr. When required, they should be steamed or boiled a further 2 or 3 hr.

7 Turn out on a hot dish, put a sprig of holly in the centre, pour brandy round and set light to it.
8 Hand brandy or hard sauce (pp. 73, 74) or whipped cream and castor sugar.

Note These puddings may be made several months in advance. If they are to be stored, the cooking cloth must be replaced with a clean one, and puddings boiled without a basin should be hung up till required.

Plain plum pudding

6 persons

	Metric	Imp
flour	200 g	½ lb
breadcrumbs	100 g	4 oz
shredded suet	200 g	½ lb
brown sugar	100 g	4 oz
raisins	200 g	½ lb
currants	500 g	1¼ lb
milk	250 ml	½ pt
2 eggs		
pinch of salt		

Method

1 Sieve the flour and salt.
2 Mix all the dry ingredients together.
3 Beat up the eggs with the milk and stir into the mixture. Beat well.
4 Put mixture into a **scalded** cloth or a greased basin.
5 Boil steadily for 3 hr.
6 Boil for a further 2 hr when required.
7 To serve, see Christmas pudding (above).

Note Do not keep this pudding too long.

Plain sweet suet pudding

4 persons

	Metric	Imp
flour	100 g	4 oz
breadcrumbs	100 g	4 oz
suet	100 g	4 oz
milk	125 ml	1 gill
sweet melted butter or custard (pp. 65, 229)	250 ml	½ pt
1 tsp baking powder		
½ tsp salt		
flavouring: 2 tbsp jam, marmalade or syrup or a handful of dried fruit or chopped nuts stirred in		

Method
1 Mix the dry ingredients together.
2 Make a well in the centre and add enough milk to make a soft dough.
3 Stir in the flavouring.

4 Put into a greased basin, cover with greased paper and steam for 2½ to 3 hr.
5 Turn out on a hot dish and serve with sweet melted butter or custard.

BAKED PUDDINGS

Apple batter pudding   6 persons

	Metric	Imp
apples peeled, cored, sliced	400 g	1 lb
milk	500 ml	1¼ pt
sugar	50 g	2 oz
butter	25 g	1 oz
3 tbsp flour		
3 eggs		
1 tsp grated lemon rind		
pinch of salt		

Method
1 Sieve flour and salt into a basin.
2 Make a well in the centre and put in the eggs, unbeaten.
3 Stir flour gradually into the eggs, beat well, add a little milk. When well mixed, add rest of milk gradually.
4 Put apples in a greased pie dish, sprinkle with sugar and lemon rind.
5 Stir the batter and pour it over.
6 Bake in a fairly hot oven (200°C, 400°F, Mark 6) for ¾ hr or till batter is set.
7 Dot the top of the pudding with pieces of butter, sprinkle with castor sugar and return to the oven to brown, about 5 min.

Note Any kind of fruit prepared for stewing may be used. Apples may be peeled whole, cored and filled with sugar and a clove, covered with batter and cooked as above.

Apple charlotte   4–5 persons

	Metric	Imp
cooking apples peeled, cored and cut up	800 g	2 lb
clarified butter	75 g	3 oz
brown sugar	50 g	2 oz
margarine	25 g	1 oz
juice and rind of ½ lemon		
6 slices stale bread		
a little castor sugar		

Method
1 Stew apples gently with lemon rind, juice, sugar and margarine.
2 Grease a soufflé dish and cut 2 rounds of bread to fit top and bottom.
3 Cut fingers of bread to fit sides of dish. Dip bread in clarified butter. Line the dish with bread.
4 Pour in apple purée and put on top.
5 Put a piece of greased paper over and bake till crisp and brown in a fairly hot oven (200°C, 400°F, Mark 6) for about 45 min.
6 Serve in the dish or turn out on a hot plate and sprinkle castor sugar over.

Castle puddings   6 persons

	Metric	Imp
2 eggs		
the weight of the eggs in butter, sugar and flour		
jam or German sauce (pp. 74, 73)	250 ml	½ pt
1 tsp vanilla essence or grated lemon rind		
pinch of salt		
glacé cherries		

Method
1 Cream butter and sugar.
2 Add eggs one by one, beating well.
3 Sieve the flour with the salt, stir in lightly to the mixture with the flavouring.
4 Half fill some small greased moulds with the mixture. Place on a baking tin and bake in a fairly hot oven (200°C, 400°F, Mark 6) or steam for 30 min.
5 Turn out the puddings, top with a cherry and pour round a little jam or German sauce.

Note These may be made in one mould if desired, in which case it takes ¾ to 1 hr to cook.

Coconut pudding

4 persons

	Metric	Imp
short crust or rough puff pastry (pp. 218, 217)	150 g	6 oz
granulated or castor sugar	100 g	4 oz
butter or margarine	100 g	4 oz
desiccated coconut	200 g	½ lb
3 eggs		
½ tsp lemon juice		
pinch of nutmeg		
a little milk		

Method

1 Line a pie dish with the pastry.
2 **Cream** butter and sugar, add eggs one by one, beating well.
3 Add lemon juice, nutmeg and coconut, and a little milk if very dry.
4 Put mixture into prepared pie dish and bake in a fairly hot oven (200°C, 400°F, Mark 6) for ½ hr or till set and pastry cooked.
5 Serve hot or cold in the dish.

General satisfaction pudding

4 persons

	Metric	Imp
6 finger or boudoir sponge biscuits		
short crust or rough puff pastry (pp. 218, 217)	150 g	6 oz
butter	25 g	1 oz
flour	25 g	1 oz
milk	125 ml	1 gill
castor sugar	25 g	1 oz
2 separated eggs		
1 tsp grated lemon rind		
a little jam		

Method

1 Line a pie dish with pastry and cover with a layer of jam.
2 Cut sponge fingers in half and place on jam.
3 Melt butter in a pan, add flour, blend well and stir in milk. Stir rapidly till this thickens and forms a ball in the centre of the pan. Cool slightly.
4 Add egg yolks, grated lemon rind and sugar. Beat well.
5 Beat egg whites stiff, fold in to mixture.
6 Put into prepared pie dish.
7 Bake in moderate oven (175°C, 350°F, Mark 4) for ½ hr or till set.
8 Serve hot.

Queen of puddings

4–5 persons

	Metric	Imp
milk	500 ml	1 pt
breadcrumbs	100 g	4 oz
sugar	40 g	1½ oz
butter	50 g	2 oz
castor sugar	40 g	1½ oz
2 separated eggs		
rind and juice of 1 lemon		
vanilla essence		
3 tbsp jam		
sugar for the meringue		

Method

1 Boil the milk with the lemon rind and butter; strain over the breadcrumbs.
2 Add the lemon juice and sugar and leave it to soak for a few minutes.
3 Beat up egg yolks, stir all well together.
4 Put into a greased pie dish and bake in a moderate oven (175°C, 350°F, Mark 4) till firm (20–25 min.).
5 Whisk up egg whites stiffly, add sugar and flavour with vanilla.
6 Spread jam over the pudding, cover with meringue, sprinkle with castor sugar and return to the oven for a few minutes till brown.

Note Cake or biscuit crumbs may be used instead of bread for this pudding.

Yorkshire or baked batter pudding

4–5 persons

	Metric	Imp
milk	625 ml	1¼ pt
flour	200 g	8 oz
4 eggs		
pinch of salt		

Method

1 Sieve flour and salt into a basin.
2 Make a well in the centre, add eggs gradually, stir flour into them, add a little milk, beat well for 10 min.
3 Stir in the rest of the milk.
4 Put in a greased pie dish and bake in a hot oven (220°C, 425°F, Mark 7) for ¾ hr.

Note If served with meat, this is baked in the tin under the meat.

SOUFFLÉS

Soufflés are very light puddings, the foundation of which is a panada, to which the yolks and whites of eggs, beaten separately, and any ingredient or flavouring desired, are added.

A soufflé must be cooked directly it is mixed, and served as quickly as possible before it has time to fall, therefore see that everything is ready before beginning to cook it. If steamed, the water must be boiling in the saucepan. If baked, the oven must be at the right heat.

To prepare the moulds   For a steamed soufflé, a tin with straight sides is generally used. This should be brushed over thickly with **clarified** butter. A double band of paper deep enough to stand 7 to 10 cm (3 or 4 in.) above the tin, and long enough to fold right round it and just overlap, should be greased with the butter and tied round the outside of the tin. Grease another round of paper to cover the top.

For baked soufflés, fireproof china, glass or earthenware soufflé dishes are used. These are dished on a doily on another dish or are put into a silver frame.

Small soufflés are usually baked and served in small china or paper cases. The dishes and paper cases are greased with **clarified** butter. Put them on to a baking tin and cook them in a moderate oven until well risen and firm when touched.

A soufflé mixture should only three-parts fill the mould to allow room for rising.

If baking a soufflé, put it into a moderate oven and keep the oven at a steady heat. Avoid opening the oven door as much as possible, as a sudden rush of cold air might cause the soufflé to fall.

A soufflé must be served directly it is cooked, as if kept waiting it will sink.

Steamed soufflés are turned out on to a hot dish and the sauce poured round them. Baked soufflés are served in the dish in which they were cooked.

Chocolate soufflé
4 persons

	Metric	Imp
butter	25 g	1 oz
flour	25 g	1 oz
grated chocolate	75 g	3 oz
milk	125 ml	1 gill
castor sugar	25 g	1 oz
3 yolks and 4 whites of eggs		
custard sauce (p. 73)	250 ml	½ pt
½ tsp vanilla essence		

Method
1 Melt butter in a pan, add flour and mix well. Cook for 1 min., then remove from heat.
2 Add chocolate and milk, blend smoothly.
3 Return to heat and boil till mixture thickens and leaves the side of the pan, stirring continuously. Cool slightly.
4 Beat in egg yolks one by one, add sugar and vanilla.
5 Whisk egg whites stiff, fold into mixture.
6 Put in a greased soufflé tin, round which a band of paper has been tied. Steam gently for 1 hr or bake in a moderate oven (175°C, 350°F, Mark 4) for ½ hr.
7 Turn out the steamed soufflé and serve with custard sauce. Serve the baked soufflé in the dish.

Cornflour soufflé
3 persons

	Metric	Imp
butter	25 g	1 oz
milk	125 ml	1 gill
cornflour	10 g	½ oz
castor sugar	50 g	2 oz
½ tsp vanilla essence **or** 1 tsp rose water		
3 separated eggs		
crystallized rose petals or flaked almonds		

Method
1 Blend the cornflour with the milk, put with butter into a small pan.
2 Stir over fire till mixture boils, stir rapidly till mixture leaves the edges of the pan.
3 Remove from heat, stir in egg yolks, one by one. Beat well.

4 Stir in sugar and vanilla essence or rose water.
5 Whip egg whites stiffly, **fold in** lightly.
6 Put in small greased fireproof dishes and bake in a moderate oven (175°C, 350°F, Mark 4) for 15 min.
7 Serve in the dishes, sprinkle with crystallized rose petals or flaked almonds.

Omelette soufflé

4 persons

	Metric	**Imp**
3 separated eggs		
castor sugar	50 g	2 oz
1 tsp flour		
vanilla essence		
salt		
a little jam		

Method

1 Beat egg yolks and sugar till creamy.
2 Add 15 drops vanilla essence and shake in flour lightly.
3 Whip egg whites with a pinch of salt till stiff. Stir into yolks with a metal spoon.
4 Butter a shallow, fireproof dish, put in the mixture and put the pan into a fairly hot oven (200°C, 400°F, Mark 6) and cook for about 8 min.
5 Turn out on to a heated dish, spread with jam and fold over. Sprinkle with sugar and serve.

Note A little warm, stewed fruit may be used instead of jam and liqueur sprinkled over. A rum omelette is made with 1 tsp rum instead of flavouring essence, and warmed rum poured over and set alight as soon as the omelette is served.

Vanilla soufflé

4 persons

	Metric	**Imp**
milk	500 ml	1 pt
flour	100 g	4 oz
butter	100 g	4 oz
castor sugar	50 g	2 oz
custard or German sauce (p. 73)	250 ml	½ pt
5 eggs		
1 tsp vanilla or almond essence		
glacé cherries		

Method

1 Grease a soufflé mould; cut cherries in half and decorate the bottom with them. Tie a piece of greased paper round the mould.
2 Melt the butter in a saucepan, add flour, blend well. Add milk, stir till mixture boils, then stir very quickly till it forms a ball.
3 Remove from heat, beat in 4 egg yolks, one by one. Add flavouring and sugar.
4 Whisk 5 egg whites stiff, stir into mixture.
5 Put into prepared mould, cover with greased paper, steam for 1 to 1½ hr.
6 Let pudding stand for 2 min., remove paper and turn out on to a hot dish.
7 Serve with custard or German sauce.

Note This soufflé may be baked, in which case use only 75 g (3 oz) of flour and cook in a moderate oven (175°C, 350°F, Mark 4) for ½ hr.

BATTERS AND FRITTERS

Sweet fritters are composed of a light batter which is either incorporated with, or encloses, some sweet mixture. Fritter batters must be thick enough to coat the article to be fried but should not be stodgy. Always let the batter stand for about half an hour before using it. The success of fritters greatly depends upon the frying. A deep saucepan and plenty of fat must be used, and the fat must be properly hot before putting in the fritters. It may be tested by dropping in a small spoonful of the batter, which should at once rise to the surface and frizzle; the fritters will then puff out and become crisp. If the fat is not hot enough it sinks into the batter, which becomes greasy and indigestible. Do not put too many fritters into the pan at once, or the fat becomes chilled. Reheat the fat before adding the second batch of fritters. Drain them well on soft white paper, and keep hot while frying the remainder. Turn the fritters when browned on one side, in order to brown the other side. Lift them out of the pan with a perforated spoon.

A pancake batter is more liquid than a fritter batter, and may be made more or less rich according to the number of eggs used. It should also stand a short while before using it to allow the starch grains to burst and aerate the batter before cooking it. Pancakes are fried in a very little fat.

Cream pancakes
4 persons

	Metric	Imp
flour	100 g	4 oz
milk	125 ml	1 gill
cream or more milk	125 ml	1 gill
castor sugar	25 g	1 oz
2 eggs		
lemon juice		
butter to fry		
pinch of salt		

Method
1 Sieve the flour and salt into a basin.
2 Make a well in the centre, drop the eggs in and add a little milk. Stir well, add more milk gradually. Beat till smooth, leave to stand for ½ hr.
3 Stir in rest of milk, cream and sugar. Mix well.
4 Cover the bottom of a small frying pan with a little butter and turn this out, leaving the pan well greased.
5 When the pan is hot, pour in just enough batter to cover the bottom thinly. Turn the pan a little to coat it evenly, cook the batter gently till set and brown (5 min.).
6 Toss, then fry the second side.
7 Turn the pancake on to sugared paper, **dredge** it lightly with sugar and sprinkle with a little lemon juice. Roll up and keep hot by placing on a plate over a saucepan of boiling water, covered with a lid.
8 Just enough fresh butter must be put into the pan between cooking each pancake to grease the pan.
9 Serve with cut slices of lemon or orange and hand castor sugar.

Note Apple pancakes may be made by adding 2 peeled, cored and finely chopped apples to the batter before frying the pancakes.

To toss a pancake Loosen the pancake from the pan and shake it gently towards the edge opposite the handle, and give the pan a quick toss, when the pancake should turn over neatly and fall brown-side uppermost in the pan.

French pancakes
5–6 persons

	Metric	Imp
milk	250 ml	½ pt
flour	100 g	4 oz
castor sugar	25 g	1 oz
2 separated eggs		
1 tsp grated lemon rind		
jam		
pinch of salt		

Method
1 Sieve flour and salt into a bowl.
2 Stir yolks into the flour with a little milk. Beat well, add rest of the milk gradually. Leave for ½ hr.
3 Whip egg whites stiff, add sugar and lemon rind and stir into batter.
4 Grease some saucers or shallow tins, put a little batter into each, place on a baking tin and bake in a moderate oven (175°C, 350°F, Mark 4) 20 min.
5 Serve with 1 tsp jam on each pancake and doubled over.

Note If desired, 1 tsp ground ginger may be sieved in with the flour in place of lemon rind.

PANCAKE VARIATIONS

The pancakes may be filled with whipped cream, flavoured with vanilla or with grated chocolate mixed with whipped cream or with apple marmalade made like apple sauce.

Savoury pancakes may be made with a filling of mince of any kind of poultry, game, meat or fish mixed with a savoury sauce. Grated cheese may be added to the batter for savoury pancakes, which should be made smaller than sweet ones. Cooked mushrooms, tomatoes, asparagus tips or green peas are also excellent served inside pancakes. Needless to say, if a savoury mixture is put in the pancakes, no sugar must be added to the batter.

A spoonful of rum, brandy or any liqueur may be added to the pancakes, if desired.

A pancake batter is made richer by adding more eggs and less milk, or 25 g (1 oz) of melted butter may be stirred into the mixture before frying. Pancakes may also be sprinkled over with grated cinnamon and castor sugar.

Cleaned currants may be added to the pancakes just before frying.

Fritter batter no 1

	Metric	Imp
flour	200 g	½ lb
tepid water	250 ml	½ pt
2 tbsp salad oil or melted butter		
2 egg whites		
pinch of salt		

Method
1 Sieve the flour and salt into a basin.
2 Mix the oil or butter with the water.
3 Stir into the flour, beat till smooth, let stand for ½ hr.
4 Whisk egg whites stiff, stir in lightly, just before using.

Fritter batter no 2

	Metric	Imp
flour	100 g	4 oz
milk	125 ml	1 gill
pinch of salt		
1 egg		

Method
1 Sieve flour and salt into a basin. Make a well in the centre.
2 Put in the egg and a little of the milk, beat till smooth.
3 Add the rest of the milk, beat well and leave for at least ½ hr before using.

American fritters
(Doughnuts)

12 doughnuts

	Metric	Imp
flour	200 g	8 oz
milk	75 ml	3 oz
castor sugar	50 g	2 oz
margarine	40 g	1½ oz
1½ tsp baking powder		
1 egg		
pinch of salt		
cinnamon (optional)		

Method
1 Sieve the flour, salt and baking powder into a bowl.
2 Rub in the margarine, add the sugar.
3 Add egg and enough milk to make a soft dough.
4 Roll out to 1 cm (⅓ to ½ in.) and stamp out in rings.
5 Fry in deep fat for 5 to 7 min., turning once.
6 Drain well.
7 Toss in sugar and cinnamon.

Apple fritters

6 persons

	Metric	Imp
3 apples peeled, cored and cut into rings		
fritter batter	250 ml	½ pt
castor sugar		
lemon juice		
lard for frying		

Method
1 Sprinkle apple rings with sugar and lemon juice.
2 Heat lard in a deep frying pan till faint blue haze rises.
3 Dip each ring in batter and drop in the fat. Fry for about 6 min. Lower heat after first minute, so apple may cook through.
4 Drain on soft paper. Sprinkle with sugar and serve.

Note Pineapple and bananas are excellent made into fritters, the latter sliced lengthways then across.

Bread and butter fritters

Small jam sandwiches with the crusts cut off may be dipped in batter and fried and served like apple fritters. Stale cake may be used up in the same way.

Currant fritters

4–5 persons

	Metric	Imp
flour	200 g	½ lb
butter	25 g	1 oz
sugar	50 g	2 oz
milk	250 ml	½ pt
currants	50 g	2 oz

1 tsp baking powder
pinch of salt
2 egg yolks
grated rind of ½ lemon
vanilla or almond essence
lard for frying

Method

1 Sieve the flour, salt and baking powder.
2 Beat butter and sugar to a cream, add egg yolks one by one.
3 Stir in the flour and milk alternately.
4 Add currants, lemon rind and a few drops vanilla or almond essence.
5 Drop teaspoonful of the mixture into deep fat and fry till pale brown (6 min.), turning once.
6 Drain and sprinkle with castor sugar.

COLD SWEETS, JELLIES AND CREAMS

Cold puddings and sweets – creams, soufflés and mousses –
jellies – fruit compôtes and salads

Jellies, creams and blancmanges should be made sufficiently stiff to turn out of the mould without breaking, but they should not be too stiff or the sweet will be rubbery and unpalatable.

Gelatine should always be dissolved in water, fruit juice or syrup. It is possible to dissolve it in milk, but there is always the danger of its curdling if the milk is allowed to boil. In warm weather more gelatine is required than in cold, and for picnics, where the sweets have to be carried, more gelatine should be used when making them.

Jellies and creams set in large moulds require to be slightly stiffer than if set in small moulds; and where fruit or any other solid substance is mixed with the jelly, it would also require stiffening a little more. A cream or custard mixture requires less gelatine than a clear jelly, as the eggs thicken it.

Creams and mousses should be quite cold and almost set before putting them into the mould, otherwise the gelatine is apt to sink to the bottom of the mould instead of being suspended throughout the cream. The mould must always be rinsed out in cold water before putting the jelly or cream into it. If setting creams or jellies in different coloured layers, one layer must be completely set before putting in another, otherwise they become mixed. All cold sweets should be made several hours before use, but putting them in the refrigerator when cooled will accelerate setting.

To decorate a mould for creams or jellies

Required   A little clear jelly; any decoration suitable, such as glacé cherries, angelica, pistachio nuts, crystallized fruits, crystallized violets or rose petals, almonds, etc., may be used.

Rinse the mould out in cold water, pour in a little cold but liquid jelly, and leave this in a cold place or on ice to set, then arrange the decorations on the jelly in any design liked; pour more jelly very carefully over the decorations with a spoon. Care must be taken not to dislodge the decorations when setting them with the jelly. Leave them to set.

To coat the sides of the mould too, proceed as follows. Allow the decorations at the bottom of the mould to set, then pour in a little more cold jelly, turn the mould round and round slowly so that the sides may become coated. (To coat the sides of the mould satisfactorily and quickly it is better to use a little ice. Break the ice into fairly small pieces, put these into a basin, keeping the surface as flat as possible. Place the mould on this and turn it round slowly.) When a coating of the jelly has set all over the sides, place the mould on the ice sideways, arrange the decorations on one side, then pour a spoonful of the jelly over carefully and allow it to set. Proceed in the same manner for the other sides of the mould. Small moulds are coated in the same way, but the sides of small moulds are rarely decorated.

To turn out moulds, jellies or cold sweets

Dip the mould into a basin of hot but not boiling water. Move the mould about for a second or two, lift it out quickly and dab the top with a clean cloth. Place the dish over the top of the mould, reverse both of them, holding the thumbs on the mould and the fingers under the dish. Give a sharp downward shake to loosen the jelly, then withdraw the mould very gently from the jelly. If the mould does not leave the jelly, after shaking it two or three times, again dip it in warm water and repeat the process. Always shake downwards, not up and down. Should the water be so hot that the jelly begins to melt and runs down on to the dish, put the dish at once into a very cold place to check any further melting. If an earthenware mould is used, the water should be hotter and the immersion longer than for a metal mould.

COLD PUDDINGS AND SWEETS

Banana chartreuse   4 persons

	Metric	Imp
whipped cream	250 ml	½ pt
sugar	50 g	2 oz
gelatine	2·5 ml	½ oz
lemon jelly unset	125 ml	1 gill
water	125 ml	1 gill
pistachio nuts **blanched** and chopped	25 g	1 oz
6 bananas		
a little chopped lemon jelly for decoration		

Method
1 Pour a little of the lemon jelly in the bottom of a Charlotte mould, arrange 2 bananas cut in thin rounds and the pistachio nuts in a pattern and pour a little jelly carefully over the top. Decorate the sides of the mould in the same way, as described on p. 244.
2 Sieve the rest of the bananas, or put in blender.
3 Dissolve the gelatine and the sugar in the water and strain into the purée. Leave 5 min. to cool.
4 Fold in the whipped cream.
5 Fill the prepared mould and leave in a cold place to set.
6 Turn out mould on to a dish and garnish with a little chopped jelly.

Chocolate charlotte russe   4 persons
Use a straight-sided soufflé tin which holds 500 ml (1 pt)

	Metric	Imp
sponge fingers		
cream	375 ml	¾ pt
gelatine	12 g	½ oz
chocolate	75 g	3 oz
water	125 ml	1 gill
castor sugar	25 g	1 oz
1 tbsp brandy		
vanilla essence		
1 egg white		
melted lemon jelly		

Method
1 Pour a thin layer of lemon jelly in the rinsed out soufflé tin.

2 Cut the sponge fingers so they are straight-sided and the height of the soufflé tin. Arrange them round the mould with the outside of the biscuit against the edge of the tin.
3 Dissolve the chocolate over low heat in half the water and the gelatine in the other half. Leave to cool.
4 Whip up 250 ml (½ pt) of the cream with the sugar and strain chocolate and gelatine into the cream.
5 Add brandy, a few drops of vanilla essence and **fold in** beaten egg white.
6 When quite cold, turn into prepared mould and leave in a cold place to set.
7 Turn out on to a glass dish and top with the rest of the cream, whipped.

Note Almost any cream mixture to which gelatine has been added may be used for filling a Charlotte Russe prepared in the foregoing manner. Coffee, pineapple, vanilla, ginger, strawberry, raspberry, loganberry creams are all equally suitable for this purpose. The top of the mould may be decorated as desired with the clear jelly and glacé cherries and angelica in the place of the cream garnish. A very excellent Charlotte Russe can be made with chestnut cream, the top being decorated with *marrons glacés*, or the sides of the mould may be ornamented with pink and white biscuits, placed alternately round the tin, the centre being filled with strawberry or vanilla cream. When turned out, decorate the top with crystallized fruits. Sometimes, after a Charlotte Russe is turned out, a piece of ribbon is tied round the biscuits.

Cornflour blancmange   4 persons

	Metric	Imp
cornflour	40 g	1½ oz
sugar	25 g	1 oz
milk	500 ml	1 pt
2 bay leaves or strip of lemon rind or few drops vanilla essence		

Method
1 Blend cornflour with a little of the milk.
2 Put the rest of the milk and the bay leaf, lemon rind or vanilla essence in a pan and bring slowly to the boil.
3 Strain over the cornflour, stirring well.
4 Return to pan, add sugar and cook over low heat for about 8 min., stirring continuously.
5 Pour into a wet mould and leave in a cold place to set.
6 When set, turn out carefully on to a dish and serve with stewed fruit, or jam sauce (p. 74).

Note Ground rice or arrowroot may be made into a blancmange in the same way, using any flavouring essence desired.

An inexpensive blancmange

4 persons

	Metric	Imp
milk	500 ml	1 pt
castor sugar	50 g	2 oz
gelatine	12 g	½ oz
1 tbsp boiling water		
grated rind of 1 lemon		
1 stick cinnamon		
few drops vanilla essence		

Method
1 Melt the gelatine in the water.
2 Mix the lemon rind and sugar.
3 Put the milk, cinnamon and sugar mixture into a pan, bring to the boil.
4 Strain in the gelatine. Remove the cinnamon.
5 Pour all into a basin and leave till nearly cold, stirring occasionally. Add the vanilla.
6 Pour into a rinsed mould and leave in a cold place to set.
7 Turn out on to a dish when set and serve with a compôte of fruit or with cream.

Creamed rice pudding

4 persons

	Metric	Imp
carolina rice	50 g	2 oz
milk	500 ml	1 pt
sugar	50 g	2 oz
glacé cherries	25 g	1 oz
angelica	25 g	1 oz
strip of lemon peel		

Method
1 Wash rice well and soak in milk for 1 hr.
2 Put into a double saucepan with the lemon peel and simmer till rice is soft and liquid has been absorbed (15–20 min.), stirring occasionally.
3 Remove peel and stir in sugar; add some of the cherries and angelica, chopped, and stir well.
4 Pour into a wet mould and leave till cold.
5 Turn out of mould and decorate with the rest of the cherries and angelica.

Note 1 tbsp cream or evaporated milk may be added to the rice before putting it in the mould. This pudding may also be made in small moulds and served with stewed fruit.

Devonshire junket

4 persons

	Metric	Imp
milk	500 ml	1 pt
1 tsp rennet		
1 dssp sugar		
cinnamon or grated nutmeg to taste		
1 tbsp brandy or rum		
clotted cream (optional)		

Method
1 Warm milk to blood heat with the sugar.
2 Pour into a glass dish, add the rum or brandy, stir in the rennet lightly and leave in a warm room till set.
3 Spread some clotted cream over if desired, and sprinkle with cinnamon or nutmeg.

Note Vanilla or any other essence may be added instead of the cinnamon or nutmeg.
Coffee junket is made in the same way, using 1 tsp coffee essence in the milk or replacing a small quantity of milk with strong coffee.
Caramel junket is made by adding 1 tbsp black treacle to the milk while heating, and stirring it well.

Gooseberry fool

4 persons

	Metric	Imp
washed gooseberries	800 g	2 lb
water	125 ml	1 gill
sugar	200 g	½ lb
cream or custard	250 ml	½ pt

Method

1 Put gooseberries in a pan with the water and sugar and bring to the boil. Simmer till soft. Rub through a sieve and cool.
2 Stir in cream or custard and leave in a cold place.
3 Serve in a glass bowl or in custard cups.

Note Any fruit such as blackberries alone or with apples, blackcurrants, redcurrants alone or with raspberries, tinned apricots, and peaches all make excellent fool if cooked in this manner. Cream is better than custard with strawberries and raspberries; these should be hulled and sprinkled with sugar overnight and rubbed through a hair sieve without cooking.

Green caps

4 persons
Cooking time: 25 min.

	Metric	Imp
4 baking apples peeled and cored		
water	125 ml	1 gill
castor sugar	75 g	3 oz
custard (p. 229)	250 ml	½ pt
3 egg whites		
6 drops vanilla essence		
2 glacé cherries		

Method

1 Put the apples in a baking tin with the water, cover with greased paper and bake in a moderate oven (175°C, 350°F, Mark 4) till soft but not broken (15 min.). Remove from the oven and cool.
2 Whisk the egg whites very stiff, add the vanilla and 1 tbsp sugar, and coat the apples with this meringue.
3 Sift the rest of the sugar over them and return to the oven for a few minutes.
4 Arrange in a glass dish, pour custard round and top each one with a half cherry.

Note Meringue pears may be made in this way.

Honeycomb mould

4–5 persons

	Metric	Imp
milk	750 ml	1 ½ pt
gelatine	25 g	1 oz
water	60 ml	½ gill
castor sugar	40 ml	1 ½ oz
4 separated eggs		
grated rind of 1 lemon		
2 bay leaves		

Method

1 Boil the milk with the bay leaves.
2 Beat up the egg yolks with the sugar, strain the hot milk over, stir well; return to pan and stir over low heat till mixture thickens.
3 Pour in a basin to cool.
4 Melt gelatine in water, strain into custard, add grated lemon rind and stir often till cold.
5 Whip egg whites stiffly, **fold into** custard.
6 Pour into wet mould and leave in a cold place to set.
7 Turn out on to a glass dish.

Pear condé

4 persons

	Metric	Imp
4 pears peeled, halved and cored		
carolina rice	50 g	2 oz
milk	500 ml	1 pt
sugar	100 g	4 oz
butter	25 g	1 oz
water	125 ml	1 gill

Method

1 Make the rice, milk and half the sugar into a creamed rice pudding (p. 246) and leave to cool.
2 Meanwhile, put the pears, butter, rest of the sugar and water in a casserole and stew gently till pears are soft, but not broken, about 25 to 30 min.
3 Remove pears and leave to cool.
4 Turn rice out on a dish and surround with pears.
5 Serve very cold.

Note Apricots and peaches are very good made into a condé and tinned fruit may be used instead of fresh.

Pears à la duchesse   4 persons

	Metric	Imp
4 pears peeled, cored and		
left whole		
sugar	75 g	3 oz
water	125 ml	1 gill
cream	125 ml	1 gill
6 drops vanilla essence		
4 cloves		
cochineal		

Method

1 Put sugar and water in a pan, stir till melted, then bring to the boil. Put in the pears with a clove stuck in the end of each.
2 Simmer till pears are soft, 30 to 40 min.
3 Lift out pears carefully, drain well.
4 Boil up syrup till thick. Colour with a few drops cochineal.
5 Remove cloves. Paint each pear with cochineal.
6 Whip cream, sweeten to taste and flavour with vanilla.
7 With a forcing bag, fill pears with cream till it shows at the other end.
8 Pour syrup around.

Note Apples may be cooked in the same manner.

Prune mould   4 persons

	Metric	Imp
prunes washed and soaked		
overnight	200 g	½ lb
gelatine	21 g	¾ oz
water	250 ml	½ pt
sugar	350 g	¾ lb
½ tsp cinnamon		
wineglassful of claret		
juice and grated rind of 1 lemon		
cream		

Method

1 Stew the prunes in the soaking water with the cinnamon, sugar and lemon rind till tender (approx. 20 min.).

2 Dissolve gelatine in a little prune syrup and strain into the prunes with the lemon juice, claret and rest of the syrup. Leave to cool.
3 When cold, put in a wet mould and leave in a cool place to set.
4 Turn out and decorate with whipped cream.

Strawberry shortcake   5–6 persons

	Metric	Imp
flour	200 g	½ lb
butter	50 g	2 oz
castor sugar	200 g	½ lb
strawberries hulled	400 g	1 lb
1 tsp baking powder		
pinch of salt		
2 egg yolks		
3 egg whites		
little milk		

Method

1 Sieve flour, baking powder, salt on to a piece of paper.
2 **Cream** the butter and half the sugar together, add egg yolks one by one, beat well.
3 Stir in flour and milk alternately, adding enough milk to make a soft dough.
4 Turn into 2 greased and lined sandwich tins and bake in a hot oven (220°C, 425°F, Mark 7) for about 15 min.
5 Turn out cakes on to a wire tray and cool.
6 Put half the strawberries on top of one cake, sprinkle with a little sugar.
7 Whip egg whites stiff, add 50 g (2 oz) of the sugar and spread a little of the meringue on top of the strawberries.
8 Cover with the second cake and repeat the process with the rest of the strawberries, meringue and sugar.
9 Return cake to the oven for 2 min. to set the meringue.
10 Decorate with a few strawberries. Serve at once.

Note Whipped cream may be used in the place of meringue, and raspberries, loganberries, tinned peached or apricots may be used instead of strawberries.

Summer pudding

4 persons

To be made the day before

	Metric	Imp
about ½ loaf of stale bread		
mixed fruit such as blackcurrants, redcurrants, raspberries, gooseberries	600 g	1½ lb
sugar	75 g	3 oz
custard sauce (p. 73) or cream	250 ml	½ pt

Method

1 Stew the fruit in very little water with the sugar.
2 Cut the bread in approximately 1 cm (½ in.) thick slices. Trim off the crusts.
3 Cut 2 rounds of bread to fit the top and bottom of a basin.
4 Line the basin with the bread. Fill with the hot stewed fruit. Cover with bread. There must be no gaps in the bread surround.
5 Cover with a plate with a weight on it, and set aside overnight.
6 Turn out and serve with custard sauce or cream.

Tipsy cake

4 persons

	Metric	Imp
1 large stale sponge cake		
blanched shredded almonds	75 g	3 oz
custard	500 g	1 pt
sherry	60 ml	½ gill
juice of ½ lemon		
apricot or strawberry jam		

Method

1 Cut the cake into thick slices without spoiling the shape.
2 Spread each slice with jam and put back to the original shape.
3 Place cake in a glass bowl; mix lemon juice and sherry and pour over cake. Leave for 2 hr.
4 Stick shredded almonds all over the cake.
5 Pour custard around.

Note Trifle is made by putting the slices of cake flat in the dish. Coat with jam, sprinkle with crushed macaroons or ratafias, soak in the sherry for ½ hr, then coat with cool custard. Pile whipped cream on top. Decorate with glacé cherries, angelica and blanched almonds.

CREAMS, SOUFFLÉS AND MOUSSES

Cold chocolate soufflé

5–6 persons

	Metric	Imp
milk	375 g	¾ pt
unsweetened cooking chocolate	100 g	4 oz
sugar	75 g	3 oz
3 separated eggs		
3 tbsp water or coffee		
3 tbsp whipped cream		
pistachio nuts		

Method

1 Put milk and chocolate in a pan and bring slowly to the boil, whisking well.
2 Beat egg yolks with the sugar, pour over the hot milk, stir well and return to pan.
3 Thicken over heat without boiling, strain into pan and cool.

4 When cold, whisk cream and egg whites separately, and **fold in** to chocolate mixture.
5 Turn at once into a soufflé dish that has a band of lightly oiled paper tied round it. The mixture should come a little way above the dish. Leave to set.
6 When set, remove the paper and decorate with cream and chopped pistachio nuts.

Coffee mousse

5–6 persons

	Metric	Imp
gelatine	12 g	½ oz
milk	500 g	1 pt
2 separated eggs		
3 tbsp castor sugar		
2 tbsp black coffee		

Method

1 Beat together sugar and egg yolks.
2 Warm milk slightly in a double saucepan and stir it into the sugar and egg yolks. Mix well.
3 Cook for 4 min. stirring continuously in the double saucepan. Remove from heat.
4 Soften gelatine in coffee and add to custard. Stir till dissolved.
5 Leave mixture to cool.
6 When almost set, fold in the stiffly beaten egg whites.

Lemon mousse

4 persons

	Metric	Imp
lemon juice	125 ml	1 gill
loaf sugar	100 g	4 oz
water	600 g	1½ pt
gelatine	25 g	1 oz

thinly pared rind of 2 lemons
3 egg whites
glacé cherries or angelica

Method

1 Put rind, gelatine, water and sugar in a pan and dissolve slowly over heat.
2 Strain into a basin and cool a little.
3 Add strained lemon juice.
4 When cold, add lightly beaten egg whites and whisk all till frothy and white and beginning to stiffen.
5 Put in a wet mould and leave in a cold place to set and turn out on a glass dish or put in a glass bowl and decorate with glacé cherries or angelica.

Note Orange mousse is made the same way, using half orange and half lemon juice.

Loganberry cream

4 persons

	Metric	Imp
loganberry purée	250 ml	½ pt
water	125 ml	1 gill
castor sugar	100 g	4 oz
gelatine	25 g	1 oz
double cream	250 ml	½ pt

cochineal
squeeze of lemon juice

Method

1 Melt gelatine and sugar in water and strain into purée.
2 Add lemon juice and cochineal if the colour is poor.
3 Whip the cream and stir lightly into the mixture.
4 When nearly setting, pour into a glass dish. Decorate with fresh loganberries.

Note Strawberries, blackcurrants, redcurrants, blackberries and apples or raspberries may be made into a cream in the same way, using less sugar for the sweeter fruits.

JELLIES

General rules for making jellies

Home-made jellies are not often made these days as commercially prepared ones are so easy to mix. However, the flavour of home-made jellies is particularly good and for those who wish to try making them, the rules are as follows:

1 The best quality gelatine available should be used as the cheaper ones can taste of glue.
2 The pan, whisk and jelly bag or cloth must be **scalded** before use. A large pan should be used to allow room for the liquid to rise.
3 Loaf sugar is best for clear jellies as it gives a more brilliant finish.
4 2 egg whites, lightly whisked to a froth and 2 washed and crushed egg shells are added to the jelly mixture when dissolved, and this is whisked and allowed to boil up, then drawn from the heat for a minute to settle. It is then returned to the heat and the process of whisking, boiling up and leaving to settle off the heat is repeated 2 or 3 times, then the jelly is strained. This process is carried out in order to clear the jelly. The jelly may be strained through a jelly bag, but it is simpler to strain it through a clean tea cloth which should be tied

on to the legs of an inverted chair. Always **scald** the cloth before pouring the jelly in by pouring boiling water through it into a basin underneath. Remove the basin and empty it; put it back under the cloth and then pour the jelly through the cloth. If it does not run through clear at first, another basin should be held underneath the cloth while the contents of the first basin are gently poured back into the cloth. Continue changing the basins in this way until the jelly runs through quite clear. Strain the jelly in a warm place and cover it while straining, as it is liable to set before it has all run through the cloth. The jelly should be cold before being put into the mould, as if put in hot it is apt to become cloudy.

Apple jelly

4–5 persons

	Metric	Imp
apples washed and cut in pieces without peeling or coring	800 g	2 lb
sugar	100 g	4 oz
gelatine	25 g	1 oz
water	250 ml	½ pt
very thinly peeled rind of 1 lemon		
cochineal		

Method

1 Stew apples with the lemon rind, water and sugar to a pulp.
2 Rub through a sieve.
3 Make up pulp to 500 ml (1 pt) with water.
4 Dissolve gelatine in a little water and strain into the purée.
5 Add a few drops of cochineal if required.
6 Put in a rinsed mould and leave in a cold place to set.
7 Turn out and serve with cream or custard.

Note Rhubarb jelly may be made in the same way, using rhubarb in place of apples.

Lemon jelly

5–6 persons

	Metric	Imp
thinly pared rind of 4 lemons		
lemon juice	250 ml	½ pt
cold water	750 ml	1½ pt
gelatine	50 g	2 oz
loaf sugar	200 g	½ lb
small stick cinnamon		
whites and shells of 2 eggs		
2 cloves		

Method

1 Put the water, sugar, gelatine, cloves and cinnamon in a **scalded** saucepan. Add lemon peel without pith, strained lemon juice, slightly whisked egg whites and washed and crushed shells.
2 Whisk the jelly over heat till just on boiling point, remove the whisk and boil up to the top of the pan.
3 Draw aside and repeat twice more.
4 Pour through a jelly bag or a **scalded** tea cloth.
5 Put in a wetted mould and leave in a cold place. Turn out when set.

Note Wine may be added, the jelly taking its name from the wine used, e.g. claret jelly. Equal quantities of wine and water are used.

Orange jelly

4 persons

	Metric	Imp
4 oranges		
1 lemon		
water	125 ml	¼ pt
gelatine	25 g	1 oz
loaf sugar	100 g	4 oz
whipped cream		

Method

1 Wipe fruit. Pare the rind very thinly without pith.
2 Put rind in a pan with gelatine, loaf sugar and water. Stir over low heat till gelatine is melted, then simmer 10 min.
3 Skim and strain.
4 Add 250 ml (½ pt) strained juice of the fruit and stir often till cool.
5 Pour into a wet mould and leave in a cold place to set.
6 Turn out when set and serve with whipped cream.

Note The jelly may also be set in cups made of scooped-out halves of oranges. Notch the edges of each half of the orange peel and arrange a handle of angelica over them.

FRUIT COMPÔTES

In all compôtes, the syrup should be prepared first by dissolving the sugar in the water and then adding the fruit. If all three are put in together, the result will be watery and lacking in flavour.

The juicy fruits such as raspberries, plums, cherries should be cooked in a small quantity of thick syrup and the less juicy fruits like apples and pears cooked in a large amount of thinner syrup.

Apples in syrup

4 persons

	Metric	Imp
4 apples peeled, cored and left whole		
sugar	100 g	4 oz
water	125 ml	1 gill
redcurrant jelly		
rind of 1 lemon or a few cloves		
cochineal (optional)		

Method

1 Put the sugar and water in a pan, stir till dissolved, then boil fast to a syrup.
2 Skim and put in apples with a piece of lemon rind or a clove in each one.
3 Cover the pan and simmer very gently till cooked but not broken (30–40 min.). Cool a little. Remove lemon peel or cloves.
4 Put apples in a glass dish.
5 Boil up syrup, colour with cochineal if desired and pour round the apples.
6 Fill the centre of the apples with redcurrant jelly.

Note Pears, quinces, apricots, peaches and any stone fruit may be cooked this way.

Wine or liqueurs may be added instead of cloves.

Stewed prunes

4 persons

	Metric	Imp
prunes soaked in water (500 ml (1 pt)) overnight	400 g	1 lb
juice and thinly pared rind of ½ lemon		
Demerara or granulated sugar	100 g	4 oz

Method

1 Put prunes in a pan with the water they were soaked in, add sugar, strained lemon juice and lemon rind.
2 Bring to the boil and simmer very gently till soft (¾ hr). Leave till cold.
3 Serve with custard or cream.

Note Prunes may be cooked in a casserole in a slow oven and flavoured with cinnamon or cloves, or for a special dish a little red wine or port may be added to them.

FRUIT SALADS

Almost any kind of fruit may be used for making salads, or several kinds mixed. In winter, when fresh fruit is difficult to obtain, bottled or tinned fruit may be used, and dried fruit may also be made into fruit salads. The fruit must be prepared as for cooking, i.e. stones should be removed from stone fruit; apples, pears, bananas should be peeled, cored and cut into slices; cherries are stalked and sometimes stoned; fresh peaches or apricots are skinned and stoned; strawberries and raspberries are hulled, and the stalks removed from currants. Grapes are sometimes served whole in fruit salads, while at other times they are skinned and the stones removed.

Different coloured fruits should be mixed judiciously, and where colourless fruit is made into a salad it may be garnished with pistachio nuts, glacé cherries or any crystallized fruits. The syrup for fruit salad is made of sugar and water, boiled to a syrup, to which is added red or white wine, brandy, rum, gin or any liqueur preferred. Fruit salad may be served in a salad bowl, or in small glass or china individual bowls, custard cups or wine glasses. It should be eaten very cold.

Orange salad   *4 persons*

	Metric	Imp
6 oranges		
castor sugar	100 g	4 oz

Method

1 Peel the oranges and remove all the pith.
2 Cut in 4 vertically and slice down the length of the quarters to remove the white membrane and take out the pips.
3 Cut across the quarters in thin slices.
4 Arrange in a bowl and **dredge** with the sugar. Leave for 2 hours in a very cold place.

Note Bananas may be added to the oranges. A sprinkling of desiccated coconut or **blanched** almond slivers on top of the salad makes a change.

Strawberry salad   *4 persons*
Prepare 1½ hr before use

	Metric	Imp
strawberries hulled	400 g	1 lb
castor sugar	100 g	4 oz
orange juice	125 ml	1 gill
cream		

Method

1 Sprinkle sugar over strawberries and leave ½ hr.
2 Strain orange juice over and divide into individual bowls. Leave another hour.
3 Serve with a spoonful of whipped cream on top of each bowl.

Note Raspberries may be used in place of strawberries, and bananas will mix with either. Any fruit juice may be used, and maraschino or kirsch added.

Summer fruit salad   *5–6 persons*

	Metric	Imp
3 bananas		
strawberries	200 g	½ lb
raspberries	200 g	½ lb
cherries	200 g	½ lb
redcurrants	200 g	½ lb
chopped almonds	25 g	1 oz
loaf sugar	100 g	4 oz
water	125 ml	1 gill
red wine	125 ml	1 gill
1 tbsp brandy		
cream		

Method

1 Prepare the fruit as for cooking and put in a salad bowl. Mix well.
2 Put the sugar and water in a pan, stir till dissolved then boil up to a thick syrup, add the wine and brandy and spoon over the fruit.
3 Serve very cold in the bowl it was mixed in.
4 Offer cream separately.

Winter fruit salad   *5–6 persons*

	Metric	Imp
grapes	200 g	½ lb
shelled walnuts chopped finely	25 g	1 oz
pineapple syrup	125 ml	1 gill
sugar	100 g	4 oz
water	125 ml	1 gill
2 slices of tinned pineapple diced		
3 bananas peeled and sliced		
2 oranges peeled and segmented		
glacé cherries quartered		
1 apple peeled, cored and sliced		
juice of 1 lemon		
2 tbsp sherry		

Method

1 Mix all the fruits together in a bowl.
2 Put the sugar, water and pineapple syrup in a pan. Stir till melted, then boil up fast for a few minutes.
3 Add strained lemon juice and sherry and boil again.
4 Spoon over the fruit salad and allow to become cold.
5 Serve in a glass bowl, sprinkle with walnuts and serve with cream and sponge fingers.

SAVOURIES AND COCKTAIL
SNACKS

Savouries used always to follow the sweet course at the end of dinner; now they are very often served as an alternative to the sweet. They are the perfect way of finishing up the wine at the end of a meal. Savouries should be served piping hot, in very small quantities. They should be strong and hot in taste and flavour, and not be made of ingredients which form one of the other courses of a dinner. For example, if oysters figure as an hors d'oeuvre or in the fish course, an oyster savoury should not be given.

The remains of all sorts of ingredients may be used in making savouries, provided they are well-seasoned. Many after-dinner savouries are the same as hors d'oeuvres, but are larger in size.

Angels on horseback

These are oysters rolled in bacon, fastened with a skewer, and either grilled or baked in a hot oven (220°C, 425°F, Mark 7) for 5 to 6 minutes. Allow two rolls per person and serve on hot, buttered toast.

Cheese straws

6 persons

	Metric	Imp
flour	100 g	4 oz
grated cheese	75 g	3 oz
butter	50 g	2 oz
1 egg yolk		
a little water		
salt, cayenne		

Method

1 Sift the flour, salt and cayenne.
2 **Rub in** the butter; add the cheese mixed with the beaten egg yolk and a little water, and mix to a stiff paste.
3 **Knead** slightly and roll out on a floured board.
4 Cut into strips 7 cm long (3 in.) and 6 mm thick (¼ in.).
5 Cut out some rings of pastry also.
6 Bake on a greased baking tin in a fairly slow oven (150°C, 300°F, Mark 2) till quite crisp and golden brown (about 15 min.).
7 Serve on a hot plate with the strips in bundles, passed through the rings.

Note These may be eaten cold, if desired, and they will keep for some time in a tin with a well-fitting lid. They are very short and break very easily, therefore care must be taken when handling them after they are cooked. Parmesan cheese is the best to use for these, but any dry well-flavoured cheese may be substituted. Care must be taken when adding salt, in case the cheese is already very salt; but savouries are always highly seasoned.

Cheese allumettes or matches are made of this pastry, but are cut the size of a match and consequently take a shorter time to cook.

Anchovy straws are made in this manner, adding a teaspoonful of anchovy essence and a few drops of cochineal in place of cheese. This anchovy pastry may also be used for lining small moulds, thus forming cases for small savouries.

Finnan haddock croûtons

6 persons

	Metric	Imp
smoked haddock cooked and flaked	200 g	½ lb
butter	25 g	1 oz
1 tbsp milk or cream		
6 small round **croûtons** of fried bread		
3 anchovy fillets chopped		
yolk of 1 hard-boiled egg sieved		
1 tsp lemon juice		
pepper, cayenne		

Method

1 Pound the anchovies, haddock and butter.
2 Season well and rub through a wire sieve.
3 Add the milk and lemon juice.
4 Heat, without boiling, and pile on **croûtons**. Sprinkle with the egg yolk. Garnish with lemon and serve immediately.

Devilled ham

6 persons

	Metric	Imp
ham minced	75 g	3 oz
1 gherkin chopped		
2 tbsp curry sauce (p. 66)		
1 tsp anchovy essence		
6 **croûtons** of fried bread		
salt, pepper, cayenne		
parsley		

Method

1 Mix ham, gherkin, anchovy essence and curry sauce in a saucepan and heat.
2 Season well. Pile mixture thickly on **croûtons** and warm in oven a few minutes.
3 Serve on a hot dish, garnished with parsley.

Note Tongue or corned beef may be used in place of ham.

Devils on horseback

6 persons

12 cooked prunes cooled and stoned
12 stuffed olives **or** 12 anchovies each wrapped round an almond
6 thin rashers of bacon
12 small rounds of buttered toast
watercress

Method

1 Fill each prune with either an olive or an anchovy wrapped round an almond.
2 Cut the bacon rashers in half, flatten and roll round a prune.
3 Place on a baking tin and bake in a hot oven (220°C, 425°F, Mark 7) for 7 to 10 min.
4 Set each on a piece of buttered toast and serve garnished with watercress.

Herring roes on toast

6 persons

	Metric	Imp
about 6 herring roes		
6 fingers of buttered toast		
butter	40 g	1½ oz
salt, pepper		
squeeze of lemon juice		
parsley		

Method

1 Wash the roes, dry and cut in halves.
2 Heat the butter in a pan, fry the roes lightly.
3 Season well with salt, pepper and lemon juice and place on the toast.
4 Put in a hot oven (220°C, 425°F, Mark 7) for 3 min., or under the grill.
5 Serve on a hot dish, garnished with parsley.

Note Hard roes may be cooked in the same way, but they should be pounded first and mixed with a little cream or thick savoury sauce.

Mushrooms on toast

6 persons

	Metric	Imp
flat mushrooms, preferably field ones	300 g	12 oz
butter	50 g	2 oz
salt, pepper		
6 pieces of toast		

Method

1 Peel the mushrooms, if field ones, otherwise wipe clean and remove the stalks.
2 Put the best ones in a buttered dish, hollow side up.
3 Chop any broken ones, and season well. Fill the cups with them and dot generously with butter.
4 Bake in a moderate oven (160°C, 325°F, Mark 3) till done, about 15 min.
5 Serve hot, on hot buttered toast.

Sardine croûtons

6 persons

	Metric	Imp
4 sardines skinned, boned and mashed		
butter	15 g	½ oz
6 **croûtons** of fried bread		
2 tbsps milk		
1 tsp anchovy essence		
1 egg yolk		
salt, pepper		
parsley		

Method

1 Melt the butter in a pan, add the sardines, beaten egg yolk, anchovy essence and milk.
2 Season well, and stir till mixture thickens.
3 Serve hot on **croûtons** and garnish with parsley.

Stuffed eggs   4–6 persons

	Metric	Imp
6 hard-boiled eggs		
tinned tuna fish	25 g	1 oz
anchovy fillets	25 g	1 oz
stoned black olives	25 g	1 oz
capers	25 g	1 oz
1 level tsp French mustard		
4 tbsp olive oil		
6 drops lemon juice		
black pepper		
watercress		

Method

1 Shell eggs and halve lengthwise. Remove yolks carefully.
2 Pound tuna, anchovies, olives and capers together till smooth. Blend in mustard.
3 Add oil, lemon juice and pepper to taste.
4 Sieve egg yolks and blend into fish mixture.
5 Pile stuffing into egg whites, or pipe through a rosette nozzle.
6 Serve with watercress.

Note A simpler version of stuffed eggs is made by mixing the sieved egg yolks with 3 tbsp mayonnaise and 1 tsp curry powder. Blend well and stuff egg whites as above.

Welsh rarebit   4 persons

	Metric	Imp
butter	15 g	½ oz
grated cheddar cheese	100 g	4 oz
1 tsp made mustard		
2 tbsp milk or ale		
4 small slices of toast		

Method

1 Melt the butter in a small pan.
2 Mix the other ingredients into the melted fat, cook very gently till smooth and creamy.
3 Spread on the hot toast.
4 Grill till golden brown. Serve at once.

IDEAS FOR VARIOUS SAVOURIES

The following make excellent savouries, and take their name from the mixture with which they are filled. They should be highly seasoned, and kept as small as possible.

Line small boat-shaped or oval or round moulds with thinly rolled-out short crust or cheese pastry (p. 218). Bake these and then fill them with various savoury mixtures such as cooked oysters, shrimps, lobster or crab, or any kind of cooked fish mixed with a suitable sauce.

SANDWICHES

The original sandwich consisted of a slice of beef between two slices of bread, but now a sandwich can vary from an open Danish one to a whole filled loaf, and can include fried or toasted ones, sandwiches cut in fancy shapes or made into rolls or pinwheels, multi-decked ones and even pastry ones.

Sandwiches can be used for almost any meal by adapting the size and the thickness of the bread to the occasion.

Any kind of bread may be used for sandwiches; if it is to be cut with a knife, i.e. not bought ready sliced, it should be at least one day old. The butter or margarine should be soft enough to spread easily; some fillings are best mashed with the butter first and then spread as a mixture on to the bread.

To soften a hard block of butter   Put the butter on a flat plate, take a basin that is large enough to cover the butter, fill it with boiling water, empty it and invert it immediately over the butter and leave for a few minutes. The steam will soften the butter without oiling it.

Meat fillings should be cut into narrow strips or minced, to make them easier to eat, salad fillings should be shredded.

To keep sandwiches fresh, wrap them in polythene or foil, keeping each kind separate.

Use imagination when making and serving sandwiches. Remember that variations in shape and filling are important and that brown bread can be used as well as white. Instead of serving them in the usual piles on separate plates, set them out in rows on a large tray that has been covered with a cloth.

Sandwich fillings

Savoury

Cheese   Pound some butter with 3 times the amount of grated cheese, add salt, pepper and a little made mustard, moisten with a little beer or cream.

Cream cheese   Season some cream cheese with cayenne and extra salt, if necessary. Add finely chopped walnuts and mix well. Use with chopped watercress in brown bread.

Cream cheese mixed with finely chopped celery and apple instead of walnuts.

Minced chicken and ham mixed with well-drained chopped pineapple.

Hard-boiled eggs mashed with mayonnaise, with chopped gherkins added.

Cold scrambled egg mixed with chopped shrimps and chopped parsley and well-seasoned.

Minced cold or *tinned meat* mixed with chutney.

Sardines, boned and mashed with a little vinegar.

Tuna fish and thin slices of cucumber, well-seasoned.

Sweet

Mashed banana with a little lemon juice.

Chocolate   Spread the buttered bread with a little sweetened whipped cream that has been flavoured with vanilla. Sprinkle liberally with grated chocolate.

Fresh strawberries or *raspberries*, sprinkled with sugar and a little lemon juice and mixed with whipped cream.

Minced dates, figs and *almonds*, moistened with lemon or orange juice.

Peanut butter mixed with grated raw apple.

Rolled sandwiches

Use thinly cut fresh bread and remove the crusts. It helps to cut a fresh loaf by dipping a very sharp knife in a jug of boiling water and shaking off the drops before cutting each slice. Place a cooked cocktail sausage, an asparagus tip, or a slice of smoked salmon or ham on each piece of buttered bread, roll it up and chill to set the butter and keep the shape.

Pinwheels

Cut slices 6 mm (¼ in.) thick from the full length of a fresh sandwich loaf that has had its crusts removed. Spread each long slice with a creamy and colourful savoury filling. Roll up tightly. Store in foil overnight in the refrigerator. When needed, slice into little pinwheels.

Open sandwiches or smoerrebroeds

These consist of a single slice of bread with the filling piled on top. White, brown or rye bread may be used and the sandwiches served on a large tray on lettuce leaves.

Fillings for open sandwiches
Pickled herring strips and fine rings of raw onions.
Chopped celery, liver sausage and sliced tomato.
Diced ham on a lettuce leaf, topped with asparagus tips, sliced egg and chopped chives.
Crisp fried bacon covered with liver paste, tomato slices and topped with aspic and horseradish.
Fried calf's liver with cucumber slices.
Smoked eel topped with cold scrambled egg and sprinkled with chopped chives.
Diced cooked fish mixed in curry mayonnaise.

Stuffed loaf

Cut the crust from one end of a fresh sandwich loaf or split a French loaf in half lengthwise. Remove the crumb without breaking the shell. Butter the inside well and line it with chopped lettuce or sliced cucumber. Fill the centre with a moist filling such as an omelette put in hot, scrambled egg or minced poultry or flaked fish mixed with mayonnaise. Close the loaf, wrap in foil. When needed, cut in thick slices.

Toasted sandwiches

These are either ordinary sandwiches toasted on both sides, or they can be made with one thick slice of toast which is split in half and filled at once with a warmed filling.

Fried sandwiches

Stale sandwiches may be used up by frying them in a little hot fat till brown on both sides, or they may be dipped in fritter batter (p. 240), fried in hot oil and served with a mushroom, tomato or cheese sauce (pp. 67, 68).

Garlic bread

This can be eaten with almost any picnic meal, or cold buffet dish or with soup.
    Take a long French stick loaf; cut down diagonally at intervals of about 5 cm (2 in.) to within a fraction of the base crust. Spread garlic butter (p. 75) liberally in each cut; press loaf back into its original shape; wrap in kitchen foil and heat in a moderate oven (175°C, 350°F, Mark 4) for about 12 min. just before serving. For picnics, wrap the heated loaf still in its foil in several cloths or put in an insulated bag to keep warm.

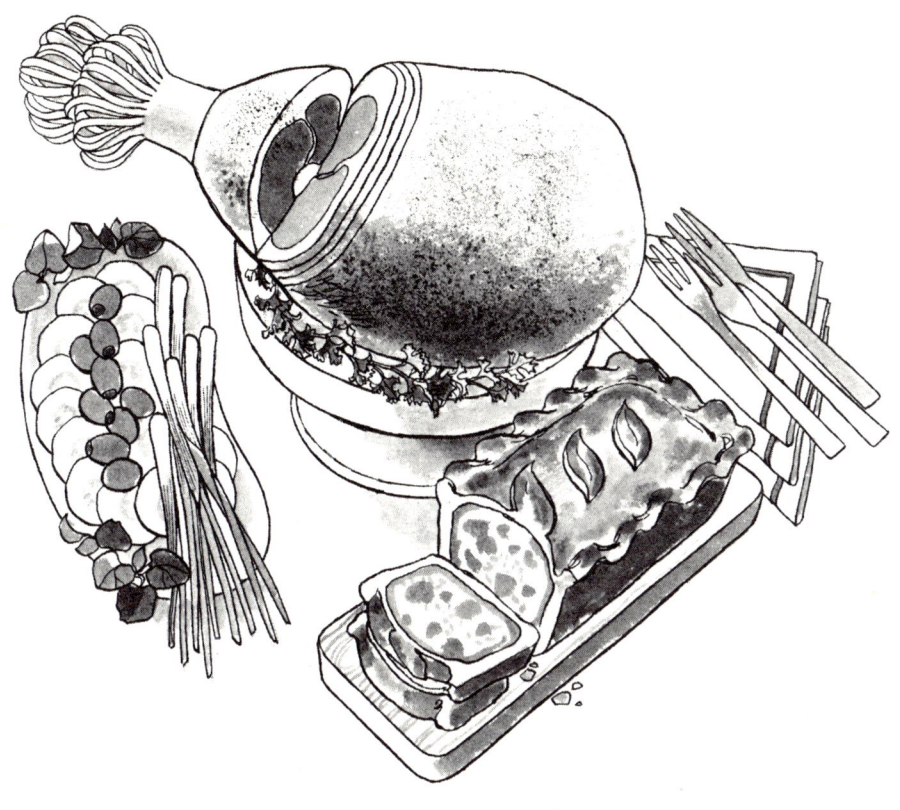

THE COLD TABLE

Recipes for cold dishes – buffet dishes made with fish, meat, poultry and game

The traditional cold table as seen at formal receptions or large country house parties is almost a thing of the past as far as the ordinary housewife is concerned. However, it may be that a *pièce de résistance* is wanted for a cold buffet or that a particular joint of meat has been given which needs to be spiced, or a lobster acquired, so recipes for these special dishes are given, even if they appear to be beyond the average budget for a party. It is worth remembering, however, that meat will go further if it is carved cold rather than hot. Some dishes suggested for buffet meals are quite economical, though nearly all of them involve quite lengthy preparation.

Dishes suitable for cold luncheons, suppers, balls and wedding breakfasts may be found in other parts of the book and include:

Pressed beef	Boiled ham	Cold ox tongue (glazed or
Spiced beef	Brisket of beef	unglazed)
Boiled tongue	York ham	

Any kind of cold pie, such as:

Hare	Veal and ham	Game
Rabbit	Pork	Chicken
Pigeon		

Any poultry or game roasted whole, eaten cold and served with salad

Cold roast beef	Boiled beef	Brawn
Cold veal	Boiled salt beef	

FISH

Timbale of cod

4–5 persons

	Metric	Imp
cooked cod skinned and flaked	200 g	½ lb
cooked rice	50 g	2 oz
gelatine	6 g	¼ oz
aspic jelly (p. 80)	250 ml	½ pt
2 tsp anchovy essence		
1 tbsp chutney		
1 tbsp piquante sauce (p. 71)		
1 tsp lemon juice		
8 prawns		
1 hard-boiled egg		
salt, cayenne		

Method

1 Mix anchovy essence, chutney, piquante sauce and lemon juice together. Add fish, rice and season well.

2 Melt gelatine in a very little water; strain into mixture.

3 Line a wetted mould with aspic; when set decorate with prawns and shapes cut out of egg-white. Cover with a little more aspic and add the remainder of the aspic to the fish.

4 When lining of mould has set, put fish mixture into mould. Leave in a very cold place to set (1–2 hr).

5 Turn out carefully and decorate with small salad.

Note This may be made with any cold cooked white fish or with salmon. Cooked macaroni may be used instead of rice.

Lobster in aspic

about 8 moulds

	Metric	Imp
the meat of 1 cooked lobster diced		
aspic jelly (p. 80)	250 ml	½ pt
4 hard-boiled eggs		
chopped chervil or parsley		
2 chillies		

Method

1 Rinse out some small moulds and set a little aspic jelly at the bottom. Decorate with slices of egg, chopped herbs and shapes cut from chilli skins. Sprinkle lobster coral over and set with more aspic.

2 Fill moulds with alternate slices of lobster and egg. Set each layer with aspic jelly and wait for it to set before adding the next layer. Place in refrigerator till required.

3 Arrange on a serving dish in a circle with the centre filled with a green salad dressed with mayonnaise or French dressing.

Note Shrimps or prawns may be set in aspic in this way.

Lobster cutlets

6 moulds

	Metric	Imp
the meat of 1 cooked lobster cut in slices		
aspic jelly (p. 80)	500 ml	1 pt
shrimp butter (p. 75)	25 g	1 oz
gelatine	6 g	¼ oz
thick tomato sauce (p. 67)	60 ml	½ gill
2 anchovies chopped		
a few cooked green peas		
1 hard-boiled egg		
salt, pepper, nutmeg		
parsley		

Method

1 Melt gelatine in a spoonful of water and stir into half of the aspic jelly. Add tomato sauce and mix well. Leave till cold.

2 Line some wetted shallow moulds with plain aspic jelly.

3 When set decorate with green peas and shapes cut from hard-boiled egg whites. Cover with more aspic. Leave to set.

4 Coat the moulds with the tomato aspic, fill with the lobster and anchovies, and season well. Pour the rest of the tomato aspic over. Leave in a cold place to set.

5 Turn out when set on to a bed of lettuce and garnish with parsley and small pats of shrimp butter.

Lobster mayonnaise or salad

4 persons

	Metric	Imp
1 cooked lobster		
mayonnaise sauce (p. 72)	250 ml	½ pt
1 hard-boiled egg		
2 anchovy fillets cut in strips		
capers		
lettuce		
cooked beetroot		

Method

1 Split the lobster in half lengthwise, remove all the meat, keep back any coral for decoration, take the meat from the claws as whole as possible. Cut the rest of the meat in neat pieces.

2 Line a salad bowl with washed lettuce pieces.

3 Mix the lobster pieces with shredded lettuce and mayonnaise and pile in the centre of the salad bowl.

4 Pour over more mayonnaise and decorate with pieces of claws, quarters of hard-boiled egg, anchovy, capers and beetroot cut in fancy shapes.

5 Sprinkle the lobster coral over and serve very cold. This may be decorated with the head and claws of the lobster.

Lobster mousse

4 persons

	Metric	Imp
the meat of 1 cooked lobster finely chopped		
aspic jelly (p. 80)	125 ml	¼ pt
gelatine	6 g	¼ oz
whipped cream	125 ml	1 gill
mayonnaise (p. 72)	125 ml	1 gill
white sauce (p. 65)	125 ml	1 gill
salt, pepper		

Method

1 Mix the lobsters into the hot white sauce. Cool slightly.

2 Dissolve the gelatine into the aspic; stir into the lobster and leave till cold.

3 **Fold in** the mayonnaise and the cream. Season to taste.

4 Pour into a soufflé mould that has a band of paper tied round the top. Put in the refrigerator to set, but not till too cold (about 2 hr).

5 Remove paper band, sprinkle the top with lobster coral, serve at once.

Mayonnaise of whole salmon

25 persons

	Metric	Imp
1 whole salmon cooked very carefully in **court-bouillon** (p. 93)	4 kg	8 lb
mayonnaise sauce (p. 72)	500 ml	1 pt
aspic jelly (p. 80)	2 l	2 qt
2 hard-boiled eggs		
cucumber and chilli skins		

Method

1 Drain the cooked salmon very well and put on a cloth to absorb the moisture.
2 Arrange it carefully on a large dish; skin it carefully and coat with mayonnaise sauce. Leave in a cold place to set.
3 Pour over some cold and nearly setting aspic jelly. When set decorate down the centre of the salmon with cucumber and chilli skins used as petals, and hard-boiled egg. Set with more aspic.
4 When the decorations are set, wipe the edges of the dish carefully and garnish with quarters of hard-boiled egg and chopped aspic.

Note Mayonnaise may be coloured green with vegetable colouring, and decorated with white of egg and blanched almonds, or coloured red with tomato purée. Salmon mayonnaise may be made with cold cooked salmon broken into small pieces, mixed with lettuce, coated with mayonnaise and garnished with hard-boiled egg and mustard and cress.

MEAT

Beef mould

5–6 persons

	Metric	Imp
lean stewing beef minced	400 g	1 lb
1 packet aspic jelly powder		
hot water	250 ml	½ pt
stock (any kind)	250 ml	½ pt
1 sheep's kidney chopped		
1 onion minced		
2 small carrots minced		
a little beef dripping		
1 tsp tomato purée		
salt, pepper		

Method

1 Melt dripping, fry onion, add beef, carrots, kidney, season, fry till brown.
2 Mix tomato purée and stock. Dissolve aspic powder in 250 ml (½ pt) hot water and add to mould.
3 Stir well and pour into a wetted mould. Turn out when set. Serve with green salad.

Galantine of beef

8–9 persons

	Metric	Imp
lean beef trimmed of gristle and skin and minced	600 g	1½ lb
diced bacon	200 g	½ lb
breadcrumbs	150 g	6 oz
stock (any kind)	185 ml	1½ gills
2 eggs		
1 tbsp chopped parsley		
½ tsp chopped thyme and marjoram mixed		
salt, pepper		
glaze (p. 62)		
butter		

Method

1 Mix beef, bacon, breadcrumbs, parsley and herbs. Season well.
2 Beat up eggs with stock and add. Mix very thoroughly.
3 Tie in a **scalded** floured cloth in a roly-poly shape. Tie at both ends and boil gently in a large pan of boiling water for 2½ hr (stand the roll on a plate to prevent sticking).
4 When cooked, untie the cloth, re-tie it very tightly and press galantine between two boards with a weight on top till cold.
5 When cold, remove cloth, trim the ends and brush with **glaze**. If more than one coat is needed, leave each one to dry before applying the next. Decorate with butter put through a forcing bag.

Galantine of pork (or veal) and ham

12 persons

	Metric	Imp
breast of veal or pork fillet	1600 g	4 lb
sausage meat	1200 g	3 lb
fat bacon cut in strips	200 g	½ lb
ham cut in strips	400 g	1 lb
1 onion, 2 carrots, chopped		
2 blades mace		
12 peppercorns		
1 bunch herbs		
¼ tsp allspice		
salt, pepper		
glaze (p. 62)		
potato salad (p. 202)		

Method

1 Bone breast of veal, remove all fat and lay flat on table skin side down, or divide pork lengthwise to flatten it out. Cut 10 small incisions without cutting through meat.
2 Spread sausage meat over it, season with salt, pepper and allspice.
3 Lay on strips of bacon and ham.
4 Roll up meat tightly, tie it up, and wrap in a **scalded** cloth.
5 Put an upturned dish in the bottom of a saucepan. Lay the roll on it, cover with water, and add vegetables, herbs and seasoning and bones if available. Simmer for 3 hr. Cool slightly.
6 Tighten cloth, press under a dish with a weight on top, leave till next day.
7 Remove from cloth, trim ends and brush with **glaze**.
8 Serve in thin slices accompanied by potato salad.

Ham mousse

4 persons

	Metric	Imp
cooked lean ham minced	300 g	¾ lb
Espagnole or brown sauce (pp. 65, 64)	375 g	¾ pt
cream	250 ml	½ pt
gelatine	15 g	¾ oz
stock (any kind)	60 ml	½ gill
aspic jelly (p. 80)	250 ml	½ pt
pinch of nutmeg		

Method

1 Add sauce to ham and liquidize or rub through a sieve.
2 Whip cream slightly and add to ham gradually, season with nutmeg.
3 Melt gelatine in stock and strain into ham mixture.
4 Put into a souffle mould with a band of paper tied round the top. Leave to set in a very cold place.
5 When cold, pour liquid aspic over.
6 When set, remove paper and serve in the mould.

Mutton cutlets en chaudfroid

8 persons

	Metric	Imp
best end of neck of mutton	1200 g	3 lb
gelatine	6 g	¼ oz
white sauce (p. 65)	500 ml	1 pt
aspic jelly (p. 80)	500 ml	1 pt
tomato sauce (p. 67)	500 ml	1 pt
green pea purée made with 200 g (½ lb) dried green peas (p. 208)		
1 small tin foie gras		
salt, pepper		

Method

1 Cut off the long rib bone and **chine** bone. Remove all skin and superfluous fat and braise the joint. Let it cool.
2 Cut into cutlets, trim away most fat and cut bones short.
3 Sprinkle with salt and pepper and spread one side with fois gras. See that the bones all turn the same way.
4 Melt gelatine in 125 ml water (1 gill) and add half to tomato sauce and half to white sauce. When cool, coat half cutlets in one sauce and half in the other and leave to set.
5 When set, pour over a thin layer of aspic jelly and leave till cold. Decorate with green pea purée, piped, and put a cutlet frill on each bone, arranging them in alternate colours.

Terrine maison

10 persons

	Metric	Imp
6 to 8 rashers streaky bacon		
minced liver	300 g	¾ lb
sausage meat	300 g	¾ lb
lean veal, pork or game cut in fine strips	300 g	¾ lb

	Metric	Imp
jellied stock	about 430 ml	¾ pt
2 hard-boiled eggs chopped		
1 small onion minced		
1 clove garlic minced		
1 tsp chopped herbs		
4 bay leaves		
salt, pepper		

Method

1 Line a small earthenware terrine with bacon.

2 Mix sausage meat, liver, onion, garlic, eggs, and herbs, season well and spread a layer of this over the bacon.

3 Cover with a layer of meat strips.

4 Continue with alternating layers of meat and liver mix, ending with the liver.

5 Arrange the bay leaves on top.

6 Put the lid on, or cover tightly with foil so it is airtight and bake, standing on a baking tin of water, in a moderate oven (175°C, 350°F, Mark 4) for 1½ hr.

7 Take out, remove the lid and put a weight on the top. Leave overnight.

8 The next day, fill the sides of the terrine with good jellied stock.

9 Leave till quite cold, then turn out.

Veal cake   *4–5 persons*

	Metric	Imp
lean veal diced	600 g	1½ lb
ham or bacon diced	100 g	4 oz
water	250 ml	½ pt
white stock	125 ml	1 gill
gelatine	12 g	½ oz
2 hard-boiled eggs sliced		
1 tbsp chopped parsley		
1 tsp grated lemon rind		
salt, pepper		

Method

1 Grease a soufflé tin or round cake tin. Decorate the bottom with pieces of egg.

2 Put in a layer of veal, a layer of ham, sprinkle with parsley, salt, pepper, lemon rind and rest of egg. Continue in layers till meat is used up. Fill tin nearly to the top with water. Cover with greased paper.

3 Bake on a baking sheet in a fairly hot oven (200°C, 400°F, Mark 6) for one hour; lower the temperature to 160°C, 325°F, Mark 3 and bake another hour.

4 Dissolve gelatine in white stock and pour into tin. Leave in a cold place to set.

5 Turn out on a dish and garnish with parsley.

Note Rabbit cake is made the same way, cutting all the meat from the bones.

Veal cream   *8–9 persons*

	Metric	Imp
cooked veal minced	200 g	½ lb
cooked ham minced	75 g	3 oz
aspic jelly (p. 80)	125 g	1 gill
mayonnaise sauce (p. 72)	250 ml	½ pt
tomatoes sliced	200 g	½ lb
water	250 ml	½ pt
gelatine	12 g	½ oz
cream	125 ml	1 gill
béchamel sauce (p. 64)	185 ml	1½ gills
10 peppercorns		
2 cloves		
salt		
2 egg whites		

Method

1 Put the water, gelatine, peppercorns, cloves, salt in a pan. Add tomatoes and egg whites and whisk over low heat till almost boiling. Boil up, then simmer for 20 min.

2 Strain through a jelly bag or **scalded** cloth tied to the legs of an inverted chair. Leave till cold but not set.

3 Line 8 or 9 small wetted moulds with a little of the tomato jelly.

4 Pound the veal and ham in a mortar or liquidize them, add the béchamel sauce, and aspic jelly. Season well.

5 Whip the cream, stir into the mixture. Put in prepared moulds. Pour more tomato jelly on top; leave to set in a cold place.

6 Turn out on to a bed of lettuce and hand mayonnaise separately.

Note Tongue may be used instead of ham, and rabbit, fowl or turkey may be made into creams in this way. Aspic jelly or aspic mixed with cream or white **chaudfroid** sauce may be used instead of tomato jelly.

POULTRY

Chaudfroid of chicken
5–6 persons

	Metric	Imp
1 boiling chicken		
aspic jelly (p. 80)	250 ml	½ pt
white stock	500 ml	1 pt
white **chaudfroid** sauce		
(p. 71)	500 ml	1 pt
chilli skins or beetroot		

Method

1 Truss the bird for boiling (p. 142). Boil till tender (approx. 1½ hr) in white stock. Take it out, remove the skin and let it become cold.
2 Coat chicken completely in **chaudfroid** sauce.
3 Decorate breast of chicken with chilli skins or beetroot.
4 Pour a little cold but liquid aspic very carefully with a spoon over the fowl, taking care not to move decorations. Allow to set.
5 Serve the chicken on a bed of lettuce; garnish with chopped aspic.

Note If preferred, the chicken may be jointed first and then coated as above. Cooked turkey and pheasant may also be treated this way.

Chicken cream
6–8 persons

	Metric	Imp
cooked chicken meat		
chopped	200 g	½ lb
butter	12 g	½ oz
tomatoes sliced	200 g	½ lb
whipped cream	125 ml	1 gill
aspic jelly (p. 80)	125 ml	1 gill
ham chopped	50 g	2 oz
white sauce	60 ml	½ gill
salt, pepper		
chervil		

Method

1 Melt butter in a pan, cook tomatoes in it for 10 min., season with salt and pepper, rub through a sieve.
2 Stir in 3 tablespoons stiff aspic jelly.
3 Pound chicken and ham together and liquidize or rub through a coarse sieve.

4 Mix with white sauce and about 2 tbsp stiff aspic.
5 Season well and **fold in** cream.
6 Pour a little aspic in the bottom of small wetted moulds. Leave to set.
7 When tomato purée is cold and nearly setting, line moulds with it.
8 Fill with chicken purée. Leave in a cold place to set.
9 Turn out on a dish and garnish with chervil and chopped aspic.

Note Turkey or game may be cooked in the same manner.

Chicken mayonnaise
6 persons

	Metric	Imp
1 cooked chicken jointed		
mayonnaise sauce (p. 72)	500 ml	1 pt
lettuce and watercress		
4 hard-boiled eggs quartered		

Method

1 Remove skin from chicken, chop off any protruding bones, pile the joints in a pyramid in the centre of a dish.
2 Arrange lettuce round chicken, garnish with watercress.
3 Arrange eggs round salad.
4 Just before serving, pour mayonnaise sauce over chicken.

Chaudfroid of pigeons
8 persons

	Metric	Imp
2 pigeons plucked, cleaned		
and singed		
brown stock	250 g	½ pt
sherry	125 ml	1 gill
liver farce (p. 79)	200 g	½ lb
brown chaudfroid sauce		
(p. 71)	750 g	1½ pt
1 bunch herbs		
1 onion, 1 carrot, 1 turnip		

Method

1 Remove breastbone and backbone. Stuff birds with liver farce restoring their original shape, truss as for roasting.

2 Tie each in a piece of muslin.
3 Put stock, sherry, vegetables, herbs in a sauté pan, bring to the boil, add the pigeons, cover with greased paper and the lid of the pan. Simmer for 45 to 60 min.
4 Leave the birds till cold, remove muslin, cut in quarters.
5 Place on a wire rack, pour **chaudfroid** sauce over.
6 Serve with a green salad and French dressing.

Note Quails may be cooked and served in the same way, but are cut in halves, not quarters.

GAME

Game cutlets
5–6 persons

	Metric	Imp
cooked game minced	200 g	½ lb
cooked rice	100 g	4 oz
liver farce (p. 79).	100 g	4 oz
gelatine	12 g	½ oz
game sauce (p. 66)	185 ml	1 ½ gills
aspic jelly (p. 80)	500 ml	1 pt
a few cooked peas		
tomato ketchup		
salt, pepper, cayenne		

Method
1 Melt gelatine in a very little hot water; strain into sauce.
2 Pound game in a mortar or put in blender. Mix with farce and sauce. Season well and rub through sieve.
3 Line some flat wetted moulds with aspic jelly, leave to set.
4 Decorate with peas and set with a little more aspic.
5 Fill the moulds with game purée and leave in a cold place to set.
6 Line a ring mould with aspic and when set put in the rice mixed with tomato ketchup.

Leave till cold.
7 Turn the rice ring out on a dish, turn out the cutlets and arrange on the rice and fill the centre of the ring with salad.

Game or poultry in aspic
4 persons

	Metric	Imp
cold game or poultry cut in neat slices	400 g	1 lb
aspic jelly	125 ml	1 gill
2 hard-boiled eggs sliced		

Method
1 Rinse out a mould in cold water and put in some aspic jelly which is nearly setting. Leave to set.
2 Arrange some egg slices on the aspic and cover with a little more jelly and allow to set.
3 Put a layer of meat on this, then eggs, then more aspic. Continue till all ingredients are used up. Leave in a cold place to set.
4 Turn out on a bed of lettuce on a dish. Serve a green salad with French dressing separately.

RABBIT

Galantine of rabbit
6–7 persons

	Metric	Imp
1 rabbit soaked for ½ hr in cold water, then the meat removed and minced		
breadcrumbs	150 g	6 oz
fat bacon minced	200 g	½ lb
ham minced	100 g	4 oz
stock (any kind)	125 g	1 gill
glaze or white **chaudfroid** sauce (pp. 62, 71)	500 ml	1 pt
1 tsp chopped mixed herbs		
1 dssp chopped parsley		
2 eggs		
2 onions, 2 carrots, chopped		
bouquet garni		
salt, pepper, nutmeg		

Method

1 Combine rabbit, ham and bacon. Mix with breadcrumbs, parsley, herbs, nutmeg and seasoning.

2 Add beaten eggs to stock and stir into rabbit mixture.

3 Mix well and shape into a roll. Tie in a **scalded** cloth.

4 Put in a large pan containing boiling water with **bouquet garni**, seasoning and carrots and onions, and simmer gently for 3 hr.

5 Lift out carefully, tighten the cloth and leave under a board with weights on top till cold.

6 Remove the cloth, trim the ends of the galantine and brush with glaze or white **chaudfroid** sauce.

7 Serve on a cold plate, garnished with parsley.

BREAKFAST AND SUPPER DISHES

Eggs

Eggs may be stored in a cool place or in the refrigerator. It is advisable to let them return to room temperature before boiling them or they will crack, and they should also be at room temperature for beating or else put into a warmed bowl and beaten with a warmed whisk.

Standard eggs, which are used in all the recipes unless otherwise stated, weigh approximately 55 g (2 oz). The time for cooking large or small eggs should be increased or decreased slightly to allow for the difference in size.

Boiled eggs

Lightly boiled	3–3 ½ min.
Moderately soft	4–4 ½ min.
Hard-boiled	10 min.

Method
1 Bring enough water to boil to cover the eggs.
2 Put in the eggs gently with a spoon. Leaving the spoon in the pan helps to prevent eggs cracking.
3 Simmer for time required.

Hard-boiled eggs
1 Place in cold water.
2 Bring to boil. Boil for 10 min.
3 Place in cold water immediately after cooking.

Baked eggs
Method
1 Melt a little butter in an individual fire-proof dish.
2 Break egg carefully in dish. Season. If desired, a little cream or melted butter may be added.
3 Bake in hot oven (220°C, 425°F, Mark 7) till white is set (10–15 min.).

Note This may be sprinkled with grated cheese before cooking, or the dish lined with a layer of chopped mushrooms or chives or cooked meat such as ham or tongue before breaking the egg in it.

Fried eggs
Method
1 Break eggs in a saucer.
2 Melt a little butter, oil or bacon fat in a frying pan.
3 When hot, slide egg in.
4 Cook egg gently, basting with hot fat using a metal spoon.
5 Lift out with fish slice, draining well.

Omelettes

Ideally, a pan should be especially reserved for making omelettes. A heavy, non-stick type is the best. If, however, no special pan is available, an old pan can be used if it is 'proved' first.

To prove an omelette pan
1 Clean it thoroughly with salt to make the surface smooth.
2 Put in a piece of lard the size of a large pea, heat it till it begins to smoke, then rub it clean with paper.

To cook an omelette   Beat the eggs lightly with a fork, add the seasoning. Heat the butter in the pan, and when it begins to foam and is slightly brown at the edges, pour in the egg mixture. With one hand, shake the pan back and forth regularly and with a fork in the other, lift the edges of the omelette and pass the flat of the fork over the base of the pan. Tilt the pan occasionally to let the liquid centre run to the edges. An omelette should be creamy in the middle and more set at the sides. When it has reached the right consistency, fold it in half quickly with a spatula or fish slice. Have ready a hot dish and tip it and the frying pan at an angle to each other so that the omelette can be slipped straight on to the dish. It should take about 2 to 3 minutes to make an omelette.

Plain omelette

1 person

	Metric	Imp
2 eggs		
butter	15 g	½ oz
salt, pepper		

Method
1 Prove the pan if necessary (see p. 274).
2 Heat the butter in the pan.
3 Beat the eggs lightly with the seasoning.
4 When butter is hot, pour in eggs, stirring as described above.
5 While still creamy, fold in half.
6 Serve at once on a hot dish.

Cheese omelette

Add 40 g (1½ oz) of grated cheese to the eggs before pouring them into the pan.

Herb omelette

(Fines herbes)
Add 1 tsp finely chopped herbs (parsley, chives and tarragon) or dried mixed herbs into the egg mixture.

Kidney, mushroom, onion, bacon omelettes

Chop the filling finely and cook separately for a few minutes, keep hot. As soon as the omelette is cooked, before folding, put in the filling.

Spanish omelette

2 persons

	Metric	Imp
4 eggs		
mushrooms (optional)	50 g	2 oz
lean ham or bacon chopped	50 g	2 oz
½ green pepper chopped		
1 small onion chopped		
1 clove garlic crushed		
1 small tin tomatoes **or** 3 fresh ones sliced		
1 tsp olive oil		
salt, pepper		
grated parmesan cheese		
chopped parsley		

Method
1 Put tomatoes, with a little water if they are fresh, green pepper, sliced mushrooms, garlic, onion, ham or bacon and seasoning in a pan. Simmer till the mixture becomes a soft purée.
2 Beat eggs lightly with a little salt.
3 Heat the oil in a frying pan till really hot.
4 Pour in the eggs, add the purée immediately and mix it up with the eggs. When the bottom is set and gently browned, sprinkle the top with chopped parsley and parmesan cheese.
5 Brown under a hot grill. Serve unfolded on a hot dish.

Note Spanish omelettes are more solid in texture than classic omelettes. They may be eaten hot or cold.

Soufflé omelette

2 persons

	Metric	Imp
4 separated eggs		
water	60 ml	½ gill
cheese or mushroom sauce (pp. 68, 67)	250 ml	½ pt
salt, pepper		
1 tbsp butter		

Method
1 Beat egg yolks with the water till thick; add the seasoning.
2 Beat egg whites stiffly.

3 Melt butter in a pan.
4 **Fold** egg yolks **into** whites and pour into pan. Cook slowly for 5 min.
5 Put under a slow grill for about 10 min.
6 Serve with a hot savoury sauce, e.g. cheese or mushroom.

Poached eggs

1 or 2 eggs per person

	Metric	Imp
eggs		
water	1 l	1 qt
1 tbsp vinegar (when using an open pan)		

Method
1 Half fill frying pan with water. Add vinegar. Bring to boil.
2 Break eggs in saucer one by one and slide into simmering water gently.
3 Simmer for about 4 min., till white is firm.
4 Lift out with a perforated spoon and drain well.
5 Serve on rounds of buttered toast.

Note Eggs may be cooked inside a greased egg poacher. Poached eggs may be served on a bed of cooked spinach with grated cheese on top, or coated with cheese sauce; they may be served on a cream of smoked haddock, and covered with Hollandaise sauce (p. 70), the whole being served on croûtes of fried bread.

Scrambled eggs   *3 or 4 persons*

	Metric	Imp
4 eggs		
butter	25 g	1 oz
2 tbsp milk		
salt, pepper		

Method
1 Beat the eggs with the milk, salt and pepper.
2 Heat the butter in a saucepan, add the egg mixture and stir over low heat till the eggs are just beginning to set.
3 Have ready some rounds of buttered toast. Pile eggs on to these while they are still a little moist.

Note Scrambled eggs can be varied by spreading the toast with shrimp, anchovy or bloater paste before piling the egg on, or by adding chopped parsley or herbs to the eggs before cooking them. A small quantity of chopped ham or corned beef, chopped cooked kidneys, chicken livers, mince of game or poultry, chopped cooked mushrooms or a little curry powder may be added to the eggs before cooking them. The eggs may be dished on spinach, sorrel, endive or sliced grilled tomatoes. Only a little of these ingredients should be added, but they will vary the flavour and make the dish go farther.

Birds' nests   *4 persons*

	Metric	Imp
mashed potatoes	600 g	1 ½ lb
grated cheese **or** ½ tsp		
curry powder	50 g	2 oz
butter	50 g	2 oz
hot milk	125 ml	¼ pt
8 eggs		
salt, pepper		

Method
1 Add the milk and butter to the potato, mix well and season. Add cheese or curry powder, reserving a little cheese for the top of the dish.
2 Grease a shallow fireproof dish, put in the mashed potato.
3 Make 8 depressions with a spoon, gently break an egg into each hollow.
4 Sprinkle with rest of cheese, if used, and dot with small pieces of butter.
5 Bake in a moderate oven (175°C, 350°F, Mark 4) for about 20 min., till whites are set but yolks still runny.
6 Serve at once.

Scotch eggs   *4 persons*

	Metric	Imp
4 hard-boiled eggs		
sausage meat	100 g	4 oz
a little flour		
beaten egg and breadcrumbs		
deep fat for frying		

Method
1 Shell the eggs, dry well and dust lightly in flour.
2 Divide the sausage meat into 4 and wrap 1 portion round each egg, shaping well.
3 Roll egg in beaten egg and coat in breadcrumbs.
4 Fry in deep fat at 180°C (350°F) for 8 to 10 min., rolling it round occasionally, till sausage meat is cooked through.
5 Drain well. Serve cold either whole or cut in half lengthwise.

Muesli

The night before, soak some rolled oats in enough milk to cover. Stir in some grated raw eating apple, raisins, hazel nuts and sugar to taste. Leave overnight.

Serve with cream, a little lemon juice and chopped banana.

Porridge

4 persons

	Metric	Imp
oatmeal	100 g	4 oz
water	500 ml	1 pt
salt		

Method
1 Bring water to boil in a double saucepan, add salt.
2 Sprinkle in oatmeal, stirring all the time with a wooden spoon.
3 Continue to stir till porridge begins to thicken and is free from lumps.
4 Simmer for about an hour. Add a little more boiling water if porridge becomes too thick.
5 Serve in hot bowls and offer hot milk or cream; syrup, brown or white sugar; or salt.

Note The cooking time depends on whether coarse, medium or fine oatmeal is used, the fine taking the least time. Rolled oats porridge is made in the same way, but takes only 20 to 30 min. to cook. Certain patent preparations take as little as 5 min. to cook. Porridge may be cooked very successfully overnight in a tightly covered casserole in the bottom oven of an Aga cooker, starting with the first three stages as above.

Fried or grilled bacon or ham

Back or streaky bacon is best for frying, though some people prefer rather lean bacon. The bacon is cut into thin slices or rashers. Remove the rind and rust and any small pieces of bone or gristle.

To fry Heat a frying pan, place the bacon in it and cook over low heat until the fat is transparent, turning the rashers once or twice. If cooked too quickly the bacon becomes scorched and hard. It is difficult to give an exact time for frying bacon, as some people prefer it crisp and dry, and others rather under-cooked.

To dish Serve the bacon on a hot dish and garnish it with small pieces of bread fried in the bacon fat.

Variations Cut some tomatoes in slices and fry these in the bacon fat, adding them just before the bacon is cooked. In this case they are dished either on the rashers of bacon or in the centre of the dish with the bacon arranged round. After dishing the bacon, eggs may be fried in the fat and dished on each rasher of bacon. Grilled mushrooms or kidneys make an excellent accompaniment to bacon; or left-over potatoes, if fried in the bacon fat and well drained, may be dished with it.

Grilled bloaters or kippers

4 persons

	Metric	Imp
4 kippers or bloaters		
butter	50 g	2 oz

Method
1 Remove the heads. Bloaters may be grilled closed, in which case they should be scored; or split open like kippers.
2 Wipe fish with a damp cloth.
3 Place fish skin side down on the grill pan. Place small pieces of butter on cut side.
4 Grill about 5 min. Test gently with a fork to see if they are soft.

Note A certain amount of the oiliness of a kipper can be removed by plunging them in and out of boiling water and drying them well before grilling. Kippers may also be fried, poached in a little water in a frying pan or baked with a little butter in a moderate oven (175°C, 350°F, Mark 4) for about 15 min.

Smoked haddock on toast

4 persons

	Metric	Imp
smoked haddock fillet	400 g	1 lb
butter	40 g	1½ oz
milk and water mixed	250 ml	½ pt
1 tbsp flour		
pepper, cayenne		
a little chopped parsley		
toast		

Method
1 Cut the fish in 3 pieces. Place in a pan and pour boiling water over to cover it. Leave for 5 min. Drain.
2 Add the milk and water and ⅓ of the butter. Cover and simmer another 5 min.
3 Take out fish carefully and keep hot, reserving liquor.
4 Melt remaining butter in a pan, stir in flour.
5 Remove from heat, stir in fish liquor gradually, add seasoning and return to heat. Stir till thick.
6 Flake the fish, add to sauce, sprinkle with parsley and serve on toast.

Note Smoked haddock may also be simply cooked in the milk and water mixture, drained and **flaked**, and mixed with melted butter.

To fry sausages

4 persons

	Metric	Imp
sausages (about 8 large ones)	450 g	1 lb
dripping	25 g	1 oz

Method
1 Prick the sausages well.
2 Melt the dripping.
3 Fry the sausages slowly, turning constantly, for about 15 min.
4 When browned and cooked through, serve on a hot dish.

Note Stale bread can be fried in the fat after the sausages, or cold, cooked potatoes, cut in slices. Halved tomatoes, apples or bananas may be fried and served with the sausages.

INVALID COOKERY

General hints – soups – fish – poultry – meat – sweet dishes – beverages

The recipes suggested for invalids are light and easy to digest. These are not recipes for special diets, which would come in a separate book, but merely recipes for tempting the appetite of the really sick and building up a convalescent.

When planning meals for the sick remember:

1 Serve small quantities of food in an appetising way, preferably in individual portions, and remove all left-over food from the sick-room as soon as the meal is over.

2 Serve food very punctually and see that cold food is really cold and hot food properly hot. All utensils must be scrupulously clean.

3 Bear the invalid's likes and dislikes in mind, following them as far as is compatible with a prescribed diet.

4 Avoid monotony. Where certain foods are a necessity, serve them in various ways, using different dishes or moulds. Colour helps tempt a jaded appetite, so use may be made of some of the harmless vegetable colourings available.

5 Cook all foods lightly and avoid fried and highly spiced foods. Eggs and milk are especially valuable in restoring strength to an invalid and can be introduced in all sorts of dishes, e.g. milk in a soup or jelly, eggs in a savoury custard or soufflé.

6 Fruit is important and if the patient cannot tolerate it in solid form, it can be offered in the form of rosehip or blackcurrant syrup poured over a sweet, or in a drink.

Note Beef tea and all meat soups for invalids should be made of fresh meat and not from stock made in the stockpot. All fat should be carefully removed and the soup or broth served in a soup cup. Fingers or cubes of thin crisp toast should be handed.

For convalescents, the broths or soups may be made more savoury by the addition of an onion, a little celery or tomato. Thick soups made with milk and eggs are nourishing, though a little heavier than broths and clear soups, therefore they are less suited to extreme cases of illness.

The following invalid recipes are intended for one person, though the whole amount in some cases would not be eaten at one meal.

SOUPS

Quickly made beef tea

	Metric	Imp
lean beef	200 g	½ lb
water	250 ml	½ pt
pinch of salt		

Method

1 Remove all fat and skin from the meat, shred it with a sharp knife. Put at once into a pan so as not to lose any juice.

2 Add water and salt to pan.

3 Simmer over low heat for about 15 min., stirring with a wooden spoon, pressing meat against the side of the pan to extract juice.

4 When liquid is brown and meat white, strain through coarse strainer.

5 Remove all fat with tissue paper.

6 Serve as required.

Ordinary beef tea

The same quantities as above, but dice the meat and put into a covered jar with the water in a warm oven (160°C, 325°F, Mark 3) for 4 hours. Add salt to taste after it is cooked, as if added before, it hardens the meat. Keep in a cold place and warm as required.

Note Skim off all trace of fat. The yolk of an egg beaten up may be added to any beef tea, and makes it more nourishing, and in some cases milk may be added.

Mutton and veal tea may be made like beef tea, using fillets from the legs of either. Sometimes mutton, veal and beef are mixed, making a very strong broth. Use 400 g (1 lb) of each to 3 litres (3 qt) of water.

Chicken broth

	Metric	Imp
1 boiling fowl cut up		
water	1 ½ l	3 pt
1 small onion		
1 blade mace		
salt, pepper		
1 tsp finely chopped parsley		

Method
1 Put the fowl, neck, gizzard and liver in a pan with the water and salt.
2 Bring to the boil and skim.
3 Add onion and mace and simmer 4 hr.
4 Strain, return to the pan, bring to the boil and skim.
5 Check seasoning, add parsley and serve.

Mutton broth

	Metric	Imp
very lean mutton	200 g	½ lb
rice or barley	10 g	½ oz
cold water	500 ml	1 pt
1 tbsp chopped parsley		
salt		

Method
1 Wash meat, remove fat and put in pan with water and salt.
2 Bring to boil and skim.
3 Simmer for 1 ½ hr. Add rice or barley.
4 Simmer another ½ hr. Season to taste. Leave till cold.
5 Remove all fat. Dice meat very small.
6 Reheat, add parsley and serve.

Veal broth

	Metric	Imp
knuckle of veal	600 g	1 ½ lb
water	750 ml	1 ½ pt
cooked rice	25 g	10 oz
1 onion		
1 blade mace		
2 pieces celery sliced		
1 spray parsley		
salt, pepper		

Method
1 Simmer all the ingredients except the rice in a pan till the liquid is reduced to 500 ml (1 pt), about 1 ½ hr.
2 Take out the meat and add the rice.
3 Reheat and serve.

Note The veal can be served with parsley and butter sauce.

FISH

Baked fillet of fish

Lay fish fillet in a buttered fireproof dish. Season with salt, pepper and a little lemon juice. Cover with buttered cooking paper and bake for 10 minutes in a hot oven (220°C, 425°F, Mark 7). Remove paper, sprinkle with breadcrumbs and serve with a little white sauce.

Poached fillet of fish

Put fish in a pan that just fits it. Cover with milk. Add a pinch of salt. Simmer till tender. Take out fish and keep on a hot dish. Make a sauce with a little butter and flour and the fish liquor, and pour over fish.

Steamed fillet of fish

Spread a little butter on a plate. Place fish on it. Squeeze over some lemon juice, season with salt and pepper. Cover with a piece of buttered paper, then another plate. Put the plates over a pan of boiling water and cook till the fish looks white and opaque, about 10 to 15 minutes. Serve on a hot plate and pour liquor round. Garnish with cut lemon or parsley.

Baked haddock in custard

	Metric	Imp
haddock fillet	150 g	6 oz
milk	250 ml	½ pt
butter	10 g	½ oz
1 egg		
lemon juice		
a little chopped parsley		
salt, pepper		

Method

1 Cut the fillet in two lengthwise.
2 Sprinkle with salt, pepper and lemon juice. Roll up.
3 Place in a buttered pie-dish.
4 Beat up the egg with the milk, season with salt and pepper, strain over the fish and sprinkle with parsley.
5 Bake in a slow oven (150°C, 300°F, Mark 2) 20 to 30 min. till set.
6 Serve in the dish.

Fish soufflé

	Metric	Imp
cooked white fish	100 g	4 oz
butter	15 g	½ oz
milk	60 ml	½ gill
white sauce (p. 65)		
1 separated egg		
squeeze of lemon juice		
1 dssp flour		
salt, pepper		
shrimps, parsley		

Method

1 Melt the butter, stir in the flour.
2 Add the milk and cook, stirring, till the mixture leaves the sides of the pan.
3 **Flake** the fish and mix well with the panada.
4 Add the egg yolk, mix well. Season.
5 Whip egg white stiff, fold into the mixture. Add lemon juice.
6 Grease a small soufflé mould. Fill three parts full with mixture. Cover with greased paper.
7 Steam gently for 20 to 30 min.
8 Turn out on a hot dish. Coat with white sauce. Garnish with shrimps and parsley.

POULTRY AND MEAT

Chicken cream

	Metric	Imp
cooked chicken chopped finely	100 g	4 oz
white sauce (p. 65)	60 ml	½ gill
milk or cream	60 ml	½ gill
béchamel sauce (p. 64)	125 ml	1 gill
1 egg		
salt, pepper		
parsley		

Method

1 Pound the chicken in a mortar or put in blender.
2 Add the egg and white sauce gradually.
3 Sieve the mixture, stir in milk or cream, season.
4 Turn into small greased moulds and cover with greased paper.
5 Steam very gently till firm, 30 to 40 min.
6 Turn out moulds and coat with échamel sauce. Garnish with parsley.

Chicken soufflé

	Metric	Imp
cooked chicken minced finely	50 g	2 oz
white sauce (p. 65)	125 g	¼ pt
béchamel sauce (p. 64)	250 ml	½ pt
1 tsp chopped parsley		
1 separated egg		
pinch of mixed herbs		
salt, pepper		

Method

1 Mix the sauce, chicken, parsley and herbs. Season well and stir over heat till mixture boils.
2 Remove from heat and add egg yolk, lightly beaten.
3 Whip egg white stiff and fold in.
4 Grease small soufflé mould and put in mixture.
5 Place mould on a baking tin and bake in a

moderately hot oven (175°C, 350°F, Mark 4) about 15 min. till risen and brown, but still soft inside.

6 Serve at once with béchamel sauce handed separately.

Steamed chicken fillets

2 fillets of chicken breast
butter
toast
salt, pepper
lemon juice

Method

1 Skin fillets and sprinkle with lemon juice, salt and pepper.
2 Grease a plate with butter, put on the fillets, cover with another plate.
3 Place over a saucepan of boiling water. Steam till tender (about ¾ hr).
4 Serve on a hot plate with any juice from the cooking. Hand fingers of toast.

Note Mutton or lamb cutlets or small chops may be cooked in the same way, turning them over when half-cooked. This is an excellent way of cooking meat for invalids as it is very easily digested.

Lamb chop en papillote

1 lamb loin chop trimmed of fat
salt, pepper

Method

1 Sprinkle the chop with salt and pepper.
2 Grease a piece of foil and fold the chop in it, sealing the edges carefully.
3 Bake in a hot oven (220°C, 425°F, Mark 7) for 15 min.
4 Serve on a hot plate in the foil.

Note A tender fillet steak just large enough for one may be cooked in the same way.

Raw beef croquettes

	Metric	Imp
lean beef	200 g	½ lb
butter	10 g	½ oz
1 tsp beef tea or *bouillon*		

Method

1 Remove all skin and fat; shred beef finely; rub through a sieve.
2 Season lightly and add the beef tea.
3 Shape mixture into small balls.
4 Heat butter in a pan. Put in the balls; stir them round till the outside changes colour, but the inside remains uncooked (3–4 min.).
5 Drain on soft paper and serve.

Note Raw beef sandwiches are prepared in the same way, spreading the mixture between thin bread and butter, or bread alone if butter is not allowed, without cooking it at all.

Savoury custard

	Metric	Imp
1 egg		
beef tea or chicken broth	125 ml	1 gill
salt, pepper		

Method

1 Bring the broth to the boil.
2 Pour over the beaten egg, beating the whole time.
3 Season and pour into a greased jar or basin.
4 Cover with greased paper, put in a steamer or stand on an inverted saucer in a pan of boiling water that reaches half-way up the basin.
5 Simmer gently for 15 to 20 min. or till custard is set.
6 Take it out. Let stand for a minute. Turn out gently on to a plate.

SWEET DISHES

Banana cream

	Metric	Imp
3 bananas		
milk	250 g	½ pt
castor sugar	40 g	1½ oz
1 separated egg		
rind and juice of ½ lemon		
few drops vanilla essence		

Method
1 Slice bananas and put in a glass dish.
2 Sprinkle with lemon juice and 1 dssp sugar.
3 Boil lemon rind in the milk with 1 tsp sugar.
4 Strain on to beaten egg yolk and stir over low heat for 5 min., without boiling. Cool.
5 Pour over bananas and leave till cold.
6 Whip egg white stiffly, fold in rest of sugar and vanilla essence. Pile on custard.

Egg jelly

	Metric	Imp
1 egg		
gelatine	12 g	½ oz
loaf sugar	50 g	2 oz
water	250 ml	½ pt
rind and juice of 1 lemon		

Method
1 Rub sugar on lemon rind. Squeeze and strain lemon juice.
2 Put gelatine, sugar and water in a pan and stir over low heat till melted. Bring just to the boil.
3 Strain water mixture over beaten egg stirring all the time.
4 Add lemon juice and return to pan.
5 Stir over low heat till mixture thickens without boiling.
6 Put in a basin to cool.
7 When cold, put in 2 wetted moulds.
8 Turn out when set.

Snow cream

	Metric	Imp
milk	250 ml	½ pt
ground rice	25 g	1 oz
butter	25 g	1 oz
granulated sugar	15 g	½ oz
few drops flavouring essence		

Method
1 Blend rice with a little cold milk.
2 Put in pan with other ingredients and boil till smooth (15 min.), stirring all the time.
3 Turn the mixture into a small mould. Leave till cold.
4 Turn out and decorate with jam, jelly or pour over a little rosehip or blackcurrant syrup.

BEVERAGES

Albumen water

	Metric	Imp
white of an egg		
water	125 ml	1 gill
a little glucose or salt		

Method
1 Mix the unbeaten egg white and water together very well.
2 Strain through muslin.
3 Add glucose or salt.

Note This is nourishing and may be given in extreme cases of illness. It may be added to either warm milk or beef tea, in which case only 1 tbsp water is added to the white of egg. Care must be taken that the beef tea is not too hot or the egg may cook or curdle.

Blackcurrant tea

	Metric	Imp
1 tbsp blackcurrant jam		
boiling water	250 ml	½ pt
sugar to taste		
squeeze of lemon juice		

Method
1 Put the jam, sugar and lemon juice in a jug.
2 Pour over the boiling water.
3 Stir, cover and leave to stand in a warm place 20 to 30 min.
4 Strain through a piece of muslin and drink hot or cold.

Camomile tea

6 camomile flowers
breakfast-cupful boiling water

Method
1 Put the camomile flowers in a small teapot or jug.
2 Pour on the boiling water.
3 Infuse in a warm place for 10 min.
4 Pour through a strainer and serve with or without sugar.

Beaten egg with tea

1 egg yolk
1 cup of tea
1 dssp milk
1 tsp brandy or sherry
sugar (optional)

Method
1 Beat up the egg yolk in a cup.
2 Gradually add milk and brandy.
3 Fill up cup with hot tea, beating all the time.
4 Add sugar to taste if required and serve.

Egg nog

1 egg white
castor sugar to taste
1 tbsp milk
1 tbsp brandy or sherry

Method
1 Put the brandy or sherry in a tumbler.
2 Add milk and sugar; beat well.
3 Whisk egg white stiff; stir into tumbler and serve.

Gruel

	Metric	Imp
1 tbsp fine oatmeal		
water or milk and water mixed	500 ml	1 pt
sugar to taste		
pinch of salt		

Method
1 Mix oats in a basin with enough water to blend them.
2 Boil remainder of water and pour it on to the blended oatmeal.
3 Return to pan and stir till boiling. Simmer for ½ hr, stirring frequently.
4 Strain. Add a pinch of salt and sugar to taste.

Note If desired, a strip of lemon peel may be added to this.

Gruel made with patent oats

	Metric	Imp
1 tbsp patent oats		
water	500 ml	1 pt
brandy or white wine	60 ml	½ gill
nutmeg (optional)		

Method
1 Mix oats in a basin with enough water to blend them.
2 Add rest of the water, boiling, stirring all the time.
3 Stir over low heat till thick (about 10 min.).
4 Sweeten to taste, add brandy or wine and a little nutmeg if desired.

To prepare Iceland and Irish moss

Wash the moss and soak it in water for several hours. It is wise to add a pinch of soda to water in which Iceland moss is soaked. After soaking, lift the moss out of the water and put it into a saucepan with 2 litres (2 qt) of water, simmer gently for about 4 hours. Strain and add sugar to taste and a little strained lemon juice.

Irish moss is sometimes made into a jelly.

Lemon barley water

	Metric	Imp
rind and juice of 2 lemons		
loaf sugar	50 g	2 oz
pearl barley	100 g	4 oz
boiling water	1 l	1 qt

Method
1 Wash barley, put in pan and just cover with cold water.
2 Bring to boil, boil for 4 min., strain off 1 slice crusty bread
3 Put barley in jug.
4 Rub off yellow part of rind on to sugar and add to barley.
5 Pour over 1 litre (1 qt) boiling water. Stir to dissolve sugar.
6 Leave till quite cold, stir in juice of lemons. Strain and serve.

Milk and rum

1 tbsp rum to 250 ml (1 pt) milk

Method
Warm milk, mix rum in and pour it from one cup to another twice.

An egg yolk may be beaten up with the rum first and the hot milk stirred gently into it. Sweeten to taste and serve in a glass.

Prairie oyster

For a hangover
1 egg
1 tsp Worcestershire sauce
1 tsp tomato ketchup
½ tsp vinegar
pinch of pepper
a shake of tabasco sauce

Method
Put the whole egg in a glass. Add the other ingredients. Gulp down.

Stomach settler

To help stop vomiting

	Metric	Imp
fruit juice diluted with water	125 ml	¼ pt
¼ tsp salt		
2 tsp sugar		
½ egg white		

Method
1 Put all ingredients together in the blender or beat very thoroughly till emulsified.
2 Give 1 tsp every half hour.

Toast water

	Metric	Imp
1 slice crusty bread		
water	500 ml	1 pt
a little lemon juice		

Method
1 Toast bread till deep brown but not burnt.
2 Put some very fresh cold water in a jug; add toast in pieces.
3 Cover and leave till water is colour of sherry (about ½ hr).
4 Add lemon juice.

Treacle posset

Good for colds

	Metric	Imp
1 tbsp golden syrup or treacle		
milk	125 ml	1 gill

Method
1 Boil up milk; add syrup and boil again, stirring.
2 Strain and serve hot.

Whey

	Metric	Imp
milk	500 ml	1 pt
1 tsp rennet		

Method
1 Make the milk lukewarm, stir in the

rennet; leave in a warm place to set.

2 When cool, break it up and strain whey through muslin. Lemon juice may also be added to the milk.

White wine whey

	Metric	Imp
milk	125 ml	1 gill
½ wineglassful sherry		
sugar to taste		

Method

1 Bring milk to boil, add wine and heat slowly till milk curdles (5 min.).

2 Strain through muslin and use whey, adding sugar to taste.

Note Whey is very easily digested and makes a pleasing drink for people with digestive troubles.

OTHER DISHES SUITABLE FOR INVALIDS

Cream of barley soup
Consommé
Artichoke soup
Spinach soup
Boiled, grilled or fried fish
Fish croquettes, cutlets
Omelettes
Kedgeree
Fillets of sole baked or steamed
Baked whiting
Asparagus
Celery à la creme
Green pea purée
Spinach cream
Roast, boiled or spatchcock chicken
Lightly cooked rabbit
Various tripe dishes
Delicate dishes with mutton or lamb cutlets
Grilled cutlets or steak
Steamed or boiled mutton or veal
Soufflés of any kind of meat, game or
poultry
Various dishes made with brains, calves' feet and sweetbreads
All simple milk puddings
Custard puddings
Caramel rice
Various fruit purées
Stewed fruit
Soufflés, omelettes, jellies
Blancmanges
Junkets
Fruit fools
Custard of any kind
Simple creams
Lemonade

BREAD AND CAKE MAKING

General remarks – recipes for bread, buns, scones, biscuits, cakes, almond paste, icings

POINTS TO REMEMBER

1 The flour for bread-making should be plain, never self-raising. If possible, use strong flour which can be bought in all health food stores and many grocers now. Strong flour is also best for yeast cakes and buns, soft flour for cakes and biscuits. Keep the flour in a really dry place, preferably an airtight bin.

2 Bread should be baked in a hot oven 200°C–230°C (400°F–450°F), Mark 6 or 7. A little steam can be provided by placing a meat tin with boiling water in it on the oven floor; this helps the bread to rise. For a soft crust, brush a little oil over the loaves before baking and dust with flour. For a crisp crust, brush a little salt water over the loaves before baking, and bake a little longer than normal, starting in a hot oven and reducing the heat to 190°C (375°F), Mark 5 after about 20 minutes.

3 When cooked, bread will have shrunk from the sides of the tin. When knocked out of the tin, it will sound hollow if rapped with the knuckles. To test if cakes are cooked, run a fine skewer into the top of the cake; if it comes out clear, the cake is cooked. The top of the cake should be firm but springy to the touch.

4 Bread should be rested on a wire rack to cool when removed from the oven to allow the steam to evaporate. Some cakes, such as rich fruit cakes, which need to be really moist, are left to cool completely in the tin before turning out; others, such as gingerbread, are left for 10 or 15 minutes and then turned out, whereas sponges are removed from the tin and placed on a rack as soon as they come out of the oven.

5 *Yeast* Either fresh or dried yeast can be bought. Fresh yeast is obtained from the baker and can sometimes be bought frozen from grocers with deep-freeze cabinets. It should be stored in a jar with a screw top and will keep up to a month in a refrigerator. In a freezer, it will keep a year. Dried baker's yeast is obtained from health food shops and chemists; this comes in a tin and should keep 6 months.

Yeast is a sort of fungus which begins to grow at a certain temperature, and this growth causes chemical changes to take place in the flour, which produce carbonic acid gas and aerate the dough, thus causing the bread to rise. Yeast requires a certain amount of warmth to start this growth, but should too great heat be employed, it checks the growth and causes the bread to stop rising. It is important, therefore, that warm basins should be used when mixing the yeast, and that it is mixed with lukewarm water or milk.

Fresh yeast should not be **creamed** with a little sugar but simply dissolved in a little of the warm, sweet liquid which will be used for mixing and left till frothy. Frozen fresh yeast may be grated and used without thawing.

Dried yeast can be used in the same way as fresh yeast, if it is just mixed with sugar and flour and water and allowed to stand for 5 minutes, then mixed with the warm sweetened liquid in the same way as fresh yeast. The proportions should be as follows: 1 teaspoonful of flour and 1 of sugar mixed with 6 teaspoonsful of dried yeast and 6 of water will give the equivalent of 12 teaspoonsful or 60 g of fresh yeast. The amount of yeast used depends on the length of time the dough can be left to rise – less yeast being needed for a longer rise. Dough can be left to rise overnight in the refrigerator, for 2 or 3 hours in a cool larder or for ½ hour in an airing cupboard. Cover with polythene while rising to keep the dough moist.

To prepare cake and bread tins

To line a round cake tin with paper White kitchen paper should be used for this. Fold a double band of paper about 5–7 cm (2–3 in.) deeper than the cake tin and just long enough to fit round the inside of the tin, and wrap over a little at the joint. Cut this and then fold up about 2 cm (1 in.) at the folded side, open out the fold and make slanting cuts on the edge that has been folded at little intervals apart. Cut a doubled round of the paper to fit the bottom of the tin exactly. Melt a little butter or margarine in a small pan, remove any scum that rises, and then, with a clean brush, brush the butter round the inside of the cake tins and over the band of paper. Arrange the band inside the cake tin, putting the notched part of the paper flat on the tin. Place the doubled round of paper inside the tin, covering the notched piece of the band and press it down well, perfectly flat. If making a very large cake, three or four folds of paper should be used.

To line a square flat tin Take a piece of paper larger than the tin, so that the sides will stand up 2–5 cm (1 or 2 in.) all round. Grease the tin and then the paper and press it smoothly into the bottom of the tin. Notch the corners and see that the paper stands up at least 2 cm (1 in.) above the edge of the tin all round.

To prepare small patty pans or cake tins Brush them over well with **clarified** butter or margarine. Sometimes 1 tbsp flour and 1 tbsp castor sugar are mixed together, and a spoonful of this is put into the small cake tins and shaken well all over them. Shake out all the loose flour.

Large sponge cake tins are sometimes treated in the above manner. A double band of any kind of paper should be fastened round the outside of a sponge cake tin, projecting 5–7 cm (2 or 3 in.) above the top.

For scones, buns or small cakes baked without a tin, brush the baking tin well over with **clarified** butter or margarine.

Sandwich cake tins are greased, or they may be dusted out with a mixture of flour and sugar. In other cases, they are lined with greased paper. Should the sides of the tin be 5–7 cm (2 or 3 in.) high, the paper must be put in the same as in lining a round cake tin.

Bread tins are sometimes greased; in other cases they are dusted out with flour. If the bread is made into Coburg or cottage loaves, they are placed upon a greased and floured baking tin.

To shape the loaves

Dough that is baked in tins may be a little softer than that which is made up into loaves without support.

When the loaves are shaped they should be put into a warm place to 'prove' before baking them. When weighing dough it must be remembered that a good deal of weight is lost by evaporation during baking, so if a loaf is to weigh 800 g (2 lb) when cooked, the dough must weigh 885 g (2 lb 3½ oz).

To make a **Cottage Loaf** take two pieces of dough, one larger than the other, shape them into balls, put the smaller ball on the top of the larger one and flour the finger or thumb and press it right through the centre of both. Then make four or five cuts round the sides of the bread with the back of the knife. Put the loaves on a greased and floured tin.

For a **Coburg Loaf** shape the dough into an oval shape and make several deep cuts across the tops. If baking the bread in tins, grease and flour the tins and only half fill them.

Brown bread

	Metric	Imp
wholemeal flour	750 g	1¾ lb
strong white flour	750 g	1¾ lb
fresh yeast **or**	50 g	2 oz
dried yeast	25 g	1 oz
lukewarm water	1100 ml	2 pt
1 tbsp salt		
1 tsp sugar		
1 tsp flour		

Method

1 Mix flours and salt together in a warm basin. Make a well in the centre.

2 Mix yeast, sugar, 1 tsp flour and a little of the lukewarm water together. Leave 5 min. till frothy.

3 Pour into the well in the flour all at once together with the rest of the water, mix to a soft dough with the fingers till the dough leaves the sides of the basin clean.

4 Place dough on a floured surface, **knead** well and divide into four.

5 Place in 4 greased and floured tins (750 g size or 1½ lb), or shape into 4 cobs by making a round ball and flattening it on greased and floured baking sheets.

6 Brush the tops with oil and put to rise inside a loosely wrapped sheet of polythene, till double the size.

7 Brush tops with salt water for a crusty finish or with oil and flour for a soft finish and bake in a hot oven (220°C, 425°F, Mark 7), middle shelf, for 40–50 min.

Note Wholemeal or brown meal flour only may be used for making this bread, but a lighter bread results when white flour is added to it.

White bread

	Metric	Imp
strong plain flour	1·5 kg	3½ lb
lard	25 g	1 oz
fresh yeast	50 g	2 oz
or dried yeast	25 g	1 oz
lukewarm water	1100 ml	2 pt
1 tbsp salt		
1 tsp sugar		
1 tsp flour		

Method

1 Mix flour and salt, rub in lard, make a well in the centre.

2 Mix sugar and 1 tsp flour with yeast and some of the warm water. Leave 5 min. till frothy.

3 Pour yeast liquid and rest of the water all at once into the flour and make a firm dough, adding extra flour or water if needed till the dough leaves the sides of the bowl clean.

4 Knead dough on a lightly floured surface till firm and not sticky, about 10 min. This may be done with a dough hook on an electric mixer for 3 min. on minimum speed.

5 Place to rise in a large lightly oiled polythene bag, loosely tied, or in a glass bowl, lightly covered, till double the size and springy when pressed with a finger. This will take ½–¾ hr in a warm place, 2 hr at room temperature, 4–6 hr in a cool larder and overnight in a refrigerator.

6 Knock back the dough by turning it on a lightly floured board and **kneading** it to a firm dough.

7 Divide the dough into four and place in greased floured tins (750 g or 1½ lb), put inside a lightly greased polythene bag and leave till dough reaches the top of the tins.

8 Bake in the centre of a hot oven (220°C, 425°F, Mark 7) for 40–45 min., till the bread shrinks from the sides of the tin. It should sound hollow if tapped at the bottom.

9 Cool on a wire rack.

To **knead** bread properly, flour the hands and fold the fingers over the thumbs, thus making a fist. Then beat and pummel the dough, first with one hand, then with the other, all over, turning it over and working it well until it ceases to stick to the hands (from 15 to 20 min.). Flour a basin and return the dough to it, making a cross on the top, and let it stand until well risen. It should be nearly double its original size. The dough may be set to rise overnight if covered close and kept in a warm place.

Breakfast cakes may be made from this dough, adding a beaten egg and 25 g (1 oz) of melted butter or margarine to 400 g (1 lb) of dough. Shape the mixture into balls and bake in a hot oven for 20 min.

Baking powder bread
(a good emergency bread)

	Metric	Imp
white flour	800 g	2 lb
fresh or sour milk	about 750 ml	1¼ pt
4 heaped tsp baking powder		
½ tsp salt		

Method

1 Sieve together the flour, baking powder and salt.

2 Add milk to make a soft dough.

3 Turn out on a floured board, **knead** lightly.

4 Divide into two, shape into rounds, place on a greased baking tray.

5 Bake in a moderate oven (175°C, 350°F, Mark 4) for about ¾ hr. Eat very fresh.

Note This may be made into rolls, in which case bake for 15 to 20 min.

Milk rolls

	Metric	Imp
strong plain flour	500 g	1 lb
butter or margarine	50 g	2 oz
4 tsp dried yeast **or**		
fresh yeast	25 g	1 oz
warm milk	300 ml	½ pt
2 tsp salt		
1 tsp sugar		
1 tsp flour		
1 egg		

Method

1 Sieve flour and salt into a basin, **rub in** the fat.

2 Mix yeast, sugar, 1 tsp flour and milk together and stand for 5 min.

3 Add beaten egg. Save a little for **glazing** the top of the rolls.

4 Make a well in the flour, pour in liquid and mix to a soft dough.

5 Knead on a floured board till firm and not sticky. Put in a greased polythene bag to rise.

6 When double the bulk, turn on to a floured board and shape into rolls, either elongated like bridge rolls or round baps. It should make about 14 rolls (imperial measure) or 16 (metric).

7 Put on a greased baking tin. Leave in a warm place about 10 min. to 'prove', inside a polythene bag.

8 Brush with egg and salt.

9 Bake in a fairly hot oven (200°C, 400°F, Mark 6) about 15 min.

Buns

	Metric	Imp
flour	700 g	1½ lb
warm milk	about 300 ml	¾ pt
yeast	60 g	2 oz
lard or butter	50 g	2 oz
sugar	100 g	4 oz
currants	100 g	4 oz
1 egg		
pinch of salt		
1 tsp grated lemon rind		
a little grated nutmeg		

Method

1 Melt the fat in a pan with the milk; when warm, pour it on to the crumbled yeast.

2 Sieve the flour, salt and nutmeg into a basin; make a well in the centre.

3 Pour the yeast mixture into the well, gradually mix in the flour and beat to a dough. Cover and leave to rise for 1½ hr. It should double its size.

4 Add the sugar, lemon peel, currants and beaten egg to the dough.

5 Mix well and shape on an oiled board into approximately 24 buns.

6 Put on a greased baking sheet, cover with a polythene bag and leave in a warm place for about ½ hr to rise.

7 Bake in a hot oven (220°C, 425°F, Mark 7) for 15 to 20 min. Just before removing them, brush over with a little milk mixed with sugar.

8 Cool on a rack.

Note Hot Cross Buns are made in the same way, adding a large pinch of mixed spice and 50 g (2 oz) chopped peel to the recipe. Form a cross with the back of a knife on each bun after shaping it.

Drop scones

	Metric	Imp
plain flour	200 g	½ lb
1 tsp bicarbonate of soda		
1 tsp cream of tartar		
pinch of salt		
1 egg		
2 dssp golden syrup		
milk to mix		

Method

1 Sieve the dry ingredients.

2 Drop in the beaten egg and a little milk. Mix quickly and add golden syrup.

3 Add more milk, gradually till a thick batter is made.

4 Grease a hot girdle or thick frying pan with very little butter.

5 Drop on the mixture in small rounds.

6 When the surface rises in bubbles, turn each scone with a knife.

7 Cook till golden brown (about 10 min.). Remove and cool on a wire rack.

8 Butter and serve with jam or honey.

Plain scones

	Metric	Imp
plain flour	200 g	½ lb
castor sugar (for sweet scones)	25 g	1 oz
margarine or butter	40 g	2 oz
4 tsp baking powder		
pinch of salt		
1 egg		
milk or sour milk to mix		

Method

1 Sieve the dry ingredients, **rub in** the fat.
2 Add beaten egg and enough milk to make a soft dough.
3 Turn out on a floured board and **knead** a little.
4 Roll out to about 1 ½ cm (½ in.) thick.
5 Cut in rounds (12 to 16 scones). Brush with milk.
6 Place on a greased tin and bake in a hot oven (220°C, 425°F, Mark 7) about 15 min.

Note About 40 g (2 oz) of currants or sultanas may be added to the dough to make fruit scones.

Potato scones

Replace half the quantity of flour with an equivalent amount of sieved cooked potato. Add the potato after rubbing in the margarine. Roll out on to a floured board and cut into rounds. Put them on a greased girdle or frying pan and bake for about 10 min., turning once. Split in half, butter and serve hot.

Wholemeal scones

Replace half the white flour with wholemeal flour and proceed as for plain scones.

BISCUITS

Flapjacks

	Metric	Imp
porridge oats	200 g	8 oz
syrup	50 g	2 oz
soft brown sugar	75 g	3 oz
butter	125 g	5 oz
squeeze of lemon juice		
pinch of salt		

Method

1 Melt butter, sugar, syrup in saucepan.
2 Stir in lemon juice, oats and salt.
3 Spread mixture in well-greased tin, pressing down.
4 Cook in moderate oven (175°C, 350°F, Mark 4) 25 to 30 min., till golden brown.
5 Cut in segments while still warm.

Ginger biscuits

	Metric	Imp
flour	200 g	½ lb
butter	100 g	¼ lb
castor sugar	100 g	¼ lb
1 tsp ground ginger		
2 eggs		
pinch of salt		

Method

1 Sieve the flour, salt and ginger.
2 Beat the butter and sugar to a cream.
3 Add the beaten eggs one by one, beating each in well, then gradually stir in the flour. If the mixture is too dry, add a little milk.
4 Drop spoonsful of the mixture on greased paper on a greased tin fairly well spaced out.
5 Bake in a fairly slow oven (160°C, 325°F, Mark 3) for 15 to 20 min., till pale brown.

Note Ginger biscuits do not become crisp till cold.

Milk biscuits

	Metric	Imp
flour	400 g	1 lb
milk	250 ml	½ pt
butter	25 g	1 oz
pinch of salt		

Method

1 Sieve flour and salt and **rub in** the butter.
2 Gradually stir in enough milk to make a paste that will roll out easily.

3 Flour a board and roll out paste thin.

4 Stamp out with a round cutter the size of a tumbler.

5 Put the biscuits on a lightly greased baking tin and bake in a hot oven (220°C, 425°F, Mark 7) till very pale brown, about 15 min.

6 Cool on a rack.

Shrewsbury biscuits (or **Easter cakes**)

	Metric	**Imp**
flour	200 g	½ lb
castor sugar	100 g	¼ lb
butter	100 g	¼ lb
currants	50 g	2 oz

2 egg yolks and 1 egg white
¼ tsp cinnamon
pinch of salt

Method

1 Sieve the flour, salt and cinnamon. **Rub in** the butter.

2 Add the sugar.

3 Beat up the egg yolks and stir lightly in. If too dry, add 1 egg white.

4 Add the currants and mix all to a stiff paste.

5 Roll out very thinly and cut into cakes with a fluted cutter about 8 cm (3 in.) in diameter.

6 Put on to a greased baking tin and bake in a cool oven (130°C, 275°F, Mark 1) till very pale brown, about 10 to 15 min.

Note Caraway seeds may be used in the place of currants, or the biscuits flavoured with ground ginger. The cinnamon may be omitted.

CAKES

Note Some of the cake recipes give a smaller quantity of eggs with the metric ingredients than with the imperial ones. This is to maintain the right balance of eggs to other ingredients. The metric recipe will make a slightly smaller cake, and will consequently need a slightly shorter cooking time.

Christmas cake

(See **Note** above)

	Metric	**Imp**
flour	400 g	1 lb
castor sugar	200 g	½ lb
sultanas	400 g	1 lb
currants	400 g	1 lb
candied peel	200 g	½ lb
almonds **blanched** and chopped	100 g	¼ lb
eggs	5	6

wineglass of brandy
1 tsp mixed spice
pinch of salt

Method

Prepare, make and bake this cake according to the directions for Rich Wedding Cake (p. 299). This quantity requires a tin about 20 cm (8 in.) in diameter. This cake improves with keeping, so should be made two or three months before Christmas. A few days before it is required cover it with almond paste and ice with royal icing.

Coconut drop cakes

	Metric	**Imp**
desiccated coconut	50 g	2 oz
self-raising flour	150 g	6 oz
castor sugar	75 g	3 oz
margarine	75 g	3 oz

1 egg
pinch of bicarbonate of soda
grated rind of 1 lemon

Method

1 **Cream** the fat and sugar.

2 Stir together the flour, soda and coconut. Add the beaten egg and lemon rind.

3 Blend with the creamed mixture.

4 Arrange in small heaps on a greased baking sheet and bake in a hot oven (220°C, 425°F, Mark 7) for 15 to 20 min.

Foundation cake

(See **Note** on previous page)

	Metric	Imp
flour	400 g	1 lb
castor sugar	200 g	½ lb
butter or margarine	200 g	½ lb
milk	60–100 ml	up to 1 gill
1 tsp baking powder		
pinch of salt		
4 eggs		
any flavouring essence		

Method

1 Sieve the flour, baking powder and salt.
2 Cream butter and sugar, add eggs one by one alternating with a little flour to prevent curdling.
3 Stir in the flour lightly, alternately with the milk to a dropping consistency.
4 Add any flavouring essence liked.
5 Put in a greased tin lined with greased paper. Bake in a moderate oven (175°C, 350°F, Mark 4) for about 1 hour.
6 Turn on to a rack to cool.

Note This cake forms a good foundation for various other cakes. Mixed dried fruits and almonds may be added, or sultanas or currants only. Any kind of nuts or preserved ginger, glacé cherries, coconut, caraway seeds, nuts, candied peel, and so on may also be added, the cake taking its name from the fruit, etc., added, such as sultana, currant, seed, cherry, plum cake. The amount of fruit may be varied according to the richness of the cake. This cake may be made richer or plainer by adding more eggs and a little less milk, or fewer eggs and a little more baking powder and milk. Dripping may be used in place of butter.

Genoese pastry

	Metric	Imp
flour	150 g	6 oz
castor sugar	200 g	½ lb
butter	150 g	6 oz
eggs	6	7
any flavour desired		
pinch of salt		

Method

1 Melt the butter and remove the scum that rises.
2 Sieve the flour and salt.
3 Put the eggs in a basin; whisk for 5 min., then add the sugar and whisk again.
4 Place the basin over a pan of boiling water and continue to whisk till the eggs become thick and frothy. Do not let the mixture get too hot or the eggs will cook, but remove the basin from the pan and whisk away from the heat occasionally.
5 Add flour and butter alternately with a metal spoon, and then the flavouring.
6 Put mixture in a greased shallow tin lined with greased paper.
7 Bake in a hot oven (220°C, 425°F, Mark 7) for 15 to 20 min. till firm when pressed.
8 Turn out on to a rack to cool.

Note This may be made into a Swiss roll (p. 299) or it may be made in two sandwich tins and made into a layer cake with any filling preferred, and iced if desired. It is also sometimes made into small fancy cakes or it may be baked in one round tin lined with greased paper. In this case, it takes a little longer to bake, being thicker.

Inexpensive gingerbread

	Metric	Imp
flour	400 g	1 lb
lard	100 g	4 oz
treacle or golden syrup	400 g	1 lb
milk	125 ml	1 gill
candied peel	50 g	2 oz
1 tsp ginger		
1 tsp bicarbonate of soda		
pinch of salt		
2 eggs		

Method

1 Sieve the flour, ginger, salt and bicarbonate of soda into a basin.
2 Put the lard, treacle or syrup and milk into a pan and stir over low heat till mixed.
3 Beat up the eggs, make a well in the centre of the flour, pour in the treacle mixture and the beaten eggs and mix well.

4 Add the peel and put mixture in a 22 cm (9 in.) greased tin lined with greased paper. Bake for ¾ to 1 hr in a very moderate oven (160°C, 325°F, Mark 3).

Madeira cake

(See **Note** on p. 295)

	Metric	Imp
flour	200 g	8 oz
butter or margarine	150 g	6 oz
castor sugar	150 g	6 oz
candied peel	40 g	1½ oz
eggs	3	4
1 tsp baking powder		
grated peel of ½ lemon		
pinch of salt		

Method

1 Cream the fat and sugar. Sieve flour, baking powder and salt.
2 Add eggs and flour alternately, mix very lightly.
3 Stir in the lemon peel and the mixed peel.
4 Put the mixture into a greased cake tin lined with 2 or 3 thicknesses of greased paper. Place a slice of candied peel on top.
5 Bake in a moderate oven (175°C, 350°F, Mark 4) for about 1 hr or till the cake is firm when pressed.
6 Cool on a wire rack.

Rice cakes

	Metric	Imp
ground rice	100 g	4 oz
flour	100 g	4 oz
butter	150 g	6 oz
castor sugar	200 g	8 oz
3 separated eggs		
pinch of salt		
vanilla or almond essence		

Method

1 Sieve the flour and salt. Stir in the ground rice.
2 Cream the butter and sugar, add the egg yolks one by one.
3 Whip the egg whites stiffly and stir in lightly alternately with the flour.
4 Put mixture into greased patty pans dusted out with flour and sugar and bake in a

hot oven (220°C, 425°F, Mark 7) for 20 to 30 min.

Rock cakes

	Metric	Imp
flour	200 g	½ lb
Demerara sugar	100 g	¼ lb
butter or margarine	100 g	¼ lb
currants	100 g	¼ lb
1 egg		
pinch of salt		
lemon juice or milk to mix		

Method

1 Sieve the flour and salt.
2 Rub the fat **in**, stir in the sugar and currants.
3 Mix in the beaten egg and if too stiff, add a little lemon juice or milk. Mixture must be dry enough to form rocky heaps on the baking tin.
4 Grease a tin and pile in rough heaps a short distance apart from each other.
5 Bake for 20 to 30 min. in a fairly hot oven (200°C, 400°F, Mark 6).

Sand cake

	Metric	Imp
butter	100 g	4 oz
castor sugar	100 g	4 oz
flour	50 g	2 oz
ground rice	50 g	2 oz
arrowroot	50 g	2 oz
1 tsp baking powder		
pinch of salt		
2 separated eggs		

Method

1 Sieve the flour, baking powder and salt, add the ground rice and arrowroot.
2 Beat the sugar and butter to a cream, add egg yolks one at a time.
3 Whip egg whites stiffly and stir in lightly, alternately with the flour.
4 Put the mixture in a square bread tin that has been dusted out with equal parts of flour and sugar.
5 Place the tin on a baking sheet and put in a fairly hot oven (200°C, 400°F, Mark 6) for

about 10 min. Lower the temperature to moderate (175°C, 350°F, Mark 4) and continue cooking for about 1 hr.

Real Scottish shortbread

	Metric	Imp
butter	100 g	4 oz
flour	300 g	12 oz
sugar	100 g	4 oz
pinch of salt		
strips of candied peel		
a few **blanched** split almonds		

Method

1 **Cream** butter and sugar.
2 Sieve flour and salt together. Add to the butter mixture by degrees quickly and lightly.
3 As soon as they are mixed together, roll out lightly to a round 1·5 cm (¾ in.) thick and pinch round the edges with the fingers.
4 Put the shortbread on a greased baking tin and prick all over with a fork. Cut the peel in strips and use for decoration with the almonds.
5 Bake in a cool oven (130°C, 275°F, Mark 1) till pale biscuit colour for 25 to 30 min.
6 Leave to cool in the tin as it stiffens and is less liable to break.

Simnel (or Easter) cake

	Metric	Imp
flour	300 g	12 oz
butter	200 g	8 oz
sugar	200 g	8 oz
sultanas	150 g	6 oz
currants	150 g	6 oz
chopped peel	150 g	6 oz
almond paste (p. 300)	500 g	1¼ lb
½ tsp baking powder		
1 dssp black treacle		
4 eggs		

Method

1 **Cream** the butter and sugar. Add the beaten eggs gradually, beating well.
2 Put all the dry ingredients together and add to the mixture, stirring well. Add treacle.
3 Roll out 200 g (½ lb) of almond paste and shape into a round the size of the cake tin.
4 Put half the cake mixture in a greased and lined tin, then put in the round of almond paste and press down well. Put in the rest of the mixture.
5 Bake in a moderate oven (175°C, 350°F, Mark 4) for 2½–3 hr.
6 When cold, roll out another 200 g (½ lb) of almond paste to fit the top, sticking it with melted syrup.
7 Roll the rest of the paste into little balls and put them round the edge, painting with a little egg yolk to make them stick. Paint the paste with egg yolk and put the cake in a very hot oven (240°C, 475°F, Mark 9) till the paste is golden brown (5–10 min.).
8 Remove cake from oven and cool on a rack.
9 When quite cold, place decorations in the centre, small sugar eggs, chickens, etc.

Soda cake

	Metric	Imp
flour	400 g	1 lb
butter or margarine	150 g	6 oz
sugar	100 g	4 oz
currants	200 g	½ lb
1 tsp bicarbonate of soda		
2 eggs		
milk to mix		
pinch of salt		

Method

1 Sieve the flour, salt and bicarbonate of soda.
2 **Rub in** the butter and add the sugar and currants.
3 Beat up the eggs with a little milk and add. Add more milk to a stiff dropping consistency.
4 Put in a greased tin lined with greased paper.
5 Bake in a moderate oven (175°C, 350°F, Mark 4) for 1¼ to 1½ hours.

Sponge cake

5 separated eggs
their weight in castor sugar
the weight of 3 eggs in flour
1 tbsp lemon juice

Method

1 Take 1 tbsp sugar away from the total quantity for every egg white.
2 Whisk the remaining sugar and egg yolks in a bowl over low heat till white and fluffy.
3 Add the lemon juice.
4 Whisk the whites stiffly, **fold in** the remaining sugar and **fold into** the mixture with the sifted flour.
5 Turn at once into a lined, greased and sugared cake tin and bake in a slow to moderate oven (160°C, 325°F, Mark 3) for 40 min. to 1 hr.

Swiss roll

	Metric	Imp
2 eggs		
castor sugar	50 g	2 oz
flour	50 g	2 oz
a few drops vanilla essence		
about 2 tbsp tepid water		
a little warmed jam		

Method

1 Grease a Swiss roll tin and line with greased paper.
2 Warm and sieve the flour.
3 Beat the eggs and sugar until thick and creamy, over moderate heat, or in a warm bowl with an electric beater.
4 Add vanilla, **fold in** the flour.
5 Add tepid water to make a pouring consistency.
6 Put in the prepared tin.
7 Bake in a hot oven (220°C, 425°F, Mark 7) 8 to 10 min.
8 Turn on to a damp cloth covered with sugared paper; trim edges; spread with warm jam and roll up.
9 Sprinkle with castor sugar when cold.

Note A Genoese pastry (p. 296) or simple sponge cake mixture may be used for Swiss roll in place of the above.

Chocolate Swiss Roll is made in the same way, adding to the mixture just before stirring in the flour 50 g (2 oz) of grated chocolate melted over low heat in 1 tbsp of water. When baked, roll according to the directions for Swiss roll. When cold, unroll and spread over butter icing (p. 300) flavoured with vanilla and roll again.

Victoria sandwich

	Metric	Imp
3 eggs		
butter	150 g	6 oz
castor sugar	150 g	6 oz
flour	150 g	6 oz
1 tsp baking powder		
grated rind of 1 lemon **or** 1 tsp vanilla essence		
pinch of salt		
milk to mix		

Method

1 **Cream** the butter and sugar.
2 Add eggs one by one, beating thoroughly. Add flavouring.
3 Sieve the flour, baking powder and salt.
4 Lightly **fold in** the flour alternately with milk. The mixture should be soft enough to drop easily from the spoon.
5 Put in two prepared 18 cm (7 in.) sandwich tins.
6 Bake in a moderate oven (175°C, 350°F, Mark 4) 20 to 30 min. Turn out on to a rack.
7 When cold, sandwich the two sponges with jam or butter icing in the middle and **dredge** with castor or icing sugar.

Rich wedding cake
(See **Note** on page 295)

	Metric	Imp
flour	1·6 kg	4 lb
butter	1·6 kg	4 lb
castor sugar	800 g	2 lb
mace and nutmeg mixed	25 g	1 oz
sultanas	400 g	1 lb
currants	800 g	2 lb
raisins	1·6 kg	4 lb

	Metric	Imp
mixed peel	200 g	½ lb
almonds **blanched** and chopped	400 g	1 lb
eggs	20	24
brandy	250 ml	½ pt
1 tsp salt		

2 baking tins about 25 cm (10 in.) and 15 cm (6 in.) will be needed.

Method

1 Sieve the flour with the salt and spices.
2 Soften the butter in a warm basin, do not let it oil, and cream it. Add the sugar and beat till creamy.
3 Add the eggs two at a time, alternating with a little flour to keep it from curdling.
4 Mix a little flour with all the fruit and add to the mixture. Beat in the almonds.
5 Stir in the flour lightly with the brandy. Do not beat.
6 Put in prepared cake tins that have been lined with three layers of greased paper.
7 Bake in a moderate oven (175°C, 350°F, Mark 4) for the first half hour, then lower the temperature a little (160°C, 325°F, Mark 3). The larger cake will take 4 to 5 hr, the smaller less in proportion.
8 Cool in the tins, then wrap in white paper and store in an airtight tin for 3 or 4 months.
9 When required, ice the cakes first with almond icing then with royal icing (p. 299).

Almond paste or marzipan

TO coat a cake 20 cm (8 in.) in diameter. To cover the top only, use half quantities.

	Metric	Imp
ground almonds	400 g	1 lb
sieved icing sugar (or ½ icing and ½ castor)	600 g	1 ½ lb
2 small eggs		
juice of ½ lemon		

Method

1 Pound the almonds with the lemon juice. Add the sugar.
2 Add the egg whites or yolks or whole eggs gradually, pounding until a fairly stiff paste is formed. (The yolks make a richer, yellower paste and the whites a drier, paler paste).

When well mixed, **knead** till smooth and soft.

3 Roll paste out to 2 cm (1 in.) in thickness.
4 Level top of cake, turn upside down and brush top over with slightly whipped egg white. Roll out paste in a round to fit top of cake and overhang the edges by 2 cm (1 in.).
5 Brush the sides of the cake with melted apricot jam and press round them a strip of almond paste the depth and circumference of the cake.
6 Leave for 24 hours to dry before icing, or put in a cool oven to dry and when cold, cover with glacé or royal icing.

Butter icing

	Metric	Imp
butter	100 g	4 oz
icing sugar	200 g	½ lb

Method

1 **Cream** butter and sugar till white and soft.
2 Add flavouring and colouring if desired.
3 Use inside layer cakes or piped on top of large or small fancy cakes.

For **mocha** or **coffee icing**, add a very little strong black coffee or essence.
For **chocolate icing**, dissolve 50 g (2 oz) grated chocolate in 1 tbsp hot milk or water. When cool, add to the icing.

Glacé icing

	Metric	Imp
icing sugar	200 g	½ lb
2–3 tbsp water or other liquid		
flavouring, colouring		

Method

1 Rub the icing sugar through a sieve into a very clean saucepan.
2 Add the water gradually and mix to a rather liquid paste.
3 Add flavouring or colouring as required, and stir with a wooden spoon over a low heat till the sugar melts. Do not let it get too hot.
4 When it coats the back of the spoon, pour it over the cake at once.

5 Do not touch the top of the cake, but smooth the sides and lift any icing that has run off with a knife dipped in cold water.

6 Decorate before the icing sets.

Chocolate glacé icing

	Metric	Imp
icing sugar	200 g	½ lb
grated chocolate	75 g	3 oz
3 tsp water		

Method

1 Put the water and the chocolate into a saucepan.

2 Stir over the fire till the chocolate melts; boil for 5 min.

3 Cool slightly, then stir in the icing sugar.

4 Stir over very low heat for a minute to melt the sugar, then pour the icing over the cake.

Royal icing

	Metric	Imp
icing sugar	400 g	1 lb
1 tsp lemon juice		
2 egg whites		
¼ tsp glycerine		

Method

1 Sieve the sugar.

2 Place the egg whites in a grease-free basin.

3 Work in half the sugar, add the lemon juice and the glycerine.

4 Continue adding sugar till it pours from the spoon.

5 Beat till glossy. For piping it must be stiff enough to stand up in points.

6 Cover the bowl with a damp cloth.

7 Beat the icing occasionally while using it and re-cover with the damp cloth.

Note All equipment must be free from grease.

To ice a cake with royal icing   The cake must be perfectly flat. If it is not, the cake should be cut straight and turned upside down, as the bottom is always level. If a revolving cake stand is available, place the cake on this; if not, place it on an inverted plate put on a dish. Have ready a jug of cold water and a broad-bladed knife. Pile sufficient icing on the cake to cover it, then with the knife dipped in cold water smooth this, making it perfectly even. Place the point of the knife on the centre of the cake and move the stand round until a complete circle has been made, when the top of the cake should be perfectly smooth. If no revolving stand is available, a little practice is required to smooth the cake evenly, but the knife should be brought smoothly across the cake in one direction.

To ice the sides of the cake place some icing on the sides and spread it round roughly with a knife, then hold the knife in a slanting position against the sides of the cake and turn the stand round. Allow this icing to dry. For a wedding, birthday or christening cake, two or three layers of icing are put on, but each coat must be dry before putting on the next. The cake may then be decorated according to taste. If decorated with the icing, this must be put into a forcing bag or tube, which is supplied together with various pipe attachments to make shell and rose motifs and for writing. The icing is forced through the bag or tube and through the pipe attachment to form the required design. It is essential to obtain the right amount of pressure when forcing icing through a tube, and it is as well to practise a design or motif before attempting to apply the decoration to a cake. Simple designs are often the most effective; it is a good plan to mark the intended positions of rosettes, shells, etc., by pricking the icing base on the cake with a fine needle. Icing which is used for practising purposes may be used over and over again provided it is beaten up and not allowed to harden. Any royal icing which drops down on to the dish while icing may be returned to the basin, beaten up and used again. This icing may be coloured and flavoured as desired.

PRESERVES AND PICKLES

Jams – jellies – marmalades – preserves – pickles – chutneys

General rules for jam and jelly making

1 Use perfectly sound, just ripe fruit, freshly picked (and on a fine day if possible).

2 Use the best sugar; loaf, preserving or granulated. Good quality sugar is cleaner and makes less scum.

3 Weighing and measuring must be absolutely accurate: too much sugar will spoil the flavour of the fruit, too little means waste as the jam has to be boiled so long that it wastes considerably.

4 Jam must always be stirred once the sugar is in, using a wooden spoon. Do not let the mixture boil till all the sugar has dissolved.

5 When the sugar is dissolved boil the jam rapidly. Keep the jam skimmed.

6 As the jam thickens and the fruit becomes clear test for setting by dropping a little on a saucer and leaving in a cold place. If a thin skin forms on it, it is ready. Remove the pan from the heat while testing the jam. If the jam does not set, return the pan and boil a little longer.

7 In some jam the fruit is apt to rise to the surface, leaving the syrup at the bottom of the jars. In this case, let the jam cool a bit in the pan and give it a stir before pouring it out.

To pot and cover jam

1 The jars should be scrupulously clean, dry and warmed a little in the oven since cold jars may crack when hot jam is put in them.

2 Fill the jars very full as jam sinks when it cools and air should be excluded from the jars as much as possible. Wipe the tops and sides while still hot.

3 Cover the jam either directly they are filled, while the jam is still hot; or when the jam has become quite cold; they must not be covered while the jam is lukewarm. Press a small round of wax paper inside the top of the jar. Cover the top with a cellophane circle. It should be slightly damped on the outside and dried on a cloth just before use; it will then dry taut when held in place with an elastic band.

4 Label the jars with the date and type of preserve. Jams should keep perfectly for a year if stored in a cool dry place.

Remedies

If signs of fermentation or mould appear on the top of any jars of jam, open the jars, skim off the affected part and re-boil the rest. Put it back into perfectly clean dry jars. If badly fermented, however, nothing can be done to save the jam.

If jam does not set when boiling, this is usually because it has not been boiled fast enough or too much water has been added to it. Half an ounce of seed pearl tapioca may then be added to each pound of jam. Soak the tapioca for 12 hours, then return the jam to the pan, bring to the boil, put in the tapioca, and boil until it is clear. Put it into pots and cover. Jam treated in this way will not keep long.

Useful tips

Some jams lose weight considerably. Watery fruits yield a much smaller proportion of jam than dry, hard fruits, as it takes longer to set and wastes a good deal during the boiling. Gooseberries, plums, damsons, greengages, blackcurrants, blackberries, if made with 3 parts of sugar to 4 of fruit should not lose more than 1/7th of their value when boiling. 8 parts of any of the plums and 6 parts of sugar should yield 12 parts of jam. Soft berries such as strawberries, raspberries, redcurrants (especially strawberries) yield a much smaller portion of jam, as they are very watery, and in wet weather the yield is still less – 10 parts of fruit and sugar often give only 7 parts of jam.

Some berries contain so much juice that very little water is required. The drier fruits, such as apples, pears and plums, require more water.

JAMS

Apple jam

	Metric	Imp
apple pulp made from peeled and cored apples cooked till soft with the minimum of water	500 ml	1 pt
granulated sugar	300 g	¾ lb
pinch each of powdered cinnamon and cloves		

Method
1 Measure the apple pulp carefully. Add sugar and spices in a large pan and stir over low heat till melted.
2 Boil up for 30 min., stirring all the time to prevent burning.
3 Put in a warm, dry jars; cover tightly and store.

Blackberry and apple jam
equal quantities of blackberries and cooking apples
3 parts of sugar to 4 parts of fruit
a very little water

Method
1 Prepare the fruit as for boiling, put it into a pan with sufficient water to keep it from burning and simmer till soft.
2 Add sugar, stir till boiling.
3 Boil fast till jam sets when tested. Remove all scum.
4 Cover and store.

Blackberry and marrow jam may be made in the same way, using marrow instead of apples, but if desired, when the fruit is soft, it may be rubbed through a hair sieve and the sugar added to the pulp.

Blackcurrant jam
allow 3 parts of sugar to 4 of fruit

Method
1 Use dry, ripe fruit, remove the stalks and weigh.
2 Put into a deep dish, cover with sugar and leave overnight.

3 Put in a pan and finish as for blackberry and apple jam.

Whitecurrant and redcurrant jam
The same proportions of sugar and fruit are used, but as their skins are not so tough, they may be cooked without the overnight steeping that is necessary for blackcurrants.

Cherry jam

	Metric	Imp
fruit	400 g	1 lb
sugar	300 g	¾ lb
3 tbsp water		

Method
1 Put half the sugar in a preserving pan.
2 Remove stalks from cherries and place on sugar. Cover with rest of sugar.
3 Add water or redcurrant juice and place over low heat.
4 Bring to the boil, shaking the pan constantly, but do not stir. Boil quickly, shaking often. Remove scum.
5 When cherries look clear and syrup sets when tested, put into pots.
6 Cover and store.

Green gooseberry jam

	Metric	Imp
fruit	400 g	1 lb
sugar	300 g	¾ lb
water	125 ml	¼ pt

Method
1 Select gooseberries that are fully grown but not ripe.
2 Wash, top and tail the fruit.
3 Dissolve the sugar in the cold water.
4 Bring to the boil, simmer for 15 min., skimming when necessary.
5 Add the fruit, boil for 35 to 40 min. or till jam sets when tested.
6 Pour into clean, dry pots. Cover and store.

Ripe gooseberry jam

Method

1 Put fruit in a preserving pan with just enough water to prevent it burning.
2 Bring to the boil, skim and weigh.
3 Add 3 parts sugar to 4 parts fruit.
4 Finish as for green gooseberry jam.

Plum jam

	Metric	Imp
fruit	400 g	1 lb
sugar	300 g	¾ lb
water – to each 2400 g (6 lb)		
fruit	500 ml	1 pt

Method

1 Wash and dry the plums, cut in half and remove the stones or make a slit in them and skim off the stones as they rise.
2 Put them in a preserving pan with the water, bring to the boil and simmer gently till soft.
3 Add the sugar, and finish according to the directions for blackberry and apple. This jam takes from 20 to 30 min. to stiffen.

Note All kinds of plums, greengages and damsons may be made into jam according to this recipe. In making greengage jam a few of the stones may be cracked and the kernels skinned and added to the jam.

Plum and apple, and damson and apple jam may be made in the same manner, allowing equal quantities of each fruit. Peel, core and slice the apples, add them to the stoned plums, put them into a preserving pan with 250 ml (½ pt) of water, and simmer until soft; then add 300 g (¾ lb) of sugar to each 400 g (1 lb) of fruit, and finish as above.

Raspberry or loganberry jam

	Metric	Imp
fruit	400 g	1 lb
preserving sugar	350 g	14 oz

Method

1 Pick over the fruit and reject any unsound berries.

2 Remove the stalks, put fruit in a preserving pan over low heat and simmer gently for a few minutes. Press against the pan with a wooden spoon.
3 Simmer 20 min. Add sugar, stir till dissolved then boil fast till jam sets when tested.
4 Put into warm jars. Cover and store.

Note Raspberry jam is much improved by the addition of redcurrants. Allow 1 part of redcurrants to 2 of raspberries and 300 g (¾ lb) of sugar to 400 g (1 lb) of fruit.

Rhubarb and ginger jam

	Metric	Imp
rhubarb (without leaves)	400 g	1 lb
sugar	300 g	¾ lb
To every 1600 g (4 lb) rhubarb allow:		
½ tsp citric acid		
1 tsp ground ginger		
bruised root ginger	25 g	1 oz

Strawberry jam

allow 3 parts of sugar to 4 of fruit
juice of 1 lemon for every 1200 g (3 lb) of fruit

Method

1 Pick over the fruit carefully and use only what is just ripe and dry.
2 Remove the stalks, put fruit in a preserving pan over low heat till juice flows freely, about ½ hr. Stir constantly.
3 Add sugar and lemon juice, stir till dissolved. Boil fast for ½ hr or till jam sets when tested. Remove scum as it rises.
4 Put jam in pots. Cover and store.

Vegetable marrow jam

	Metric	Imp
marrow	400 g	1 lb
sugar	300 g	¾ lb
1 lemon		
¼ tsp ground ginger		

Method

1 Peel marrow, remove seeds, cut pulp into small dice and weigh.

2 Grate rind and extract juice of lemon.

3 Put rind, pulp and juice with sugar and ginger and leave overnight.

4 Next day, strain off juice into a pan, bring to boil and add marrow.

5 Boil for about 1½ hr till pulp becomes transparent and syrup sets when tested.

6 Put into pots and store.

Note Oranges may be used in place of lemons.

Cucumber or **pumpkin jam** may be made the same way.

MARMALADES

Grapefruit marmalade

	Metric	Imp
2 grapefruits		
4 lemons		
water	2 l	4 pt
sugar	900 g	2¼ lb

Method

1 Wipe grapefruits and lemons. Squeeze juice from fruit and strain it.

2 Scrape out inside skins and pith and put in a muslin bag with pips.

3 Shred peel finely. Put in preserving pan with muslin bag, juice and water.

4 Boil all together till peel is tender and mixture reduced to about half.

5 Remove muslin bag, add sugar, stir till boiling.

6 Boil fast for 10 min. Test for setting.

7 When ready, pot and cover.

Lemon marmalade

	Metric	Imp
lemons	400 g	1 lb
sugar	800 g	2 lb
water	500 ml	1 pt

Method

1 Wipe lemons, put in water and boil for 2 hr.

2 Change the water once, replacing with the same quantity of boiling water.

3 Cut the lemons into thin slices and remove all pips.

4 To every 400 g (1 lb) of sugar required allow 250 ml (½ pt) of liquor in which lemons were boiled.

5 Put both in a pan and when sugar has

melted add the fruit and boil for ½ hr or till marmalade sets when tested.

6 Cover and store.

Orange marmalade (1)

To every 6 Seville oranges, add 1 large lemon and 2 sweet oranges. 600 g (1½ lb) of preserving sugar to each 400 g (1 lb) of pulp. 750 ml (1½ pt) of water to every 400 g (1 lb) of fruit.

Method

1 Remove the yellow rind from fruit and shred finely.

2 Take off all the pith and slice the pulp.

3 Put the pips in a basin with 500 ml (1 pt) cold water and leave overnight.

4 Put the pulp and orange rind into another basin with the water and leave overnight also.

5 The next day, put the fruit and water in a preserving pan, add strained liquor from lemon pips and boil all for an hour.

6 Pour into a basin and leave till the next day.

7 Weigh this pulp and to every 400 g (1 lb) add 600 g (1½ lb) sugar.

8 Put all in preserving pan, stir till the sugar has melted and boil fast till the marmalade sets when tested.

9 Put in pots. Cover and store.

Orange marmalade (2)

To every 4 Seville oranges allow 4 sweet oranges and 2 lemons. 500 ml (1 pt) of water for the pips, 2400 g (6 lb) sugar and 4 litres (8 pt) water.

Method

1 Wipe fruit and grate as much as possible of coloured and white skin directly into the water in a large pan.

2 Remove any remaining pith, shred it finely and add to water.

3 Cut the pulp in fine slices, remove pips and centre white core. Place the fruit slices and juice with the water and peel.

4 Put the pips in 500 ml (1 pt) of water and leave overnight.

5 Put the fruit and water in a preserving pan, add strained water from pips, bring to boil and simmer for 1 hr. Skim well.

6 Add sugar, stir till dissolved then boil very fast for 1 hr or till marmalade sets when tested.

7 Cover and store.

JELLIES

In making fruit jellies, remember that under-ripe fruits contain a vegetable jelly called pectose, which loses its power of setting if the fruit becomes overripe. The same thing happens if the fruit juice is over-cooked, and no amount of boiling will then make a jelly set. It only turns syrupy.

Apple juice contains so much more pectose than other fruits that very often it is added to fruits which are deficient in pectose. A proprietary liquid pectin can be bought from chemists and health food shops that will ensure setting.

Loaf sugar is best for making jelly, though it can be made with granulated sugar. Under-ripe, perfectly sound fruit, gathered on a dry day, must always be chosen. Warm the sugar in the oven before adding it to the fruit juice.

Jellies must always be put into small jars, as they do not set well in large ones.

Jellies are tested in the same way as jams. For covering and storing see the rules for jams (p. 29).

Straining jellies

When making jelly, it is essential to have a good jelly bag or to use a clean tea cloth which has been tied to the legs of an inverted chair. Always **scald** the bag or cloth before using it.

The whole contents of the pan should be put into the jelly bag. Let it drip all night into a basin. Never squeeze the bag or try to hurry up the dripping process. If you do, the jelly will be cloudy instead of clear.

Apple jelly

	Metric	Imp
apples	1200 g	3 lb
water	1½ l	3 pt
1 lemon		
sugar to each pint of juice	400 g	1 lb

Method

1 Wipe apples, cut in quarters, put into a pan with water without peeling or coring and simmer till soft.

2 Strain through a jelly bag or cloth all night.

3 Next day, measure juice; put 400 g (1 lb) sugar to every 500 ml (1 pt) of juice and 1 teaspoon lemon juice into a pan.

4 Stir till sugar melts, bring to the boil and boil fast till jelly sets when tested, about 20 min. Skim.

5 Put into small jars. Cover and store.

Note The jelly may be made from the cores and peels of apples only. Put them into a jar and cover with water. Cover the jar and leave it in a moderate oven (175°C, 350°F, Mark 4) for about 12 hr, or all night. If the water evaporates, add more water. After the peels have soaked for 12 to 24 hr, strain the water through muslin, measure and put it into a pan. Bring to the boil, and add 300 g (¾ lb) of sugar to each 500 ml (1 pt) of juice. Warm the sugar and add it to the juice, stir until it has melted and boil fast until the jelly sets when tested. Apple jelly may be flavoured with a little stick cinnamon or a few cloves when cooking the fruit or soaking the peel.

Apple marmalade may be made with the pulp of the fruit after the juice has been strained from it. Rub the pulp through a sieve and to each 400 g (1 lb) allow 300 g (¾ lb) of sugar and 60 ml (½ gill) water. Put all into a preserving pan, stir until boiling, then boil from ¾ to 1 hr, stirring almost continuously. Put into pots and cover.

Crab apple jelly

500 ml (1 pt) water to each 800 g (2 lb) of apples; 300 g (¾ lb) sugar to every 500 ml (1 pt) of juice.

Method
Make in the same way as apple jelly but do not cut up the apples. Put them whole in the pan. On no account let them get mashed or the jelly will be too acid.

Blackcurrant jelly

To every 500 ml of blackcurrant juice allow 400 g (1 lb) of sugar.

Method
1 Wash the fruit, remove the stalks, put into a jar, cover and place jar in a pan of boiling water.
2 Bring to the boil and simmer till the juice flows freely.
3 Strain through a jelly bag or cloth all night.
4 Next day, warm the sugar in the oven.
5 Measure the strained juice, place in a pan, bring to the boil and boil for 5 min.
6 Add the sugar, stir till melted and boil fast till the jelly sets when tested.

Elderberry jelly is made in the same way, but to every 400 g (1 lb) of elderberries allow 200 g (½ lb) of apples. The apples are stewed in 250 ml (½ pt) of water to each 400 g (1 lb).

Then this water is strained through muslin and added to the elderberry juice.

Blackberry jelly is made in the same way, but if desired, 250 ml (½ pt) of apple water may be added to every 500 ml (1 pt) of blackberry juice.

Redcurrant jelly

Allow 400 g (1 lb) sugar to every 500 ml (1 pt) of currant juice.

Method
This is made according to the directions for blackcurrant jelly. 1½ litres (3 pt) of currants will yield about 500 ml (1 pt) juice. This jelly is much improved by adding 500 ml (1 pt) of raspberry or white currant juice to 1½ litres (3 pt) of the red.

White currant, raspberry and **strawberry jelly** may be made in the same manner, allowing equal weights of sugar and raspberry or strawberry juice. These are improved by the addition of 1 measure of redcurrant juice to every 3 measures of raspberry or strawberry juice.

Green gooseberry jelly

2400 g gooseberries (6 lb); 400 g (1 lb) of sugar to each 500 ml (1 pt) of juice; 2 litres (4 pt) of water.

Method
1 Top, tail and wash gooseberries.
2 Put in a preserving pan with the water and simmer till well broken.
3 Leave to drip through a jelly bag or cloth all night. Do not press.
4 Measure juice and boil fast for 15 min.
5 Allow 400 g (1 lb) of sugar, warmed, to every 500 ml (1 pt) of juice. Stir it in the juice till melted.
6 Boil fast 15 to 20 min. or till jelly sets when tested.
7 Skim, pot and cover.

Black grape jelly

To every 500 ml (1 pt) juice allow 300 g (¾ lb) of loaf sugar.

Method

1 Put fruit in a saucepan over very gentle heat and press till juice flows freely.
2 Strain through muslin overnight without further pressing.
3 Measure the juice and finish as for gooseberry jelly.

Note 2 litres (2 qt) of grapes makes about 500 ml (1 pt) of juice.

Mint jelly

	Metric	Imp
cooking apples	800 g	2 lb
water	1 l	1 qt
½ tsp tartaric acid		

sugar
green colouring
fresh mint

Method

1 Wash apples and slice without peeling or coring.
2 Put slices in a pan with water, tartaric acid and a few sprigs of fresh mint.
3 Bring to the boil; stir occasionally till mixture becomes a soft pulp.
4 Strain pulp through fine muslin.
5 Measure resulting liquid, bring to the boil; add 400 g (1 lb) sugar for every 500 g (1 pint). Add freshly chopped mint.
6 Boil, test for setting; add a dash of green colouring.
7 Pot and cover.

PRESERVES

Almack's preserve

equal quantities of apples, plums and pears
equal quantities of sugar and fruit

Method

1 Peel, core and slice apples and pears. Slit plums and remove stones.
2 Weigh and put all in a stone jar in layers.
3 Place in a cool oven (130°C, 275°F, Mark 1) and cook till fruit is tender (1–2 hr, depending on variety and ripeness of fruit).
4 Rub through a coarse sieve, put in a preserving pan, add the sugar and stir over moderate heat till boiling.
5 Simmer, stirring constantly till jam sets when tested.
6 Put into small jars. Cover and store.

Note This jam should be thick as damson cheese and cut into slices when used.

Apple ginger

	Metric	Imp
apples weighed after peeling and coring	1200 g	3 lb
water	750 ml	1½ pt
sugar	1200 g	3 lb
whole ginger	100 g	4 oz
juice of 2 lemons		

Method

1 Bruise ginger well. Put in a pan with sugar, water, lemon juice, stir till sugar has melted, bring slowly to the boil.
2 Add apples, peeled, cored and quartered, to boiling syrup and simmer gently till apples are clear.
3 Remove ginger, lift apples carefully with a perforated spoon, put into jars and pour syrup over. Syrup must completely cover the apples.
4 Cover and store.

Damson cheese

damsons
sugar
water

Method

1 Wipe damsons; remove stalks.
2 Place in a pan with a very little water to prevent burning.
3 Cook very gently till soft, stirring from time to time.
4 Rub fruit through a sieve, measure the pulp and add 400 g (1 lb) sugar to every 500 ml (1 pt) of purée.
5 Return to preserving pan, cook gently till sugar has dissolved.

6 Boil for about ¾ hr till pulp becomes stiff. It is essential to stir almost continuously.

7 Turn into small oiled jars and cover tightly.

Note All hard fruits may be made into cheese in this way, though sweeter fruits than damsons require less sugar in proportion to the purée. Use 3 parts to 4 for apple, plum and apple or quince and apple cheese, 2 parts to 4 for cherry or apricot cheese.

Imitation preserved ginger

	Metric	Imp
vegetable marrow or cucumber	800 g	2 lb
whole ginger	25 g	1 oz
loaf sugar	800 g	2 lb
water	250 ml	½ pt

Method

1 Peel vegetable, remove seeds, cut into cubes.

2 Put sugar and water into a pan, stir till sugar is melted, then boil to the thread state (110°C, 225°F). When a little syrup is dropped from the spoon, a very fine thread is seen.

3 Put the ginger and pieces of pulp into the syrup and simmer till the pulp looks clear, then leave for 24 hr.

4 Strain and boil the syrup again to the thread stage.

5 Add the pieces of pulp and ginger and boil gently for an hour. Leave overnight again.

6 Repeat process next day; remove ginger; put pieces of pulp in pots with syrup. Cover and store.

Note Lettuce stalks or rhubarb may be made into imitation preserved ginger in the same manner, using the same quantity of lettuce stalks going to seed or rhubarb as marrow. Wash, wipe and in the case of rhubarb string the stalks and cut into lengths about 5 cm (2 in.) long.

Lemon curd

	Metric	Imp
rind and juice of 2 lemons		
castor sugar	200 g	8 oz
butter	50 g	2 oz
3 eggs		

Method

1 Grate lemon rind and strain juice. Beat eggs slightly.

2 Put all ingredients in a double saucepan and cook slowly, stirring with a wooden spoon till mixture thickens slightly. (It will thicken more when it cools).

3 Pot at once in hot jars and seal while hot.

Mincemeat

	Metric	Imp
chopped suet	400 g	1 lb
currants	400 g	1 lb
mixed peel	200 g	½ lb
peeled and cored apples	400 g	1 lb
chopped raisins	400 g	1 lb
Demerara sugar	100 g	¼ lb
brandy	60 ml	½ gill
sherry	60 ml	½ gill
1 tsp salt		
½ tsp allspice		
½ tsp ground ginger		
½ tsp ground cloves		
juice of 1 lemon		

Method

1 Mince apples, add all other ingredients and mix well in a basin. Cover and leave for 12 to 24 hr.

2 Mix thoroughly again.

3 Press into jars, press down well.

4 Cover and store in a cool place.

Rhubarb and orange preserve

	Metric	Imp
5 oranges		
rhubarb	2 kg	5 lb
loaf or granulated sugar	600 g	1½ lb
1 lemon		

Method

1 Peel oranges and lemon carefully, removing all pith. Chop peel finely.
2 Slice pulp into a pan, removing pips, add peel.
3 Wash, dry and cut rhubarb finely, add with sugar.
4 Stir over low heat till sugar has melted.
5 Boil fast till it sets when tested.
6 Put into clean, dry jars, cover and store.

Strawberries preserved whole

	Metric	Imp
fruit	400 g	1 lb
loaf or preserving sugar	300 g	¾ lb

Method

1 Choose fine ripe fruit. Hull and place the fruit in deep dishes; cover the fruit thoroughly with half the sugar and leave overnight.
2 Next day, strain off the syrup and put it with the remainder of the sugar in a pan. Boil till it jellies.
3 Add fruit and simmer ¾ hr. Stir very carefully without breaking fruit. Skim.
4 Put into jars and fill up with syrup.
5 Cover and store.

Preserved tomatoes

	Metric	Imp
small plum-shaped tomatoes	2800 g	7 lb
water	875 ml	1¾ pt
granulated sugar	2100 g	5¼ lb
2 lemons		

Method

1 Pour boiling water over tomatoes, leave to soak 2 or 3 min. and remove skins.
2 Put sugar and water in a pan, stir over low heat till sugar dissolves, then bring to the boil.
3 Put in tomatoes and simmer gently till tender (about 1 hr).
4 Boil lemons in water till peel is tender, drain and cut in thin slices. Remove pips.
5 Add lemons to tomatoes and simmer till tomatoes are clear and syrup thickens (about 1 hr).
6 Remove tomatoes carefully from syrup; leave to cool.
7 Boil syrup till thick, let cool.
8 Put tomatoes into jars, strain the syrup and pour it over them. Cover and store.

PICKLES

Rules to be observed

Always use the best vinegar. Malt vinegar gives pickles the best flavour. Use glass bottles where possible. If using earthenware jars they must be unglazed, as the action of the vinegar on the glaze produces a mineral poison. Never use a metal pan, fork or spoon when making pickles, as the action of the vinegar on the metal also produces a poison. It is best to use enamel pans or unglazed earthenware pans. If the vinegar evaporates in the bottles, add more vinegar, which should be first boiled and allowed to become cold.

Vegetables must be covered for at least 2 cm (1 in.) above the surface. Cork the bottles, then cover them with jam pot covers, or even with paraffin wax. Store pickles in a cool, dry place.

Pickled red cabbage

	Metric	Imp
1 red cabbage		
whole ginger	15 g	½ oz
malt vinegar	1 l	1 qt
salt		
peppercorns		

Method

1 Remove coarse outside leaves and stalks from a firm red cabbage. Wash and slice finely across cabbage.
2 Put in a large dish and sprinkle thickly with salt. Leave 24 hr.
3 Rinse; drain well; put into jars.

4 Boil vinegar with ginger, salt and peppercorns; strain it.
5 When cold, pour over cabbage.
6 Cover jars with jam pot covers, paraffin wax or use screw top jar.
7 The pickle is fit to use after a week. If kept too long, it becomes discoloured and soft.

Pickled cauliflowers

	Metric	Imp
cauliflowers		
malt vinegar	2 l	2 qt
whole ginger	15 g	½ oz
mustard seed	15 g	½ oz
nutmeg	6 g	¼ oz
mace	6 g	¼ oz
6 cloves		
salt		

Method

1 Tie spices in a muslin bag; boil in vinegar for 10 min; remove spices.
2 Choose white, firm cauliflowers; break into sprigs; wash in salted water; place in a pan of salt and water and bring almost to the boil.
3 Drain; cover with a cloth; leave till cold.
4 Sprinkle with salt; leave for 24 hr.
5 Drain well; put in jars.
6 Pour prepared vinegar over, which must cover cauliflower completely.
7 Divide spices into separate muslin bags; place one in each jar. Cover and store.

Pickled onions

	Metric	Imp
small silver-skinned		
onions	1 l	1 qt
wine vinegar	1 l	1 qt
spices as for pickled cauliflower (p. 311)		
salt		

Method

1 Prepare vinegar as for pickled cauliflower.
2 Peel onions and pack between layers of salt in a bowl.
3 Cover with water and leave for 24 hr.
4 Drain onions and rinse well with cold water and dry thoroughly.

5 Pack tightly in clean jars. Cover with vinegar. Seal jars.

Piccalilli

A selection of vegetables such as sprigs of cauliflower, pickling onions, French beans, gherkins, green tomatoes, nasturtium seeds, etc.

	Metric	Imp
salt		
spiced vinegar as in stage 1		
of cauliflower pickle (p. 311)	1 l	1 qt
For the thickened vinegar		
malt vinegar	1½ l	3 pt
mustard seed bruised	100 g	4 oz
root ginger finely sliced	100 g	4 oz
garlic cloves crushed	100 g	4 oz
turmeric	100 g	4 oz
sugar (optional)	100 g	4 oz
flour	20 g	¾ oz
peppercorns	15 g	½ oz

Method

1 Prepare and clean vegetables. Sprinkle with salt. Leave for 24 hr.
2 Meanwhile simmer all ingredients for thickened vinegar except flour for 15 min. Cool, leave for 24 hr.
3 Mix flour with a little cold liquid. Boil up vinegar mixture, add flour to it and stir till thickened. Cool.
4 Drain vegetables, cover with clear, spiced vinegar and simmer 10 min. Drain.
5 Add thickened vinegar, stir in thoroughly.
6 Pot and cover.

Vegetable marrow pickle

	Metric	Imp
To every 400 g (1 lb)		
marrow allow:		
1 clove garlic		
2 chillies		
sugar	200 g	½ lb
mustard powder	25 g	1 oz
root ginger	25 g	1 oz
turmeric	12 g	½ oz
malt vinegar	1 l	1 qt
salt		

Method

1 Peel marrow, remove seeds, cut pulp into strips. Sprinkle with salt, leave overnight.
2 Drain thoroughly and dry on a cloth.
3 Mix mustard powder smoothly with a little vinegar, add rest of ingredients and bring to the boil.
4 Stir in pulp; boil for 20 min. Leave till cool.
5 Put marrow into bottles; pour vinegar over. Cover and store.

Note **Cucumber** and **melon** may be pickled in this way.

Pickled walnuts

The walnuts must be picked about the end of June before the inside shell has formed. Try 1 or 2 of the walnuts with a darning needle, inserting it in every direction. If no shell can be felt, the nuts are right for picking. Use rubber gloves to deal with walnuts as their juice stains indelibly.

walnuts
brine – 150 g (6 oz) of salt
to 1 litre (1 qt) of water

	Metric	Imp
mace, cloves (each)	12 g	½ oz
allspice, ground ginger	25 g each	1 oz each
mustard seed, black	25 g	1 oz
and white peppercorns	each	each
malt vinegar	2 l	2 qt
root ginger bruised	40 ml	1½ oz
1 tsp salt		
2 tbsp grated horseradish		

Method

1 Put walnuts in cold water; bring to boil. Drain and rub off skin with a cloth.
2 Put in a basin. Cover with brine. Leave for 9 days; stir twice daily and change brine every 3 days.
3 Drain well; spread on trays in the sun till dry and black.
4 Pound all seasonings and spices together except horseradish and root ginger.
5 Put walnuts in jars with pounded spices sprinkled between each layer.
6 Boil vinegar with horseradish and root ginger. Leave to cool.
7 Strain over walnuts. Cover and store.

CHUTNEYS

These are an Indian preparation, consisting of sweet, sour and hot ingredients. A good imitation of an Indian chutney may be made in England, though it is not exactly the same, as the Indian fruits cannot easily be obtained in this country.

Apple chutney

	Metric	Imp
unripe sour apples	2 kg	5 lb
Demerara sugar	200 g	½ lb
garlic	12 g	½ oz
dry chillies	12 g	½ oz
raisins	100 g	4 oz
salt	25 g	1 oz
onions	100 g	4 oz
ground ginger	100 g	4 oz
mustard seed	25 g	1 oz
malt vinegar	1 l	1 qt

Method

1 Peel, core and slice apples. Put in a pan with sugar and vinegar, simmer till apples are soft.
2 Wash mustard seed with a little vinegar and dry in a cool oven.
3 Stone and chop raisins, peel and mince onions, garlic, chillies. Pound with ginger and mustard seeds.
4 When apples are soft, add other ingredients, mix well and put into small bottles. Cover and store. Keep for at least three months before using.

Cucumber mangoes

(A very hot chutney)

	Metric	Imp
4 large under-ripe cucumbers		
malt vinegar	2 l	2 qt
To flavour vinegar		
black peppercorns	25 g	1 oz
root ginger crushed	25 g	1 oz
mustard seed	25 g	1 oz
mace	12 g	½ oz
cloves	12 g	½ oz
grated horseradish	12 g	½ oz
1 clove garlic		
To stuff cucumbers		
grated horseradish	25 g	1 oz
mustard seed	25 g	1 oz
white peppercorns	25 g	1 oz
1 clove garlic		

Method

1 Cut a piece out of the side of each cucumber, remove seeds with a teaspoon.
2 Pound ingredients for stuffing cucumbers; put mixture in hollow, tie strips of peel back over hole.
3 Boil vinegar and when hot, pour over cucumbers. Leave till next day and drain off.
4 Boil up vinegar again and pour over cucumbers again. Boil up the vinegar each day for 3 days and pour over cucumbers.
5 Strain off vinegar and boil up with spices and seasoning.
6 Put cucumbers in jars and pour boiling vinegar over. Cover and store.

Green gooseberry chutney

	Metric	Imp
fully grown under-ripe gooseberries	1½ l	3 pt
onions sliced	400 g	1 lb
sultanas	100 g	4 oz
salt	25 g	1 oz
ground ginger	25 g	1 oz
raisins chopped	200 g	8 oz
Demerara sugar	300 g	¾ lb
malt vinegar	1 l	1 qt
mustard seed	6 g	¼ oz
½ level saltspoon cayenne		
¼ tsp turmeric		

Method

1 Top, tail, slice gooseberries.
2 Put all ingredients in an enamel pan, place over very gentle heat and bring to the boil.
3 Simmer for 1 hr, stirring often.
4 Put in jars; cover and store.

Lemon chutney

	Metric	Imp
4 large lemons sliced		
seedless raisins	100 g	4 oz
Demerara sugar	400 g	1 lb
onions peeled and chopped	400 g	1 lb
malt vinegar	500 ml	1 pt
salt	25 g	1 oz
mustard seed crushed	12 g	¼ oz
1 tsp ground ginger		
½ saltspoonful cayenne pepper		

Method

1 Put lemons and onions on a dish, sprinkle with salt and leave 24 hr.
2 Put in a preserving pan, add all other ingredients, bring to the boil; simmer till tender (1½ hr).
3 Turn into dry jars, tie down when cold.

Note This is delicious chutney to eat with cold beef.

Green tomato chutney

	Metric	Imp
green tomatoes	1200 g	3 lb
sultanas	400 g	1 lb
green apples peeled, cored and chopped	800 g	2 lb
chopped dates (optional)	200 g	½ lb
Demerara sugar	300 g	¾ lb
malt vinegar	375 ml	¾ pt
mustard seed	12 g	½ oz
6 shallots sliced		
2 cloves garlic chopped		
salt, pepper		

Method

1 Put all the dry ingredients into a preserving pan.
2 Pour over vinegar and boil mixture to a pulp (1½ hr).
3 Put into jars and cover.

PRESERVING FRUIT AND

VEGETABLES

BOTTLING FRUIT

Some people feel that it is a waste of time and energy to bottle fruit at home when they can buy a wide selection of canned or frozen fruit throughout the year. But tinned and frozen fruits in family sizes are a serious drain on the housekeeping budget. Fruit can be bottled cheaply while it is in season and a wise shopper will take advantage of lower prices while supplies are good.

Preserving jars are available, usually in two sizes, and are fitted with metal lids and clips, or with glass stoppers and metal screw tops. A rubber ring is placed between the jar and the lid to ensure that the contents remain sealed and airtight. The jars and metal or glass tops will last for many years. It is advisable, however, to buy new rubber rings each season, rather than run the risk of using old ones which may have perished.

Special containers are available for sterilizing, in sizes which will take eight or more bottles, although any bucket, small bath or boiler may be used, provided it is deep enough to allow for the almost complete immersion of the jars.

A thermometer is almost essential as it is important, when sterilizing, to maintain the correct temperature according to the fruit.

Most fruits bottle well, but there are a few exceptions which often prove disappointing. Strawberries sometimes lose their flavour and invariably become soft and spongy. Pumpkins and melons have a high water content and are therefore not very successful, while grapes are often insipid.

Whole fruit for bottling should be slightly under-ripe, and perfect. If a large quantity of fruit is damaged it is a good plan to make it into a purée (p. 319) and bottle that, for use in jellies, moulds, sauces and tarts.

Directions are given below for sterilizing fruit by two of the most popular methods.

Sterilizing under water

1 Wipe the fruit and prepare it as required. Remove large stones as in peaches or apricots.

2 Pack the fruit into the jars (which must be absolutely clean and dry). Use the handle of a wooden spoon to pack the sections of fruit tightly into the jars.

3 Fill the jars with cold water or with syrup (made from 150 g (6 oz) sugar to 500 ml (1 pt) of water, boiled, and allowed to cool).

4 Soak the rubber bands in cold water, fix one to the top of each jar and put the lid on. (If screw bands are used, screw them tightly, then loosen them by a half-turn, to allow for expansion.)

5 Put a folded newspaper or an old cloth at the bottom of the sterilizing container, so that the jars will not crack. Arrange the jars in the container so that they do not touch one another, and pour in sufficient cold water to reach the necks of the jars.

6 Put the sterilizer over a slow heat and in ¾ hr bring the temperature gradually to 75°C (160°F). Adjust the heat to allow the temperature to drop to 70°C (150°F), and maintain the latter for 2 hours. Should a thermometer not be available, heat gently to slow simmering and maintain for 1½ hours.

7 Use a cloth, or tongs, to remove the jars from the container, and stand them on a wooden surface, tighten screw bands if necessary, and leave them for 24 hours. At the end of this time, remove clips or screw bands and gently invert the jar to test that it is properly sealed. If juice oozes from the jar, or if the stopper is loose, the process of sterilizing must be repeated.

Jars can also be sterilized in water, in a pressure cooker. They should be arranged on the rack, with ½ to 2 litres (1 to 4 pt) of water according to the size of the cooker. Fix the lid and bring to L (5 lb) pressure within 10 minutes. Close the vent and maintain pressure for 1 minute for soft fruits, 3 to 4 minutes for peaches; 5 minutes for pears and whole tomatoes.

The jars should be stored in a cool, dry place.

Sterilizing in the oven

This method is useful if a deep container is not available, although it is not recommended for apples, pears and peaches, which are liable to become discoloured.

1 Wipe the fruit and prepare it as required. Large stones, as in plums, should be removed to facilitate packing.

2 Pack the fruit into clean, dry preserving jars, using the handle of a wooden spoon to push the fruit into place.

3 Stand the jars on a baking sheet and put them in a slow oven at 130°C (250°F, Mark ½) for about an hour, or until the juice starts to flow from them.

4 If the fruit has shrunk very much, use the contents of one jar to top up the others and return the now full jars to the oven for a further 5 minutes. Remove them, one at a time, fill them up with boiling water or syrup made from 150 g (6 oz) sugar to 500 ml (1 pt) water, and fasten the tops immediately. After 24 hours test the sealing of the jars by removing the clips or screw bands and picking them up by the lids. If the lids are secure, the jars are sealed satisfactorily.

FRUIT PULPS AND PURÉES

Pulps and purées can be made from the sound parts cut from fruit which is bruised or misshapen. For example, an excellent apple purée can be made from bruised windfalls which might otherwise be wasted.

Fruit pulp

Peel the fruit and cut out any bruised parts. Remove large stones, as in plums. Put the fruit in a saucepan with just sufficient water to prevent burning, and cook gently until tender. Pour the boiling pulp into warm, dry preserving jars and seal as for bottled fruit, with rubber rings and lids. If metal screw bands are used, loosen them by a half-turn. Stand the jars on a cloth in a sterilizing container, previously filled with hot water. Bring the water to boiling point and boil for five minutes. Remove the jars and stand them on a wooden surface. Tighten the screw bands and allow the jars to stand for 24 hours before testing the seal.

Fruit purée

Prepare and cook the fruit as for pulp and put in blender, or cook without peeling and when tender force it through a hair or nylon sieve, and return it to the saucepan. Bring the purée to boiling point again before transferring it to warm preserving jars.

BOTTLING VEGETABLES

Vegetables must be sterilized at a temperature which is higher than boiling point, and the only way to achieve this successfully and safely is to process them in a pressure cooker which can be adjusted to give a constant pressure of M (10 lbs). Only fresh and tender vegetables should be used.

1 Prepare them according to type and dice or slice them as necessary.

2 **Blanch** them by putting them in a thin muslin bag and immersing them in boiling water for 3 to 4 minutes.

3 Plunge them into cold water and allow them to drain.

4 Pack them into clean preserving jars and cover them with brine made from 60 g (2 ½ oz) salt dissolved in 4 litres (1 gallon) of water. Secure the tops and loosen screw bands by a half-turn.

5 Place the jars in the cooker with 2 cm (1 in.) of water. Fix the lid and heat to M (10 lb) pressure. Close the vent and process at this pressure for 30 minutes, or according to directions given by the maker of the cooker.

When a jar of bottled vegetables is opened for use there should be no smell but that of the actual food, and the vegetables should be quite unspoiled, and without discoloration. If there is the slightest suspicion that the food has spoiled in any way, the whole contents of the jar should be discarded without even a sample taste being taken.

All vegetables preserved in this way must be boiled before they are used. Do not attempt even to taste them before they are boiled.

The book of instructions supplied with every pressure cooker should be consulted carefully before any attempt is made to use it for sterilizing bottled fruit and vegetables.

Salting beans

	Metric	Imp
runner beans or French beans	1 ½ kg	4 lb
cooking salt	500 g	1 ¼ lb

Method
1 Wash, dry and remove strings from beans.
2 Slice runner beans. Leave French beans whole.
3 Crush salt with a rolling pin or grind to a powder.
4 Pack salt and beans in layers in clean jars, beginning and ending with salt.
5 Press beans well down and fill jars to top.
6 Cover jars and leave for a few days.
7 Fill to the top again ending with salt.
8 Cover and store in a dark place.

FREEZING

The housewife who acquires a freezer for the first time will be well advised to get one of the many books that specialize in deep-freezing. These will have sections on freezer care, containers and wrapping materials, instructions for the straightforward freezing of foodstuffs in their natural state and recipes for made-up dishes that will do well in the freezer.

Freezing is a quick and simple method of preserving food, which in the case of some, such as meat, fish and bread, is the only way it can be done easily at home. Freezing enables the housewife to buy foodstuffs in bulk when prices are low, to preserve surplus garden produce, to save left-overs, and to shop and cook ahead.

Every housewife will discover with experience which foodstuffs are the most usefully stored in the freezer for her particular household. To get the best use of a freezer, the turnover of contents should be fairly rapid rather than be hoarded for long periods. As in all preserving, only best quality materials should be used; it is a waste of money to store second-rate stuff. Cleanliness must naturally be observed and everything should be carefully labelled. If an inventory of the contents is kept and the different types of food stored in definite areas of the freezer, it should be easy to keep a check on the stock and replace it when necessary.

BEVERAGES

*To make tea, coffee and cocoa – soft drinks – syrups – guidance
for choosing wine – party drinks and long cold drinks*

To make tea

Water for making tea must be freshly boiled. A teapot must be kept properly clean and must never be put away with the tea leaves in it. Always warm the teapot before making the tea by pouring in a little boiling water or by letting the teapot stand in a warm place. The usual proportion of tea is 1 teaspoonful per person and 1 for the pot, but if tea is being made for a large number of people, a smaller proportion may be allowed.

Put the tea into the warmed pot, then half fill the teapot with absolutely boiling water. Let it stand for 3 minutes in a warm place, fill up the teapot with boiling water and pour out the tea at once. Tea should never be allowed to stand.

Teabags must be used in the same way, with boiling water in a warmed pot.

China tea will be made weaker than Indian and will look much paler. Slices of lemon should be offered as an alternative to milk.

Russian tea is served in heat-proof glasses in special holders. It is made of Indian tea and served with a slice of lemon instead of milk, and sugar is offered.

Coffee

Ideally, one should grind one's own coffee, but if a mill is not available it is advisable to buy coffee in small quantities only from a reliable dealer, where it is roasted daily.

Some people prefer chicory blended with coffee. Chicory gives a slightly bitter flavour, and its addition is a matter of personal taste.

Vacuum-packed ground coffee is the next best thing, but only a small quantity should be bought at a time, as the flavour deteriorates fast once the vacuum is released. Keep the remainder of the ground coffee in an airtight jar in a cool place.

Make sure the coffee maker is really clean; the oils of the coffee will cling to the pot and soon turn rancid.

There are various kinds of coffee pot on the market, most of them being fitted with a percolator of some sort. Put the coffee in the percolator and pour on the boiling water, letting it filter slowly through. Some electric or gas percolators are filled with cold water, which is heated up and then filters through the coffee. Always use fresh cold water from the cold tap to bring to the boil and never water which has previously boiled in the kettle. An earthenware jug can be used for coffee-making. The jug is warmed, the coffee put in, boiling water poured over, the liquid stirred with a wooden spoon and allowed to stand for 5 minutes.

Measure the coffee carefully. A reasonable formula is 2 level tablespoons coffee to 150 ml (6 fluid oz) water. For weaker coffee use fewer grains rather than add water.

Coffee is better if it can be made without letting it boil after the water has touched it.

Coffee is served with hot milk (café-au-lait), cream or plain black.

Turkish coffee

This should ideally be made in a special copper or brass pot, with a spout on one side and a long handle. Put 2 tablespoons of freshly ground coffee in the pot for each cup to be served. Add 75 ml (3 fl oz) of cold water. In Turkey, coffee is ordered without sugar, semi-sweet or very sweet, and the sugar is added or not at the time of making. In the case of very sweet coffee, 1 tablespoon castor sugar is added with the coffee into the pot before the water is poured on. The water should rise to about 5 cm (2 in.) from the top of the pot. Put the pot over heat, bring to the boil. Remove and put it back twice more to boil up. Let it stand a few minutes. A little of the foam from the top should go into each cup.

Viennese coffee

This is very good strong coffee served very hot with a spoonful of whipped cream on the top of each cup.

Iced coffee

There are two methods of making iced coffee. In the first case, the coffee should be made extra strong, using half the amount of water to the usual measurements, and should be poured hot on to a tall glass full of ice-cubes just before serving. Cream and sugar are passed. In the second case, regular strength coffee is made and chilled in the refrigerator till the very last minute, then cream or top of the milk whisked into it. Sugar, or better still, syrup made from equal quantities of sugar and water, boiled for a minute and cooled, is offered separately.

Gaelic coffee

1 part Irish whiskey to 3 parts double-strength coffee
sugar

Method
1 Warm some goblets.
2 Put about 40 ml (1½ fl oz) whiskey and 1 level tsp sugar in each goblet.
3 Add three times the quantity of very hot, black coffee. The glasses must not be too full. Stir till sugar dissolves.
4 Fill the glasses to the brim with chilled double cream, poured on to the coffee over the back of a spoon.
5 Allow to stand for a minute, then drink coffee through the cream.

Cocoa

Put 1½ tsp cocoa in a breakfast cup, add a little cold milk; mix to a smooth paste; pour on boiling milk. Return to the pan, boil up and serve.

SOFT DRINKS

Ginger beer

	Metric	Imp
loaf sugar	1 kg	2½ lb
water	6 l	6 qt
ground ginger	75 g	3 oz
5 lemons		
2 tsp brewer's yeast		
a slice of toast		

Method
1 Boil sugar, ginger and water for 1 hr.
2 When cold, add juice and thinly peeled rind of lemons.
3 Put yeast on toast and add.
4 Put into a tub and cover with a thick cloth for 2 or 3 days.
5 Strain through a cloth, bottle and cork securely. Keep in a cool place.
6 This is ready to drink in 4 or 5 days.

Note More ginger may be added for a stronger flavour.

Lemonade

	Metric	Imp
4 lemons		
loaf sugar	75 g	3 oz
boiling water	1 l	1 qt

Method

1 Wipe lemons with a damp cloth; rub sugar on the rind till all yellow is removed.
2 Put sugar in a jug, pour boiling water over, let it stand for an hour.
3 Squeeze lemon juice, remove pith and pips, add to water.
4 Strain and serve quite cold, with ice if desired.

Orangeade

	Metric	Imp
4 oranges		
sugar	50 g	2 oz
boiling water	500 ml	1 pt

Method

1 Remove peel very thinly from oranges, put into a jug and pour boiling water over.
2 Cover and leave till cold.
3 Put sugar and 60 ml (½ gill) water into a pan, stir till sugar is melted, boil to a thin syrup 10 min.
4 Skim; add strained juice of the oranges, then strain in water from peel.
5 If too strong, add more water. Serve with crushed ice if desired.

Milk shakes

These can be made with 250 ml (½ pt) of milk and a 1 tbsp flavouring syrup or jam and 2 tbsp crushed ice and the whole put in the blender till smooth; or they can be made in the same way, substituting ice cream for the syrup and crushed ice, and blending into the milk.

SYRUPS

Blackberry syrup

	Metric	Imp
blackberry juice made by simmering blackberries in a jar standing in a pan of boiling water till the juice flows out (about 8 to 10 litres or quarts of blackberries)	2 l	2 qt
sugar	1600 g	4 lb
water	2 l	2 qt
2 tsp nutmeg		
2 wineglasses brandy		

Method

1 Strain and measure the juice.
2 Put sugar and water into a pan, stir till sugar has melted then boil without stirring till thick and syrupy, about 15 to 20 min.
3 Strain into blackberry juice, add grated nutmeg.
4 Bring to the boil, boil for 15 to 20 min., add brandy.
5 Cork securely.

Raspberry syrup

Method

1 Choose ripe juicy raspberries, remove stalks, put fruit into a basin and bruise well. Leave in a cold place for 24 hr. Strain off all the juice, measure, and to every 500 ml (1 pt) add 200 g (½ lb) loaf sugar.
2 Boil gently for ½ hr.
3 Remove all scum. When cold, put into dry bottles and cork well.

WINE

There are no hard and fast rules for choosing the right wine for a dish – as one becomes more experienced so one becomes less rigid in one's choice.

However for the complete beginner the most important thing to remember when choosing a wine is the flavour of the dish. For example, roast duck cooked with stuffing and a fairly spicy seasoning, would probably go best with a claret, but a duck 'à l'orange', sweeter and flavoured with the fruit, might well be better with a sweetish hock or Riesling.

When buying wine for immediate consumption, i.e. not to lay down in a cellar, try to buy the wine at least a day before it is needed so that it can settle.

The temperature that wine is drunk at is very important. Champagne should be very cold, white wine and rosé, cold, and clarets and burgundies at room temperature. (Have the bottles of red wine in the kitchen for at least the day of the party, and uncork them several hours before they are needed, to breathe.)

Remember that older wine is not necessarily better wine; some, such as Beaujolais and Chianti do not improve after 18 months, rosés can be drunk as young as possible, and many whites do not improve after 3 years. Some of the reds, however, are at their best after 20 years of maturing (the Bordeaux of St Julien and St Estephe, for example), but different years mature at different rates and it takes a great deal of knowledge and experience and possibly a little luck to choose a wine when it is absolutely right for drinking.

For simple guidance, a few suggestions are made:

1 Champagne will go with everything and should be drunk really cold.

2 Dry white wine will go with most dishes, especially pastas, shellfish, fish (cooked plain or in a white wine sauce), chicken cooked in a cream sauce and, occasionally, pork.

3 A medium white wine (moselle or hock) might be preferable for plain chicken, veal and fish or poultry cooked with a fruity sauce.

4 Rosé must be drunk cold; it is essentially a summer drink, and most suited to cold chicken dishes or veal.

5 Red Bordeaux is for lamb, beef and pork cooked without too much seasoning or spice.

6 Red Burgundy for the 'high' dishes; jugged hare, game, steak and kidney pudding and the richer beef dishes.

7 Sauternes and other sweet white wines are suitable for accompanying some sweets, particularly Christmas pudding.

PARTY DRINKS AND LONG COLD DRINKS

The fashion in apéritifs changes so frequently, and the variety of sherries, spirits and fortified wines is so great that it is impossible to mention them all without sounding like a wine merchant's list.

For the host who wants to be prepared for most tastes, a stock of sherry, medium and dry, whisky, gin, vodka and brandy, with some tonic water, bitter lemon and possibly dry ginger, a little beer, and lemon, ice and soda water should cover most needs, though some people would consider white rum and vermouths essential to their basic drinks cupboard.

There are countless recipes for cocktails, but these usually need the addition of various liqueurs, fresh fruit juice and refinements such as olives, maraschino cherries, or angostura bitters, so they are not mentioned here, but it is left to each host to work out his own speciality and stock up the necessary ingredients. It is definitely simpler for all concerned if the guest is offered a choice of 3 or 4 basic drinks, e.g. sherry, whisky or gin, and then chooses the accompaniments such as water or soda, lemon, ice, etc.

With a large number of guests it is difficult to cater for different tastes and it is quite acceptable to make up a punch or wine cup to offer around, making sure, however, that there is some sherry and whisky in reserve for the guest who quite firmly refuses it.

Always make sure you have non-alcoholic drinks in stock which can be served without making the guest feel that he is being awkward by not drinking alcohol. Chilled tomato juice, fresh orange juice, bitter lemon are good stand-bys, and if for a large party a punch or something similar has been made, prepare a small quantity of non-alcoholic fruit cup as well.

An excellent starter to a party is champagne, if one can afford a good one – nothing gives people a headache quicker than a cheap champagne – but again, a reserve of whisky and sherry is necessary as there will always be someone who says he cannot take champagne.

Naturally, the type of party given will influence the choice of drinks provided – a Christmas party suggests a mulled wine or a hot punch; a barbecue: beer and cider; a summer luncheon party in the garden: cool wine or a wine cup; an oyster party: black velvet (⅓ Guinness, ⅔ champagne).

Your wine merchant will always help you decide on quantities needed, and most of them will provide drinks on a sale or return basis.

Cider cup

6 persons

	Metric	Imp
3 apples peeled and thinly sliced		
brandy	100 ml	4 fl oz
sweet vermouth	200 ml	8 fl oz
medium dry cider	1 ½ l	3 pt
1 dssp sugar		

Method
1 Place apples in a jug; sprinkle sugar over, add brandy and vermouth. Leave for about an hour.
2 Add cider, iced. Stir and serve.

Cold claret cup

6 persons

	Metric	Imp
1 bottle claret		
sherry	60 ml	½ gill
½ lemon thinly peeled		
a few slices of cucumber unpeeled		
a sprig of borage		
sugar to taste		
soda water		

Method
1 Put lemon peel, cucumber and borage into a jug.
2 Pour claret and sherry over, and sugar to taste. Refrigerate till required.
3 Add soda water to taste at the last minute, and crushed ice if desired.

Planter's punch

1 person

	Metric	Imp
juice of 2 limes or 2 lemons		

	Metric	Imp
soda water	50 ml	2 fl oz
rum	65 ml	2 ½ fl oz
angostura bitters		
2 tsp sugar		
a cherry, piece of pineapple, or slice of orange		

Method
1 Put fruit juice, sugar and soda water into a tall glass.
2 Add plenty of crushed ice and stir.
3 Add 2 dashes of bitters and rum. Stir.
4 Serve with cherry, pineapple or orange slice, with a straw.

Vermouth cassis

1 person

	Metric	Imp
dry vermouth	125 ml	1 gill
crème de cassis	40 ml	1 ½ fl oz
crushed ice		
soda water		
a twist of lemon		

Method
1 Put vermouth and cassis in a tall glass with lots of ice.
2 Fill with soda water, add a twist of lemon. Serve at once.

Virginia egg nog

About 12 servings

	Metric	Imp
12 separated eggs		
½ bottle brandy		
castor sugar	100 g	4 oz
milk	500 ml	1 pt
rum	25 g	1 oz
double cream	250 ml	½ pt
nutmeg		

Method
1 Beat egg yolks; add sugar gradually and beat till sugar has dissolved.
2 Add brandy gradually, then rum and milk.
3 Whip cream lightly and fold in.
4 Beat egg whites stiffly and fold in.
5 Serve very cold in small glasses, with nutmeg grated over.

Whisky sour
1 person

	Metric	Imp
whisky	60 ml	½ gill
juice of ½ lemon		
1–2 tsp sugar		
soda water		
a slice of orange		
a cherry		

Method
1 Shake lemon juice, sugar and whisky well together.
2 Strain into a glass.
3 Add a squirt of soda water, orange, cherry and ice.

Milk punch
1 person

	Metric	Imp
rum	40 ml	1 ½ oz
very hot milk	100 ml	4 oz
1 tsp sugar		
1 tbsp curaçao		
a dash of orange juice		
slice of orange		
a few grains of nutmeg		

Method
1 Mix rum, orange, juice, curaçao and sugar in a tall glass.
2 Pour on milk.
3 Add orange slice and nutmeg. Serve at once.

Mulled ale

	Metric	Imp
ale	500 ml	1 pt
4 egg yolks		
3 cloves		
sugar to taste		
a grate of nutmeg		

Method
1 Put ale minus 2 tbsp in a pan with cloves, nutmeg and sugar. Bring to the boil. Cool slightly.
2 Beat up egg yolks with remaining cold ale; stir into warm ale.
3 Pour it backwards and forwards from pan to basin 2 or 3 times.
4 Stir over low heat till hot, but not boiling.
5 Serve with dry toast.

Mulled wine

	Metric	Imp
2 bottles claret		
rum, whisky, curaçao or		
cherry brandy	60 ml	½ gill
water	125 ml	¼ pt
thinly peeled rind of 1 orange and 1 lemon		
4 tbsp Demerara sugar		
½ tsp ground cinnamon		
1 tsp ground nutmeg		

Method
1 Simmer peel, sugar and spices in water for 15 min.
2 Add wine and spirit, and heat gently till hot but not boiling.
3 Strain into a bowl.

Note A few slices of orange and 4 or 5 cloves may be added with the wine for extra flavour.

Sailor's punch

	Metric	Imp
ale	1 l	1 qt
boiling water	500 ml	1 pt
¼ bottle of whisky		
¼ bottle of rum		
¼ bottle of gin		
2 tbsp soft brown sugar		
pinch each of cinnamon, cloves, nutmeg		
1 ½ lemons thinly sliced		

Method
1 Put slices of one lemon in a large pan, pour boiling water over.
2 Add other ingredients, bring nearly to the boil.
3 Strain. Serve hot with the rest of the lemon slices floating on the top.

MENUS

Seasonable menus for the family – party menus – Christmas dinners – wedding breakfast – buffet refreshments for large numbers – vegetarian menus – quantities for entertaining – laying the table and serving

It is well worth the trouble to sit down once a week before shopping and plan the week's menus. In this way, the most efficient way of shopping will be worked out, lists made for different shops and for different days, and the last-minute panics of what to eat will be avoided.

Plan the meals day by day to get a good balance of foodstuffs. Suggestions are given for family meals for the different seasons of the year. These are for a cooked breakfast, a main meal, which can be taken at midday or in the evening, and a lighter meal which is either lunch or supper, according to the family's needs.

Party menus are suggested in the second half of the chapter.

FOUR MENUS FOR A SPRING DAY

1

Breakfast
Orange juice
Scrambled eggs on toast

Main meal
Asparagus with melted butter
Lamb cutlets
Creamed potatoes
Glazed carrots
Rhubarb fool

Light meal
Cauliflower cheese
Fresh fruit

2

Breakfast
Fresh grapefruit
Grilled sausage and tomato

Main meal
Spinach soup
Stuffed baked haddock
Anchovy sauce
New potatoes
Orange salad

Light meal
Stuffed peppers
Honeycomb mould

3

Breakfast
Sliced bananas and cereal
Sardines on toast

Main meal
Egg mayonnaise
Beef rissoles
Spring cabbage
Sauté potatoes
Fresh fruit salad

Light meal
Creamed kidneys
New carrots
Cheese and French bread

4

Breakfast
Stewed figs
Poached egg on toast

Main meal
Vichyssoise
Calves' liver à la française
Spinach
Chipped potatoes
Lemon mousse

Light meal
Grilled herrings
Green salad
Fresh fruit

FOUR MENUS FOR A SUMMER DAY

1

Breakfast
Pineapple juice
Mushrooms on toast

Main meal
Cold consommé
Baked sweetbreads
New potatoes, broad beans
Strawberries and cream

Light meal
Scotch eggs
Salade Niçoise
Cheese and biscuits

2

Breakfast
Muesli
Boiled egg

Main meal
Tomato salad
Grilled trout and almonds
New potatoes
Summer pudding and cream

Light meal
Ham mousse
Sweet corn fritters
Melon

3

Breakfast
Orange juice
Grilled bacon and tomatoes

Main meal
Iced curry soup
Fricassée of chicken
Boiled rice
Peas
Gooseberry pie and cream

Light meal
Pancakes stuffed with smoked haddock in
parsley sauce
Fresh peaches

4

Breakfast
Apple juice
Baked eggs with grated cheese

Main meal
Chicken curry
Rice
Sliced bananas, tomatoes
Chutneys, poppadums, cucumber in
yoghourt
Sliced fresh pineapple

Light meal
Quiche Lorraine
Green salad
Apricot fool

FOUR MENUS FOR AN AUTUMN DAY

1

Breakfast
Grapefruit juice
Bacon and egg

Main meal
Tomato soup
Fried chicken
Sauté potatoes
Runner beans
Blackberry and apple pie

Light meal
Cornish pasties
Mixed salad
Fresh fruit

2

Breakfast
Stewed prunes
Kippers

Main meal
Cold ratatouille
Liver and bacon
Creamed potatoes
Cauliflower
Pear condé

Light meal
Ravioli
Apple jelly
Ice cream

3

Breakfast
Stewed apples
Sausages and mushrooms

Main meal
Avocado vinaigrette
Cod au gratin
Mashed potatoes
Runner beans
Plum pie and custard

Light meal
Nut cutlets
Spinach à la crème
Cheese and biscuits

4

Breakfast
Slice of lemon
Kedgeree

Main meal
Corn on the cob
Rabbit à la poulette
Boiled potatoes with parsley
Carrots
Pears à la duchesse

Light meal
Gnocchi
Celery and apple salad
Fresh fruit

FOUR MENUS FOR A WINTER DAY

1

Breakfast
Porridge
Fish cakes

Main meal
Grapefruit and orange cocktail
Roast pheasant
Potato crisps
Sweet and sour red cabbage
Queen's pudding

Light meal
Baked potatoes stuffed with cheese
Cole-slaw salad
Bananas and cream

2

Breakfast
Orange juice
Fried bread, bacon and tomato

Main meal
Carrot soup
Steak and kidney pudding
Jerusalem artichokes
Baked apples and cream

Light meal
Curried eggs and rice
Winter fruit salad

3

Breakfast
Grapefruit
Baked beans on toast

Main meal
Artichoke soup
Fried plaice
Chipped potatoes
Brussels sprouts
Mince pies

Light meal
Moussaka
Fresh fruit

4

Breakfast
Tomato juice
Fried egg and breakfast sausage

Main meal
Baked aubergines
Mock goose
Turnips
Prune mould

Light meal
Macaroni cheese
Baked bananas

PARTY MENUS

Planning is the keynote to any successful party.

1 Plan the type of party it is to be – degree of informality, number of guests, time of day. This will affect the menus. Make it clear to the guests what type of party it is to be, the sort of clothes to be worn, the type of food to be offered, the time to arrive.

2 The above points will affect the seating arrangements, whether at a formal dinner table, an informal supper table, on small separate tables, standing buffet, indoors or out.

3 The menu will then be chosen according to what can be coped with. Equally important to consider are the cooker's capacity, the help and time available, the space for eating and sitting afterwards.

A Menu for a breakfast party
Grapefruit
Kedgeree   Kidneys on toast
Creamed mushrooms
Croissants, bread rolls, toast
Marmalade   Black cherry jam
Butter
Tea   Coffee
Champagne

A Menu for a Luncheon Party
Gazpacho
Chicken à la bourgeoise
Fried rice   Green salad
Coffee mousse
Coffee

A Menu for a Dinner Party
Avocado vinaigrette
Creamed scallops
Roast crown of lamb   Forcemeat balls
Potato croquettes
Peas cooked by the French method
Lemon meringue pie
Cheese and biscuits
Coffee

A Menu for a Picnic Party
Cucumber soup in a thermos – either iced or hot according to the weather
Cold roast chicken flavoured with tarragon
French bread, butter, tomatoes
Melon   Cheese straws
Shrewsbury biscuits
Mint chocolate
Coffee   Hock

A Menu for a Barbecue
Sausages   Steak
Hamburgers (cooked on the grill)
Jacket potatoes (partly cooked before and finished on the grill)
Green salad   Grilled tomatoes
Cheese board
Beer   Cider   and   Red wine
Coffee

FAMILY CHRISTMAS DINNER 1

Consommé jardinière
Roast turkey   Chestnut stuffing
Boiled ham
Cranberry sauce   Bread sauce
Chipolatas
Roast potatoes   Brussels sprouts
Plum pudding   Mince pies
Orange sponge
Coffee

FAMILY CHRISTMAS DINNER 2

Grapefruit cocktail
Roast goose   Red cabbage
Roast potatoes   Sage and onion stuffing
Plum pudding   Brandy butter
Ice cream   Mince pies
Stilton   Coffee

CHRISTMAS DINNER FOR TWO

Consommé à la royale
Roast chicken
Chestnut stuffing   Bread sauce
Potatoes   Lettuce salad
Individual plum puddings
Pears à la duchesse
Devilled prunes
Dessert   Coffee

Note In place of roast chicken, substitute:
1. Roast duck   Rice and nut stuffing   onion sauce
2 Roast pigeons with chestnuts

WEDDING BREAKFAST FOR 100 GUESTS

Salmon mayonnaise
6·5–8 kg (16–20 lb) of fish
Lobster in aspic
(40 small moulds)
Chicken pie
(3 pies)
Chaudfroid of turkey
(1 turkey)
or
Oyster or shrimp patties
(40)
Tongue
(2 tongues)
York ham
(1)
Salads
(4)
WEDDING CAKE
Trifle
(2 dishes)
Fruit salad
6·5 kg (16 lb)

Cold chocolate soufflé
2 litres (2 qt) soufflés
Lemon jelly
3 litres (3 qt)
Éclairs
(2½ dozen)
Fancy pastries
1600 g (4 lb)
Cream buns
(2½ dozen)
Ices
5 litres (5 pt)
Asparagus and smoked salmon rolls
(100)
Coffee
1200 g (3 lb)
Champagne or cider or hock cup
12·5 litres (25 pt)
Whisky and soda
(3 bottles of whisky, 4 syphons of soda)

EVENING BRIDGE REFRESHMENTS

Assorted sandwiches
Quiche Lorraine, cut in segments
Sausage rolls
Assorted cut cake
Coffee   Claret or cider cup
Whisky and soda

BUFFET REFRESHMENTS FOR A DANCE FOR 100 PEOPLE

Sandwiches (ham, lobster, cheese and
celery)
(50 of each)
Shrimp patties
(50)
Veal and ham patties
(75)
Wine jelly
10 litres (10 qt)
Chicken creams
(50)
Fruit salad
10 kg (25 lb)
Trifle
(3 dishes)
Fancy pastries
(150)
Ice cream (two flavours)
2·5 litres (5 pt) each
Soup (on leaving)
14 litres (3½ gallons)
Coffee
800 g (2 lb) coffee,
3 litres (3 qt) milk
Lemonade
16 litres (16 qt)
Claret or cider cup
16 litres (16 qt)

VEGETARIAN MENUS

1

Palestine soup
Savoury omelette
Haricot bean croquettes with tomato sauce
Fried potatoes   Asparagus
Fruit pie and cream

2

Grapefruit salad
Carrot soup
Baked aubergines with poached eggs
Vegetable cutlets and tomato salad
Apple pudding
Cheese   Biscuits

3

Cream of barley soup
Cheese omelette
Boiled chestnuts
Potato croquettes   Brussels sprouts
Cornflour blancmange   Fruit salad
Cheese

MENU FOR CHILDREN'S PARTY TEA

Egg sandwiches
Cream cheese and tomato sandwiches
Sausages on sticks   Buttered scones
Small Swiss rolls
Flapjacks   Potato crisps
Chocolate biscuits
Ice cream   Birthday cake
Orangeade   Iced chocolate milk

QUANTITIES FOR ENTERTAINING

5 to 6 large sandwich loaves will make about 200 sandwiches with 1200 g (3 lb) of butter. Allow 2 sandwiches per head and 2 savouries, at an afternoon buffet party. 400 g (1 lb) of cake will cut into 8 or 9 slices, and it is customary to allow 3 small cakes for 2 people. Where several kinds of fancy cakes are served, 50 of each kind should prove sufficient for 100 people, as each guest rarely chooses the same kind of cake.

A litre (1 qt) mould of either sweets or savouries will make about 10 helpings where 2 or 3 different kinds figure on the menu. If only one kind be given, a similar mould will make only eight helpings.

5 litres (5 qt) of ice cream are sufficient for 100 people, that is allowing 20 small helpings per litre.

It is usual to allow 300 g (¾ lb) of fruit salad per head and about 250 ml (½ pt) of lemonade per head.

A little more than ¾ of a teacupful of soup is usually allowed when giving soup on the departure of guests after a dance or evening party.

In calculating the amount of tea per person, it is well to remember that the more people there are the less tea is required, in proportion. It is usual to allow about 5 teaspoonful of tea for 4 persons, but 400 g (1 lb) of tea will be ample for 100 people, and if coffee is handed at the same time, probably 200 g (½ lb) of tea will be sufficient for 100 people.

400 g (1 lb) of coffee is sufficient for 100 people when tea is served, but should coffee be served alone, about 800 g (2 lb) will be required. 800 g (2 lb) of loaf sugar and about 4 litres (4 qt) of milk should be ample for 100 people for either tea or coffee.

Quantities per person

Cocktail party	4–5 savouries; nuts, olives 3–4 drinks
Buffet party	1 helping of starter; 1½ of main dish; 2 different sweets 2–3 aperitifs, 3–4 glasses wine
Wedding reception	4–5 savouries; 2 cakes 3–4 drinks
Children's tea party	4–5 savouries; 2 cakes or biscuits; 1 portion of ice cream; 2 drinks

Quantities per bottle

Sherry, vermouth, port	12–16 glasses
Spirits	16–20 glasses
Wine	6–7 glasses
Concentrated fruit squash	20 drinks
Splits of tonic, bitter lemon	2 drinks

LAYING THE TABLE AND SERVING

It is not necessary to have fine bone china and silver for entertaining. A beautiful table can be set with wooden and pottery dishes and stainless steel cutlery, and on modern heat and stainproof tables, place mats can be dispensed with altogether or a tablecloth used without any sort of underfelt or heatproof mat. Colour is all important: a bright cloth looks most effective with white china, flowers and candles; or dark china on a lighter toning cloth; a homespun look is splendid in a cottage setting or out of doors: rush mats, brown glazed pottery, wooden platters and bowls, with perhaps a yellow check cloth and a bowl of orange flowers.

For those who wish to give a formal dinner party, however, the following guidelines are set out, but it must be emphasized that today, anything goes.

A FORMAL DINNER PARTY

1 A fine cloth in damask, linen, lace or some smooth material, beautifully laundered, or heat-proof mats, either large pictorial ones or small ones covered with a lace or embroidered place mat. Napkins to match.

2 Table decorations. These should be low and fit in with the colour scheme, but can consist of anything decorative: flowers, fruit, china, glass or silver ornaments, driftwood or gourds: any attractive arrangement making up one centre piece or several small ones according to the shape of the table. Candles can be bought in any colour and should also complement the colour scheme, and are an important part of the formal dinner table.

3 Cutlery in silver or stainless steel is placed in order of use on either side of the diner's place, starting from the outside and working inwards. This will consist of a soup spoon or a knife for pâté on the right on the outside, or a fork for a savoury starter on the left outside, a fish knife and fork next (the knife on the right), a large knife and fork and a small spoon and fork, which can alternatively be placed above the plate. Should more forks and spoons be necessary, they are placed on the table in the order required. A small knife for spreading butter is placed by the side plate.

4 Glasses, which should be uncoloured, are arranged on the right-hand side, and it is usual to place one tumbler and as many wine glasses as there will be wines drunk, to each cover. There used to be rules for special shaped glasses for each wine, e.g. hock, claret, burgundy, champagne, etc., but it is quite acceptable now to use a tulip-shaped glass for any of these.

5 China or pottery. Side plates are placed to the left of the cover. These can be small round or crescent-shaped plates. Soup is usually served in small bowls with or without lids. The soup can be poured out immediately before the guests come to the dining room, so they find it at their place, or it may be served with a ladle from a tureen on the sideboard and offered to the guests once seated. Other specially shaped dishes exist for oysters, corn on the cob, and so on.

Hors d'oeuvres are usually placed in china or glass dishes on the table or on individual plates, before the guests are seated. Other first courses are served on a smaller version of the main dinner plate.

The main course is either carved from the side on to plates which are handed to each guest, or if it consists of food already divided into portions, the dish is handed to each person who helps himself. Salad is usually handed round in a bowl, preferably wooden, or placed on individual salad plates.

The sweet may be served at table on flat dessert plates or previously set out in individual glass bowls or coupes. Cheese is eaten from clean side plates.

Between courses, everything should be removed that is no longer required, dirty plates, sauces, salt and pepper, etc.

SERVING AT A DINNER PARTY

At a large dinner party, begin with the lady on the right-hand side of the host and go right round. With fewer guests, serve the right-hand lady first, then the left, then other women guests and repeat the process with the men guests, ending with members of the family, the hostess and finally the host. Offer food to the left of the guest and clear away from the right.

It is no longer taken for granted that the women shall leave the table before the men, leaving them to drink port alone. This is entirely a matter for the hostess to decide on, and many people feel it is an insult to women to do this.

Coffee is usually served in the sitting room, but may be taken at table at the end of the meal if everyone is comfortable and one does not wish to interrupt the conversation.

INDEX